Collected Works
of
Thomas Troward

Collected Works
of
Thomas Troward

This book was written in the prevailing style of that period. Language and spelling have been left original in an effort to give the full flavor of this classic work.

Bottom of the Hill Publishing

Memphis, TN

www.BottomoftheHillPublishing.com

ISBN: 978-1-61203-427-0

Contents

THE CREATIVE PROCESS IN THE INDIVIDUAL

FOREWORD

In the present volume I have endeavored to set before the reader the conception of a sequence of creative action commencing with the formation of the globe and culminating in a vista of infinite possibilities attainable by everyone who follows up the right line for their unfoldment.

I have endeavored to show that, starting with certain incontrovertible scientific facts, all these things logically follow, and that therefore, however far these speculations may carry us beyond our past experience, they nowhere break the thread of an intelligible connection of cause and effect.

I do not, however, offer the suggestions here put forward in any other light than that of purely speculative reasoning; nevertheless, no advance in any direction can be made except by speculative reasoning going back to the first principles of things which we do know and thence deducing the conditions under which the same principles might be carried further and made to produce results hitherto unknown. It is to this method of thought that we owe all the advantages of civilization from matches and post-offices to motor-cars and aeroplanes, and we may therefore be encouraged to hope such speculations as the present may not be without their ultimate value. Relying on the maxim that Principle is not bound by Precedent we should not limit our expectations of the future; and if our speculations lead us to the conclusion that we have reached a point where we are not only able, but also required, by the law of our own being, to take a more active part in our personal evolution than heretofore, this discovery will afford us a new outlook upon life and widen our horizon with fresh interests and brightening hopes.

If the thoughts here suggested should help any reader to clear some mental obstacles from his path the writer will feel that he has not written to no purpose. Only each reader must think out these suggestions for himself. No writer or lecturer can convey an idea into the minds of his audience. He can only put it before them, and what they will make of it depends entirely upon themselves--assimilation is a process which no one can carry out for us.

To the kindness of my readers on both sides of the Atlantic, and in Australia and New Zealand, I commend this little volume, not, indeed, without a deep sense of its many shortcomings, but at the same time encouraged by the generous indulgence extended to my previous books.

T.T.

June, 1910.

I say no man has ever yet been half devout enough, None has ever yet adored or worship'd half enough, None has begun to think how divine he himself is, and how certain the future is. I say that the real and permanent grandeur of these States must be their religion, Otherwise there is no real and permanent grandeur. —WALT WHITMAN.

CHAPTER I

THE STARTING-POINT

It is an old saying that "Order is Heaven's First Law," and like many other old sayings it contains a much deeper philosophy than appears immediately on the surface. Getting things into a better order is the great secret of progress, and we are now able to fly through the air, not because the laws of Nature have altered, but because we have learnt to arrange things in the right order to produce this result--the things themselves had existed from the beginning of the world, but what was wanting was the introduction of a Personal Factor which, by an intelligent perception of the possibilities contained in the laws of Nature, should be able to bring into working reality ideas which previous generations would have laughed at as the absurd fancies of an unbalanced mind. The lesson to be learnt from the practical aviation of the present day is that of the triumph of principle over precedent, of the working out of an idea to its logical conclusions in spite of the accumulated testimony of all past experience to the contrary; and with such a notable example before us can we say that it is futile to enquire whether by the same method we may not unlock still more important secrets and gain some knowledge of the unseen causes which are at the back of external and visible conditions, and then by bringing these unseen causes into a better order make practical working realities of possibilities which at present seem but fantastic dreams? It is at least worthwhile taking a preliminary canter over the course, and this is all that this little volume professes to attempt; yet this may be sufficient to show the lay of the ground.

Now the first thing in any investigation is to have some idea of what you are looking for--to have at least some notion of the general direction in which to go--just as you would not go up a tree to find fish though you would for birds' eggs. Well, the general direction in which we all want to go is that of getting more out of Life than we have ever got out of it--we want to be more alive in ourselves and to get all sorts of improved conditions in our environment. However happily any of us may be circumstanced we can all conceive something still better, or at any rate we should like to make our present good permanent; and since we shall find as our studies advance that the prospect of increasing possibilities keeps opening out more and more widely before us, we may say that what we are in search of is the secret of getting more out of Life in a continually progressive degree. This means that what we are looking for is something personal, and that it is to be obtained by producing conditions which do not yet exist; in other words it is nothing less than the exercise of a certain creative power in the sphere of our own particular world. So, then, what we want is to introduce our own Personal Factor into the realm of unseen causes. This is a big thing, and if it is possible at all it must be by some sequence of cause and effect, and this sequence it is our object to discover. The law of Cause and Effect is one we can never get away from, but by carefully following it up we may find that it will lead us further than we had anticipated.

Now, the first thing to observe is that if we can succeed in finding out such a sequence of cause and effect as the one we are in search of, somebody else may find out the same creative secret also; and then, by the hypothesis of the case, we should both be armed with an infallible power, and if we wanted to employ this power against each other we should be landed in the "impasse" of a conflict between two powers each of which was irresistible. Consequently it follows that the first principle of this power must be Harmony. It cannot be antagonizing itself from different centers--in other words its operation in a simultaneous order at every point is the first necessity of its being. What we are in search of, then, is a sequence of cause and effect so universal in its nature as to include harmoniously all possible variations of individual expression. This primary necessity of the Law for which we are seeking should be carefully borne in mind, for it is obvious that any sequence which transgresses this primary essential must be contrary to the very nature of the Law itself, and consequently cannot be conducting us to the exercise of true creative power.

What we are seeking, therefore, is to discover how to arrange things in such an order as to set in motion a train of causation that will harmonize our own conditions without antagonizing the exercise of a like power by others. This therefore means that all individual exercise of this power is the particular application of a universal power which itself operates creatively on its own account independently of these individual applications; and the harmony between the various individual applications is brought about by all the individuals bringing their own particular action into line with this independent creative action of the original power. It is in fact another application of Euclid's axiom that things which are equal to the same thing are equal to one another; so that though I may not know for what purpose someone may be using this creative power in Pekin, I do know that if he and I both realize its true nature, we cannot by any possibility be working in opposition to one another. For these reasons, having now some general idea of what it is we are in search of, we may commence our investigation by considering this common factor which must be at the back of all individual exercise of creative power, that is to say, the Generic working of the Universal Creative Principle.

That such a Universal Creative Principle is at work we at once realize from the existence of the world around us with all its inhabitants, and the inter-relation of all parts of the cosmic system shows its underlying Unity--thus the animal kingdom depends on the vegetable, the vegetable kingdom on the mineral, the mineral or globe of the earth on its relation to the rest of the solar system, and possibly our solar system is related by a similar law to the distribution of other suns with their attendant planets throughout space. Our first glance therefore shows us that the All-originating Power must be in essence Unity and in manifestation Multiplicity, and that it manifests as Life and Beauty through the unerring adaptation of means to ends--that is so far as its cosmic manifestation of ends goes: what we want to do is to carry this manifestation still further by operation from an individual standpoint. To do this is precisely our place in the Order of Creation, but we must defer the question why we hold this place till later on.

One of the earliest discoveries we all make is the existence of Matter. The bruised shins of our childhood convince us of its solidity, so now comes the question, Why does Matter exist? The answer is that if the form were not expressed in solid substance, things would be perpetually flowing into each other so that no identity could be maintained for a single moment. To this it might be replied that a condition of matter is conceivable in which, though in itself a plastic substance, in a fluent state, it might yet by the operation of will be held in any particular forms desired. The idea of such a condition of matter is no doubt conceivable, and when the fluent matter was thus held in particular forms you would have concrete matter just as we know it now, only with this difference, that it would return to its fluent state as soon as the supporting will was withdrawn. Now, as we shall see later on, this is precisely what matter really is, only the will which holds it together in concrete form is not individual but cosmic.

In itself the Essence of Matter is precisely the fluent substance we have imagined, and as we shall see later on the knowledge of this fact, when realized in its proper order, is the basis of the legitimate control of mind over matter. But a world in which every individual possessed the power of concreting or fluxing matter at his own sweet will irrespective of any universal coordinating principle is altogether inconceivable--the conflict of wills would prevent such a world remaining in existence. On the other hand, if we conceive of a number of individuals each possessing this power and all employing it on the lines of a common cosmic unity, then the result would be precisely the same stable condition of matter with which we are familiar--this would be a necessity of fact for the masses who did not possess this power, and a necessity of principle for the few who did. So under these circumstances the same stable conditions of Nature would prevail as at present, varied only when the initiated ones perceived that the order of evolution would be furthered, and not hindered, by calling into action the higher laws. Such occasions would be of rare occurrence, and then the departure from the ordinary law would be regarded by the multitude as a miracle. Also we may be quite sure that no one who had attained this knowledge in the legitimate order would ever perform a "miracle" for his own personal aggrandizement or for the purpose of merely astonishing the beholders--to do so would be contrary to the first principle of the higher teaching which is that of profound reverence for the Unity of the All-originating Principle. The conception, therefore, of such a power over matter being possessed by certain individuals is in no way opposed to our ordinary recognition of concrete matter, and so we need not at present trouble ourselves to consider these exceptions.

Another theory is that matter has no existence at all but is merely an illusion projected by our own minds. If so, then how is it that we all project identically similar images? On the supposition that each mind is independently projecting its own conception of matter a lady who goes to be fitted might be seen by her dressmaker as a cow. Generations of people have seen the Great Pyramid on the same spot; but on the supposition that each individual is projecting his own material world in entire independence of all other individuals there is no reason why any two persons should ever see the same thing in the same place. On the supposition of such an independent action by each separate mind, without any common factor binding them all to one particular mode of recognition, no intercourse between individuals would be possible--then, without the consciousness of relation to other individuals the consciousness of our own individuality would be lost, and so we should cease to have any conscious existence at all. If on the other hand we grant that there is, above the individual minds, a great Cosmic Mind which imposes upon them the necessity of all seeing the same image of Matter, then that image is not a projection of the individual minds but of the Cosmic Mind; and since the individual minds are themselves similar projections of the Cosmic Mind, matter is for them just as much a reality as their own existence. I doubt not that material substance is thus projected by the all-embracing Divine Mind; but so also are our own minds projected by it, and therefore the relation between them and matter is a real relation and not a merely fictitious one.

I particularly wish the student to be clear on this point, that where two factors are projected from a common source their relation to each other becomes an absolute fact in respect of the factors themselves, notwithstanding that the power of changing that relation by substituting a different projection must necessarily always continue to reside in the originating source. To take a simple arithmetical example--by my power of mental projection working through my eyes and fingers I write 4 X 2. Here I have established a certain numerical relation which can only produce eight as its result. Again, I have power to change the factors and write 4 X 3, in which case 12 is the only possible result, and so on. Working in this way calculation becomes possible. But if every time I wrote 4 that figure possessed an independent power of setting down a different number by which to multiply itself, what would be the result? The first 4 I wrote might set down 3 as its multiplier, and the next might set down 7, and so on. Or if I want to make a box of a certain size and cut lengths of plank accordingly, if each length could capriciously change its width at a moment's notice, how could I ever make the box? I myself may change the shape and size of my box by establishing new relations between the bits of wood, but for the pieces of wood themselves the proportions determined by my mind must remain fixed quantities, otherwise no construction could take place.

This is a very rough analogy, but it may be sufficient to show that for a cosmos to exist at all it is absolutely necessary that there should be a Cosmic Mind binding all individual minds to certain generic unities of action, and so producing all things as realities and nothing as illusion. The importance of this conclusion will become more apparent as we advance in our studies.

We have now got at some reason why concrete material form is a necessity of the Creative Process. Without it the perfect Self-recognition of Spirit from the Individual standpoint, which we shall presently find is the means by which the Creative Process is to be carried forward, would be impossible; and therefore, so far from matter being an illusion, it is the necessary channel for the self-differentiation of Spirit and its Expression in multitudinous life and beauty. Matter is thus the necessary Polar Opposite to Spirit, and when we thus recognize it in its right order we shall find that there is no antagonism between the two, but that together they constitute one harmonious whole.

CHAPTER II

THE SELF-CONTEMPLATION OF SPIRIT

If we ask how the cosmos came into existence we shall find that ultimately we can only attribute it to the Self-Contemplation of Spirit. Let us start with the facts now known to modern physical science. All material things, including our own bodies, are composed of combinations of different chemical elements such as carbon, oxygen, nitrogen, &c. Chemistry recognizes in all about seventy of these elements each with its peculiar affinities; but the more advanced physical science of the present day finds that they are all composed of one and the same ultimate substance to which the name of Ether has been given, and that the difference between an atom of iron and an atom of oxygen results only from the difference in the number of etheric particles of which each is composed and the rate of their motion within the sphere of the atom, thus curiously coming back to the dictum of Pythagoras that the universe has its origin in Number and Motion. We may therefore say that our entire solar system together with every sort of material substance which it contains is made up of nothing but this one primary substance in various degrees of condensation.

Now the next step is to realize that this ether is everywhere. This is shown by the undulatory theory of light. Light is not a substance but is the effect produced on the eye by the impinging of the ripples of the ether upon the retina. These waves are excessively minute, ranging in length from 1-39,000th of an inch at the red end of the spectrum to 1-57,000th at the violet end. Next remember that these waves are not composed of advancing particles of the medium but pass onwards by the push which each particle in the line of motion gives to the particle next to it, and then you will see that if there were a break of one fifty-thousandth part of an inch in the connecting ether between our eye and any source of light we could not receive light from that source, for there would be nothing to continue the wave-motion across the gap. Consequently as soon as we see light from any source however distant, we know that there must be a continuous body of ether between us and it. Now astronomy shows us that we receive light from heavenly bodies so distant that, though it travels with the incredible speed of 186,000 miles per second, it takes more than two thousand years to reach us from some of them; and as such stars are in all quarters of the heavens we can only come to the conclusion that the primary substance or ether must be universally present.

This means that the raw material for the formation of solar systems is universally distributed throughout space; yet though we find that millions of suns stud the heavens, we also find vast interstellar spaces which show no sign of cosmic activity. Then something has been at work to start cosmic activity in certain areas while passing over others in which the raw material is equally available. What is this something? At first we might be inclined to attribute the development of cosmic energy to the etheric particles themselves, but a little consideration will show us that this is mathematically impossible in a medium which is equally distributed throughout space, for all its particles are in equilibrium and so no one particle possesses per se a greater power of originating motion than any other. Consequently the initial movement must be started by something which, though it works on and through the particles of the primary substance, is not those particles themselves. It is this "Something" which we mean when we speak of "Spirit."

Then since Spirit starts the condensation of the primary substance into concrete aggregation, and also does this in certain areas to the exclusion of others, we cannot avoid attributing to Spirit the power of Selection and of taking an Initiative on its own account.

Here, then, we find the initial Polarity of Universal Spirit and Universal Substance, each being the complementary of the other, and out of this relation all subsequent evolution proceeds. Being complementary means that each supplies what is wanting in the other, and that the two together thus make complete wholeness. Now this is just the case here. Spirit supplies Selection and Motion. Substance supplies something from which selection can be made and to which Motion can be imparted; so that it is a sine qua non for the Expression of Spirit.

Then comes the question, How did the Universal Substance get there? It cannot have made itself, for its only quality is inertia, therefore it must have come from some source having power to project it by some mode of action not of a material nature. Now the only mode of action not of a material nature is Thought, and therefore to Thought we must look for the origin of Substance. This places us at a point antecedent to the existence even of primary substance, and consequently the initial action must be that of the Originating Mind upon Itself, in other words, Self-contemplation.

At this primordial stage neither Time nor Space can be recognized, for both imply measurement of successive intervals, and in the primary movement of Mind upon itself the only consciousness must be that of Present Absolute Being, because no external points exist from which to measure extension either in time or space. Hence we must eliminate the ideas of time and space from our conception of Spirit's initial Self-contemplation.

This being so, Spirit's primary contemplation of itself as simply Being necessarily makes its presence universal and eternal, and consequently, paradoxical as it may seem, its independence of Time and Space makes it present throughout all Time and Space. It is the old esoteric maxim that the point expands to infinitude and that infinitude is concentrated in the point. We start, then, with Spirit contemplating itself simply as Being. But to realize your being you must have consciousness, and consciousness can only come by the recognition of your relation to something else. The something else may be an external fact or a mental image; but even in the latter case to conceive the image at all you must mentally stand back from it and look at it--something like the man who was run in by the police at Gravesend for walking behind himself to see how his new coat fitted. It stands thus: if you are not conscious of something you are conscious of nothing, and if you are conscious of nothing, then you are unconscious, so that to be conscious at all you must have something to be conscious of.

This may seem like an extract from "Paddy's Philosophy," but it makes it clear that consciousness can only be attained by the recognition of something which is not the recognizing ego itself--in other words consciousness is the realization of some particular sort of relation between the cognizing subject and the cognized object; but I want to get away from academical terms into the speech of human beings, so let us take the illustration of a broom and its handle--the two together make a broom; that is one sort of relation; but take the same stick and put a rake-iron at the end of it and you have an altogether different implement. The stick remains the same, but the difference of what is put at the end of it makes the whole thing a broom or a rake. Now the thinking and feeling power is the stick, and the conception which it forms is the thing at the end of the stick, so that the quality of its consciousness will be determined by the ideas which it projects; but to be conscious at all it must project ideas of some sort.

Now of one thing we may be quite sure, that the Spirit of Life must feel alive. Then to feel alive it must be conscious, and to be conscious it must have something to be conscious of; therefore the contemplation of itself as standing related to something which is not its own originating self in propria persona is a necessity of the case; and consequently the Self-contemplation of Spirit can only proceed by its viewing itself as related to something standing out from itself, just as we must stand at a proper distance to see a picture--in fact the very word "existence" means "standing out." Thus things are called into existence or "outstandingness" by a power which itself does not stand out, and whose presence is therefore indicated by the word "subsistence."

The next thing is that since in the beginning there is nothing except Spirit, its primary feeling of aliveness must be that of being alive all over; and to establish such a consciousness of its own universal livingness there must be the recognition of a corresponding relation equally extensive in character; and the only possible correspondence to fulfill this condition is therefore that of a universally distributed and plastic medium whose particles are all in perfect equilibrium, which is exactly the description of the Primary Substance or ether. We are thus philosophically led to the conclusion that Universal Substance must be projected by Universal Spirit as a necessary consequence of Spirit's own inherent feeling of Aliveness; and in this way we find that the great Primary Polarity of Being becomes established.

From this point onward we shall find the principle of Polarity in universal activity. It is that relation between opposites without which no external Motion would be possible, because there would be nowhere to move from, and nowhere to move to; and without which external Form would be impossible because there would be nothing to limit the diffusion of substance and bring it into shape. Polarity, or the interaction of Active and Passive, is therefore the basis of all Evolution.

This is a great fundamental truth when we get it in its right order; but all through the ages it has been a prolific source of error by getting it in its wrong order. And the wrong order consists in making Polarity the originating point of the Creative Process. What this misconception leads to we shall see later on; but since it is very widely accepted under various guises even at the present day it is well to be on our guard against it. Therefore I wish the student to see clearly that there is something which comes before that Polarity which gives rise to Evolution, and that this something is the original movement of Spirit within itself, of which we can best get an idea by calling it Self-contemplation.

Now this may seem an extremely abstract conception and one with which we have no practical concern. I fancy I can hear the reader saying "The Lord only knows how the world started, and it is His business and not mine," which would be perfectly true if this originating faculty were confined to the Cosmic Mind. But it is not, and the same action takes place in our own minds also, only with the difference that it is ultimately subject to that principle of Cosmic Unity of which I have already spoken. But, subject to that unifying principle, this same power of origination is in ourselves also, and our personal advance in evolution depends on our right use of it; and our use of it depends on our recognition that we ourselves give rise to the particular polarities which express themselves in our whole world of consciousness, whether within or without. For these reasons it is very important to realize that Evolution is not the same as Creation. It is the unfolding of potentialities involved in things already created, but not the calling into existence of what does not yet exist--that is Creation.

The order, therefore, which I wish the student to observe is, first the Self-contemplation of Spirit producing Polarity, and next Polarity producing Manifestation in Form--and also to realize that it is in this order his own mind operates as a subordinate center of creative energy. When the true place of Polarity is thus recognized, we shall find in it the explanation of all those relations of things which give rise to the whole world of phenomena; from which we may draw the practical inference that if we want to change the manifestation we must change the polarity, and to change the polarity we must get back to the Self-contemplation of Spirit. But in its proper place as the root-principle of all secondary causation, Polarity is one of those fundamental facts of which we must never lose sight. The term "Polarity" is adopted from electrical science. In the electric battery it is the connecting together of the opposite poles of zinc and copper that causes a current to flow from one to the other and so provides the energy that rings the bell. If the connection is broken there is no action. When you press the button you make the connection. The same process is repeated in respect of every sort of polarity throughout the universe. Circulation depends on polarity, and circulation is the manifestation of Life, which we may therefore say depends on the principle of polarity. In relation to ourselves we are concerned with two great polarities, the polarity of Soul and Body and the polarity of Soul and Spirit; and it is in order that he may more clearly realize their working that I want the student to have some preliminary idea of Polarity as a general principle.

The conception of the Creative Order may therefore be generalized as follows. The Spirit wants to enjoy the reality of its own Life--not merely to vegetate, but to enjoy giving--and therefore by Self-contemplation it projects a polar opposite, or complementary, calculated to give rise to the particular sort of relation out of which the enjoyment of a certain mode of self-consciousness will necessarily spring. Let this sentence be well pondered over until the full extent of its significance is grasped, for it is the key to the whole matter Very well, then: Spirit wants to Enjoy Life, and so, by thinking of itself as having the enjoyment which it wishes, it produces the conditions which, by their re-action upon itself, give rise to the reality of the sort of enjoyment contemplated. In more scientific language an opposite polarity is induced, giving rise to a current which stimulates a particular mode of sensation, which sensation in turn becomes a fresh starting-point for still further action; and in this way each successive stage becomes the stepping-stone to a still higher degree of sensation--that is, to a Fuller Enjoyment of Life.

Such a conception as this presents us with a Progressive Series to which it is impossible to assign any limit. That the progression must be limitless is clear from the fact that there is never any change in the method. At each successive stage the Creating Power is the Self-consciousness of the Spirit, as realized at that stage, still reaching forward for yet further Enjoyment of Life, and so always keeping on repeating the one Creative Process at an ever-rising level; and since these are the sole working conditions, the progress is one which logically admits of no finality. And this is where the importance of realizing the Singleness of the Originating Power comes in, for with a Duality each member would limit the other; in fact, Duality as the Originating Power is inconceivable, for, once more to quote "Paddy's Philosophy," "finality would be reached before anything was begun."

This Creative Process, therefore, can only be conceived of as limitless, while at the same time strictly progressive, that is, proceeding stage by stage, each stage being necessary as a preparation for the one that is to follow. Let us then briefly sketch the stages by which things in our world have got as far as they have. The interest of the enquiry lies in the fact that if we can once get at the principle which is producing these results, we may discover some way of giving it personal application.

On the hypothesis of the Self-contemplation of Spirit being the originating power, we have found that a primary ether, or universal substance, is the necessary correspondence to Spirit's simple awareness of its own being. But though awareness of being is the necessary foundation for any further possibilities it is, so to say, not much to talk about. The foundation fact, of course, is to know that I Am; but immediately on this consciousness there follows the desire for Activity--I want to enjoy my I Am-ness by doing something with it. Translating these words into a state of consciousness in the Cosmic Mind they become a Law of Tendency leading to localized activity, and, looking only at our own world, this would mean the condensation of the universal etheric substance into the primary nebula which later on becomes our solar system, this being the correspondence to the Self-contemplation of Spirit as passing into specific activity instead of remaining absorbed in simple awareness of Being. Then this self-recognition would lead to the conception of still more specific activity having its appropriate polar opposite, or material correspondence, in the condensation of the nebula into a solar system.

Now at this stage Spirit's conception of itself is that of Activity, and consequently the material correspondence is Motion, as distinguished from the simple diffused ether which is the correspondence of mere awareness of Being, But what sort of motion? Is the material movement evolved at this stage bound to take any particular form? A little consideration will show us that it is. At this initial stage, the first awakening, so to say, of Spirit into activity, its consciousness can only be that of activity absolute; that is, not as related to any other mode of activity because as yet there is none, but only as related to an all-embracing Being; so that the only possible conception of Activity at this stage is that of Self-sustained activity, not depending on any preceding mode of activity because there is none. The law of reciprocity therefore demands a similar self-sustained motion in the material correspondence, and mathematical considerations show that the only sort of motion which can sustain a self-supporting body moving in vacuo is a rotary motion bringing the body itself into a spherical form. Now this is exactly what we find at both extremes of the material world. At the big end the spheres of the planets rotating on their axes and revolving round the sun; and at the little end the spheres of the atoms consisting of particles which, modern science tells us, in like manner rotate round a common center at distances which are astronomical as compared with their own mass. Thus the two ultimate units of physical manifestation, the atom and the planet, both follow the same law of self-sustained motion which we have found that, on a priori grounds, they ought in order to express the primary activity of Spirit. And we may note in passing that this rotary, or absolute, motion is the combination of the only two possible relative modes of motion, namely, motion from a point and motion to it, that is to say centrifugal and centripetal motion; so that in rotary, or absolute, motion we find that both the polarities of motion are included, thus repeating on the purely mechanical side the primordial principle of the Unity including the Duality in itself.

But the Spirit wants something more than mechanical motion, something more alive than the preliminary Rota, and so the first step toward individualized consciousness meets us in plant life. Then on the principle that each successive stage affords the platform for a further outlook, plant life is followed by animal life, and this by the Human order in which the liberty of selecting its own conditions is immensely extended. In this way the Spirit's expression of itself has now reached the point where its polar complementary, or Reciprocal, manifests as Intellectual Man--thus constituting the Fourth great stage of Spirit's Self-recognition. But the Creative Process cannot stop here, for, as we have seen, its root in the Self-contemplation of Spirit renders it of necessity an Infinite Progression. So it is no use asking what is its ultimate, for it has no ultimate--its word is "Excelsior"--ever Life and "Life more Abundant." Therefore the question is not as to finality where there is none, but as to the next step in the progression. Four kingdoms we know: what is to be the Fifth? All along the line the progress has been in one direction, namely, toward the development of more perfect Individuality, and therefore on the principle of continuity we may reasonably infer that the next stage will take us still further in the same direction. We want something more perfect than we have yet reached, but our ideas as to what it should be are very various, not to say discordant, for one person's idea of better is another person's idea of worse. Therefore what we want to get at is some broad generalization of principle which will be in advance of our past experiences. This means that we must look for this principle in something that we have not yet experienced, and the only place where we can possibly find principles which have not yet manifested themselves is in gremio Dei--that is, in the innermost of the Originating Spirit, or as St. John calls it, "in the bosom of the Father." So we are logically brought to personal participation in the Divine Ideal as the only principle by which the advance into the next stage can possibly be made. Therefore we arrive at the question, What is the Divine Ideal like?

CHAPTER III

THE DIVINE IDEAL

What is the Divine Ideal? At first it might appear hopeless to attempt to answer such a question, but by adhering to a definite principle we shall find that it will open out, and lead us on, and show us things which we could not otherwise have seen--this is the nature of principle, and is what distinguishes it from mere rules which are only the application of principle under some particular set of conditions. We found two principles as essential in our conception of the Originating Spirit, namely its power of Selection and its power of Initiative; and we found a third principle as its only possible Motive, namely the Desire of the LIVING for ever increasing Enjoyment of Life. Now with these three principles as the very essence of the All-originating Spirit to guide us, we shall, I think, be able to form some conception of that Divine Ideal which gives rise to the Fifth Stage of Manifestation of Spirit, upon which we should now be preparing to enter.

We have seen that the Spirit's Enjoyment of Life is necessarily a reciprocal--it must have a corresponding fact in manifestation to answer to it; otherwise by the inherent law of mind no consciousness, and consequently no enjoyment, could accrue; and therefore by the law of continuous progression the required Reciprocal should manifest as a being awakening to the consciousness of the principle by which he himself comes into existence.

Such an awakening cannot proceed from a comparison of one set of existing conditions with another, but only from the recognition of a Power which is independent of all conditions, that is to say, the absolute Self-dependence of the Spirit. A being thus awakened would be the proper correspondence of the Spirit's Enjoyment of Life at a stage not only above mechanical motion or physical vitality, but even above intellectual perception of existing phenomena, that is to say at the stage where the Spirit's Enjoyment consists in recognizing itself as the Source of all things. The position in the Absolute would be, so to speak, the awakening of Spirit to the recognition of its own Artistic Ability. I use the word "Artistic" as more nearly expressing an almost unstatable idea than any other I can think of, for the work of the artist approaches more closely to creation ex nihilo than any other form of human activity. The work of the artist is the expression of the self that the artist is, while that of the scientist is the comparison of facts which exist independently of his own personality. It is true that the realm of Art is not without its methods of analysis, but the analysis is that of the artist's own feeling and of the causes which give rise to it. These are found to contain in themselves certain principles which are fundamental to all Art, but these principles are the laws of the creative action of mind rather than those of the limitations of matter. Now if we may transfer this familiar analogy to our conception of the working of the All-Originating Mind we may picture it as the Great Artist giving visible expression to His feeling by a process which, though subject to no restriction from antecedent conditions, yet works by a Law which is inseparable from the Feeling itself--in fact the Law is the Feeling, and the Feeling is the Law, the Law of Perfect Creativeness.

Some such Self-contemplation as this is the only way in which we can conceive the next, or Fifth, stage of Spirit's Self-recognition as taking place. Having got as far as it has in the four previous stages, that is to the production of intellectual man as its correspondence, the next step in advance must be on the lines I have indicated--unless, indeed, there were a sudden and arbitrary breaking of the Law of Continuity, a supposition which the whole Creative Process up to now forbids us to entertain. Therefore we may picture the Fifth stage of the Self-contemplation of Spirit as its awakening to the recognition of its own Artistic Ability, its own absolute freedom of action and creative power--just as in studio parlance we say that an artist becomes "free of his palette." But by the always present Law of Reciprocity, through which alone self-consciousness can be attained, this Self-recognition of Spirit in the Absolute implies a corresponding objective fact in the world of the Relative; that is to say, the coming into manifestation of a being capable of realizing the Free Creative Artistry of the Spirit, and of recognizing the same principle in himself, while at the same time realizing also the relation between the Universal Manifesting Principle and its Individual Manifestation.

Such, it appears to me, must be the conception of the Divine Ideal embodied in the Fifth Stage of the progress of manifestation. But I would draw particular attention to the concluding words of the last paragraph, for if we miss the relation between the Universal Manifesting Principle and its Individual Manifestation, we have failed to realize the Principle altogether, whether in the Universal or in the Individual--it is just their interaction that makes each become what it does become--and in this further becoming consists the progression. This relation proceeds from the principle I pointed out in the opening chapter which makes it necessary for the Universal Spirit to be always harmonious with itself; and if this Unity is not recognized by the individual he cannot hold that position of Reciprocity to the Originating Spirit which will enable it to recognize itself as in the Enjoyment of Life at the higher level we are now contemplating--rather the feeling conveyed would be that of something antagonistic, producing the reverse of enjoyment, thus philosophically bringing out the point of the Scriptural injunction, "Grieve not the Spirit." Also the re-action upon the individual must necessarily give rise to a corresponding state of inharmony, though he may not be able to define his feeling of unrest or to account for it. But on the other hand if the grand harmony of the Originating Spirit within itself is duly regarded, then the individual mind affords a fresh center from which the Spirit contemplates itself in what I have ventured to call its Artistic Originality--a boundless potential of Creativeness, yet always regulated by its own inherent Law of Unity.

And this Law of the Spirit's Original Unity is a very simple one. It is the Spirit's necessary and basic conception of itself. A lie is a statement that something is, which is not. Then, since the Spirit's statement or conception of anything necessarily makes that thing exist, it is logically impossible for it to conceive a lie. Therefore the Spirit is Truth. Similarly disease and death are the negative of Life, and therefore the Spirit, as the Principle of Life, cannot embody disease or death in its Self-contemplation. In like manner also, since it is free to produce what it will, the Spirit cannot desire the presence of repugnant forms, and so one of its inherent Laws must be Beauty. In this threefold Law of Truth, Life, and Beauty, we find the whole underlying nature of the Spirit, and no action on the part of the individual can be at variance with the Originating Unity which does not contravert these fundamental principles.

This it will be seen leaves the individual absolutely unfettered except in the direction of breaking up the fundamental harmony on which he himself, as included in the general creation, is dependent. This certainly cannot be called limitation, and we are all free to follow the lines of our own individuality in every other direction; so that, although the recognition of our relation to the Originating Spirit safeguards us from injuring ourselves or others, it in no way restricts our liberty of action or narrows our field of development. Am I, then, trying to base my action upon a fundamental desire for the opening out of Truth, for the increasing of Livingness, and for the creating of Beauty? Have I got this as an ever present Law of Tendency at the back of my thought? If so, then this law will occupy precisely the same place in My Microcosm, or personal world, that it does in the Macrocosm, or great world, as a power which is in itself formless, but which by reason of its presence necessarily impresses its character upon all that the creative energy forms. On this basis the creative energy of the Universal Mind may be safely trusted to work through the specializing influence of our own thought[1] and we may adopt the maxim "trust your desires" because we know that they are the movement of the Universal in ourselves, and that being based upon our fundamental recognition of the Life, Love, and Beauty which the Spirit is, their unfoldments must carry these initial qualities with them all down the line, and thus, in however small a degree, becomes a portion of the working of the Spirit in its inherent creativeness.

This perpetual Creativeness of the Spirit is what we must never lose sight of, and that is why I want the student to grasp clearly the idea of the Spirit's Self-contemplation as the only possible root of the Creative Process. Not only at the first creation of the world, but at all times the plane of the innermost is that of Pure Spirit,[2] and therefore at this, the originating point, there is nothing else for Spirit to contemplate excepting itself; then this Self-contemplation produces corresponding manifestation, and since Self-contemplation or recognition of its own existence must necessarily go on continually, the corresponding creativeness must always be at work. If this fundamental idea be clearly grasped we shall see that incessant and progressive creativeness is the very essence and being of Spirit. This is what is meant by the Affirmativeness of the Spirit. It cannot per se act negatively, that is to say uncreatively, for by the very nature of its Self-recognition such a negative action would be impossible. Of course if we act negatively then, since the Spirit is always acting affirmatively, we are moving in the opposite direction to it; and consequently so long as we regard our own negative action as being affirmative, the Spirit's action must appear to us negative, and thus it is that all the negative conditions of the world have their root in negative or inverted thought: but the more we bring our thought into harmony with the Life, Love, and Beauty which the Spirit is, the less these inverted conditions will obtain, until at last they will be eliminated altogether. To accomplish this is our great object; for though the progress may be slow it will be steady if we proceed on a definite principle; and to lay hold of the true principle is the purpose of our studies. And the principle to lay hold of is the Ceaseless Creativeness of Spirit. This is what we mean when we speak of it as The Spirit of the Affirmative, and I would ask my readers to impress this term upon their minds. Once grant that the All-originating Spirit is thus the Spirit of the Pure Affirmative, and we shall find that this will lead us logically to results of the highest value.

If, then, we keep this Perpetual and Progressive Creativeness of the Spirit continually in mind we may rely upon its working as surely in ourselves as in that great cosmic forward movement which we speak of as Evolution. It is the same power of Evolution working within ourselves, only with this difference, that in proportion as we come to realize its nature we find ourselves able to facilitate its progress by offering more and more favorable conditions for its working. We do not add to the force of the Power, for we are products of it and so cannot generate what generates us; but by providing suitable conditions we can more and more highly specialize it. This is the method of all the advance that has ever been made. We never create any force (e.g. electricity) but we provide special conditions under which the force manifests itself in a variety of useful and beautiful ways, unsuspected possibilities which lay hidden in the power until brought to light by the cooperation of the Personal Factor.

Now it is precisely the introduction[3] of this Personal Factor that concerns us, because to all eternity we can only recognize things from our own center of consciousness, whether in this world or in any other; therefore the practical question is how to specialize in our own case the generic Originating Life which, when we give it a name, we call "the Spirit." The method of doing this is perfectly logical when we once see that the principle involved is that of the Self-recognition of Spirit. We have traced the modus operandi of the Creative Process sufficiently far to see that the existence of the cosmos is the result of the Spirit's seeing itself in the cosmos, and if this be the law of the whole it must also be the law of the part. But there is this difference, that so long as the normal average relation of particles is maintained the whole continues to subsist, no matter what position any particular particle may go into, just as a fountain continues to exist no matter whether any particular drop of water is down in the basin or at the top of the jet. This is the generic action which keeps the race going as a whole. But the question is, What is going to become of ourselves? Then because the law of the whole is also the law of the part we may at once say that what is wanted is for the Spirit to see itself in us--in other words, to find in us the Reciprocal which, as we have seen, is necessary to its Enjoyment of a certain Quality of Consciousness. Now, the fundamental consciousness of the Spirit must be that of Self-sustaining Life, and for the full enjoyment of this consciousness there must be a corresponding individual consciousness reciprocating it; and on the part of the individual such a consciousness can only arise from the recognition that his own life is identical with that of the Spirit--not something sent forth to wander away by itself, but something included in and forming part of the Greater Life. Then by the very conditions of the case, such a contemplation on the part of the individual is nothing else than the Spirit contemplating itself from the standpoint of the individual consciousness, and thus fulfilling the Law of the Creative Process under such specialized conditions as must logically result in the perpetuation of the individual life. It is the Law of the Cosmic Creative Process transferred to the individual.

This, it seems to me, is the Divine Ideal: that of an Individuality which recognizes its Source, and recognizes also the method by which it springs from that Source, and which is therefore able to open up in itself a channel by which that Source can flow in uninterruptedly; with the result that from the moment of this recognition the individual lives directly from the Originating Life, as being himself a special direct creation, and not merely as being a member of a generic race. The individual who has reached this stage of recognition thus finds a principle of enduring life within himself; so then the next question is in what way this principle is likely to manifest itself.

CHAPTER IV

THE MANIFESTATION OF THE LIFE PRINCIPLE

We must bear in mind that what we have now reached is a principle, or universal potential, only we have located it in the individual. But a principle, as such, is not manifestation. Manifestation is the growth proceeding from the principle, that is to say, some Form in which the principle becomes active. At the same time we must recollect that, though a form is necessary for manifestation, the form is not essential, for the same principle may manifest through various forms, just as electricity may work either through a lamp or a tram-car without in any way changing its inherent nature. In this way we are brought to the conclusion that the Life-principle must always provide itself with a body in which to function, though it does not follow that this body must always be of the same chemical constitution as the one we now possess. We might well imagine some distant planet where the chemical combinations with which we are familiar on earth did not obtain; but if the essential life-principle of any individual were transported thither, then by the Law of the Creative Process it would proceed to clothe itself with a material body drawn from the atmosphere and substance of that planet; and the personality thus produced would be quite at home there, for all his surroundings would be perfectly natural to him, however different the laws of Nature might be there from what we know here.

In such a conception as this we find the importance of the two leading principles to which I have drawn attention--first, the power of the Spirit to create ex nihilo, and secondly, the individual's recognition of the basic principle of Unity giving permanence and solidity to the frame of Nature. By the former the self-recognizing life-principle could produce any sort of body it chose; and by the latter it would be led to project one in harmony with the natural order of the particular planet, thus making all the facts of that order solid realities to the individual, and himself a solid and natural being to the other inhabitants of that world. But this would not do away with the individual's knowledge of how he got there; and so, supposing him to have realized his identity with the Universal Life-Principle sufficiently to consciously control the projection of his own body, he could at will disintegrate the body which accorded with the conditions of one planet and constitute one which accorded just as harmoniously with those of another, and could thus function on any number of planets as a perfectly natural being on each of them. He would in all respects resemble the other inhabitants with one all-important exception, that since he had attained to unity with his Creative Principle he would not be tied by the laws of matter as they were.

Anyone who should attain to such a power could only do so by his realization of the all-embracing Unity of the Spirit as being the Foundation of all things; and this being the basis of his own extended powers he would be the last to controvert his own basic principle by employing his powers in such a way as to disturb the natural course of evolution in the world where he was. He might use them to help forward the evolution of others in that world, but certainly never to disturb it, for he would always act on the maxim that "Order is Heaven's First Law."

Our object, however, is not to transfer ourselves to other planets but to get the best out of this one; but we shall not get the best out of this one until we realize that the power which will enable us to do so is so absolutely universal and fundamental that its application in this world is precisely the same as in any other, and that is why I have stated it as a general proposition applicable to all worlds.

The principle being thus universal there is no reason why we should postpone its application till we find ourselves in another world, and the best place and time to begin are Here and Now. The starting point is not in time or locality, but in the mode of Thought; and if we realize that this Point of Origination is Spirit's power to produce something out of nothing, and that it does this in accordance with the natural order of substance of the particular world in which it is working, then the spiritual ego in ourselves, as proceeding direct from the Universal Spirit, should be able first, to so harmoniously combine the working of spiritual and physical laws in its own body as to keep it in perfect health, secondly to carry this process further and renew the body, thus eradicating the effects of old age, and thirdly to carry the process still further and perpetuate this renewed body as long as the individual might desire.

If the student shows this to one of his average acquaintances who has never given any thought to these things, his friend will undoubtedly exclaim "Tommy rot!" even if he does not use a stronger expletive. He will at once appeal to the past experience of all mankind, his argument being that what has not been in the past cannot be in the future; yet he does not apply the same argument to aeronautics and is quite oblivious of the fact that the Sacred Volume which he reverences contains promises of these very things. The really earnest student must never forget the maxim that "Principle is not bound by Precedent"--if it were we should still be primitive savages.

To use the Creative Process we must Affirm the Creative Power, that is to say, we must go back to the Beginning of the series and start with Pure Spirit, only remembering that this starting-point is now to be found in ourselves, for this is what distinguishes the individual Creative Process from the cosmic one. This is where the importance of realizing only ONE Originating Power instead of two interacting powers comes in, for it means that we do not derive our power from any existing polarity, but that we are going to establish polarities which will start secondary causation on the lines which we thus determine. This also is where the importance comes in of recognizing that the only possible originating movement of spirit must be Self-contemplation, for this shows us that we do not have to contemplate existing conditions but the Divine Ideal, and that this contemplation of the Divine Ideal of Man is the Self-contemplation of the Spirit from the standpoint of Human Individuality.

Then the question arises, if these principles are true, why are we not demonstrating them? Well, when our fundamental principle is obviously correct and yet we do not get the proper results, the only inference is that somewhere or other we have introduced something antagonistic to the fundamental principle, something not inherent in the principle itself and which therefore owes its presence to some action of our own. Now the error consists in the belief that the Creative Power is limited by the material in which it works. If this be assumed, then you have to calculate the resistances offered by the material; and since by the terms of the Creative Process these resistances do not really exist, you have no basis of calculation at all--in fact you have no means of knowing where you are, and everything is in confusion. This is why it is so important to remember that the Creative Process is the action of a Single Power, and that the interaction of two opposite polarities comes in at a later stage, and is not creative, but only distributive--that is to say, it localizes the Energy already proceeding from the Single Power. This is a fundamental truth which should never be lost sight of. So long, however, as we fail to see this truth we necessarily limit the Creative Power by the material it works in, and in practice we do this by referring to past experience as the only standard of judgment. We are measuring the Fifth Kingdom by the standard of the Fourth, as though we should say that an intellectual man, a being of the Fourth Kingdom, was to be limited by the conditions which obtain in the First or Mineral Kingdom--to use Scriptural language we are seeking the Living among the dead.

And moreover at the present time a new order of experience is beginning to open out to us, for well authenticated instances of the cure of disease by the invisible power of the Spirit are steadily increasing in number. The facts are now too patent to be denied--what we want is a better knowledge of the power which accounts for them. And if this beginning is now with us, by what reason can we limit it? The difference between the healing of disease and the renewal of the entire organism and the perpetuation of life is only a difference of degree and not of kind; so that the actual experience of increasing numbers shows the working of a principle to which we can logically set no limits.

If we get the steps of the Creative Process clearly into our minds we shall see why we have hitherto had such small results.

Spirit creates by Self-contemplation; Therefore, What it contemplates itself as being, that it becomes. You are individualized Spirit; Therefore, What you contemplate as the Law of your being becomes the Law of your being.

Hence, contemplate a Law of Death arising out of the Forces of the Material reacting against the Power of the Spirit and overcoming it, and you impress this mode of self-recognition upon Spirit in yourself. Of course you cannot alter its inherent nature, but you cause it to work under negative conditions and thus make it produce negative results so far as you yourself are concerned.

But reverse the process, and contemplate a Law of Life as inherent in the very Being of the Spirit, and therefore as inherent in spirit in yourself; and contemplate the forces of the Material as practically non-existent in the Creative Process, because they are products of it and not causes--look at things in this way and you will impress a corresponding conception upon the Spirit which, by the Law of Reciprocity, thus enters into Self-contemplation on these lines from the standpoint of your own individuality; and then by the nature of the Creative Process a corresponding externalization is bound to take place. Thus our initial question, How did anything come into existence at all, brings us to the recognition of a Law of Life which we may each specialize for ourselves; and in the degree to which we specialize it we shall find the Creative Principle at work within us building up a healthier and happier personality in mind, body, and circumstances.

Only we must learn to distinguish the vehicles of Spirit from Spirit itself, for the distinction has very important bearings. What distinguishes the vehicles from the Spirit is the Law of Growth. The Spirit is the Formless principle of Life, and the vehicle is a Form in which this principle functions. Now the vehicle is a projection by the Spirit of substance coordinate with the natural order of the plane on which the vehicle functions, and therefore requires to be built up comformably to that order. This building up is what we speak of as Growth; and since the principle which causes the growth is the individualized Spirit, the rate at which the growth will go on will depend on the amount of vitalizing energy the Spirit puts into it, and the amount of vitalizing energy will depend on the degree in which the individualized Spirit appreciates its own livingness, and finally the degree of this appreciation will depend on the quality of the individual's perception of the Great All-originating Spirit as reflecting itself in him and thus making his contemplation of It nothing else than the Creative Self-contemplation of the Spirit proceeding from an individual and personal center. We must therefore not omit the Law of Growth in the vehicle from our conception of the working of the Spirit. As a matter of fact the vehicle has nothing to say in the matter for it is simply a projection from the Spirit; but for this very reason its formation will be slow or rapid in exact proportion to the individual spirit's vitalizing conception. We could imagine a degree of vitalizing conception that would produce the corresponding form instantaneously, but at present we must allow for the weakness of our spiritual power--not as thinking it by any means incapable of accomplishing its object, but as being far slower in operation now than we hope to see it in the future--and so we must not allow ourselves to be discouraged, but must hold our thought knowing that it is doing its creative work, and that the corresponding growth is slowly but surely taking place--thus following the Divine precept that men ought always to pray and not to faint. Gradually as we gain experience on these new lines our confidence in the power of the Spirit will increase, and we shall be less inclined to argue from the negative side of things, and thus the hindrances to the inflow of the Originating Spirit will be more and more removed, and greater and greater results will be obtained.

If we would have our minds clear on this subject of Manifestation we should remember its threefold nature:--First the General Life-Principle, secondly the Localization of this principle in the Individual, and thirdly the Growth of the Vehicle as it is projected by the individualized spirit with more or less energy. It is a sequence of progressive condensation from the Undifferentiated Universal Spirit to the ultimate and outermost vehicle--a truth enshrined in the esoteric maxim that "Matter is Spirit at its lowest level."

The forms thus produced are in true accord with the general order of Nature on the particular plane where they occur, and are therefore perfectly different from forms temporarily consolidated out of material drawn from other living organisms. These latter phantasmal bodies are held together only by an act of concentrated volition, and can therefore only be maintained for a short time and with effort; while the body which the individualized spirit, or ego, builds for itself is produced by a perfectly natural process and does not require any effort to sustain it, since it is kept in touch with the whole system of the planet by the continuous and effortless action of the individual's sub-conscious mind.

This is where the action of sub-conscious mind as the builder of the body comes in. Sub-conscious mind acts in accordance with the aggregate of suggestion impressed upon it by the conscious mind, and if this suggestion is that of perfect harmony with the physical laws of the planet then a corresponding building by the sub-conscious mind will take place, a process which, so far from implying any effort, consists rather in a restful sense of unity with Nature.[4]

And if to this sense of union with the Soul of Nature, that Universal Sub-conscious Mind which holds in the cosmos the same place that the sub-conscious mind does in ourselves--if to this there be superadded a sense of union with the All-creating Spirit from which the Soul of Nature flows, then through the medium of the individual's sub-conscious mind such specialized effects can be produced in his body as to transcend our past experiences without in any way violating the order of the universe. The Old Law was the manifestation of the Principle of Life working under constricted conditions: the New Law is the manifestation of the same Principle working under expanding conditions. Thus it is that though God never changes we are said to "increase with the increase of God."

CHAPTER V
THE PERSONAL FACTOR

I have already pointed out that the presence of a single all-embracing Cosmic Mind is an absolute necessity for the existence of any creation whatever, for the reason that if each individual mind were an entirely separate center of perception, not linked to all other minds by a common ground of underlying mentality independent of all individual action, then no two persons would see the same thing at the same time, in fact no two individuals would be conscious of living in the same world. If this were the case there would be no common standard to which to refer our sensations; and, indeed, coming into existence with no consciousness of environment except such as we could form by our own unaided thought, and having by the hypothesis no standard by which to form our thoughts, we could not form the conception of any environment at all, and consequently could have no recognition of our own existence. The confusion of thought involved even in the attempt to state such a condition shows it to be perfectly inconceivable, for the simple reason that it is self-contradictory and self-destructive. On this account it is clear that our own existence and that of the world around us necessarily implies the presence of a Universal Mind acting on certain fixed lines of its own which establish the basis for the working of all individual minds. This paramount action of the Universal Mind thus sets an unchangeable standard by which all individual mental action must eventually be measured, and therefore our first concern is to ascertain what this standard is and to make it the basis of our own action.

But if the independent existence of a common standard of reference is necessary for our self-recognition simply as inhabitants of the world we live in, then a fortiori a common standard of reference is necessary for our recognition of the unique place we hold in the Creative Order, which is that of introducing the Personal Factor without which the possibilities contained in the great Cosmic Laws would remain undeveloped, and the Self-contemplation of Spirit could never reach those infinite unfoldments of which it is logically capable.

The evolution of the Personal Factor is therefore the point with which we are most concerned. As a matter of fact, whatever theories we may hold to the contrary, we do all realize the same cosmic environment in the same way; that is to say, our minds all act according to certain generic laws which underlie all our individual diversities of thought and feeling. This is so because we are made that way and cannot help it. But with the Personal Factor the case is different. A standard is no less necessary, but we are not so made as to conform to it automatically. The very conception of automatic conformity to a personal standard is self-contradictory, for it does away with the very thing that constitutes personality, namely freedom of volition, the use of the powers of Initiative and Selection. For this reason conformity to the Standard of Personality must be a matter of choice, which amounts to the same thing as saying that it rests with each individual to form his own conception of a standard of Personality; but which liberty, however, carries with it the inevitable result that we shall bring into manifestation the conditions corresponding to the sort of personality we accept as our normal standard.

I would draw attention to the words "Normal Standard." What we shall eventually attain is, not what we merely wish, but what we regard as normal. The reason is that since we sub-consciously know ourselves to be based upon the inherent Law of the Universal Mind we feel, whether we can reason it out or not, that we cannot force the All-producing Mind to work contrary to its own inherent qualities, and therefore we intuitively recognize that we cannot transcend the sort of personality which is normal according to the Law of Universal Mind. This thought is always at the back of our mind and we cannot get away from it for the simple reason that it is inherent in our mental constitution, because our mind is itself a product of the Creative Process; and to suppose ourselves transcending the possibilities contained in the Originating Mind would involve the absurdity of supposing that we can get the greater out of the less.

Nevertheless there are some who try to do so, and their position is as follows. They say in effect, I want to transcend the standard of humanity as I see it around me. But this is the normal standard according to the Law of the Universe, therefore I have to get above the Law of the Universe. Consequently I cannot draw the necessary power from that Law, and so there is nowhere else to get it except from myself. Thus the aspirant is thrown back upon his own individual will as the ultimate power, with the result that the onus lies on him of concentrating a force sufficient to overcome the Law of the Universe. There is thus continually present to him a suggestion of struggle against a tremendous opposing force, and as a consequence he is continually subjecting himself to a strain which grows more and more intense as he realizes the magnitude of the force against which he is contending. Then as he begins to realize the inequality of the struggle he seeks for extraneous aid, and so he falls back on various expedients, all of which have this in common that they ultimately amount to invoking the assistance of other individualities, not seeing that this involves the same fallacy which has brought him to his present straits, the fallacy, namely, of supposing that any individuality can develop a power greater than that of the source from which itself proceeds. The fallacy is a radical one; and therefore all efforts based upon it are fore-doomed to ultimate failure, whether they take the form of reliance on personal force of will, or magical rites, or austerity practiced against the body, or attempts by abnormal concentration to absorb the individual in the universal, or the invocation of spirits, or any other method--the same fallacy is involved in them all, that the less is larger than the greater.

Now the point to be noted is that the idea of transcending the present conditions of humanity does not necessarily imply the idea of transcending the normal law of humanity. The mistake we have hitherto made has been in fixing the Standard of Personality too low and in taking our past experiences as measuring the ultimate possibilities of the race. Our liberty consists in our ability to form our own conception of the Normal Standard of Personality, only subject to the conditions arising out of the inherent Law of the underlying Universal Mind; and so the whole thing resolves itself into the question, What are those fundamental conditions? The Law is that we cannot transcend the Normal; therefore comes the question, What is the Normal?

I have endeavored to answer this question in the chapter on the Divine Ideal, but since this is the crucial point of the whole subject we may devote a little further attention to it. The Normal Standard of Personality must necessarily be the reproduction in Individuality of what the Universal Mind is in itself, because, by the nature of the Creative Process, this standard results from Spirit's Self-contemplation at the stage where its recognition is turned toward its own power of Initiative and Selection. At this stage Spirit's Self-recognition has passed beyond that of Self-expression through a mere Law of Averages into the recognition of what I have ventured to call its Artistic Ability; and as we have seen that Self-recognition at any stage can only be attained by the realization of a relation stimulating that particular sort of consciousness, it follows that for the purpose of this further advance expression through individuals of a corresponding type is a necessity. Then by the Law of Reciprocity such beings must possess powers similar to those contemplated in itself by the Originating Spirit, in other words they must be in their own sphere the image and likeness of the Spirit as it sees itself.

Now we have seen that the Creating Spirit necessarily possesses the powers of Initiative and Selection. These we may call its active properties--the summing up of what it does. But what any power does depends on what it is, for the simple reason that it cannot give out what it does not contain; therefore at the back of the initiative and selective power of the Spirit we must find what the Spirit is, namely, what are its substantive properties. To begin with it must be Life. Then because it is Life it must be Love, because as the undifferentiated Principle of Life it cannot do otherwise than tend to the fuller development of life in each individual, and the pure motive of giving greater enjoyment of life is Love. Then because it is Life guided by Love it must also be Light, that is to say, the primary all-inclusive perception of boundless manifestations yet to be. Then from this proceeds Power, because there is no opposing force at the level of Pure Spirit; and therefore Life urged forward by Love or the desire for recognition, and by Light or the pure perception of the Law of Infinite Possibility, must necessarily produce Power, for the simple reason that under these conditions it could not stop short of action, for that would be the denial of the Life, Love, and Light which it is. Then because the Spirit is Life, Love, Light, and Power, it is also Peace, again for a very simple reason, that being the Spirit of the Whole it cannot set one part in antagonism against another, for that would be to destroy the wholeness. Next the Spirit must be Beauty, because on the same principle of Wholeness it must duly proportion every part to every other part, and the due proportioning of all parts is beauty. And lastly the Spirit must be Joy, because, working on these lines, it cannot do otherwise than find pleasure in the Self-expression which its works afford it, and in the contemplation of the limitlessness of the Creative Process by which each realized stage of evolution, however excellent, is still the stepping-stone to something yet more excellent, and so on in everlasting progression.

For these reasons we may sum up the Substantive Being of the All-originating Spirit as Life, Love, Light, Power, Peace, Beauty, and Joy; and its Active Power as that of Initiative and Selection. These, therefore, constitute the basic laws of the underlying universal mentality which sets the Standard of Normal Personality--a standard which, when seen in this light, transcends the utmost scope of our thought, for it is nothing else than the Spirit of the Infinite Affirmative conceived in Human Personality. This standard is therefore that of the Universal Spirit itself reproduced in Human Individuality by the same Law of Reciprocity which we have found to be the fundamental law of the Creative Process--only now we are tracing the action of this Law in the Fifth Kingdom instead of in the Fourth.

This Standard, then, we may call the Universal Principle of Humanity, and having now traced the successive steps by which it is reached from the first cosmic movement of the Spirit in the formation of the primary nebula, we need not go over the old ground again, and may henceforward take this Divine Principle of Humanity as our Normal Standard and make it the starting point for our further evolution. But how are we to do this? Simply by using the one method of Creative Process, that is, the Self-contemplation of Spirit. We now know ourselves to be Reciprocals of the Divine Spirit, centers in which It finds a fresh standpoint for Self-contemplation; and so the way to rise to the heights of this Great Pattern is by contemplating it as the Normal Standard of our own Personality.

And be it noted that the Pattern thus set before us is Universal. It is the embodiment of all the great principles of the Affirmative, and so in no way interferes with our own particular individuality--that is something built up upon this foundation, something additional affording the differentiating medium through which this unifying Principle finds variety of expression, therefore we need be under no apprehension lest by resting upon this Pattern we should become less ourselves. On the contrary the recognition of it sets us at liberty to become more fully ourselves because we know that we are basing our development, not upon the strength of our own unaided will, nor yet upon any sort of extraneous help, but upon the Universal Law itself, manifesting through us in the proper sequence of the Creative Order; so that we are still dealing with Universal principles, only the principle by which we are now working is the Universal Principle of Personality.

I wish the student to get this idea very clearly because this is really the crux of the passage from the Fourth Kingdom into the Fifth. The great problem of the future of evolution is the introduction of the Personal Factor. The reason why this is so is very simple when we see it. To take a thought from my own "Doré Lectures" we may put it in this way. In former days no one thought of building ships of iron because iron does not float; yet now ships are seldom built of anything else, though the relative specific gravities of iron and water remain unchanged. What has changed is the Personal Factor. It has expanded to a more intelligent perception of the law of flotation, and we now see that wood floats and iron sinks, both of them by the same principle working under opposite conditions, the law, namely, that anything will float which bulk for bulk is lighter than the volume of water displaced by it, so that by including in our calculations the displacement of the vessel as well as the specific gravity of the material, we now make iron float by the very same law by which it sinks. This example shows that the function of the Personal Factor is to analyze the manifestations of Law which are spontaneously afforded by Nature and to discover the Universal Affirmative Principle which lies hidden within them, and then by the exercise of our powers of Initiative and Selection to provide such specialized conditions as will enable the Universal Principle to work in perfectly new ways transcending anything in our past experience. This is how all progress has been achieved up to the present; and is the way in which all progress must be achieved in the future, only for the purpose of evolution, or growth from within, we must transfer the method to the spiritual plane.

The function, then, of the Personal Factor in the Creative Order is to provide specialized conditions by the use of the powers of Selection and Initiative, a truth indicated by the maxim "Nature unaided fails"; but the difficulty is that if enhanced powers were attained by the whole population of the world without any common basis for their use, their promiscuous exercise could only result in chaotic confusion and the destruction of the entire race. To introduce the creative power of the Individual and at the same time avoid converting it into a devastating flood is the great problem of the transition from the Fourth Kingdom into the Fifth. For this purpose it becomes necessary to have a Standard of the Personal Factor independent of any individual conceptions, just as we found that in order for us to attain self-consciousness at all it was a necessity that there should be a Universal Mind as the generic basis of all individual mentality; only in regard to the generic build of mind the conformity is necessarily automatic, while in regard to the specializing process the fact that the essence of that process is Selection and Initiative renders it impossible for the conformity to the Standard of Personality to be automatic--the very nature of the thing makes it a matter of individual choice.

Now a Standard of Personality independent of individual conceptions must be the essence of Personality as distinguished from individual idiosyncrasies, and can therefore be nothing else than the Creative Life, Love, Beauty, etc., viewed as a Divine Individuality, by identifying ourselves with which we eliminate all possibility of conflict with other personalities based on the same fundamental recognition; and the very universality of this Standard allows free play to all our particular idiosyncrasies while at the same time preventing them from antagonizing the fundamental principles to which we have found that the Self-contemplation of the Originating Spirit must necessarily give rise. In this way we attain a Standard of Measurement for our own powers. If we recognize no such Standard our development of spiritual powers, our discovery of the immense possibilities hidden in the inner laws of Nature and of our own being, can only become a scourge to ourselves and others, and it is for this reason that these secrets are so jealously guarded by those who know them, and that over the entrance to the temple are written the words "Eskato Bebeloi"--"Hence ye Profane."

But if we recognize and accept this Standard of Measurement then we need never fear our discovery of hidden powers either in ourselves or in Nature, for on this basis it becomes impossible for us to misuse them. Therefore it is that all systematic teaching on these subjects begins with instruction regarding the Creative Order of the Cosmos, and then proceeds to exhibit the same Order as reproduced on the plane of Personality and so affording a fresh starting point for the Creative Process by the introduction of Individual Initiative and Selection. This is the doctrine of the Macrocosm and the Microcosm; and the transition from the generic working of the Creative Spirit in the Cosmos to its specific working in the Individual is what is meant by the doctrine of the Octave.

CHAPTER VI

THE STANDARD OF PERSONALITY

We have now got some general idea as to the place of the personal factor in the Creative Order, and so the next question is, How does this affect ourselves? The answer is that if we have grasped the fundamental fact that the moving power in the Creative Process is the self-contemplation of Spirit, and if we also see that, because we are miniature reproductions of the Original Spirit, our contemplation of It becomes Its contemplation of Itself from the standpoint of our own individuality--if we have grasped these fundamental conceptions, then it follows that our process for developing power is to contemplate the Originating Spirit as the source of the power we want to develop. And here we must guard against a mistake which people often make when looking to the Spirit as the source of power. We are apt to regard it as sometimes giving and sometimes withholding power, and consequently are never sure which way it will act. But by so doing we make Spirit contemplate itself as having no definite action at all, as a plus and minus which mutually cancel each other, and therefore by the Law of the Creative Process no result is to be expected. The mistake consists in regarding the power as something separate from the Spirit; whereas by the analysis of the Creative Process which we have now made we see that the Spirit itself is the power, because the power comes into existence only through Spirit's self-contemplation. Then the logical inference from this is that by contemplating the Spirit as the power, and vice versa by contemplating the power as the Spirit, a similar power is being generated in ourselves.

Again an important conclusion follows from this, which is that to generate any particular sort of power we should contemplate it in the abstract rather than as applied to the particular set of circumstances we have in hand. The circumstances indicate the sort of power we want but they do not help us to generate it; rather they impress us with a sense of something contrary to the power, something which has to be overcome by it, and therefore we should endeavor to dwell on the power in itself, and so come into touch with it in its limitless infinitude.

It is here that we begin to find the benefit of a Divine Standard of Human Individuality. That also is an Infinite Principle, and by identifying ourselves with it we bring to bear upon the abstract conception of infinite Impersonal Power a corresponding conception of Infinite Personality, so that we thus import the Personal Factor which is able to use the Power without imposing any strain upon ourselves. We know that by the very nature of the Creative Process we are one with the Originating Spirit and therefore one with all the principles of its Being, and consequently one with its Infinite Personality, and therefore our contemplation of it as the Power which we want gives us the power to use that Power.

This is the Self-contemplation of Spirit employed from the individual standpoint for the generating of power. Then comes the application of the power thus generated. But there is only one Creative Process, that of the Self-contemplation of Spirit, and therefore the way to use this process for the application of the power is to contemplate ourselves as surrounded by the conditions which we want to produce. This does not mean that we are to lay down a hard and fast pattern of the conditions and strenuously endeavor to compel the Power to conform its working to every detail of our mental picture--to do so would be to hinder its working and to exhaust ourselves. What we are to dwell upon is the idea of an Infinite Power producing the happiness we desire, and because this Power is also the Forming Power of the universe trusting it to give that form to the conditions which will most perfectly react upon us to produce the particular state of consciousness desired.

Thus neither on the side of in-drawing nor of out-giving is there any constraining of the Power, while in both cases there is an initiative and selective action on the part of the individual--for the generating of power he takes the initiative of invoking it by contemplation, and he makes selection of the sort of power to invoke; while on the giving-out side he makes selection of the purpose for which the Power is to be employed, and takes the initiative by his thought of directing the Power to that purpose. He thus fulfills the fundamental requirements of the Creative Process by exercising Spirit's inherent faculties of initiative and selection by means of its inherent method, namely by Self-contemplation. The whole action is identical in kind with that which produces the cosmos, and it is now repeated in miniature for the particular world of the individual; only we must remember that this miniature reproduction of the Creative Process is based upon the great fundamental principles inherent in the Universal Mind, and cannot be dissociated from them without involving a conception of the individual which will ultimately be found self-destructive because it cuts away the foundation on which his individuality rests.

It will therefore be seen that any individuality based upon the fundamental Standard of Personality thus involved in the Universal Mind has reached the basic principle of union with the Originating Spirit itself, and we are therefore correct in saying that union is attained through, or by means of, this Standard Personality. This is a great truth which in all ages has been set forth under a variety of symbolic statements; often misunderstood, and still continuing to be so, though owing to the inherent vitality of the idea itself even a partial apprehension of it produces a corresponding measure of good results. This falling short has been occasioned by the failure to recognize an Eternal Principle at the back of the particular statements--in a word the failure to see what they were talking about. All principles are eternal in themselves, and this is what distinguishes them from their particular manifestations as laws determined by temporary and local conditions.

If then, we would reach the root of the matter we must penetrate through all verbal statements to an Eternal Principle which is as active now as ever in the past, and which is as available to ourselves as to any who have gone before us. Therefore it is that when we discern an Eternal and Universal Principle of Human Personality as necessarily involved in the Essential Being of the Originating Universal Spirit--Filius in gremio Patris--we have discovered the true Normal Standard of Personality. Then because this standard is nothing else than the principle of Personality expanded to infinitude, there is no limit to the expansion which we ourselves may attain by the operation in us of this principle; and so we are never placed in a position of antagonism to the true law of our being, but on the contrary the larger and more fundamental our conception of personal development the greater will be the fulfillment which we give to the Law. The Normal Standard of Personality is found to be itself the Law of the Creative Process working at the personal level; and it cannot be subject to limitation for the simple reason that the process being that of the Self-contemplation of Spirit, no limits can possibly be assigned to this contemplation.

We need, therefore, never be afraid of forming too high an idea of human possibilities provided always that we take this standard as the foundation on which to build up the edifice of our personality. And we see that this standard is no arbitrary one but simply the Expression in Personality of the ONE all-embracing Spirit of the Affirmative; and therefore the only limitation implied by conformity to it is that of being prevented from running on lines the opposite of those of the Creative Process, that is to say, from calling into action causes of disintegration and destruction. In the truly Constructive Order, therefore, the Divine Standard of Personality is as really the basis of the development of specific personality as the Universal Mind is the necessary basis of generic mentality; and just as without this generic ultimate of Mind we should none of us see the same world at the same time, and in fact have no consciousness of existence, so apart from this Divine Standard of Personality it is equally impossible for us to specialize the generic law of our being so as to develop all the glorious possibilities that are latent in it.

Only we must never forget the difference between these two statements of the Universal Law--the one is cosmic and generic, common to the whole race, whether they know it or not, a Standard to which we all conform automatically by the mere fact of being human beings; while the other is a personal and individual Standard, automatic conformity to which is impossible because that would imply the loss of those powers of Initiative and Selection which are the very essence of Personality; so that this Standard necessarily implies a personal selection of it in preference to other conceptions of an antagonistic nature.

CHAPTER VII
RACE THOUGHT AND NEW THOUGHT

The steady following up of the successive stages of the Creative Process has led us to the recognition of an Individuality in the All-creating Spirit itself, but an Individuality which is by its very nature Universal, and so cannot be departed from without violating the essential principles on which the further expansion of our own individuality depends. At the same time it is strictly individual, for it is the Spirit of Individuality, and is thus to be distinguished from that merely generic race-personality which makes us human beings at all. Race-personality is of course the necessary basis for the development of this Individuality; but if we do not see that it is only the preliminary to further evolution, any other conception of our personality as members of the race will prevent our advance toward our proper position in the Creative Order, which is that of introducing the Personal Factor by the exercise of our individual power of initiative and selection.

It is on this account that Race-thought, simply as such, is opposed to the attempt of the individual to pass into a higher order of life. It limits him by strong currents of negative suggestion based on the fallacy that the perpetuation of the race requires the death of the individual;[5] and it is only when the individual sees that this is not true, and that his race- nature constitutes the ground out of which his new Individuality is to be formed, that he becomes able to oppose the negative power of race-thought. He does this by destroying it with its own weapon, that is, by finding in the race-nature itself the very material to be used by the Spirit for building-up the New Man. This is a discovery on the spiritual plane equivalent to the discovery on the physical plane that we can make iron float by the same law by which it sinks. It is the discovery that what we call the mortal part of us is capable of being brought under a higher application of the Universal Law of Life, which will transmute it into an immortal principle. When we see what we call the mortal part of us in this light we can employ the very principle on which the negative race-thought is founded as a weapon for the destruction of that thought in our own minds.

The basis of the negative race-thought is the idea that physical death is an essential part of the Normal Standard of Personality, and that the body is composed of so much neutral material with which death can do what it likes. But it is precisely this neutrality of matter that makes it just as amenable to the Law of Life as to the Law of Death--it is simply neutral and not an originating power on either side; so then when we realize that our Normal Standard of Personality is not subject to death, but is the Eternal Essence and Being of Life itself, then we see that this neutrality of matter--its inability to make selection or take initiative on its own account--is just what makes it the plastic medium for the expression of Spirit in ourselves.

In this way the generic or race-mind in the individual becomes the instrument through which the specializing power of the Spirit works toward the building up of a personality based upon the truly Normal Standard of Individuality which we have found to be inherent in the All-originating Spirit itself: and since the whole question is that of the introduction of the factor of personal individuality into the creative order of causation, this cannot be done by depriving the individual of what makes him a person instead of a thing, namely, the power of conscious initiative and selection.

For this reason the transition from the Fourth Kingdom into the Fifth cannot be forced upon the race either by a Divine fiat or by the generic action of cosmic law, for it is a specializing of the cosmic law which can only be effected by personal initiative and selection, just as iron can only be made to float under certain specialized conditions; and consequently the passage from the Fourth into the Fifth Kingdom is a strictly individual process which can only be brought about by a personal perception of what the normal standard of the New Individuality really is. This can only be done by the active laying aside of the old race-standard and the conscious adoption of the new one. The student will do well to consider this carefully, for it explains why the race cannot receive the further evolution simply as a race; and also it shows that our further evolution is not into a state of less activity but of greater, not into being less alive but more alive, not into being less ourselves but more ourselves; thus being just the opposite of those systems which present the goal of existence as re-absorption into the undifferentiated Divine essence. On the contrary our further evolution is into greater degrees of conscious activity than we have ever yet known, because it implies our development of greater powers as the consequence of our clearer perception of our true relation to the All-originating Spirit. It is the recognition that we may, and should, measure ourselves by this New Standard instead of by the old race-standard that constitutes the real New Thought. The New Thought which gives New Life to the individual will never be realized so long as we think that it is merely the name of a particular sect, or that it is to be found in the mechanical observance of a set of rules laid down for us by some particular teacher. It is a New Fact in the experience of the individual, the reason for which is indeed made clear to him through intellectual perception of the real nature of the Creative Process, but which can become an actual experience only by habitual personal intercourse with that Divine Spirit which is the Life, Love and Beauty that are at the back of the Creative Process and find expression through it.

From this intercourse new thoughts will continually flow in, all of them bearing that vivifying element which is inherent in their source, and the individual will then proceed to work out these new ideas with the knowledge that they have their origin in the selection and initiative power of the All-creating Spirit itself, and in this way by combined meditation and action he will find himself advancing into increasing light, liberty and usefulness. The advance may be almost imperceptible from one day to another, but it will be perceptible at longer intervals, and the one who is thus moving forward with the Spirit of God will on looking back at any time always find that he is getting more livingness out of life than he was a year previously. And this without strenuous effort, for he is not having to manufacture the power from his own resources but only to receive it--and as for using it, that is only the exercise of the power itself. So following on these lines you will find that Rest and Power are identical; and so you get the real New Thought which grows in Newness every day.

CHAPTER VIII
THE DÉNOUEMENT OF THE CREATIVE PROCESS

Then comes the question, What should logically be the dénouement of the progression we have been considering? Let us briefly recapitulate the steps of the series. Universal Spirit by Self-contemplation evolves Universal Substance. From this it produces cosmic creation as the expression of itself as functioning in Space and Time. Then from this initial movement it proceeds to more highly specialized modes of Self-contemplation in a continually ascending scale, for the simple reason that self-contemplation admits of no limits and therefore each stage of self-recognition cannot be other than the starting-point for a still more advanced mode of self-contemplation, and so on ad infinitum. Thus there is a continuous progress toward more and more highly specialized forms of life, implying greater liberty and wider scope for enjoyment as the capacity of the individual life corresponds to a higher degree of the contemplation of Spirit; and in this way evolution proceeds till it reaches a level where it becomes impossible to go any further except by the exercise of conscious selection and initiative on the part of the individual, while at the same time conforming to the universal principles of which evolution is the expression.

Now ask yourself in what way individual selection and initiative would be likely to act as expressing the Originating Spirit itself? Given the knowledge on the part of the individual that he is able by his power of initiative and selection to draw directly upon the All-originating Spirit of Life, what motive could he have for not doing so? Therefore, granted such a perfect recognition, we should find the individual holding precisely the same place in regard to his own individual world that the All-originating Spirit does to the cosmos; subject only to the same Law of Love, Beauty, &c., which we found to be necessarily inherent in the Creative Spirit--a similarity which would entirely prevent the individual from exercising his otherwise limitless powers in any sort of antagonism to the Spirit of the Great Whole.

At the same time the individual would be quite aware that he was not the Universal Spirit in propria persona, but that he was affording expression to it through his individuality. Now Expression is impossible except through Form, and therefore form of some sort is a necessity of individuality. It is just here, then, that we find the importance of that principle of Harmony with Environment of which I spoke earlier, the principle in accordance with which a person who had obtained complete control of matter, if he wished to transport himself to some other planet, would appear there in perfect conformity with all the laws of matter that obtained in that world; though, of course, not subject to any limitation of the Life Principle in himself. He would exhibit the laws of matter as rendered perfect by the Law of Originating Life. But if any one now living on this earth were thus perfectly to realize the Law of Life he would be in precisely the same position here as our imaginary visitor to another planet--in other words the dénouement of the Law of Life is not the putting off of the body, but its inclusion as part of the conscious life of the Spirit.

This does not imply any difference in the molecular structure of the body from that of other men, for by the principle of Harmony of which I have just spoken, it would be formed in strict accordance with the laws of matter on the particular planet; though it would not be subject to the limitations resulting from the average man's non-recognition of the power of the Spirit. The man who had thus fully entered into the Fifth Kingdom would recognize that, in its relation to the denser modes of matter his body was of a similar dense mode. That would be its relation to external environment as seen by others. But since the man now knew himself as not belonging to these denser modes of manifestation, but as an individualization of Primary Spirit, he would see that relatively to himself all matter was Primary Substance, and that from this point of view any condensations of that substance into atoms, molecules, tissues, and the like counted for nothing--for him the body would be simply Primary Substance entirely responsive to his will. Yet his reverence for the Law of Harmony would prevent any disposition to play psychic pranks with it, and he would use his power over the body only to meet actual requirements.

In this way, then, we are led to the conclusion that eternal life in an immortal physical body is the logical dénouement of our evolution; and if we reflect that, by the conditions of the case, the owners of such bodies could at will either transport themselves to other worlds or put off the physical body altogether and remain in the purely subjective life while still retaining the power to reclothe themselves in flesh whenever they chose, we shall see that this dénouement of evolution answers all possible questions as to the increase of the race, the final destruction of the planet, and the like.

This, then, is the ultimate which we should keep in view; but the fact remains that, though there may be hidden ones who have thus attained, the bulk of mankind have not, and that the common lot of humanity is to go through the change which we call death. In broad philosophical terms death may be described as the withdrawal of the life into the subjective consciousness to the total exclusion of the objective consciousness. Then by the general law of the relation between subjective and objective mind, the subjective mind severed from its corresponding objective mentality has no means of acquiring fresh impressions on its own account, and therefore can only ring the changes on those impressions which it has brought with it from its past life. But these may be of very various sorts, ranging from the lowest to the highest, from those most opposed to that ultimate destiny of man which we have just been considering, to those which recognize his possibilities in a very large measure, needing little more to bring about the full fruition of perfected life. But however various may be their experiences, all who have passed through death must have this in common that they have lost their physical instrument of objective perception and so have their mode of consciousness determined entirely by the dominant mode of suggestion which they have brought over with them from the objective side of life.[6] Of course if the objective mentality were also brought over this would give the individual the same power of initiative and selection that he possesses while in the body, and, as we shall see later on, there are exceptional persons with whom this is the case; but for the great majority the physical brain is a necessity for the working of the objective mentality, and so when they are deprived of this instrument their life becomes purely subjective and is a sort of dream-life, only with a vast difference between two classes of dreamers--those who dream as they must and those who dream as they will. The former are those who have enslaved themselves in various ways to their lower mentality--some by bringing with them the memory of crimes unpardoned, some by bringing with them the idea of a merely animal life, others less degraded, but still in bondage to limited thought, bringing with them only the suggestion of a frivolous worldly life--in this way, by the natural operation of the Law of Suggestion, these different classes, either through remorse, or unsatisfied desires, or sheer incapacity to grasp higher principles, all remain earth-bound, suffering in exact correspondence with the nature of the suggestion they have brought along with them. The unchangeable Law is that the suggestion becomes the life; and this is equally true of suggestions of a happier sort. Those who have brought over with them the great truth that conditions are the creations of thought, and who have accustomed themselves while in objective life to dwell on good and beautiful ideas, are still able, by reason of being imbued with this suggestion, to mold the conditions of their consciousness in the subjective world in accordance with the sort of ideas which have become a second nature to them. Within the limits of these ideas the dominant suggestion to these entities is that of a Law which confers Liberty, so by using this Law of the constructive power of thought they can determine the conditions of their own consciousness; and thus instead of being compelled to suffer the nightmare dreams of the other class, they can mold their dream according to their will. We cannot conceive of such a life as theirs in the unseen as otherwise than happy, nevertheless its range is limited by the range of the conceptions they have brought with them. These may be exceedingly beautiful and thoroughly true and logical as far as they go; but they do not go the whole way, otherwise these spirits would not be in the category which we are considering but would belong to that still higher class who fully realize the ultimate possibilities which the Law of the Expression of Spirit provides.

The otherwise happy subjective life of these more enlightened souls has this radical defect that they have failed to bring over with them that power of original selection and initiative without which further progress is impossible. I wish the student to grasp this point very clearly, for it is of the utmost importance. Of course the basis of our further evolution is conformity to the harmonious nature of the Originating Spirit; but upon this foundation we each have to build up the superstructure of our own individuality, and every step of advance depends on our personal development of power to take that step. This is what is meant by taking an initiative. It is making a New Departure, not merely recombining the old things into fresh groupings still subject to the old laws, but introducing an entirely new element which will bring its own New Law along with it.

Now if this is the true meaning of "initiative" then that is just the power which these otherwise happy souls do not possess. For by the very conditions of the case they are living only in their subjective consciousness, and consequently are living by the law of subjective mind; and one of the chief characteristics of subjective mind is its incapacity to reason inductively, and therefore its inability to make the selection and take the initiative necessary to inaugurate a New Departure. The well-established facts of mental law show conclusively that subjective mind argues only deductively. It argues quite correctly from any given premises, but it cannot take the initiative in selecting the premises--that is the province of inductive reasoning which is essentially the function of the objective mind. But by the law of Auto-suggestion this discarnate individual has brought over his premises with him, which premises are the sum-total of his inductions made during objective life, the conception of things which he held at the time he passed over, for this constituted his idea of Truth. Now he cannot add to these inductions, for he has parted with his instrument for inductive reasoning, and therefore his deductive reasoning in the purely subjective state which he has now entered is necessarily limited to the consequences which may be deducted from the premises which he has brought along with him.

In the case of the highly-developed individualities we are now considering the premises thus brought over are of a very far-reaching and beautiful character, and consequently the range of their subjective life is correspondingly wide and beautiful; but, nevertheless, it is subject to the radical defect that it is debarred from further progress for the simple reason that the individual has not brought over with him the mental faculty which can impress his subjective entity with the requisite forward movement for making a new departure into a New Order. And moreover, the higher the subjective development with which the individual passed over the more likely he will be to realize this defect. If during earth-life he had gained sufficient knowledge of these things he will carry with him the knowledge that his discarnate existence is purely subjective; and therefore he will realize that, however he may be able to order the pictures of his dream, yet it is still but a dream, and in common with all other dreams lacks the basis of solidity from which to take really creative action.

He knows also that the condition of other discarnate individualities is similar to his own, and that consequently each one must necessarily live in a world apart--a world of his own creation, because none of them possess the objective mentality by which to direct their subjective currents so as to make them penetrate into the sphere of another subjective entity, which is the modus operandi of telepathy. Thus he is conscious of his own inability to hold intercourse with other personalities; for though he may for his own pleasure create the semblance of them in his dream-life, yet he knows that these are creations of his own mind, and that while he appears to be conversing with a friend amid the most lovely surroundings the friend himself may be having experiences of a very different description. I am, of course, speaking now of persons who have passed over in a very high state of development and with a very considerable, though still imperfect, knowledge of the Law of their own being. Probably the majority take their dream-life for an external reality; and, in any case, all who have passed over without carrying their objective mentality along with them must be shut up in their individual subjective spheres and cease to function as centers of creative power so long as they do not emerge from that state.

But the highly advanced individuals of whom I am now speaking have passed over with a true knowledge of the Law of the relation between subjective and objective mind and have therefore brought with them a subjective knowledge of this truth; and therefore, however otherwise in a certain sense happy, they must still be conscious of a fundamental limitation which prevents their further advance. And this consciousness can produce only one result, an ever-growing longing for the removal of this limitation--and this represents the intense desire of the Spirit, as individualized in these souls, to attain to the conditions under which it can freely exercise its creative power. Sub-consciously this is the desire of all souls, for it is that continual pressing forward of the Spirit for manifestation out of which the whole Creative Process arises; and so it is that the great cry perpetually ascends to God from all as yet undelivered souls, whether in or out of the body, for the deliverance which they knowingly or unknowingly desire.

All this comes out of the well-ascertained facts of the law of relation between subjective and objective mind. Then comes the question, Is there no way of getting out of this law? The answer is that we can never get away from universal principles--but we can specialize them. We may take it as an axiom that any law which appears to limit us contains in itself the principle by which that limitation can be overcome, just as in the case of the flotation of iron. In this axiom, then, we shall find the clue which will bring us out of the labyrinth. The same law which places various degrees of limitation upon the souls that have passed into the invisible can be so applied as to set them free. We have seen that everything turns on the obligation of our subjective part to act within the limits of the suggestion which has been most deeply impressed upon it. Then why not impress upon it the suggestion that in passing over to the other side it has brought its objective mentality along with it?

If such a suggestion were effectively impressed upon our subjective mind, then by the fundamental law of our nature our subjective mind would act in strict accordance with this suggestion, with the result that the objective mind would no longer be separated from it, and that we should carry with us into the unseen our whole mentality, both subjective and objective, and so be able to exercise our inductive powers of selection and initiative as well there as here.

Why not? The answer is that we cannot accept any suggestion unless we believe it to be true, and to believe it to be true we must feel that we have a solid foundation for our belief. If, then, we can find a sufficient foundation for adequately impressing this suggestion upon ourselves, then the principles of mental law assure us that we shall carry our objective faculty of initiative and selection into the unseen. Therefore our quest is to find this Foundation. Then, since we cannot accept as true what we believe to be contrary to the ultimate law of the universe, if we are to find such a foundation at all it must be within that Law; and it is for this reason that I have laid so much stress upon the Normal Standard of Human Individuality. When we are convinced that this ideal completeness is quite normal, and is a spiritual fact, not dependent upon the body, but able to control the body, then we have got the solid basis on which to carry our objective personality along with us into the unseen, and the well-established laws of our mental constitution justify the belief that we can do so.

From these considerations it is obvious that those who thus pass over in possession of their complete mentality must be in a very different position from those who pass into a condition of merely subjective life, for they have brought their powers of selection and initiative with them, and can therefore employ their experiences in the unseen as a starting-point for still further development. So, then, the question arises, What lines will this further development be likely to follow?

We are now considering the case of persons who have reached a very high degree of development; who have succeeded in so completely uniting the subjective and objective portions of their spiritual being into a perfect whole that they can never again be severed; and who are therefore able to function with their whole consciousness on the spiritual plane. Such persons will doubtless be well aware that they have attained this degree of development by the Law of the Creative Process working in terms of their own individuality, and so they would naturally always refer to the original Cosmic Creation as the demonstration of the principle which they have to specialize for their own further evolution. Then they would find that the principle involved is that of the manifestation of Spirit in Form; and they would further see that this manifestation is not an illusion but a reality, for the simple reason that both mind and matter are equally projections from the Great Originating Spirit. Both alike are thoughts of the Divine Mind, and it is impossible to conceive any greater reality than the Divine Thought, or to get at any more substantial source of reality than that. Even if we were to picture the Divine Mind as laughing at its productions as being mere illusions relatively to itself (which I certainly do not), still the relation between the individual mind and material existence would be a reality for the individual, on the simple mathematical ground that like signs multiplied together invariably produce a positive result, even though the signs themselves be negative; so that, for us, at every stage of our existence substance must always be as much a reality as mind. Therefore the manifestation of Spirit in Form is the eternal principle of the Creative Process whether in the evolution of a world-system or in that of an individual.

But when we realize that by the nature of the Creative Process substance must be an eternal verity we must not suppose that this is true also of particular forms or of particular modes of matter. Substance is a necessity for the expression of Spirit, but it does not follow that Spirit is tied down to any particular mode of expression. If you fold a piece of paper into the form of a dart it will fly through the air by the law of the form which you have given it. Again, if you take the same bit of paper and fold it into the shape of a boat it will float on water by the law of the new form that you have given it. The thing formed will act in accordance with the form given it, and the same paper can be folded into different forms; but if there were no paper you could put it into any shape at all. The dart and the boat are both real so long as you retain the paper in either of those shapes; but this does not alter the fact that you can change the shapes, though your power to do so depends on the existence of the paper. This is a rough analogy of the relation between ultimate substance and particular forms, and shows us that neither substance nor shape is an illusion; both are essential to the manifestation of Spirit, only by the nature of the Creative Process the Spirit has power to determine what shape substance shall take at any particular time.

Accordingly we find the great Law that, as Spirit is the Alpha of the Creative Process, so solid material Form is its Omega; in other words the Creative Series is incomplete until solid material form is reached. Anything short of this is a condition of incompleteness, and therefore the enlightened souls who have passed over in possession of both sides of their mentality will realize that their condition, however beatific, is still one of incompleteness; and that what is wanted for completion is expression through a material body. This, then, is the direction in which such souls would use their powers of initiative and selection as being the true line of evolution--in a word they would realize that the principle of Creative Progression, when it reaches the level of fully developed mental man, necessarily implies the Resurrection of the Body, and that anything short of this would be retrogression and not progress.

At the same time persons who had passed over with this knowledge would never suppose that Resurrection meant merely the resuscitation of the old body under the old conditions; for they would see that the same inherent law which makes expression in concrete substance the ultimate of the creative series also makes this ultimate form depend on the originating movement of the spirit which produces it, and therefore that, although some concrete form is essential for complete manifestation, and is a substantial reality so long as it is maintained, yet the maintaining of the particular form is entirely dependent on the action of the spirit of which the form is the external clothing. This resurrection body would therefore be no mere illusory spirit-shape, yet it would not be subject to the limitations of matter as we now know it: it would be physical matter still, but entirely subject to the will of the indwelling spirit, which would not regard the denser atomic relations of the body but only its absolute and essential nature as Primary Substance. I want the student to grasp the idea that the same thing may be very different when looked at, so to say, from opposite ends of the stick. What is solid molecular matter when viewed from the outside is plastic primary substance when viewed from the inside. The relations of this new body to any stimulus proceeding from outside would be those of the external laws of Nature; but its relation to the spiritual ego working from within would be that of a plastic substance to be molded at will. The employment of such power would, however, at all times be based upon the reverent worship of the All-creating Spirit; and it would therefore never be exercised otherwise than in accordance with the harmonious progress of the Creative Process. Proceeding on these lines the spirit in the individual would stand in precisely the same relation to his body that the All-originating Spirit does to the cosmos.

This, then, is the sort of body which the instructed would contemplate as that in which he was to attain resurrection. He would regard it, not as an illusion, but as a great reality; while at the same time he would not need to trouble himself about its particular form, for he would know that it would be the perfect expression of his own conception of himself. He would know this because it is in accordance with the fundamental principle that external creation has its root in the Self-contemplation of Spirit.

Those passing over with this knowledge would obviously be in a very different position from those who passed over with only a subjective consciousness. They would bring with them powers of selection and initiative by which they could continue to impress fresh and expanding conceptions upon their subjective mind, and so cause it to carry on its work as the seed-ground of the whole individuality, instead of being shut up in itself as a mere circulus for the repetition of previously received ideas; and so in their recognition of the principle of physical resurrection they would have a clear and definite line of auto-suggestion. And because this suggestion is derived from the undeniable facts of the whole cosmic creation, it is one which both subjective and objective mind can accept as an established fact, and so the suggestion becomes effective. This suggestion, then, becomes the self-contemplation of the individual spirit; and because it is in strict conformity with the generic principle of the Original Creative Activity, of which the individual mind is itself a product, this becomes also the Self-contemplation of the Originating Spirit as seeing itself reflected in the individual spirit; so that, by the basic law of the Creative Process, this suggestion is bound sooner or later to work out into its corresponding fact, namely, the production of a material body free from the power of death and from all those limitations which we now associate with our physical organism.

This, then, is the hope of those who pass over in recognition of the great truth. But how about those who have passed over without that recognition? We have seen that their purely subjective condition precludes them from taking any initiative on their own account, for that requires the presence of objective mind. Their subjective mind, however, still retains its essential nature; that is, it is still susceptible to suggestion, and still possesses its inherent creativeness in working out any suggestion that is sufficiently deeply implanted in it. Here, then, opens up a vast field of activity for that other class who have passed over in possession of both sides of their mentality. By means of their powers of initiative and selection they can on the principle of telepathy cause their own subjective mind to penetrate the subjective spheres of those who do not possess those powers, and they can thus endeavor to impress upon them the great truth of the physical ultimate of the Creative Process--the truth that any series which stops short of that ultimate is incomplete, and, if insisted upon as being ultimate, must become self-destructive because in opposition to the inherent working of the Universal Creative Spirit. Then, as the perception of the true nature of the Creative Process dawned upon any subjective entity, it would by reason of accepting this suggestion begin to develop an objective mentality, and so would gradually attain to the same status as those who had passed over in full possession of all their mental powers.

But the more the objective mentality became developed in these discarnate personalities the more the need of a corresponding physical instrument would assert itself, both from their intellectual perception of the original cosmic process, and also from the inherent energy of the Spirit as centered in the ultimate ego of the individual. Not to seek material manifestation would be the contrary of all we have traced out regarding the nature of the Creative Process; and hence the law of tendency resulting from the conscious union of subjective and objective mind in the individual must necessarily be toward the production of a physical form. Only we must recollect, as I have already pointed out, that this concentration of these minds would be upon a principle and not upon a particular bodily shape. The particular form they would be content to leave to the inherent self-expressiveness of the Universal Spirit working through the particular ego, with the result that their expectation would be fixed upon a general principle of physical Resurrection which would provide a form suited to be the material instrument of the highest ideal of man as a spiritual and mental being. Then, since the subjective mind is the automatic builder of the body, the result of the individual's acceptance of the Resurrection principle must be that this mental conception will eventually work out as a corresponding fact. Whether on this planet or on some other, matters not, for, as we have already seen, the physical body evolved by a soul that is conscious of its unity with the Universal Spirit is bound to be in conformity with the physical laws of any planet, though from the standpoint of the conscious ego not limited by them.

In this way we may conceive that those who have passed over in possession of both sides of their spiritual nature would find a glorious field of usefulness in the unseen in helping to emancipate those who had passed over in possession of their subjective side only. But from our present analysis it will be seen that this can only be effected on the basis of a recognition of the principle of the Resurrection of the Body. Apart from the recognition of this principle the only possible conception which the discarnate individual could form of himself would be that of a purely subjective being; and this carries with it all the limitations of a subjective life unbalanced by an objective one; and so long as the principle of physical resurrection is denied, so long the life must continue to be merely subjective and consequently unprogressive.[7]

But it may be asked why those who have realized this great principle sufficiently to carry their objective mentality into the unseen state are liable to the change which we call death. The answer is that though they have realized the general principle they have not yet divested themselves of certain conceptions by which they limit it, and consequently by the law of subjective mind they carry those limitations into the working of the Resurrection principle itself.

They are limited by the race-belief that physical death is under all conditions a necessary law of Nature, or by the theological belief that death is the will of God; so then the question is whether these beliefs are well founded. Of course appeal is made to universal experience, but it does not follow that the universal experience of the past is bound to be the universal experience of the future--the universal experience of the past was that no man had ever flown across the English Channel, yet now it has been done. What we have to do, therefore, is not to bother about past experience, but to examine the inherent nature of the Law of Life and see whether it does not contain possibilities of further development. And the first step in this direction is to see whether what we have hitherto considered limitations of the law are really integral parts of the law itself. The very statement of this question shows the correct answer; for how can a force acting in one direction be an integral part of a force acting in the opposite direction? How can the force which pulls a thing down be an integral part of the force which builds it up? To suppose, therefore, that the limitations of the law are an integral portion of the law itself is a reductio ad absurdum.

For these reasons the argument from the past experience of the race counts for nothing; and when we examine the theological argument we shall find that it is only the old argument from past experience in another dress. It is alleged that death is the will of God. How do we know that it is the will of God? Because the facts prove it so, is the ultimate answer of all religious systems with one exception; so here we are back again at the old race-experience as the criterion of truth. Therefore the theological argument is nothing but the materialistic argument disguised. It is in our more or less conscious acceptance of the materialistic argument, under any of its many disguises, that the limitation of life is to be found--not in the Law of Life itself; and if we are to bring into manifestation the infinite possibilities latent in that Law it can only be by looking steadily into the principle of the Law and resolutely denying everything that opposes it. The Principle of Life must of necessity be Affirmative, and affirmative throughout, without any negative anywhere--if we once realize this we shall be able to unmask the enemy and silence his guns.

Now to do this is precisely the one object of the Bible; and it does it in a thoroughly logical manner, always leading on to the ultimate result by successive links of cause and effect. People will tell you that the Bible is their authority for saying that Death is the will of God; but these are people who read it carelessly; and ultimately the only reason they can give you for their manner of interpreting the Bible is that the facts prove their interpretation to be correct; so that in the last resort you will always find you have got back to the old materialistic argument from past race-experience, which logically proves nothing. These are good well-meaning people with a limited idea which they read into the Bible, and so limit its promises by making physical death an essential preliminary to Resurrection. They grasp, of course, the great central idea that Perfected Man possesses a joyous immortal Life permeating spirit, soul and body; but they relegate it to some dim and distant future, entirely disconnected from the present law of our being, not seeing that if we are to have eternal life it must necessarily be involved in some principle which is eternal, and therefore existing, at any rate latently, at the present moment. Hence, though their fundamental principle is true, they are all the time mentally limiting it, with the result that they themselves create the conditions they impose upon it, and consequently the principle will work (as principles always do) in accordance with the conditions provided for its action.

Unless, therefore, this limiting belief is entirely eradicated, the individual, though realizing the fundamental principle of Life, is bound to pass out of physical existence; but on the other hand, since he does take the recognition of this fundamental principle with him, it is bound to bear fruit sooner or later in a joyous Resurrection, while the intermediate state can only be a peaceful anticipation of that supreme event. This is the answer to the question why those who have realized the great principle sufficiently to carry their objective mentality into the unseen world are still liable to physical death; and in the last analysis it will be found to resolve itself into the remains of race belief based upon past experience. These are they who pass over in sure and certain hope of a glorious Resurrection--sure and certain because founded upon the very Being of God Himself, that inherent Life of the All-creating Divine Spirit which is the perpetual inter-action of the Eternal Love and Beauty. They have grasped the Life-giving Truth, only they have postponed its operation, because they have the fixed idea that its present fruition is an absolute impossibility.

But if we ask the reason for this idea it always comes back to the old materialistic argument from the experience of past conditions, while the whole nature of advance is in the opening up of new conditions. And in this advance the Bible is the pioneer book. Its whole purport is to tell us most emphatically that death is not the will of God. In the story of Eden God is represented as warning man of the poisonous nature of the forbidden fruit, which is incompatible with the idea of death as an essential feature of man's nature. Then from the point where man has taken the poison all the rest of the Bible is devoted to telling us how to get rid of it. Christ, it tells us, was manifested to bring Life and Immortality to light--to abolish death--to destroy the works of the devil, that is the death-dealing power, for "he that hath the power of death is the devil." It is impossible to reconcile this life-giving conception of the Bible with the idea that death at any stage or in any degree is the desire of God. Let us, therefore, start with the recognition that this negative force, whether in its minor degrees as disease or in its culmination as death, is that which it is the will of God to abolish. This also is logical; for if God be the Universal Spirit of Life finding manifestation in individual lives, how can the desire of this Spirit be to act in opposition to its own manifestation? Therefore Scripture and common-sense alike assure us that the will of God toward us is Life and not death.[8]

We may therefore start on our quest for Life with the happy certainty that God is on our side. But people will meet us with the objection that though God wills Life to us, He does not will it just yet, but only in some dim far-off future. How do we know this? Certainly not from the Bible. In the Bible Jesus speaks of two classes of persons who believe on Him as the Manifestation or Individualization of the Spirit of Life. He speaks of those who, having passed through death, still believe on Him, and says that these shall live--a future event. And at the same time He speaks of those who are living and believe on Him, and says that they shall never die--thus contemplating the entire elimination of the contingency of death (John 11:25).

Again St. Paul expresses his wish not to be unclothed but to be clothed upon, which he certainly would not have done had he considered the latter alternative a nonsensical fancy. And in another place he expressly states that we shall not all die, but that some shall be transmuted into the Resurrection body without passing through physical death. And if we turn to the Old Testament we find two instances in which this is said to have actually occurred, those of Enoch and Elijah. And we may note in passing that the Bible draws our attention to certain facts about these two personages which are important as striking at the root of the notion that austerities of some sort are necessary for the great attainment. Of Enoch we are expressly told that he was the father of a large family, and of Elijah that he was a man of like nature with ourselves--thus showing us what is wanted is not a shutting of ourselves off from ordinary human life but such a clear realization of the Universal Principle, of which our personal life is the more or less conscious manifestation, that our commonest actions will be hallowed by the Divine Presence; and so the grand dénouement will be only the natural result of our daily habit of walking with God. From the stand-point of the Bible, therefore, the attainment of physical regeneration without passing through death is not an impossibility, nor is it necessarily relegated to some far off future. Whatever anyone else may say to the contrary, the Bible contemplates such a dénouement of human evolution as a present possibility.

Then if we argue from the philosophical stand-point we arrive at precisely the same result. Past experience proves nothing, and we must therefore make a fresh start by going back to the Original Creative action of the Spirit of Life itself. Then, if we take this as our starting point, remembering that at the stage of this original movement there can be no intervention by a second power, because there is none, why should we mentally impose any restriction upon the action of the Creative Power? Certainly not by its own Law of Tendency, for that must always be toward fuller self-expression; and since this can only take place through the individual, the desire of the Spirit must always be toward the increasing of the individual life. Nor yet from anything in the created substance, for that would either be to suppose the Spirit creating something in limitation of its own Self-expression, or else to suppose that the limiting substance was created by some other power working against the Spirit; and as this would mean a Duality of powers we should not have reached the Originating Power at all, and so we might put Spirit and Substance equally out of court as both being merely modes of secondary causation. But if we see that the Universal Substance must be created by emanation from the Universal Spirit, then we see that no limitation of Spirit by substance is possible. We may therefore feel assured that no limitation proceeds either from the will of the Spirit or from the nature of Substance.

Where, then, does limitation come from? Limiting conditions are created by the same power which creates everything else, namely, the Self-contemplation of Spirit. This is why it is so important to realize that the individual mind forms a center from which the self-contemplating action of Spirit is specialized in terms of the individual's own mode of thinking, and therefore so long as the individual contemplates negative conditions as being of the essence of his own personality, he is in effect employing the Creative Power of the Self-contemplation of Spirit invertedly, destructively instead of constructively. The Law of the Self-contemplation of Spirit as the Creative Power is as true in the microcosm as in the macrocosm, and so the individual's contemplation of himself as subject to the law of sin and death keeps him subject to that law, while the opposite self-contemplation, the contemplation of himself as rejoicing in the Life of the Spirit, the Perfect Law of Liberty, must necessarily produce the opposite results.

Why, then, should not regeneration be accomplished here and now? I can see no reason against it, either Scriptural or philosophical, except our own difficulty in getting rid of the race-traditions which are so deeply embedded in our subjective minds. To get rid of these we require a firm basis on which to receive the opposite suggestion. We need to be convinced that our ideal of a regenerated self is in accord with the Normal Standard of Humanity and is within the scope of the laws of the universe. Now to make clear to us the infinitude of the truly Normal Standard of Humanity is the whole purpose of the Bible; and the Manifestation of this Standard is set before us in the Central Personality of the Scriptures who is at once the Son of God and the Son of Man--the Great Exception, if you will, to man as we know him now, but the Exception which proves the Rule. In proportion as we begin to realize this we begin to introduce into our own life the action of that Personal Factor on which all further development depends; and when our recognition is complete we shall find that we also are children of God.

CHAPTER IX
CONCLUSION

We are now in a position to see the place occupied by the individual in the Creative Order. We have found that the originating and maintaining force of the whole Creative Process is the Self-contemplation of the Spirit, and that this necessarily produces a Reciprocal corresponding to the idea embodied in the contemplation, and thus manifesting that idea in a correlative Form. We have found that in this way the externalization of the idea progresses from the condensation of the primary nebula to the production of human beings as a race, and that at this point the simple generic reproduction of the idea terminates. This means that up to, and including, genus homo, the individual, whether plant, animal, or man, is what it is simply by reason of race conditions and not by exercise of deliberate choice. Then we have seen that the next step in advance must necessarily be by the individual becoming aware that he has power to mold the conditions of his own consciousness and environment by the creative power of his thought; thus not only enabling him to take a conscious part in his own further evolution but precluding him from evolving any further except by the right exercise of this power; and we have found that the crux of the passage from the Fourth to the Fifth Kingdom is to get people so to understand the nature of their creative power as not to use it destructively. Now what we require to see is that the Creative Process has always only one way of working, and that is by Reciprocity or Reflection, or, as we might say, by the law of Action and Re-action, the re-action being always equivalent and correspondent to the action which generated it. If this Law of Reciprocity be grasped then we see how the progress of the Creative Process must at length result in producing a being who himself possesses the power of independent spiritual initiative and is thus able to carry on the creative work from the stand-point of his own individuality.

Now the great crux is first to get people to see that they possess this power at all, and then to get them to use it in the right direction. When our eyes begin to open to the truth that we do possess this power the temptation is to ignore the fact that our power of initiative is itself a product of the similar power subsisting in the All-originating Spirit. If this origin of our own creative faculty is left out of sight we shall fail to recognize the Livingness of the Greater Life within which we live. We shall never get nearer to it than what we may call its generic level, the stage at which the Creative Power is careful of the type or race but is careless of the individual; and so at this level we shall never pass into the Fifth Kingdom which is the Kingdom of Individuality--we have missed the whole point of the transition to the more advanced mode of being, in which the individual consciously functions as a creative center, because we have no conception of a Universal Power that works at any higher level than the generic, and consequently to reach a specific personal exercise of creative power we should have to conceive of ourselves as transcending the Universal Law. But if we realize that our own power of creative initiative has its origin in the similar faculty of the All-Originating Mind then we see that the way to maintain the Life-giving energy in ourselves is to use our power of spiritual initiative so as to impress upon the Spirit the conception of ourselves as standing related to It in a specific, individual, and personal way that takes us out of the mere category of genus homo and gives us a specific spiritual individuality of our own. Thus our mental action produces a corresponding re-action in the mind of the Spirit, which in its turn reproduces itself as a special manifestation of the Life of the Spirit in us; and so long as this circulation between the individual spirit and the Great Spirit is kept up, the individual life will be maintained, and will also strengthen as the circulation continues, for the reason that the Spirit, as the Original Creative Power, is a Multiplying Force, and the current sent into it is returned multiplied, just as in telegraphy the feeble current received from a distance at the end of a long line operates to start a powerful battery in the receiving office, which so multiplies the force as to give out a clear message, which but for the multiplication of the original movement could not have been done. Something like this we may picture the multiplying tendency of the Originating Mind, and consequently the longer the circulation between it and the individual mind goes on the stronger the latter becomes; and this process growing habitual becomes at last automatic, thus producing an endless flow of Life continually expanding in intelligence, love, power and joy.

But we must note carefully that all this can only proceed from the individual's recognition that his own powers are a derivative from the All-originating Spirit, and that they can continue to be used constructively only so long as they are employed in harmony with the inherent Forward Movement of the Spirit. Therefore to insure this eternally flowing stream of Life from the Universal Spirit into the individual there must be no inversion in the individual's presentation of himself to the Originating Power: for through the very same Law by which we seek Life--the Life namely, of reciprocal action and re-action--every inversion we bring with us in presenting ourselves to the Spirit is bound to be faithfully reproduced in a corresponding re-action, thus adulterating the stream of Pure Life, and rendering it less life-giving in proportion to the extent to which we invert the action of the Life-principle; so that in extreme cases the stream flowing through and from the individual may be rendered absolutely poisonous and deadly, and the more so the greater his recognition of his own personal power to employ spiritual forces.

The existence of these negative possibilities in the spiritual world should never be overlooked, and therefore the essential condition for receiving the Perfect Fullness of Life is that we should present ourselves before the Eternal Spirit free from every trace of inversion. To do this means to present ourselves in the likeness of the Divine Ideal; and in this self-presentation the initiative, so far as the individual is consciously concerned, must necessarily be taken by himself. He is to project into the Eternal Mind the conception of himself as identical with its Eternal Ideal; and if he can do this, then by the Law of the Creative Process a return current will flow from the Eternal Mind reproducing this image in the individual with a continually growing power. Then the question is, How are we to do this?

The answer is that to take the initiative for inducing this flow of Life individually it is a sine qua non that the conditions enabling us to do so should first be presented to us universally. This is in accordance with the general principle that we can never create a force but can only specialize it. Only here the power we are wanting to specialize is the very Power of Specialization itself; and therefore, paradoxical as it may seem, what we require to have shown us is the Universality of Specialization.

Now this is what the Bible puts before us in its central figure. Taking the Bible statements simply and literally they show us this unique Personality as the Principle of Humanity, alike in its spiritual origin and its material manifestation, carried to the logical extreme of specialization; while at the same time, as the embodiment of the original polarity of Spirit and Substance, this Personality, however unique, is absolutely universal; so that the Bible sets Jesus Christ before us as the answer to the philosophic problem of how to specialize the universal, while at the same time preserving its universality.

If, then, we fix our thought upon this unique Personality as the embodiment of universal principles, it follows that those principles must exist in ourselves also, and that His actual specialization of them is the earnest of our potential specialization of them. Then if we fix our thought on this potential in ourselves as being identical with its manifestation in Him, we can logically claim our identity with Him, so that what He has done we have done, what He is, we are, and thus recognizing ourselves in Him we present this image of ourselves to the Eternal Mind, with the result that we bring with us no inversion, and so import no negative current into our stream of Life.

Thus it is that we reach "the Father" through "the Son," and that He is able to keep us from falling and to present us faultless before the presence of the Divine glory with exceeding joy (Jude 24). The Gospel of "the Word made flesh" is not the meaningless cant of some petty sect nor yet the cunning device of priestcraft, though it has been distorted in both these directions; but it can give a reason for itself, and is founded upon the deepest laws of the threefold constitution of man, embracing the whole man, body, soul and spirit. It is not opposed to Science but is the culmination of all science whether physical or mental. It is philosophical and logical throughout if you start the Creative Process where alone it can start, in the Self-contemplation of the Spirit. The more carefully we examine into the claims of the Gospel of Christ the more we shall find all the current objections to it melt away and disclose their own superficialness. We shall find that Christ is indeed the Mediator between God and Man, not by the arbitrary fiat of a capricious Deity, but by a logical law of sequence which solves the problem of making extremes meet, so that the Son of Man is also the Son of God; and when we see the reason why this is so we thereby receive power to become ourselves sons of God, which is the dénouement of the Creative Process in the Individual.

These closing lines are not the place to enter upon so great a subject, but I hope to follow it up in another volume and to show in detail the logic of the Bible teaching, what it saves us from and what it leads us to; to show while giving due weight to the value of other systems how it differs from them and transcends them; to glance, perhaps, for a moment at the indications of the future and to touch upon some of the dangers of the present and the way to escape from them. Nor would I pass over in silence another and important aspect of the Gospel contained in Christ's commission to His followers to heal the sick. This also follows logically from the Law of the Creative Process if we trace carefully the sequence of connections from the indwelling Ego to the outermost of its vehicles; while the effect of the recognition of these great truths upon the individuality that has for a time put off its robe of flesh, opens out a subject of paramount interest. Thus it is that on every plane Christ is the Fulfilling of the Law, and that "Salvation" is not a silly shiboleth but the logical and vital process of our advance into the unfoldment of the next stage of the limitless capacities of our being. Of these things I hope to write in another volume, should it be permitted to me, and in the meanwhile I would commend the present abstract statement of principles to the reader's attention in the hope that it may throw some light on the fundamental nature of these momentous questions. The great thing to bear in mind is that if a thing is true at all there must be a reason why it is true, and when we come to see this reason we know the truth at first hand for ourselves and not from someone else's report--then it becomes really our own and we begin to learn how to use it. This is the secret of the individual's progress in any art, science, or business, and the same method will serve equally well in our search after Life itself, and as we thus follow up the great quest we shall find that on every plane the Way, the Truth, and the Life are ONE.

"A little philosophy inclineth a man's mind to atheism, but depth in philosophy bringeth men's minds about to religion." —Bacon. Essay 16.

CHAPTER X

THE DIVINE OFFERING

I take the present opportunity of a new edition to add a few pages on certain points which appear to me of vital importance, and the connection of which with the preceding chapters will, I hope, become evident as the reader proceeds. Assuming the existence in each individual of a creative power of thought which, in relation to himself, reflects the same power existing in the Universal Mind, our right employment of this power becomes a matter of extreme moment to ourselves. Its inverted use necessarily holds us fast in the bondage from which we are seeking to escape, and equally necessarily its right use brings us into Liberty; and therefore if any Divine revelation exists at all its purpose must be to lead us away from the inverted use of our creative faculty and into such a higher specializing of it as will produce the desired result. Now the purpose of the Bible is to do this, and it seeks to effect this work by a dual operation. It places before us that Divine Ideal of which I have already spoken, and at the same time bases this ideal upon the recognition of a Divine Sacrifice. These two conceptions are so intimately interwoven in Scripture that they cannot be separated, but at the present day there is a growing tendency to attempt to make this separation and to discard the conception of a Divine Sacrifice as unphilosophical, that is as having no nexus of cause and effect. What I want, therefore, to point out in these additional pages is that there is such a nexus, and that so far from being without a sequence of cause and effect it has its root in the innermost principles of our own being. It is not contrary to Law but proceeds from the very nature of the Law itself.

The current objection to the Bible teaching on this subject is that no such sacrifice could have been required by God, either because the Originating Energy can have no consciousness of Personality and is only a blind force, or because, if "God is Love," He could not demand such a sacrifice. On the former hypothesis we are of course away from the Bible teaching altogether and have nothing to do with it; but, as I have said elsewhere, the fact of our own consciousness of personality can only be accounted for by the existence, however hidden, of a corresponding quality in the Originating Spirit. Therefore I will confine my remarks to the question how Love, as the originating impulse of all creation, can demand such a sacrifice. And to my mind the answer is that God does not demand it. It is Man who demands it. It is the instinctive craving of the human soul for certainty that requires a demonstration so convincing as to leave no room for doubt of our perfectly happy relation to the Supreme Spirit, and consequently to all that flows from it, whether on the side of the visible or of the invisible. When we grasp the fact that such a standpoint of certainty is the necessary foundation for the building up in ourselves of the Divine Ideal then it becomes clear that to afford us this firm basis is the greatest work that the Spirit, in its relation to human personality, could do.

We are often told that the offering of sacrifices had its origin in primitive man's conception of his gods as beings which required to be propitiated so as to induce them to do good or abstain from doing harm; and very likely this was the case. The truth at the back of this conception is the feeling that there is a higher power upon which man is dependent; and the error is in supposing that this power is limited by an individuality which can be enriched by selling its good offices, or which blackmails you by threats. In either case it wants to get something out of you, and from this it follows that its own power of supplying its own wants must be limited, otherwise it would not require to be kept in good temper by gifts. In very undeveloped minds such a conception results in the idea of numerous gods, each having, so to say, his own particular line of business; and the furthest advance this mode of thought is capable of is the reduction of these various deities to two antagonistic powers of Good and of Evil. But the result in either case is the same, so long as we start with the hypothesis that the Good will do us more good and the Evil do us less harm by reason of our sacrifices, for then it logically follows that the more valuable your sacrifices and the oftener they are presented the better chance you have of good luck. Doubtless some such conception as this was held by the mass of the Hebrew people under the sacrificial system of the Levitical Law, and perhaps this was one reason why they were so prone to fall into idolatry--for in this view their fundamental notion was practically identical in its nature with that of the heathen around them. Of course this was not the fundamental idea embodied in the Levitical system itself. The root of that system was the symbolizing of a supreme ideal of reconciliation hereafter to be manifested in action. Now a symbol is not the thing symbolized. The purpose of a symbol is twofold, to put us upon enquiry as to the reality which it indicates, and to bring that reality to our minds by suggestion when we look at the symbol; but if it does not do this, and we rest only in the symbol, nothing will come of it, and we are left just where we were. That the symbolic nature of the Levitical sacrifice was clearly perceived by the deeper thinkers among the Hebrews is attested by many passages in the Bible--"Sacrifice and burnt offering thou wouldest not" (Psalms 40:6, and 51:16) and other similar utterances; and the distinction between these symbols and that which they symbolized is brought out in the Epistle to the Hebrews by the argument that if those sacrifices had afforded a sufficient standpoint for the effectual realization of cleansing then the worshiper would not need to have repeated them because he would have no more consciousness of sin (Hebrews 10:2).

This brings us to the essential point of the whole matter. What we want is the certainty that there is no longer any separation between us and the Divine Spirit by reason of sin, either as overt acts of wrong doing or as error of principle; and the whole purpose of the Bible is to lead us to this assurance. Now such an assurance cannot be based on any sort of sacrifices that require repetition, for then we could never know whether we had given enough either in quality or quantity. It must be a once-for-all business or it is no use at all; and so the Bible makes the once-for-allness of the offering the essential point of its teaching. "He that has been bathed does not need to be bathed again" (John 13:10). "There is now no condemnation to them which are in Christ Jesus" (Romans 8:1).

Various intellectual difficulties, however, hinder many people from seeing the working of the law of cause and effect in this presentment. One is the question, How can moral guilt be transferred from one person to another? What is called the "forensic" argument (i.e., the court of law argument) that Christ undertook to suffer in our stead as our surety is undoubtedly open to this objection. Suretyship must by its very nature be confined to civil obligations and cannot be extended to criminal liability, and so the "forensic" argument may be set aside as very much a legal fiction. But if we realize the Bible teaching that Christ is the Son of God, that is, the Divine Principle of Humanity out of which we originated and subsisting in us all, however unconsciously to ourselves, then we see that sinners as well as saints are included in this Principle; and consequently that the Self-offering of Christ must actually include the self-offering of every human being in the acknowledgment (however unknown to his objective mentality) of his sin. If we can grasp this somewhat abstract point of view it follows that in the Person of Christ every human being, past, present, and to come, was self-offered for the condemnation of his sin--a self- condemnation and a self-offering, and hence a cleansing, for the simple reason that if you can get a man to realize his past error, really see his mistake, he won't do it again; and it is the perpetuation of sin and error that has to be got rid of--to do this universally would be to regain Paradise. Seen therefore in this light there is no question of transference of moral guilt, and I take it this is St. Paul's meaning when he speaks of our being partakers in Christ's death.

Then there is the objection, How can past sins be done away with? If we accept the philosophical conclusion that Time has no substantive existence then all that remains is states of consciousness. As I have said in the earlier part of this book, the Self-Contemplation of Spirit is the cause of all our perception of existence and environment; and consequently if the Self-Contemplation of the Spirit from any center of individualization is that of entire harmony and the absence of anything that would cause any consciousness of separation, then past sins cease to have any part in this self-recognition, and consequently cease to have any place in the world of existence. The foundation of the whole creative process is the calling into Light out of Darkness--"that which makes manifest is light"--and consequently the converse action is that of sending out of Light into Darkness, that is, into Notbeing. Now this is exactly what the Spirit says in the Bible--"I, even I, am He that blotteth out thy transgressions" (Isaiah 43:25). Blotting out is the sending out of manifestation into the darkness of non-manifestation, out of Being into Not-being; and in this way the past error ceases to have any existence and so ceases to have any further effect upon us. It is "blotted out," and from this new standpoint has never been at all; so that to continue to contemplate it is to give a false sense of existence to that which in effect has no existence. It is that Affirmation of Negation which is the root of all evil. It is the inversion of our God-given creative power of thought, calling into existence that which in the Perfect Life of the Spirit never had or could have any existence, and therefore it creates the sense of inharmony, opposition, and separation. Of course this is only relatively to ourselves, for we cannot create eternal principles. They are the Being of God; and as I have already shown these great Principles of the Affirmative may be summed up in the two words Love and Beauty--Love in essence and Beauty in manifestation; but since we can only live from the standpoint of our own consciousness we can make a false creation built upon the idea of opposites to the all-creating Love and Beauty, which false creation with all its accompaniments of limitation, sin, sorrow, sickness, and death, must necessarily be real to us until we perceive that these things were not created by God, the Spirit of the Affirmative, but by our own inversion of our true relation to the All-creating Being.

When, then, we view the matter in this light the Offering once for all of the Divine Sacrifice for the sin of the whole world is seen not to be a mere ecclesiastical dogma having no relation of cause and effect, but to be the highest application of the same principle of cause and effect by which the whole creation, ourselves included, has been brought into existence-- the Self-Contemplation of Spirit producing corresponding manifestation, only now working on the level of Individual Personality.

As I have shown at the beginning of this book the cosmic manifestation of principles is not sufficient to bring out all that there is in them. To do this their action must be specialized by the introduction of the Personal Factor. They are represented by the Pillar Jachin, but it must be equilibrated by the Pillar Boaz, Law and Personality the two Pillars of the Universe; and in the One Offering we have the supreme combination of these two principles, the highest specialization of Law by the highest power of Personality. These are eternal principles, and therefore we are told that the Lamb was slain from the foundation of the world; and because "thoughts are things" this supreme manifestation of the creative interaction of Law and Personality was bound eventually to be manifested in concrete action in the world conditioned by time and space; and so it was that the supreme manifestation of the Love of God to meet the supreme need of Man took place. The history of the Jewish nation is the history of the working of the law of cause and effect, under the guidance of the Divine Wisdom, so as to provide the necessary conditions for the greatest event in the world's history; for if Christ was to appear it must be in some nation, in some place, and at some time: but to trace the steps by which, through an intelligible sequence of causes, these necessary conditions were provided belongs rather to an investigation of Bible history than to our present purpose, so I will not enter into these details here. But what I hope I have in some measure made clear is that there is a reason why Christ should be manifested, and should suffer, and rise again, and that so far from being a baseless superstition the Reconciling of the world to God through the One Offering once-for-all offered for the sin of the whole world, lays the immovable foundation upon which we may build securely for all the illimitable future.

CHAPTER XI

OURSELVES IN THE DIVINE OFFERING

If we have grasped the principle I have endeavored to state in the last chapter we shall find that with this new standpoint a new life and a new world begin to open out to us. This is because we are now living from a new recognition of ourselves and of God. Eternal Truth, that which is the essential reality of Being, is always the same; it has never altered, for whatever is capable of passing away and giving place to something else is not eternal, and therefore the real essence of our being, as proceeding from God and subsisting in Him has always been the same. But this is the very fact which we have hitherto lost sight of; and since our perception of life is the measure of our individual consciousness of it, we have imposed upon ourselves a world of limitation, a world filled with the power of the negative, because we have viewed things from that standpoint. What takes place, therefore, when we realize the truth of our Redemption is not a change in our essential relation to the Parent Spirit, the Eternal Father, but an awakening to the perception of this eternal and absolutely perfect relation. We see that in reality it has never been otherwise for the simple reason that in the very nature of Being it could not be otherwise; and when we see this we see also that what has hitherto been wrong has not been the working of "the Father" but our conception of the existence of some other power, a power of negation, limitation, and destructiveness, the very opposite to all that the Creative Spirit, by the very fact of Its Creativeness, must be. That wonderful parable of the Prodigal Son shows us that he never ceased to be a son. It was not his Father who sent him away from home but his notion that he could do better "on his own," and we all know what came of it. But when he returned to the Father he found that from the Father's point of view he had never been otherwise than a son, and that all the trouble he had gone through was not "of the Father" but was the result of his own failure to realize what the Father and the Home really were.[9]

Now this is exactly the case with ourselves. When we wake up to the truth we find that, so far as the Father is concerned, we have always been in Him and in His home, for we are made in His image and likeness and are reflections of His own Being. He says to us "Son, thou art ever with me and all that I have is thine." The Self-Contemplation of Spirit is the Creative Power creating an environment corresponding to the mode of consciousness contemplated, and therefore in proportion as we contemplate ourselves as centers of individualization for the Divine Spirit we find ourselves surrounded by a new environment reflecting the harmonious conditions which preexist in the Thought of the Spirit.

This, then, is the sequence of Cause and Effect involved in the teaching of the Bible. Man is in essence a spiritual being, the reflection on the plane of individual personality of that which the All-Originating Spirit is in Itself, and is thus in that reciprocal relation to the Spirit which is Love. This is the first statement of his creation in Genesis--God saw all that He had made and behold it was very good, Man included. Then the Fall is the failure of the lower mentality to realize that God IS Love, in a word that Love is the only ultimate Motive Power it is possible to conceive, and that the creations of Love cannot be otherwise than good and beautiful. The lower mentality conceives an opposite quality of Evil and thus produces a motive power the opposite of Love, which is Fear; and so Fear is born into the world giving rise to the whole brood of evil, anger, hatred, envy, lies, violence, and the like, and on the external plane giving rise to discordant vibrations which are the root of physical ill. If we analyze our motives we shall find that they are always some mode either of Love or Fear; and fear has its root in the recognition of some power other than Perfect Love, which is God the ONE all-embracing Good. Fear has a creative force which invertedly mimics that of Love; but the difference between them is that Love is eternal and Fear is not. Love as the Original Creative Motive is the only logical conclusion we can come to as to why we ourselves or any other creation exists. Fear is illogical because to regard it as having any place in the Original Creative Motive involves a contradiction in terms.

By accepting the notion of a dual power, that of Good and Evil, the inverted creative working of Fear is introduced with all its attendant train of evil things. This is the eating of the deadly tree which occasions the Fall, and therefore the Redemption which requires to be accomplished is a redemption from Fear--not merely from this or that particular fear but from the very Root of Fear, which root is unbelief in the Love of God, the refusal to believe that Love alone is the Creating Power in all things, whether small beyond our recognition or great beyond our conception. Therefore to bring about this Redemption there must be such a manifestation of the Divine Love to Man as, when rightly apprehended, will leave no ground for fear; and when we see that the Sacrifice of the Cross was the Self-Offering of Love made in order to provide this manifestation, then we see that all the links in the chain of Cause and Effect are complete, and that Fear never had any place in the Creative Principle, whether as acting in the creation of a world or of a man. The root, therefore, of all the trouble of the world consists in the Affirmation of Negation, in using our creative power of thought invertedly, and thus giving substance to that which as principle has no existence. So long as this negative action of thought continues so long will it produce its natural effect; whether in the individual or in the mass. The experience is perfectly real while it lasts. Its unreality consists in the fact that there was never any real need for it; and the more we grasp the truth of the all-embracingness of the ONE Good, both as Cause and as Effect, on all planes, the more the experience of its opposite will cease to have any place in our lives.

This truly New Thought puts us in an entirely new relation to the whole of our environment, opening out possibilities hitherto undreamt of, and this by an orderly sequence of law which is naturally involved in our new mental attitude; but before considering the prospect thus offered it is well to be quite clear as to what this new mental attitude really is; for it is our adoption of this attitude that is the Key to the whole position. Put briefly it is ceasing to include the idea of limitations in our conception of the working of the All-Creating Spirit. Here are some specimens of the way in which we limit the creative working of the Spirit. We say, I am too old now to start this or that new sort of work. This is to deny the power of the Spirit to vivify our physical or mental faculties, which is illogical if we consider that it is the same Spirit that brought us into any existence at all. It is like saying that when a lamp is beginning to burn low the same person who first filled it with oil cannot replenish it and make it burn brightly again. Or we say, I cannot do so and so because I have not the means. When you were fourteen did you know where all the means were coming from which were going to support you till now when you are perhaps forty or fifty? So you should argue that the same power that has worked in the past can continue to work in the future. If you say the means came in the past quite naturally through ordinary channels, that is no objection; on the contrary the more reason for saying that suitable channels will open in the future. Do you expect God to put cash into your desk by a conjuring trick? Means come through recognizable channels, that is to say we recognize the channels by the fact of the stream flowing through them; and one of our most common mistakes is in thinking that we ourselves have to fix the particular channel beforehand. We say in effect that the Spirit cannot open other channels, and so we stop them up. Or we say, our past experience speaks to the contrary, thus assuming that our past experiences have included all possibilities and have exhausted the laws of the universe, an assumption which is negatived by every fresh discovery even in physical science. And so we go on limiting the power of the Spirit in a hundred different ways.

But careful consideration will show that, though the modes in which we limit it are as numerous as the circumstances with which we have to deal, the thing with which we limit it is always the same--it is by the introduction of our own personality. This may appear at first a direct contradiction of all that I have said about the necessity for the Personal Factor, but it is not. Here is a paradox.

To open out into manifestation the wonderful possibilities hidden in the Creative Power of the Universe we require to do two things--to see that we ourselves are necessary as centers for focusing that power, and at the same time to withdraw the thought of ourselves as contributing anything to its efficiency. It is not I that work but the Power; yet the Power needs me because it cannot specialize itself without me--in a word each is the complementary of the other: and the higher the degree of specialization is to be the more necessary is the intelligent and willing co-operation of the individual.

This is the Scriptural paradox that "the son can do nothing of himself," and yet we are told to be "fellow-workers with God." It ceases to be a paradox, however, when we realize the relation between the two factors concerned, God and Man. Our mistake is in not discriminating between their respective functions, and putting Man in the place of God. In our everyday life we do this by measuring the power of God by our past experiences and the deductions we draw from them; but there is another way of putting Man in the place of God, and that is by the misconception that the All-Originating Spirit is merely a cosmic force without intelligence, and that Man has to originate the intelligence without which no specific purpose can be conceived. This latter is the error of much of the present day philosophy and has to be specially guarded against. This was perceived by some of the medieval students of these things, and they accordingly distinguished between what they called Animus Dei and Anima Mundi, the Divine Spirit and the Soul of the Universe. Now the distinction is this, that the essential quality of Animus Dei is Personality--not A Person, but the very Principle of Personality itself--while the essential quality of Anima Mundi is Impersonality. Then right here comes in that importance of the Personal Factor of which I have already spoken. The powers latent in the Impersonal are brought out to their fullest development by the operation of the Personal. This of course does not consist in changing the nature of those powers, for that is impossible, but in making such combinations of them by Personal Selection as to produce results which could not otherwise be obtained. Thus, for example, Number is in itself impersonal and no one can alter the laws which are inherent in it; but what we can do is to select particular numbers and the sort of relation, such as subtraction, multiplication, etc., which we will establish between them; and then by the inherent Law of Number a certain result is bound to work out. Now our own essential quality is the consciousness of Personality; and as we grow into the recognition of the fact that the Impersonal is, as it were, crying out for the operation upon it of the Personal in order to bring its latent powers into working, we shall see how limitless is the field that thus opens before us.

The prospect is wonderful beyond our present conception, and full of increasing glory if we realize the true foundation on which it rests. But herein lies the danger. It consists in not realizing that the Infinite of the Impersonal is and also that the Infinite of the Personal is. Both are Infinite and so require differentiation through our own personality, but in their essential quality each is the exact balance of the other--not in contradiction to each other, but as complementary to one another, each supplying what the other needs for its full expression, so that the two together make a perfect whole. If, however, we see this relation and our own position as the connecting link between them, we shall see only ourselves as the Personal Factor; but the more we realize, both by theory and experience, the power of human personality brought into contact with the Impersonal Soul of Nature, and employed with a Knowledge of its power and a corresponding exercise of the will, the less we shall be inclined to regard ourselves as the supreme factor in the chain of cause and effect Consideration of this argument points to the danger of much of the present day teaching regarding the exercise of Thought Power as a creative agency. The principle on which this teaching is based is sound and legitimate for it is inherent in the nature of things; but the error is in supposing that we ourselves are the ultimate source of Personality instead of merely the distributors and specializers of it. The logical result of such a mental attitude is that putting ourselves in the place of all that is worshiped as God which is spoken of in the second chapter of the Second Epistle to the Thessalonians and other parts of Scripture. By the very hypothesis of the case we then know no higher will than our own, and so are without any Unifying Principle to prevent the conflict of wills which must then arise--a conflict which must become more and more destructive the greater the power possessed by the contending parties, and which, if there were no counterbalancing power, must result in the ultimate destruction of the existing race of men.

But there is a counterbalancing power. It is the very same power used affirmatively instead of negatively. It is the power of the Personal with the Impersonal when used under the guidance of that Unifying Principle which the recognition of the ONE-ness of the Personal Quality in the Divine Spirit supplies. Those who are using the creative power of thought only from the standpoint of individual personality, have obviously less power than those who are using it from the standpoint of the Personality inherent in the Living Spirit which is the Source and Fountain of all energy and substance, and therefore in the end the victory must remain with these latter. And because the power by which they conquer is that of the Unifying Personality itself their victory must result in the establishment of Peace and Happiness throughout the world, and is not a power of domination but of helpfulness and enlightenment. The choice is between these two mottoes:— "Each for himself and Devil take the hindmost," or "God for us all." In proportion, therefore, as we realize the immense forces dormant in the Impersonal Soul of Nature, only awaiting the introduction of the Personal Factor to wake them up into activity and direct them to specific purposes, the wider we shall find the scope of the powers within the reach of man; and the more clearly we perceive the Impersonalness of the very Principle of Personality itself, the clearer our own proper position as affording the Differentiating Medium between these two Infinitudes will become to us.

The Impersonalness of the Principle of Personality looks like a contradiction in terms, but it is not. I combine these two seemingly contradictory terms as the best way to convey to the reader the idea of the essential Quality of Personality not yet differentiated into individual centers of consciousness for the doing of particular work. Looked at in this way the Infinite of Personality must have Unity of Purpose for its foundation, for otherwise it would consist of conflicting personalities, in which case we have not yet reached the ONE all-originating cause. Or to put it in another way, an Infinite Personality divided against itself would be an Infinite Insanity, a creator of a cosmic Bedlam which, as a scientific fact, would be impossible of existence. Therefore the conception of an Infinite of Personality necessarily implies a perpetual Unity of Purpose; and for the same reason this Purpose can only be the fuller and fuller expression of an Infinite Unity of Consciousness; and Unity of Consciousness necessarily implies the entire absence of all that would impair it, and therefore its expression can only be as Universal Harmony. If, then, the individual realizes this true nature of the source from which his own consciousness of personality is derived his ideas and work will be based upon this foundation, with the result that as between ourselves peace and good will towards men must accompany this mode of thought, and as between us and the strictly Impersonal Soul of Nature our increasing knowledge in that direction would mean increasing power for carrying out our principle of peace and good will. As this perception of our relation to the Spirit of God and the Soul of Nature spreads from individual to individual so the Kingdom of God will grow, and its universal recognition would be the establishing of the Kingdom of Heaven on earth.

Perhaps the reader will ask why I say the Soul of Nature instead of saying the material universe. The reason is that in using our creative power of Thought we do not operate directly upon material elements--to do that is the work of construction from without and not of creation from within. The whole tendency of modern physical science is to reduce all matter in the final analysis to energy working in a primary ether. Whence this energy and this ether proceed is not the subject of physical analysis. That is a question which cannot be answered by means of the vacuum tube or the spectroscope. Physical science is doing its legitimate work in pushing further and further back the unanalyzable residuum of Nature, but, however far back, an ultimate unanalyzable residuum there must always be; and when physical science brings us to this point it hands us over to the guidance of psychological investigation just as in the Divina Commedia Virgil transfers Dante to the guidance of Beatrice for the study of the higher realms. Various rates of rapidity of motion in this primary ether, producing various numerical combinations of positively and negatively electrified particles, result in the formation of what we know as the different chemical elements, and thus explains the phenomena of their combining quantities, the law by which they join together to form new substances only in certain exact numerical ratios. From the first movement in the primary ether to solid substances, such as wood or iron or our own flesh, is thus a series of vibrations in a succession of mediums, each denser than the preceding one out of which it was concreted and from which it receives the vibratory impulse. This is in effect what physical science has to tell us. But to get further back we must look into the world of the invisible, and it is here that psychological study comes to our aid. We cannot, however, study the invisible side of Nature by working from the outside and so at this point of our studies we find the use of the time-honored teaching regarding the parallelism between the Macrocosm and the Microcosm. If the Microcosm is the reproduction in ourselves of the same principles as exist in the Macrocosm or universe in which we have our being, then by investigating ourselves we shall learn the nature of the corresponding invisible principles in our environment. Here, then, is the application of the dictum of the ancient philosophy, "Know Thyself." It means that the only place where we can study the principles of the invisible side of Nature is in ourselves; and when we know them there we can transfer them to the larger world around us.

In the concluding chapters of my "Edinburgh Lectures on Mental Science" I have outlined the way in which the soul or mind operates upon the physical instrument of its expression, and it resolves itself into this--that the mental action inaugurates a series of vibrations in the etheric body which, in their turn, induce corresponding grosser vibrations in the molecular substance until finally mechanical action is produced on the outside. Now transferring this idea to Nature as a whole we shall see that if our mental action is to affect it in any way it can only be by the response of something at the back of material substance analogous to mind in ourselves; and that there is such a "something" interior to the merely material side of Nature is proved by what we may call the Law of Tendency, not only in animals and plants, but even in inorganic substances, as shown for instance in Professor Bose's work on the Response of Metals. The universal presence of this Law of Tendency therefore indicates the working of some non-material and, so to say, semi-intelligent power in the material world, a power which works perfectly accurately on its own lines so far as it goes, that is to say in a generic manner, but which does not possess that

Personal power of individual selection which is necessary to bring out the infinite possibilities hidden in it. This is what is meant by the Soul of Nature, and it is for this reason I employ that term instead of saying the material universe. Which term to employ all depends on the mode of action we are contemplating. If it is construction from without, then we are dealing with the purely material universe. If we are seeking to bring about results by the exercise of our mental power from within, then we are dealing with the Soul of Nature. It is that control of the lower degree of intelligence by the higher of which I have spoken in my Edinburgh Lectures.

If we realize what I have endeavored to make clear in the earlier portion of this book, that the whole creation is produced by the operation of the Divine Will upon the Soul of Nature, it will be evident that we can set no limits to the potencies hidden in the latter and capable of being brought out by the operation of the Personal Factor upon it; therefore, granted a sufficiently powerful concentration of will, whether by an individual or a group of individuals, we can well imagine the production of stupendous effects by this agency, and in this way I would explain the statements made in Scripture regarding the marvelous powers to be exercised by the Anti-Christ, whether personal or collective. They are psychic powers, the power of the Soul of Man over the Soul of Nature. But the Soul of Nature is quite impersonal and therefore the moral quality of this action depends entirely on the human operator. This is the point of the Master's teaching regarding the destruction of the fig tree, and it is on this account He adds the warning as to the necessity for clearing our heart of any injurious feeling against others whenever we attempt to make use of this power (Mark 11:20-26).

According to His teaching, then, this power of controlling the Soul of Nature by the addition of our own Personal Factor, however little we may be able to recognize it as yet, actually exists; its employment depends on our perception of the inner principles common to both, and it is for this reason the ancient wisdom was summed up in the aphorism "Know thyself." No doubt it is a wonderful Knowledge, but on analysis it will be found to be perfectly natural. It is the Knowledge of the cryptic forces of Nature. Now it is remarkable that this ancient maxim inscribed over the portals of the Temple of Delphi is not to be found in the Bible. The Bible maxim is not "Know thyself" but "Know the Lord." The great subject of Knowledge is not ourself but "the Lord"; and herein is the great difference between the two teachings. The one is limited by human personality, the other is based on the Infinitude of the Divine Personality; and because of this it includes human personality with all its powers over the Soul of Nature. It is a case of the greater including the less; and so the whole teaching of Scripture is directed to bringing us into the recognition of that Divine Personality which is the Great Original in whose image and likeness we are made. In proportion as we grow into the recognition of this our own personality will explain, and the creative power of our thought will cease to work invertedly until at last it will work only on the same principles of Life, Love and Liberty as the Divine Mind, and so all evil will disappear from our world. We shall not, as some systems teach, be absorbed into Deity to the extinction of our individual consciousness, but on the contrary our individual consciousness will continually expand, which is what St. Paul means when he speaks of our "increasing with the increase of God"--the continual expanding of the Divine element within us. But this can only take place by our recognition of ourselves as receivers of this Divine element. It is receiving into ourselves of the Divine Personality, a result not to be reached through human reasoning. We reason from premises which we have assumed, and the conclusion is already involved in the premises and can never extend beyond them. But we can only select our premises from among things that we know by experience, whether mental or physical, and accordingly our reasoning is always merely a new placing of the old things. But the receiving of the Divine Personality into ourselves is an entirely New Thing, and so cannot be reached by reasoning from old things. Hence if this Divine ultimate of the Creative Process is to be attained it must be by the Revelation of a New Thing which will afford a new starting-point for our thought, and this New Starting-point is given in the Promise of "the Seed of the Woman" with which the Bible opens. Thenceforward this Promise became the central germinating thought of those who based themselves upon it, thus constituting them a special race, until at last when the necessary conditions had matured the Promised Seed appeared in Him of whom it is written that He is the express image of God's Person (Heb. 1:3)--that is, the Expression of that Infinite Divine Personality of which I have spoken. "No man hath seen God at any time or can see Him," for the simple reason that Infinitude cannot be the subject of vision. To become visible there must be Individualization, and therefore when Philip said "Show us the Father," Jesus replied, "He that hath seen me hath seen the Father." The Word must become flesh before St. John could say, "That which was from the beginning, which we have heard, which we have seen with our eyes, which we have looked upon, and our hands have handled, of the Word of Life." This is the New Starting-point for the true New Thought--the New Adam of the New Race, each of whom is a new center for the working of the Divine Spirit. This is what Jesus meant when he said, "Except ye eat the flesh and drink the blood of the Son of Man ye have no life in you. My flesh is meat indeed, and my blood is drink indeed--" such a contemplation of the Divine Personality in Him as will cause a like receiving of the Divine Personality into individualization in ourselves--this is the great purpose of the Creative Process in the individual. It terminates the old series which began with birth after the flesh and inaugurates a New Series by birth after the Spirit, a New Life of infinite unfoldment with glorious possibilities beyond our highest conception.

But all this is logically based upon our recognition of the Personalness of God and of the relation of our individual personality to this Eternal and Infinite Personality, and the result of this is Worship--not an attempt to "butter up" the Almighty and get Him into good temper, but the reverent contemplation of what this Personality must be in Itself; and when we see it to be that Life, Love, Beauty, etc., of which I spoke at the beginning of this book we shall learn to love Him for what He IS, and our prayer will be "Give me more of Thyself." If we realize the great truth that the Kingdom of Heaven is within us, that it is the Kingdom of the innermost of our own being and of all creation, and if we realize that this innermost is the place of the Originating Power where Time and Space do not exist and therefore antecedent to all conditions, then we shall see the true meaning of Worship. It is the perception of the Innermost Spirit as eternally subsisting independently of all conditioned manifestation, so that in the true worship our consciousness is removed from the outer sphere of existence to the innermost center of unconditioned being. There we find the Eternal Being of God pure and simple, and we stand reverently in this Supreme Presence knowing that it is the Source of our own being, and wrapped in the contemplation of This, the conditioned is seen to flow out from It. Perceiving this the conditioned passes out of our consideration, for it is seen not to be the Eternal Reality--we have reached that level of consciousness where Time and Space remain no longer. Yet the reverence which the vision of this Supreme Center of all Being cannot fail to inspire is coupled with a sense of feeling quite at home with It. This is because as the Center of all Being it is the center of our own being also. It is one-with-ourselves. It is recognizing Itself from our own center of consciousness; so that here we have got back to that Self-contemplation of Spirit which is the first movement of the Creating Power, only now this Self-contemplation is the action of the All-Originating Spirit upon Itself from the center of our own consciousness. So this worship in the Temple of the Innermost is at once reverent adoration and familiar intercourse--not the familiarity that breeds contempt, but a familiarity producing Love, because as it increases we see more clearly the true Life of the Spirit as the continual interaction of Love and Beauty, and the Spirit's recognition of ourselves as an integral portion of Its own Life. This is not an unpractical dreamy speculation but has a very practical bearing. Death will some day cease to be, for the simple reason that Life alone can be the enduring principle; but we have not yet reached this point in our evolution. Whether any in this generation will reach it I cannot say; but for the rank and file of us the death of the body seems to be by far the more probable event. Now what must this passing out of the body mean to us? It must mean that we find ourselves without the physical vehicle which is the instrument through which our consciousness comes in touch with the external world and all the interests of our present daily life. But the mere putting off of the body does not of itself change the mental attitude; and so if our mind is entirely centered upon these passing interests and external conditions the loss of the instrument by which we held touch with them must involve a consciousness of desire for the only sort of life we have known coupled with a consciousness of our inability to participate in it, which can only result in a consciousness of distress and confusion such as in our present state we cannot imagine.

On the other hand if we have in this world realized the true principle of the Worship of the Eternal Source from which all conditioned life flows out--an inner communing with the Great Reality--we have already passed beyond that consciousness of life which is limited by Time and Space; and so when we put off this mortal body we shall find ourselves upon familiar ground, and therefore not wandering in confusion but quite at home, dwelling in the same light of the Eternal in which we have been accustomed to dwell as an atmosphere enveloping the conditioned life of to-day. Then finding ourselves thus at home on a plane where Time and Space do not exist there will be no question with us of duration. The consciousness will be simply that of peaceful, happy being. That a return to more active personal operation will eventually take place is evidenced by the fact that the basis of all further evolution is the differentiating of the Undifferentiated Life of the Spirit into specific channels of work, through the intermediary of individual personality without which the infinite potentialities of the Creative Law cannot be brought to light. Therefore, however various our opinions as to its precise form, Resurrection as a principle is a necessity of the creative process. But such a return to more active life will not mean a return to limitations, but the opening of a new life in which we shall transcend them all, because we have passed beyond the misconception that Time and Space are of the Essence of Life. When the misconception regarding Time and Space is entirely eradicated all other limitations must disappear because they have their root in this primary one--they are only particular forms of the general proposition. Therefore though Form with its accompanying relations of Time and Space is necessary for manifestation, these things will be found not to have any force in themselves thus creating limitation, but to be the reflection of the mode of thought which projects them as the expression of itself.

Nor is there any inherent reason why this process should be delayed till some far-off future. There is no reason why we should not commence at once. No doubt our inherited and personally engendered modes of thought make this difficult, and by the nature of the process it will be only when all our thoughts are conformed to this principle that the complete victory will be won. But there must be a commencement to everything, and the more we habituate ourselves to live in that Center of the Innermost where conditions do not exist, the more we shall find ourselves gaining control over outward conditions, because the stream of conditioned life flows out from the Center of Unconditioned Life, and therefore this intrinsic principle of Worship has in it the promise both of the life that now is and of that which is to come. Only we must remember that the really availing worship is that of the Undifferentiated Source because It is the Source, and not as a backhanded way of diverting the stream into some petty channel of conditions, for that would only be to get back to the old circle of limitation from which we are seeking to escape.

But if we realize these things we have already laid hold of the Principle of Resurrection, and in point of principle we are already living the resurrection life. What progress we may make in it depends on our practical application of the principle; but simply as principle there is nothing in the principle itself to prevent its complete working at any moment. This is why Jesus did not refer resurrection to some remote point of time but said, "I am the resurrection and the life." No principle can carry in itself an opposite and limiting principle contradictory of its own nature, and this is as true of the Principle of Life as of any other principle. It is we who by our thought introduce an opposite and limiting principle and so hinder the working of the principle we are seeking to bring into operation; but so far as the Principle of Life itself is concerned there is in it no reason why it should not come into perfect manifestation here and now.

This, then, is the true purpose of worship. It is to bring us into conscious and loving intercourse with the Supreme Source of our own being, and seeing this we shall not neglect the outward forms of worship. From what we now know they should mean more to us than to others and not less; and in especial if we realize the manifestation of the Divine Personality in Jesus Christ and its reproduction in Man, we shall not neglect His last command to partake of that sacred memorial to His flesh and blood which He bequeathed to His followers with the words "This do in remembrance of Me."

This holy rite is no superstitious human invention. There are many theories about it, and I do not wish to combat any of them, for in the end they all seem to me to bring us to the same point, that being cleansed from sin by the Divine Love we are now no longer separate from God but become "partakers of the Divine-Nature" (2 Peter 1:4). This partaking of the Divine Nature could not be more accurately represented than by our partaking of bread and wine as symbols of the Divine Substance and the Divine Life, thus made emblematic of the whole Creative Process from its beginning in the Divine Thought to its completion in the manifestation of that Thought as Perfected Man; and so it brings vividly before us the remembrance of the Personality of God taking form as the Son of Man. We are all familiar with the saying that thoughts become things; and if we affirm the creative power of our own thought as reproducing itself in outward form, how much more must we affirm the same of that Divine Thought which brings the whole universe into existence; so that in accordance with our own principles the Divine Idea of Man was logically bound to show itself in the world of time and space as the Son of God and the Son of man, not two differing natures but one complete whole, thus summing up the foundation principle of all creation in one Undivided Consciousness of Personality. Thus "the Word" or Divine Thought of Man "became flesh," and our partaking of the symbolic elements keeps in our remembrance the supreme truth that this same "Word" or Thought of God in like manner takes form in ourselves as we open our own thought to receive it. And further, if we realize that throughout the universe there is only ONE Originating Life, sending forth only ONE Original Substance as the vehicle for its expression, then it logically follows that in essence the bread is a portion of the eternal Substance of God, and the wine a portion of the eternal Life of God. For though the wine is of course also a part of the Universal Substance, we must remember that the Universal Substance is itself a manifestation of the Life of the All-Creating Spirit, and therefore this fluid form of the primary substance has been selected as representing the eternal flowing of the Life of the Spirit into all creation, culminating in its supreme expression in the consciousness of those who, in the recognition of these truths, seek to bring their heart into union with the Divine Spirit. From such considerations as these it will be seen how vast a field of thought is covered by Christ's words "Do this in remembrance of Me."

In conclusion, therefore, do not let yourselves be led astray by any philosophy that denies the Personality of God. In the end it will be found to be a foolish philosophy. No other starting-point of creation is conceivable than the Self-Contemplation of the Divine Spirit, and the logical sequence from this brings us to the ultimate result of the Creative Process in the statement that "if any man be in Christ he is a New creature," or as the margin has it "a new creation" (2 Cor. 5:17). Such vain philosophies have only one logical result which is to put yourself in the place of God, and then what have you to lean upon in the hour of trial? It is like trying to climb up a ladder that is resting against nothing. Therefore, says the Apostle Paul, "Beware lest any man spoil you through philosophy and vain deceit, after the tradition of man, after the rudiments of the world, and not after Christ." (Col. 2:8.) The teaching of the Bible is sound philosophy, sound reasoning, and sound science because it starts with the sound premises that all Creation proceeds out of God, and that Man is made in the image and likeness of his Creator. It nowhere departs from the Law of Cause and Effect, and by the orderly sequence of this law it brings us at last to the New Creation both in ourselves and in our environment, so that we find the completion of the Creative Process in the declaration "the tabernacle of God is with men" (Rev. 21:3), and in the promise "This is the Covenant that I will make with them after those days (i.e., the days of our imperfect apprehension of these things) saith the Lord, I will dwell in them, and walk in them, and I will be their God, and they shall be my people, and I will put my laws into their hearts, and in their minds will I write them, and their sins and their iniquities will I remember no more" (Heb. 10:16. 2 Cor. 6:16. Jeremiah 31:33).

Truly does Bacon say, "A little philosophy inclineth a man's mind to atheism, but depth in philosophy bringeth men's minds about to religion." —Bacon, Essay, 16.

FOOTNOTES

[1] See my Doré Lectures, 1909.

[2] See my Edinburgh Lectures on Mental Science.

[3] See my Doré Lectures, 1909.

[4] For the relation between conscious and sub-conscious mind see my "Edinburgh Lectures on Mental Science."

[5] See "Self-Synthesis" by Dr. Cornwall Round.

[6] For the relation between subjective and objective mind see my "Edinburgh Lectures on Mental Science."

[7] This view, it may be remarked, is not necessarily incompatible with the conception of reincarnation, on which theory the final resurrection or transmutation of the body would terminate the series of successive lives and deaths, thus bringing the individual out of the circle of generation, which is the circle of Karma. I may, perhaps, have the opportunity of considering this subject on some future occasion.

[8] See my "Bible Mystery and Bible Meaning."

[9] See "Bible Mystery and Bible Meaning" by the present author.

Bible Mystery
and Bible Meaning

Chapter 1

The Creation

The Bible is the Book of Emancipation of Man. The emancipation of man means his delivery from sorrow and sickness, from poverty, struggle and uncertainty, from ignorance and limitation, and finally from death itself. This may appear to be what the colloquialism of the day would call "a tall order", but nevertheless it is impossible to read the Bible with a mind unwarped by antecedent conceptions derived from traditional interpretation without seeing that this is exactly what it promises, and that it professes to contain the secret whereby this happy condition of perfect liberty may be attained.

Jesus says that if a man keeps his saying, he shall never see death (John 8:51); in the Book of Job we are told that if a man has with him "a messenger, an interpreter", he shall be delivered from going down to the pit, and shall return to the days of his youth (Job 33:23-25); the Psalms speak of our renewing our youth (Psalm 103:5); and yet again we are told in Job that by acquainting ourselves with God we shall be at peace, we shall lay up gold as dust and have plenty of silver, we shall decree a thing and it shall be established unto us (Job 22:21-28).

Now, what I propose is that we shall reread the Bible on the supposition that Jesus and these other speakers really meant what they said. Of course, from the standpoint of the traditional interpretation this is a startling proposition. The traditional explanation assumes that it is impossible for these things to be literally true, and therefore it seeks some other meaning in the words, and so gives them a "spiritual" interpretation.

But in the same manner we may spiritualize away an Act of Parliament; and it hardly seems the best way of getting at the meaning of a book to follow the example of the preacher who commenced his discourse with the words, "Beloved brethren, the text doth not mean what it saith." Let us, however, start with the supposition that these texts do mean what they say, and try to interpret the Bible on these lines. It will at least have the attraction of novelty; and I think if the reader gives his careful attention to the following pages, he will see that this method carries with it the conviction of reason.

If a thing is true at all, there is a way in which it is true, and when the way is seen, we find that to be perfectly reasonable which, before we understood the way, appeared unreasonable. We all go by railroad now, yet they were esteemed level-headed practical men in their day who proposed to confine George Stephenson (1781-1848, English inventor of an early steam-driven railway engine) as a lunatic for saying that it was possible to travel at thirty miles an hour.

The first thing to notice is that there is a common element running through the texts I have quoted: they all contain the idea of acquiring certain information, and the promised results are all contingent on our getting this information, and using it. Jesus says it depends on our keeping his saying, that is, receiving the information which he had to give and acting upon it. Job says that it depends on rightly interpreting a certain message, and again that it depends on our making ourselves acquainted with something; and the context of the passage from the Psalms makes it clear that the deliverance from death and the renewal of youth there promised are to be attained through the "ways" which the Lord "made known unto Moses".

In all these passages we find that these wonderful results come from the attainment of certain knowledge, and the Bible therefore appeals to our Reason. From this point of view we may speak of the Science of the Bible, and as we advance in our study, we shall find that this is not a misuse of terms, for the Bible is eminently scientific; only its science is not primarily physical but mental.

The Bible contemplates Man as composed of "Spirit, soul, and body" (1 Thess. 5:23), or in other words as combining into a single unity a threefold nature — spiritual, psychic, and corporeal; and the knowledge which it proposes to give us is the knowledge of the true relation between these three factors. The Bible also contemplates the totality of all Being, manifested and unmanifested, as likewise constituting a threefold unity, which may be distributed under the terms, "God", "Man", and "the Universe"; and it occupies itself with telling us of the interaction, both positive and negative, which goes on between these three. Furthermore, it bases this interaction upon two great psychological laws, namely, that of the creative power of Thought and that of the amenability of Thought to control by Suggestion; and it affirms that this Creative Power is as innately inherent in Man's Thought as in the Divine Thought.

But it also shows how through ignorance of these truths we unknowingly misuse our creative power, and so produce the evils we deplore; and it also realizes the extreme danger of recognizing our power before we have attained the moral qualities which will fit us to use it in accordance with those principles which keep the great totality of things in an abiding harmony; and to avoid this danger, the Bible veils its ultimate meaning under symbols, allegories, and parables.

But these are so framed as to reveal this ultimate meaning to those who will take the trouble to compare the various statements with one another, and who are sufficiently intelligent to draw the deductions which follow from thus putting two and two together; while those who cannot thus read between the lines are trained into the requisite obedience suited to the present extent of their capacity, and are thus gradually prepared for the fuller recognition of the Truth as they advance.

Seen in this light, the Bible is found not to be a mere collection of old-world fables or unintelligible dogmas, but a statement of great universal laws, all of which proceed simply and naturally from the initial truth that Creation is a process of Evolution. Grant the evolutionary theory, which every advance in modern science renders clearer, and all the rest follows, for the entire Bible is based upon the principle of Evolution. But the Bible is a statement of Universal law, of that which obtains in the realm of the invisible as well as that which obtains in the realm of the visible, and therefore it deals with the facts of a transcendental nature as well as with those of the physical plane; and accordingly it contemplates an earlier process anterior to Evolution — the process, namely, of Involution: the passing of Spirit into Form as antecedent to the passing of Form into Consciousness. If we bear this in mind, it will throw light on many passages which must remain wrapped in impenetrable obscurity until we know something of the psychic principles to which they refer.

The fact that the Bible always contemplates Evolution as necessarily preceded by Involution should never be lost sight of, and therefore much of the Bible requires to be read as referring to the involutionary process taking place upon the psychic plane. But Involution and Evolution are not opposed to one another; they are only the earlier and later stages of the same process: the perpetual urging onward of Spirit for Self-expression in infinite varieties of Form. And therefore the grand foundation on which the whole Bible system is built up is that the Spirit, which is thus continually passing into manifestation, is always the same Spirit. In other words, it is only ONE.

These two fundamental truths — that under whatever varieties of Form, the Spirit is only ONE; and that the creation of all forms, and consequently of the whole world of conscious relations, is the result of Spirit's ONE mode of action, which is Thought — are the basis of all that the Bible has to teach us, and therefore from its first page to its last, we shall find these two ideas continually recurring in a variety of different connections: the ONE-ness of the Divine Spirit and the Creative Power of man's Thought, which the Bible expresses in its two grand statements, that "God is ONE", and that Man is made "in the image and likeness of God".

These are the two fundamental statements of the Bible, and all its other statements flow logically from them. And since the whole argument of Scripture is built up from these premises, the reader must not be surprised at the frequency with which our analysis of that argument will bring us back to these two initial propositions. So far from being a vain repetition, this continual reduction of the statements of the Bible to the premises with which it originally sets out is the strongest proof that we have in them a sure and solid foundation on which to base our present life and our future expectations.

But there is yet another point of view from which the Bible appears to be the very opposite of a logically accurate system built up on the broad foundations of Natural Law. From this point of view it at first looks like the egotistical and arrogant tradition of a petty tribe, the narrow book of a narrow sect, instead of a statement of Universal Truth; and yet this aspect of it is so prominent that it can by no means be ignored. It is impossible to read the Bible and shut our eyes to the fact that it tells us of God making a covenant with Abraham, and thenceforward separating his descendants by a divine interposition from the remainder of mankind; for this separation of a certain portion of the race as special objects of the Divine favour forms an integral part of Scripture from the story of Cain and Abel to the description of "the camp of the saints and the beloved city" in the Book of Revelation.

We cannot separate these two aspects of the Bible, for they are so interwoven with one another that if we attempt to do so, we shall end by having no Bible left, and we are therefore compelled to accept the Bible statements as a whole or reject it altogether, so that we are met by the paradox of a combination between an all-inclusive system of Natural Law and an exclusive selection which at first appears to flatly contradict the processes of Nature. Is it possible to reconcile the two?

The answer is that it is not only possible, but that this exclusive selection is the necessary consequence of the Universal law of Evolution when working in the higher phases of individualism. It is not that those who do not come within the pale of this Selection suffer any diminution, but that those who do come within it receive thereby a special augmentation and, as we shall see by and by, this takes place by a purely natural process resulting from the more intelligent employment of that knowledge which it is the purpose of the Bible to unfold to us.

These two principles of the inclusive and the exclusive are intertwined in a double thread which runs all through Scripture, and this dual nature of its statements must always be borne in mind if we would apprehend its meaning. Asking the reader, therefore, to carefully go over these preliminary remarks as affording the clue to the reason of the Bible statements, I shall now turn to the first chapter of Genesis.

The opening announcement that "in the beginning God created the heaven and the earth" contains the statement of the first of these two propositions which are the fundamental premises from which the whole Bible is evolved. From the Master's instruction to the woman of Samaria we know that "God" means "Spirit"; not "a Spirit", as in the Authorized (King James) Version, thus narrowing the Divine Being with the limitations of individuality, but as it stands in the original Greek, simply "Spirit" — that is, all Spirit, or Spirit in the Universal. Thus the opening words of the Bible may be read, "in the beginning Spirit" — which is the statement of the underlying Universal Unity.

Here let me draw attention to the twofold meaning of the words "in the beginning". They may mean first in order of time, or first in order of causation, and the latter meaning is brought out by the Latin version, which commences with the words "in principio" — that is, "in principle". This distinction should be borne in mind, for in all subsequent stages of evolution the initial principle which gives rise to the individualized entity must still be in operation as the fons et origo (fountain and origin) of that particular manifestation just as much as in its first concentration; it is the root of the individuality, without which the individuality would cease to exist. It is the "beginning" of the individuality in order of causation, and this "beginning" is, therefore, a continuous fact, always present and not to be conceived of as something which has been left behind and done with.

The same principle was, of course, the "beginning" of the entity in point of time also, however far back in the ages we may suppose it to have first evolved into separate existence, so that whether we apply the idea to the cosmos or to the individual, the words "in the beginning" both carry us back to the primordial out-push from non-manifestation into manifestation, and also rivet our attention upon the same power as still at work as the causal principle both in ourselves and in everything else around us. In both these senses, then, the opening words of the Bible tell us that the "beginning" of everything is "God", or Spirit in the Universal.

The next statement — that God created the heaven and the earth — brings us to the consideration of the Bible way of using words. The fact that the Bible deals with spiritual and psychic matters makes it of necessity an esoteric book, and therefore, in common with all other esoteric literature, it makes a symbolic use of words for the purpose of succinctly expressing ideas which would otherwise require elaborate explanation, and also for the purpose of concealing its meaning from those who are not yet safely to be entrusted with it. But this need not discourage the earnest student, for by comparing one part of the Bible with another he will find that the Bible itself affords the clue to the translation of its own symbolical vocabulary.

Here, as in so many other instances, the Master has given us the key to the right interpretation. He says that the Kingdom of Heaven is within us; in other words, that "Heaven" is the kingdom of the innermost and spiritual; and if so, then by necessary implication "Earth" must be the symbol of the opposite extreme and must metaphorically mean the outermost and material. We are starting the history of the evolution of the world in which we live; that is to say, this Power, which the Bible calls "God", is first presented to us in the opening words of Genesis at a stage immediately preceding the commencement of a stupendous work.

Now what are the conditions necessary for the doing of any work? Obviously there must be something that works and something that is worked upon — an active and a passive factor; an energy and a material on or in which that energy operates. This, then, is what is meant by the creation of Heaven and Earth; it is that operation of the eternally subsisting ONE upon Itself which produces its dual expression as Energy and Substance. And here remark carefully that this does not mean a separation, for Energy can only be exhibited by reason of something which is energized; or, in other words, for Life to manifest at all, there must be something that lives. This is an all-important truth, for our conception of ourselves as beings separate from the Divine Life is the root of all our troubles.

In its first verse, therefore, the Bible starts us with the conception of Energy or Life inherent in substance and shows us that the two constitute a dual-unity which is the first manifestation of the Infinite Unmanifested ONE; and if the reader will think these things out for himself, he will see that these are primary intuitions the contrary of which it is impossible to conceive. He may, if he please, introduce a Demiurge as part of the machinery for the production of the world, but then he has to account for this Demiurge, which brings him back to the Undistributed ONE of which I speak, and its first manifestation as Energy-inherent-in-Substance; and if he is driven back to this position, then it becomes clear that his Demiurge is a totally unnecessary wheel in the train of evolutionary machinery. And the gratuitous introduction of a factor which does no work but what could equally be done without it is contrary to anything we can observe in Nature or can conceive of a Self-evolving Power.

But we are particularly cautioned against the mistake of supposing that Substance is the same thing as Form, for we are told that the "earth was without form". This is important because it is just here that a very prolific source of error in metaphysical studies creeps in. We see Forms which, simply as masses, are devoid of an organized life corresponding to the particular form, and therefore we deny the inherency of Energy or Life in ultimate substance itself. As well deny the pungency of pepper because it is not in the particular pepper-pot we are accustomed to.

No, that primordial state of Substance with which the opening verse of the Bible is concerned is something very far removed from any conception we can have of Matter as formed into atoms or electrons. We are here only at the first stage of Involution, and the presence of material atoms is a stage, and by no means the earliest, in the process of Evolution.

We are next told that the Spirit of God moved upon the face of the waters. Here we have two factors, "Spirit" and "Water", and the initial movement is attributed to Spirit. This verse introduces us to that particular mode of manifestation of the Universal Substance which we may denominate the Psychic. This psychic mode of the Universal Substance may best be described as Cosmic Soul-Essence — not, indeed, universal in the strictest sense otherwise than as always included in the original Primordial Essence, but universal to the particular world-system under formation, and as yet undifferentiated into any individual forms.

This is what the medieval writers spoke of as "the Soul of the Universe", or Anima Mundi, as distinguished from the Divine Self, or Animus Dei, and it is the universal psychic medium in which the nuclei of the forms hereafter to become consolidated on the plane of the concrete and material take their inception in obedience to the movement of the Spirit, or Thought. This is the realm of Potential Forms, and is the connecting link between Spirit, or pure Thought, and Matter, or concrete Form, and as such plays a most important part in the constitution of the Cosmos and of Man.

In our reading of the Bible as well as in our practical application of Mental Science, the existence of this intermediary between Spirit and Matter must never be lost sight of. We may call it the Distributive Medium, in passing through which the hitherto undistributed Energy of Spirit receives differentiation of direction and so ultimately produces differentiation of forms and relations on the outermost or visible plane. This is the Cosmic Element which is esoterically called "Water", and so long ago as the reign of Henry VIII, Dean Colet explains it thus in a letter to his friend Randulph.

Dean Colet was very far from being a visionary. He was one of the precursors of the Reformation in England, and among the first to establish the study of Greek at Oxford; and as the founder of St Paul's School in London, he took a leading part in introducing the system of public-school education which is still in operation in this country. There is no mistaking Dean Colet for any other than a thoroughly level-headed and practical man, and his opinion as to the meaning of the word "Water" in this connection therefore carries great weight.

But we have the utterance of a yet higher authority on this subject, for the Master himself concentrates his whole instruction to Nicodemus on the point that the New Birth results from the interaction of "Spirit" and "Water", especially emphasizing the fact that "the flesh" has no share in the operation. This distinction between "the flesh", or the outermost principle, and "Water" should be carefully noted. The emphasis laid by the Master on the nothingness of "the flesh" and the essentialness of "Water" must mark a distinction of the most important kind, and we shall find it very helpful in unraveling the meaning of many passages of the Bible to grasp this distinction at the outset.

The action of "Spirit" upon "Water" is that of an active upon a passive principle; and the result of any sort of Work is to reconstruct the material worked upon into a form which it did not possess before. Now the new form to be produced, whatever it may be, is a result and therefore is not to be enumerated among the causes of its own production.

Hence it is a self-obvious truism that any act of creative power must take place at a more interior level than that of the form to be created; and accordingly, whether in the Old or the New Testament, the creative action is always contemplated as taking place between the Spirit and the Water, whether we are thinking of producing a new world or a new man. We must always go back to First Cause operating on Primary Substance.

We are told that the first product of the movement of Spirit upon Water was Light, thereby suggesting an analogy with the discoveries of modern science that light and heat are modes of motion. But the statement that the Sun was not created till the fourth day guards us against the mistake of supposing that what is here meant is the light visible to the physical eye. Rather, it is that All-pervading Inner Light, of which I shall have more to say by and by, and which only becomes visible as the corresponding sense of inward vision begins to be developed; it is that psychic condition of the Universal Substance in which the auras of the potentials of all forms may be discovered and where, consciously or unconsciously, the Spirit determines the forms of those things which are to be.

Like all other knowledge, the knowledge of the Inner Light is capable of application at higher and at lower levels, and the premature recognition of its power at the lower levels, uncontrolled by the recognition of its higher phases, is one of the most dangerous acquisitions; but duly regulated by the higher knowledge, the lower is both safe and legitimate, for in its due order it also is part of the Universal Harmony.

The initial Light having thus been produced, the introduction of the firmament on the second day indicates the separation of the spiritual principles of the different members of the world-system from one another, and the third day sees the emanation of Earth from "the Water", or the production of the actual corporeal system of Nature — the commencement of the process of Evolution. Up to this point the action has been entirely upon the inner plane of "Water" — that is to say, a process of Involution — and consistently with this it was impossible for the heavenly bodies to begin giving physical light until the fourth day, for until then no physical sun or planets could have existed.

With the fourth day, however, the physical universe is differentiated into shape; and on the fifth day the terrestrial waters begin to take their share in the evolutionary process by spontaneously producing fish and fowl. And here we may remark in passing how Genesis has forestalled modern science in the discovery that birds are anatomically more closely related to fishes than to land animals. The terrestrial earth (I call it so to distinguish it from symbolic "earth"), already on the third day impregnated with the vegetable principle, takes up the evolutionary work on the sixth day, producing all those other animal races which had not already originated in the waters, and the the preparation of the world as an abode for Man is completed.

It would be difficult to give a more concise statement of Evolution. Originating Spirit subsists at first as simple Unity; then it differentiates itself into the active and passive principles spoken of as "Heaven" and "Earth", or "Spirit" and "Water". From these proceed Light, and the separation into their respective spheres of the spiritual principles of the different planets, each carrying with it the potential of the self-reproducing power.

Then we pass into the realm of realization, and the work that has been done on the interior planes is now reproduced in physical manifestation, thus marking a still further unfoldment;

and finally, in the phrases "let the waters bring forth" and "let the earth bring forth", the land and water of our habitable globe are distinctly stated to be the sources from which all vegetable and animal forms have been evolved. Thus creation is described as the self-transforming action of the ONE unanalyzable Spirit passing by successive transitions into all the varieties of manifestations that fill the Universe.

And here we may notice a point which has puzzled commentators unacquainted with the principles on which the Bible is written. This is the expression "the evening and the morning were the first, second, etc., day". Why, it is asked, does each day begin with the evening? And various attempts have been made to explain it in accordance with Jewish methods of reckoning time. But as soon as we see what the Bible statement of creation is, the reason at once becomes clear. The second verse of the Bible tells us that the starting-point was Darkness, and the coming forth of Light out of Darkness cannot be stated in any other order than the dawning of morning from night.

It is the dawning into manifestation out of non-manifestation, and this happens at each successive stage of the evolutionary process. We should notice, also, that nothing is said as to the remainder of each day. All that we hear of each day is as "the morning", thus indicating the grand truth that when once a Divine day opens, it never again descends into the shades of night. It is always "morning".

The Spiritual Sun is always climbing higher and higher, but never passes the zenith or commences to decline — a truth which Swedenborg expresses by saying that the Spiritual Sun is always seen in the eastern heavens at an angle of forty-five degrees above the horizon. What a glorious and inspiring truth: when once God begins a work, that work will never cease, but will go on forever expanding into more and more radiant forms of strength and beauty, because it is the expression of the Infinite, which is Itself Love, Wisdom, and Power.

These days of creation are still in their prime and forever will be so, and the germs of the New Heaven and the New Earth which the Bible promises are already maturing in the heaven and earth that now are, as St Paul tells us, waiting only for the manifestation of the Sons of God to follow up the old principle of Evolution to still further expansion in the glory that shall be revealed.

As himself included in the great Whole, Man is no exception to the Universal Law of Evolution. It has often been remarked that the account of his creation is twofold, the two statements being contained in the first and second chapters of Genesis respectively. But this is precisely in accordance with the method adopted regarding the rest of creation.

First we are told of the creation in the realm of the invisible and psychic — that is to say, the process of Involution; and afterwards we are told of the creation on the plane of the concrete and material — that is to say, the process of Evolution. And since Involution is the cause and Evolution the effect, the Bible observes this order both in the account of the creation of the world and in that of the creation of Man.

In regard to his physical structure, Man's body, we are told, is formed from the "earth" — that is, by a combination of the same material elements as all other concrete forms; and thus in the physical Man, the evolutionary process attains its culmination in the production of a material vehicle capable of serving as the starting-point for a further advance, which has now to be made on the Intellectual and Spiritual.

The principle of Evolution is never departed from, but its further action now includes the intelligent co-operation of the evolving Individuality itself as a necessary factor in the work. The development of merely animal Man is the spontaneous operation of Nature, but the development of the mental Man can only result from his own recognition of the Law of Self-expression of Spirit as operating in himself.

It is, therefore, for the setting forth of Man's power to use this Law that the Bible was written; and accordingly, the great fact on which it seeks to rivet our attention in its first utterance regarding Man is that he is made in the image and likeness of God. A very little reflection will show us that this likeness cannot be in the outward form, for the Universal Spirit in which all things subsist cannot be limited by shape. It is a Principle permeating all things as their innermost substance and vivifying energy, and of it the Bible tells us that "in the beginning" there was nothing else.

Now the one and only conception we can have of this Universal Life-Principle is that of the Creative Power producing infinitely varied expressions of itself by Thought, for we cannot ascribe any other initial mode of movement to Spirit but that of thought — although as taking place in the Universal, this mode of Thought must necessarily be, relatively to the individual and particular, a subconscious activity. The likeness, therefore, between God and man must be a mental likeness, and since the only fact which, up to this point, the Bible has told us regarding the Universal Mind is its Creative Power, the resemblance indicated can only consist in the reproduction of the same Creative Power in the Mind of Man.

As we progress, we shall find that the whole Bible turns on this one fundamental fact. The Creative Power is inherent in our Thought, and we can by no means divest ourselves of it; but because we are ignorant that we possess this power, or because we misapprehend the conditions for its beneficial employment, we need much instruction in the nature of our own as yet unrecognized possibilities; and it is the purpose of the Bible to give us this teaching.

A little consideration of the terms of the evolutionary process will show us that since there is no other source from which it can proceed, the Individual Mind, which is the essential entity that we call Man, can be no other than a concentration of the Universal Mind into individual consciousness. Man's Mind is, therefore, a miniature reproduction of the Divine Mind, just as fire has always the same igneous qualities whether the center of combustion be large or small; and so it is on this fact that the Bible would fix our attention from first to last, knowing that if the interior realm of Causation be maintained in a harmonious order, the external realm of Effects is certain to exhibit corresponding health, happiness, and beauty.

And further, if the human mind is the exact image and likeness of the Divine, then its creative power must be equally unlimited. Its mode is different, being directed to the individual and particular, but its quality is the same; and this becomes evident if we reflect that it is not possible to set any limit to Thought, and that its only limitations are such as are set by the limited conceptions of the individual who thinks. And it is precisely here that the difficulty comes in. Our Thought must necessarily be limited by our conceptions. We cannot think of something which we cannot conceive; and therefore, the more limited our conceptions, the more limited will be our thought, and its creations will accordingly be limited in a corresponding degree.

It is for this reason that the ultimate purpose of all true instruction is to lead us into that Divine Light where we shall see things beyond the range of any past experiences — things which have not emerged into the heart of man to conceive, revealings of the Divine Spirit opening to us untold worlds of splendour, delight, and unending achievement. But in our earlier stages of development, where we are still surrounded by the mists of ignorance, this correspondence between the range of Thought's creations and the range of our conceptions brings about the catastrophe of "the Fall", which forms the subject of our next chapter.

Chapter 2
The Fall

In the last chapter we reached the conclusion that in the nature of things, Thought must always be limited by the range of the intelligence which gives rise to it. The power of Thought as the creative agent is perfectly unlimited in itself, but its action is limited by the particular conception which it is sent forth to embody. If it is a wide conception based upon an enlarged perception of truth, the thought which dwells upon it will produce corresponding conditions. This is self-evident; it is simply the statement that an instrument will not do work to which the hand of the workman does not apply it; and if the student will only fix this very simple idea in his mind, he will find in it the key to the whole mystery of man's power of self-evolution. Let us make our first use of this key to unlock the mystery of the story of Eden.

It is hardly necessary to say that the story of Eden is an allegory: that is clearly shown by the nature of the two trees that grew in the center of the garden — the Tree of the Knowledge of Good and Evil and the Tree of Life. This allegory is one repeated in many lands and ages, as in the classical fable of the Garden of the Hesperides and in the medieval Romance of the Rose; always the idea is repeated in a garden in whose center grows some life-giving fruit or flower which is the reward of him who discovers the secret by which the center of the garden may be reached.

The meaning in all these stories is the same. The garden is the Garden of the Soul, and the Tree of Life is that innermost perception of Spirit of which the Master said that it would be a well of water springing up to everlasting life to all who realized it. It is the garden which elsewhere in Scripture is called "the garden of the Lord"; and in accordance with the nature of the garden, the plants which grow in it — and which man has to tend and cultivate — are thoughts and ideas; and the chief of them are his idea of Life and his idea of Knowledge, and these occupy the center of the garden because all our ideas must take their colour from them.

We must recollect that human life is a drama whose action takes place in three worlds, and therefore, in reading the Bible, we must always make sure which world we are at any moment reading about — the spiritual, the intellectual, or the physical. In the spiritual world, which is that of the supreme ideal, there exists nothing but the potential of the absolutely perfect; and it is on this account that in the opening chapter of the Bible we read that God saw that all his work was good — the Divine eye could find no flaw anywhere; and we should note carefully that this absolutely good creation included Man also.

But as soon as we descend to the Intellectual world, which is the world of man's conception of things, it is quite different; and until man comes to realize the truly spiritual, and therefore perfectly good, essential nature of all things, there is room for any amount of mis-conception, resulting in a corresponding misdirection of man's creative instrument of Thought, which thus produces correspondingly misinformed realities.

Now the perfect life of Adam and Eve in Eden is the picture of Man as he exists in the spiritual world. It is not the tradition of some bygone age, but a symbolical representation of what we all are in our innermost being, thus recalling the words of the Master recorded in the Gospel of the Egyptians. He was asked when the Kingdom of Heaven should come and replied, "When that which is without shall be as that which is within" — in other words, when the perfection of the innermost spiritual essence shall be reproduced in the external part. In the story of Man's pristine life of innocence and joy in Paradise, we are reading on the level of the highest of the three worlds.

The story of "the Fall" brings us to the envelopment of this spiritual nature in the lower intellectual and material natures, through which alone it can obtain perfect individualization and Man become a reality instead of remaining only a Divine dream. In the allegory, Man is warned by god that Death will be the consequence of eating the fruit of the tree of the Knowledge of Good and Evil. This is not the threat of a sentence to be passed by God, but a warning as to the nature of the fruit itself; but this warning is disregarded by Eve, and she shares the forbidden fruit with Adam, and they are both expelled from Eden and become subject to Death as the consequence.

Now if Eden is the garden of the Soul, it is clear that Adam and Eve cannot be separate personages, but must be two principles in the human individuality which are so closely united as to be represented by a wedded pair. What, then, are these principles? St Paul makes a very remarkable statement regarding Adam and Eve. He tells us that "Adam was not deceived, but the woman being deceived was in the transgression" (1 Tim. 2:14). We have, therefore, Bible warrant for saying that Adam was not deceived; but at the same time, the story of the fall clearly shows that he was expelled from Eden for partaking of the fruit of Eve's instigation.

To satisfy both statements, therefore, we require to find in Adam and Eve two principles, one of which is capable of being deceived, and is deceived, and falls in consequence of the deception; and the other of which is incapable of being deceived but yet is involved with the fall of the former. This is the problem which has to be worked out, and the names of Adam and Eve supply the solution.

Eve, we are told, was so called because she was the mother of all living (Gen. 3:20). Eve, then, is the Mother of Life, a subject to which I shall have to refer again by and by. Eve, both syllables being pronounced, is the same word which in some Oriental languages is written "Hawa", by which name she is called in the Koran, and signifies Breath — the principle which we are told in Genesis 2:7 constitutes Man a living Soul.

Adam is rendered in the margin of the Bible "earth" or "red earth", and according to another derivation the name may also be rendered as "Not-breath". And thus in these two names we have the description of two principles, one of which is "Breath" and Life-conveying, while the other is "Not-breath" and is nothing but earth.

It requires no great skill to recognize in these the Soul and the Body. Then St Paul's meaning becomes clear. Any work on physiology will tell you that the human body is made up of certain chemical materials — so much chalk, so much carbon, so much water, etc. Obviously these substances cannot be deceived because they have no intelligence, and any deception that occurs must be accepted by the soul or intellectual principle, which is Eve, the mother of the individual life.

New Thought readers will have no difficulty in following the meaning of the poet Spenser when he says:

> For the soul of the body form doth take,
> For soul is form and doth the body make.

And since the soul is "the builder of the body", the deception which causes wrong thinking on the part of the intellectual man reproduces itself in physical imperfection and in adverse external circumstances.

What, then, is the deception which causes the "Fall"? This is figured by the Serpent. The serpent is a very favourite emblem in all ancient esoteric literature and symbolism and is sometimes used in a positive and sometimes in a negative sense. In either case it means life — not the Originating Life-Principle, but the ultimate outcome of that Life-Principle in its most external form of manifestation. This, of course, is not bad in itself. Recognized in full realization of the fact that it comes from God, it is the completion of the Divine work by outward manifestation; and in this sense it becomes the serpent which Moses lifted up in the wilderness.

But without the recognition of it as the ultimate mode of the Divine Spirit (which is all that is), it becomes the deadly reptile, not lifted up, but crawling flat upon the ground: it is that ignorant conception of things which cannot see the spiritual element in them and therefore attributes all their energy of action and reaction to themselves, not perceiving that they are the creations of a higher power.

Ignorant of the Divine Law of Creation, we do not look beyond secondary causes; and therefore because our own creative thought-power is ever externalizing conditions representative of our conceptions, we necessarily become more and more involved in the meshes of a network of circumstances from which we can find no way of escape. How these circumstances come about we cannot tell. We may call it blind chance, or iron destiny, or inscrutable Providence; but because we are ignorant of the true Law of Primary Causation, we never suspect the real fact, which is that the originating power of all this inharmony is ourself.

This is the great deception. We believe the serpent, or that conception of life which sees nothing beyond secondary causation, and consequently we accept the Knowledge of Evil as being equally necessary with the Knowledge of Good; and so we eat of the tree of Knowledge of Good and of Evil. It is this dual aspect of knowledge that is deadly, but knowledge itself is nowhere condemned in Scripture; on the contrary, it is repeatedly stated to be the foundation of all progress. "Wisdom is a Tree of Life to them that lay hold upon her", says the Book of Proverbs; "salvation is of the Jews because we know what we worship", says Jesus; and so on throughout the Bible.

But what is deadly to the soul of Man is the conception that Evil is a subject of Knowledge as well as Good — for this reason: that by thinking of Evil as a subject to be studied, we thereby attribute to it a substantive existence of its own; in other words, we look upon it as something having a self-originating power which, as we advance in our studies, we shall find more and more clearly is not the case. And so, by the Law of the creative working of Thought, we bring the Evil into existence. We have not yet penetrated the great secret of the difference between causes and conditions (as explained in my Edinburgh Lectures on Mental Science).

But this knowledge of our thought-action is not reached in the earlier history of the race or of the individual, for the simple reason that all evolution takes place by Growth; and consequently the history of Adam and Eve in realization — that is, the external life of humanity as distinguished from our simultaneous existence on the supreme plane of Spirit — commences with their expulsion from Eden and their conflict with a world of sorrows and difficulties.

If the reader realizes how this expulsion results from the soul accepting Evil as a subject of Knowledge, he will now be able to understand certain further facts. We are told that "the Lord God said, 'Behold the man is become as one of us to know good and evil'; and now lest he put forth his hand and take of the tree of life and eat and live forever, the Lord God sent him forth from the Garden of Eden" (Gen. 3:22-23). Looked at superficially, this seems like jealousy that man should have attained the same knowledge as God, and fear lest he should take the further step that would make him altogether God's equal. But such a reading of the text is babyish and indicates no conception of God as Universal All-originating Spirit, and we must therefore look for some deeper interpretation.

The First Commandment is the recognition of the Divine Unity, a fact on which Jesus laid special emphasis when he was asked which was the chief commandment of the Law; and the purpose is to guard us against the root-error from which all other forms of error spring. If the mathematical statement of Truth is that God is ONE, then the mathematical expression of error is that God is ZERO, and as the latter position has sometimes been taken by teachers of reputation, it may be well to show the student where the fallacy lies.

The conclusion that the mathematical expression of God is zero is reached in this way: as soon as you can conceive of anything as being, you can also conceive of it as not-being; in other words, the conception of any positive implies also the conception of its corresponding negative. Consequently, the conception of the positive or of the negative by itself is only half the conception, and a whole conception implies the recognition of both.

Therefore, since God contains the all, He must contain the negative as well as the positive of all potentiality, and the equal balance of positive and negative is Zero. But the radical error of this argument is the assumption that it is possible for two principles to neutralize each other, one of which is and the other of which is not.

We find the principle of neutralizing by equilibrium throughout Nature, but the equilibrium is always between two things each of which actually exists. Thus in chemistry we find an acid exactly equilibrating with an alkali and producing a neutral substance which is neither acid not alkali; but this is because the acid and the alkali both really exist; each of them is something that is. But what should we say to a chemical formula which required us to produce a neutral substance by equilibrating an acid which did exist by an alkali which did not? Yet this is precisely the sort of equilibration we are asked to accept by those who would make Zero the mathematical expression of All-originating Being. They say that a Universal Principle which is is exactly balanced by a Universal principle which is not; they affirm that Nothing is the equivalent of Something.

This is mere juggling with words and figures, and willfully shutting our eyes to the fact that the only quality of Nothing is Nothingness. Can anything be plainer than the old philosophic dictum ex nihilo nihil fit (nothing is made out of nothing)? There are disintegrating forces in Nature, but they do not proceed out of Nothing. They are the ONE positive power acting at lower levels — not the absence of the One Universal Energy but the same Energy working with less complex concentration and specific purpose than when directed by those higher modes of itself which constitute individual intelligences.

There is no such thing as a Negative Power, in the sense of power which is not the ONE All-originating Power. All energy is some mode of manifestation of the ONE, and it is always making something, though in doing so it may unmake something else; and what we loosely speak of as negative forces are the operation of the cosmic Law of Transition from one Form to another.

Above this there is a higher Law, to lead us to the realization of which is the whole object of the Bible, and that is the Law of Individual selection. It does not do away with the Law of Transition, for without transition there could be no Evolution; but it substitutes the Individual Law of conscious Life for the Impersonal Cosmic Law, and effects transition by living processes of assimilation and readjustment which more perfectly build up the individuality, instead of by a process of unbalanced disintegration which would destroy it. This is the Living Law of Liberty, which at every stage of its progress makes us not less, but more and yet more, ourselves.

It is for this reason that the Bible so strongly insists upon the mathematical statement that God is ONE, and in fact makes this the basis of all that it has to say. God is Life, Expression, reality; and how can these things comport with Nothingness? All we can know of any invisible power is through the effects we see it produce. Of electricity and chemical attraction it may truly be said that "no man hath seen them or can see them"; yet we know them by their working, and we rightly argue that if they work, they exist. The same argument applies to the Divine Spirit. It is that which is and not that which is not; and therefore I ask the student who would realize reality and not nothingness once for all to convince himself of the fallaciousness of the argument that the Divine Being is Not-being, or that Naught is the same thing as ONE.

If he starts his search for Reality by assuming what contradicts mathematics and common sense, he can never expect to find Reality, for he has denied its existence at the very outset and carries that initial denial all the way along with him. But if he realizes that all relations, whether relatively positive or negative, must necessarily be relations between factors which actually exist, and that there can be no relation with nothing, then, because he has assumed Reality in his premises, he will eventually find it in his conclusions and will learn that the Great Reality is the ONE expressing itself as the MANY, and the MANY recognizing themselves in the ONE.

The more advanced student will have no difficulty in recognizing the particular schools of teaching to which these remarks apply; their mathematics are unassailable, but the assumptions on which they make their selection of terms in the first instance are totally inapplicable to the subject-matter to which they apply them, for that subject is Life-in-itself.

Now the deception into which Eve falls is mathematically represented by saying that God = Zero, and thus attributing to Evil the same self-existence as to Good. There is no such thing as Absolute Evil; and what we recognize as Evil is the ONE Good Power working as Disintegrating Force, because we have not yet learnt to direct it is such a way that it shall perform the functions of transition to higher degrees of Life without any disintegration of our individuality either in person or circumstances. It is this disintegrating action that makes the ONE Power appear evil relatively to ourselves; and, so long as we conceive ourselves thus related to it, it does look as though it were Zero balancing in itself the two opposite forces of Life and Death, Good and Evil, and it is in this sense that "God" is said to know both.

But this is a conception very different from that of the All-productive ONE and arises, not from the true nature of Being, but from our own confused Thought. But because the action of our Thought is always creative, the mere fact of our regarding Evil as an affirmative force in itself makes it so relatively to ourselves; and therefore no sooner do we fear evil than we begin to create the evil that we fear. To extinguish evil, we must learn not to fear it, and that means to cease recognizing it as having any power of its own; and so our salvation comes from realizing that in truth there is nothing but the good.

But this knowledge can only be attained through long experience, which will at last bring Man to the place where he is able to deduce Truth from a priori principles and to learn that his past experiences of evil have proceeded from his own inverted conceptions and are not founded upon Truth but upon its opposite. If, then, it were possible for him to attain the knowledge which would enable him to live forever before gaining this experience, the result would be an immortality of misery, and therefore the Law of Nature renders it impossible for him to reach the knowledge which would place immortality within his grasp until he has gained that deep insight into the true working of causation which is necessary to make Eternal Life a prize worth having. For these reasons, man is represented as being expelled from Eden lest he should eat of the Tree of Life and live forever.

Before quitting this subject we must glance briefly at the sentences pronounced upon the man, the woman, and the serpent. The serpent, in this connection being the principle of error which results in Death, can never come into any sort of reconciliation with the Divine Spirit, which is Truth and Life, and therefore the only possible pronouncement upon the serpent is a curse — that is, a sentence of destruction; and the Bible goes on to show the stages by which this destruction is ultimately worked out. The penalty to Adam, or the corporeal body, is that of having to earn his bread by the sweat of his brow — that is, by toilsome labour, which would not be necessary if the true law of the creative exercise of our Thought were understood. The woman passes under a painful physiological law, but at the same time final deliverance and restoration from the "Fall" is promised through her instrumentality: her seed shall crush the serpent's head — that is, shall utterly destroy that false principle which the serpent represents.

Since the Woman is the Soul, or Individual Mind, her progeny must be thoughts and ideas. New ideas are not brought forth easily; they are the result of painful experiences and of long mental labour; and thus the physiological analogy contained in the text exactly illustrates the birth of new ideas into the world. And as the evolution of the Soul proceeds towards higher and higher intelligence, there is a corresponding increase in the lifeward tendency of its ideas, and thus there is enmity between the seed of "the Woman", or the enlightened conception of the principles of Life, and the seed of "the Serpent", or the opposite and unenlightened conception.

This is the same warfare which we find in Revelation between "the Woman" and "the Dragon". But in the end the victory remains with "the Woman" and her "Seed". During the progress of the struggle, the Serpent must bruise the heel of the Divine Seed — that is to say, must impede and retard the progress of Truth on the earth; but Truth must conquer at last and crush the Serpent's head so that it shall never rise up again forever. The "Seed of the Woman" — the Fruit of the spiritually enlightened Mind, which must at last achieve the final victory — is that supreme ideal which is the recognition of Man's Divine Sonship. It is the realization of the fact that he is, indeed, the image and likeness of God. This is the Truth the knowledge of which Jesus said would set us free, and each one who attains to this knowledge realizes that he is at once the Son of Man and the Son of God.

Thus the story of the Fall contains also the statement of the principle of the Rising-again. It is the history of the human race, because it is first the history of the individual soul, and to each one of us the ancient wisdom says, "de te fabula narratur" (this story is about you). These opening chapters of Genesis are, therefore, an epitome of all that the Bible afterwards unfolds in fuller detail, and the whole may be summed up in the following terms:

The great Truth concerning Man is that he is the image and likeness of God.

Man is at first ignorant of this Truth, and his ignorance is his Fall.

Man at last comes to the perfect knowledge of this Truth, and this knowledge is his Rising-again; and these principles will expand until they bring us to the full Expression of the Life that is in us in all the glories of the Heavenly Jerusalem.

Chapter 3

Israel

The space at my disposal will allow me only to touch upon a few of the most conspicuous points in that portion of the Bible narrative which takes us from the story of Eden to the Mission of Moses, for the reader will kindly bear in mind that I am not writing a commentary on the whole Bible, but only a brief introduction to its study.

The episode of Cain and Abel will be dealt with in the next chapter, and I will therefore pass on at once to the Deluge. As most of my readers probably know, this story is not confined to the Jewish and Christian Scriptures, but is met with in one form or another in all the most ancient traditions of the world, and this universal consensus of mankind leaves no doubt of the occurrence of some overwhelming cataclysm which has indelibly stamped itself upon the memory of all nations.

Whether science will ever succeed in working out the problem of its extent and of the physical conditions that gave rise to it remains to be seen, but it does not appear unreasonable to associate it with the tradition handed down to us by Plato of the sinking of the great continent of Atlantis, which is said to have once occupied the area now covered by the Atlantic Ocean. I am well aware that some geologists dispute the possibility of any radical changes having ever taken place in the distribution of the land and water surfaces of the globe, but there are at least equally good opinions on the other side, and if there is any fact in the world's history regarding which tradition is unanimous, it is the catastrophe of the Deluge.

And here I would draw attention to the fact that the Bible specially warns us against the opinion that no such catastrophe ever took place, and points out this opinion as one of the signs of the time of the end, speaking of it as determined ignorance, and telling us that a similar catastrophe, only by fire instead of water, will at some future period overwhelm the existing world (2 Peter 3); and I would add that the possible conditions for such an event may not unreasonably be inferred from certain facts in the science of astronomy. It is not my present purpose, however, to enter into the scientific and historical aspects of the Deluge tradition, but to point out its significance in that inner meaning of the Bible which I wish the student to grasp.

In the story as handed down by all nations, the Deluge is attributed to the wickedness of mankind, and according to some very ancient traditions this wickedness took largely the form of sorcery — a word which may perhaps provoke a smile in the uninitiated reader, but which holds a conspicuous place in the list of those causes which in the Book of Revelation are enumerated as leading to exclusion from the Heavenly City; and it will become sufficiently clear why it should do so when we learn what it really means. Coupling this tradition with the symbolical significance of "water", a deluge would indicate a total submergence in a psychic environment which had become too powerful to be held under control.

The psychic world is an integral part of the universe, and the psychic element is an integral part of man; and it is in this circulus that we find the plastic material which forms the nucleus for those attractions which eventually consolidate as external facts. The psychic realm is therefore the realm of tremendous potentialities, and the deeper our knowledge of its laws, the greater we see to be the need for bringing these potentialities under a higher control.

Now the opening verses of Genesis have shown us that "water" without the movement of the Spirit is darkness and the abode of chaos. The movement of the Spirit is the only power that can control the turbulence of "the waters" and bring them into that harmonious action which will result in forms of Life, Beauty, and Peace; and in the world of Man's Mind this movement of the Spirit upon "the waters" takes place exactly in proportion as the individual recognizes the true nature of the Divine Spirit, and wills to reflect its image and likeness.

Where this recognition takes place, the psychic forces are brought under the control of a harmonizing power which, reflecting itself into them, can only produce that which is Good and Beautiful, on a small scale at first because of our infantile knowledge of the powers with which we are dealing, but continually growing with our growth until the whole psychic world opens out before us as a limitless realm filled with the Glory of God and the Love of Man and the shapes of beauty to which they give rise.

But if a man forces his way into that realm on no other basis than his individual strength of will, he does so without reckoning that his will is itself a product of the psychic plane, and only one among untold organized entities and unorganized forces which sooner or later will overpower him and hurry him to age-long destruction — "age-long", for I use the Bible word aionios which, as the learned Farrar has shown in his Eternal Hope, does not mean absolutely endless; yet, if we reflect what may be included in this word — infinite periods, perhaps, of withdrawal and renewal of our whole planetary system — we may well stand aghast at such prodigious ruin.

But if such dangers are in it, may we not say that we will have nothing to do with the psychic realm? No, for by our nature we are always immersed in it; it is within us, and we are, and always must be, inhabitants of it, and we are always unconsciously using its forces and being reacted upon by them. What we need, therefore, is not to escape from what is an essential part of our nature, but to learn to vivify this otherwise dark realm with the warmth of Divine Love and the illumination of Divine Light.

But the Bible tells how very far the antediluvian world was from recognizing these Divine principles, for "the earth was filled with violence" and, except in the family of Noah, the true worship of God had ceased among men. And remark this word "violence" as the summing-up of human iniquity. Violence is the clashing of individual wills not harmonized by the recognition of any unifying principle. The ONE-ness of the Spirit from which all individualization proceeds is entirely lost sight of, and "each for himself" becomes the ruling principle — a principle which cannot but result in violence under whatever disguise it may be masked for a time.

The earth filled with violence was the outward correspondence of the inward mental state of the masses of mankind and we may, therefore, well imagine what the nature of their operations in the symbolic world of "Water" must have been. This state of things had been growing for generations until at last the inevitable result arrived, and the moral deluge produced its correspondence in the physical world.

The uninstructed reader will doubtless smile at my reference to a psychic environment, but those who have obtained at least some glimpses beyond the threshold will see the force of my argument when I direct their attention to the signs of a recurrence of a similar state of things at the present day. Research in various directions is making clearer and clearer the reality of the psychic forces, and increasing numbers are beginning to get some measure of practical insight into them; and while I rejoice to say that we see these opening powers being employed for the most part under the direction of sincere religious feeling and with charitable intention, yet there are not wanting reports of opposite uses, and this in connection with specific localities where the inverted employment of these great powers is secretly practiced according to methodized system.

I cannot too strongly warn the student against any connection with such societies, and their existence is a terrible comment upon the Master's description of the latter days which, he expressly tells us, will reproduce the character of those which immediately preceded the flood. The sole safeguard is in recognizing the Divine Spirit as the only Source of Power and in regarding every action, whether of thought, word, or deed, as being in its form and measure an act of Divine worship. This is what St Paul means when he says "Pray without ceasing". What needs to be cultivated is the habitual mental attitude that leads us to see God in all things, and it is for this reason that the foundation of conscious spiritual Life is that First Commandment to the consideration of which we are approaching.

It was, therefore, in consequence of their entire denial of the Divine Spirit that the antediluvians raised up an adverse power which at last became too strong for them to control. And here let me once for all set the student right with regard to those passages of the Bible in which God is represented as making up His mind to inflict injury, as in the announcement of the impending deluge. These expressions are figurative. They represent the entrance upon the scene of that Cosmic Law of Disintegration which necessarily comes into play as soon as the highest directing power of Intelligence is inhibited; and therefore as soon as a man willfully thrusts from himself the recognition of the Universal Spirit in its higher manifestations as the Guardian and Guide, he ipso facto calls it into action in its lower manifestations as the Universal Cosmic Force.

The reason for this will appear more clearly from a careful study of the relations between the Personal and the Impersonal modes of Spirit, but the explanation of these relations would occupy too large a space to be entered upon here, and the reader must be referred to other works on the subject. In the present connection it is sufficient to say that we can never get rid of God, for we ourselves are manifestations of His Being, and if we will not have Him as the Good, we shall be compelled to accept It as the Evil. This is what the Master meant when he said in the parable that on the lord's return to his city, he ordered those who would not accept him to reign over them to be slain before him.

Noah and his three sons are rescued from the universal overthrow by means of the Ark. As I am concerned in the present book with the inner meaning of the Bible rather than with historical facts, I must leave the reader to form his own conclusions regarding the literal measurements of that vessel; but I would take this opportunity of observing that where distinct numbers and measurements are given in the Bible, they are not introduced at haphazard. From the standpoint of ordinary arithmetic they may seem to be so, and the main argument of Bishop Colenso's great work on the Pentateuch is based on these apparent discrepancies. For instance, speaking of the sacrifices to be offered for women after childbirth, he points out that during the march through the desert these could, according to the text, only be offered by Aaron and his two sons, and that calculated on ordinary averages, the offering of these sacrifices would have occupied each of these three priests fourteen hours a day without one moment's rest or intermission (vol. 1, p. 123). From the point of view of simple arithmetic this result is unavoidable, but I cannot endorse the Bishop's conclusion that the scribes who wrote the Pentateuch under the direction of Ezra introduced any numbers that occurred to them without considering how they would work out.

On the contrary, such investigations as I have been able to make into the subject convinces me that the Bible numbers are calculated with the most rigid accuracy, and with the very deepest thoughts of the results to which they will work out — only this is done according to a certain symbolic system known as Sacred Numeration; and the very impracticability of the figures when tested by ordinary arithmetic is intended to put us upon enquiry for some deeper meaning below the surface. To explain the principles of sacred Numeration would be beyond the scope of an elementary book like the present, and probably few readers would care to undertake the requisite amount of study; but we must not suppose that the numbers given in the Bible are without significance whenever ordinary methods of calculation fail to elucidate them. The whole meaning of Scripture is not upon the surface, and in the present connection we are expressly pointed to a symbolic signification in 1 Peter 3:20,21; and the recurrence of the Ark as a sacred emblem in the great race-religions clearly indicates it as representing some universal principle.

The Zoroastrian legend of the flood throws some light upon the subject, for Yima, the Persian Noah, is bidden by Ahura Mazda, the Deity, to bring "the seeds of sheep, oxen, men and women, dogs and birds, and of every kind of tree and fruit, two of every kind, into the ark and to seal it up with a golden ring and make in it a door and a window". The significance of the Ark is that of a vehicle for the transmission of the life-principle of beings from an old to a new order of life, and all that is not included in the Ark perishes.

This is the generalized statement of relations which the Ark sets forth and, like all other generalizations, it admits of a great many particular applications, ranging from those which are purely physiological to those which are in the highest degree spiritual, and the study of comparative religion will show us that the idea has been employed in all its most varied applications; yet, however varied, they all have this common feature: they signify something which conveys individual life safely through a period of transition from one order of manifestation to another.

The Ark, as the sacred vessel, plays a conspicuous part throughout Scripture, but in the present connection we shall best realize its meaning by considering it as the opposite principle to that from which it affords deliverance. If "Water" signifies the psychic principle, then the Ark signifies that which the psychic principle supports, and which has an opposite but corresponding nature — that is to say, the Body. The Ark is not independent of the Water but is constructed for the purpose of floating upon it; and similarly, the body is expressly adapted to man's psychic nature so as to make with it and the spiritual principle of Life a Whole individuality.

Now it is precisely in the recognition of this Wholeness that refuge from all psychic entanglements is to be found. We must always remember that the body equally with the soul is the instrument of the manifestation of the Spirit. It is the union of the three into a single Whole that constitutes the full reality of Life, and it is this sacredness of the body that is typified by the sacredness of the Ark. The Ark of Noah was a solid construction, built on a pattern all the details of which were laid down to scale by the Divine Architect and it thus exemplifies the accurate proportions of the human body; and in passing it may interest the reader to note that the proportions of the human body numerically represent the principal measurements of the solar system and also form the basis of the proportions observed in such ecclesiastical architecture as is designed according to canonical rules, of which Westminster Abbey and Milan Cathedral are good examples.

I cannot, however, stop to digress into this very interesting subject, and for our present purpose it will be sufficient to say that the Ark with its living freight is typical of the fact that the full realization of Life is only attained in the Threefold Unity of body, soul, and spirit, and not by their dissociation. It is the assertion of the solid, living Reality of the work of the Spirit as distinguished from those imperfect manifestations which are the subterranean root of the true manifestation, but are not the real solid thing itself. It is the protest of healthy reality, which includes the psychic element in its proper order as the intermediary between the purely spiritual and the purely material, as against the rejection of the corporeal element and total absorption in the psychic — a condition which prevents the spirit from attaining to self-expression as a synthesis, which alone is the completion of its evolutionary work.

For this reason undue absorption in the psychic sphere is contrary to the Spirit; and however we may apply to it the word "spiritual" in the sense of not being corporeal, if the psychic element is not taken in its proper connection with the two others, it is as far from being "spiritual" in the true sense of the word as the material element itself. The true reality is in the harmonious inter-action of the Three-in-ONE. God's world is a world of Truth in which evanescent shapes do not take the place of Reality, and for these reasons the Bible everywhere insists on nothing short of the fullness of perfect realization, and the Ark is one of the figures under which it does so.

This realization of the Triple Unity of Man is the first step towards our final enfranchisement; but in the very act of escaping from the danger of the Deluge we are exposed to a danger of the opposite kind, that of regarding the corporeal side of life as everything, and this is typified by the building of the Tower of Babel. This tower, note carefully, was built of brick — that is, of a substance which is nothing but clay, the same "red earth" out of which Adam is formed; and it is therefore the very opposite to the Heavenly Jerusalem, which is built of gold and precious stones.

Now a building naturally signifies a habitation, and the building of the Tower of Babel to escape the waters of a flood is that reaction against the psychic element which denies spiritual things altogether and makes of the body and its physical environment the one and only dwelling-place of man. It is the same error as before of trying to erect the edifice of Wholeness on the foundation merely of a part, only now the part selected is the corporeal instead of the psychic. Arithmetically it is the attempt to make out that one-third is the same as ONE. The natural consequences soon follow in the confusion of tongues.

Language is the expression of Thought, and if our ideas of reality include nothing more than the infinitude of secondary causes which appear in the material world, there is no central Unit around which they can be grouped and consequently, instead of any certain knowledge, we have only a multitude of conflicting opinions based upon the ever-changing aspects of the world of ap-pearances. Quot homines tot sententiae (there are as many opinions as there are persons); and so the builders are dispersed in confusion, for theirs is not "the city that hath foundations whose builder and maker is God" (Hebrews 11:10).

From this point in the Bible story, a stretch of many ages brings us to the times of the Patri-archs Abraham, Isaac, and Jacob. We are here in the transition stage from allegory to history, and St Paul points out this intermingling of the two elements when he tells us that Hagar and Sarah represent the two covenants and the earthly and heavenly Jerusalems. And here I would impress upon the student the dual character of scriptural personages and events. Because a personage or event is typical it does not follow that it is not also historical; on the contrary, certain personages, systems, and events, become typical — that is, specially emphasize certain principles, for the very reason that they give them concrete expression. As Johnson says of the Swedish monarch:

> "He left the name at which the world grew pale.
> To point a moral or adorn a tale."

In other words, historical realities become the very summing-up and visible form of abstract principles, and therefore we are justified by the Bible itself in finding in its personages types of principles as well as historical characters.

I will not, however, here open the question whether the three Patriarchs were actual person-ages or, as some critics tell us, were merely the legendary ancestors of certain groups of wander-ing tribes, the Beni-Ibrahim, the Beni-Ishak, and the Beni-Yakub, which subsequently coalesced into the Hebrew nation. However interesting, the discussion of the historical facts would be re-mote from my present object, which is to throw some light upon the inner meaning of the Bible, and for this purpose we may be content to take the simple narrative of the text for, whether ac-tual or legendary, the only way in which Abraham, Isaac, and Jacob can affect us at the present day is as characters in a history the significance of which will become clear if we read between the lines.

But from this latter point of view the biblical statement of the national origin of Israel carries enfolded within it the hidden statement of those great principles which it is the purpose of the Bible to reveal. And here let me draw attention to the method adopted in Scripture. There are certain great universal principles which permeate all planes of being from the highest to the lowest. They are not many in number, and the relations between them are not difficult of comprehension when clearly stated; but we find difficulty in recognizing the identity of the same principles when we meet with them, so to say, at different levels, as for example on the physical and the psychic planes respectively, and consequently we are apt to imagine them much more numerous and complicated than they really are.

Now, the purpose of the Bible is to convey instruction in the nature and use of these principles to those in whose hands this knowledge would be safe and useful, while concealing it from others; and in a manner appropriate to this object, it continually repeats the same few all-embracing principles over and over again. This repetition is firstly unavoidable because the principles themselves are few in number; next it is necessary as a process of hammering-in and fixing it in our minds; and lastly it is not a bare repetition, but there is a progressive expansion of the statement so as to conduct us step by step to a further comprehension of its meaning. Now this is done in a variety of ways, and one of frequent occurrence is through the use of Names.

Sacred Nomenclature is as large a study as Sacred Numeration, and indeed the two so shade off into one another that they may be regarded as forming a single study, and I will therefore no more attempt in the present book to elucidate the one system than the other, for they require a volume to themselves; but this need not prevent us considering occasional instances of both, and the names of the Patriarchs are too important to be passed over without notice. The frequency with which God is called in Scripture the God of Abraham, of Isaac, and of Jacob shows that something more must be referred to than the mere fact that the ancestors of the Jews worshipped Him, and the consideration of some of the prominent points in the history of these allegorical personages will throw a light on the subject which will be very helpful in our further investigation.

If we realize the truth of St Paul's statement that the real object of the Bible is to convey the history of the spiritual Israel under the figure of Israel after the flesh, we shall see that the descent of Israel from the three Patriarchs must be a spiritual descent, and we may therefore expect to find in the Patriarchs themselves an adumbration of the principles which give rise to the spiritual Israel. Now we should particularly notice that the name "Israel" was bestowed on Jacob, the third Patriarch, on the occasion when he wrestled with the angel at the ford Jabbock, and he obtained this name as the result of his successful wrestling. We are told that Jacob recognized that it was the Divine Being, the Nameless ONE, with whom he wrestled, and this at once gives us the key to the allegory; for we know from the Master's instructions to the woman of Samaria that God is Universal Spirit, and though the Universal is that which gives rise to all manifestations of the particular, yet it is logically and mathematically impossible for the Universal as such to assume individual personality.

Under the figure, therefore, of wrestling with "a man", we perceive that what Jacob wrestled with was the great problem of his own relation to the Universal Spirit under its twofold aspect of Universal Energy and Universal Intelligence, allegorically represented as a powerful man; and he held on and wrestled till he gained the blessing and the New Name in which the nature of that blessing was summed up. The conditions are significant. He was alone. Father of a large family as he was, none of his dear ones could help him in the struggle. We must each solve the problem of our relation to the Infinite Mind for ourselves; and not our nearest and dearest can wrestle for us.

And the struggle takes place in the darkness. It is when we begin to find that the light we thought we possessed is not the true light, when we find that its illuminating power is gone, that we rise nerved with an energy we never knew before and commence in earnest the struggle for the Light, determined never to let go until we win the victory. And so we wrestle till the day begins to break, but even then we must not quit our hold; we must not be content until we have received the New Name which marks our possession of that principle of Light and Life which will forever expand into brighter day and fuller livingness. "To him that overcometh will I give...a New Name (Rev. 2:17).

But Jacob carries with him the mark of the struggle throughout his earthly career. The angel touched the hollow of his thigh, and thenceforward he was lame. The meaning is simple enough to those who have had some experience of the wrestling. They can never again walk in earthly things with the same step as before. They have seen the Truth, and they can never again unsee it; their whole standpoint has been altered and is no longer understood by those around them; to those who have not wrestled with the angel, they appear to walk lamely.

What, then, was the New Name that was thus gained by the resolute wrestler? His original name of Jacob was changed to Israel. The definition of Israel given in the seventy-third Psalm is "such as are of a clean heart", and Jesus expressed the same idea when he said of Nathanael, "Behold an Israelite indeed in whom is no guile"; for the emphasis laid upon the word "Israelite" at once suggests some inner meaning, since Nathanael's nationality was no more remarkable under the circumstances than that of an Englishman in Piccadilly.

The great fact about the spiritual Israel is therefore cleanness of heart and absence of guile — in other words, perfect sincerity, which again implies singleness of purpose in the right direction. It is precisely that quality which our Buddhist friends call "one-pointedness", and on which, under various similitudes, the Master laid so much stress. This, then, is the distinctive characteristic which attaches to the name of Israel, for it is this concentration of effort that is the prime factor in gaining the victory which leads to the acquisition of the Name. This is fundamental, and without it nothing can be accomplished; it indicates the sort of mental character which we must aim at, but it is not the meaning of the Name itself.

The name of Israel is composed of three syllables, each of which carries a great meaning. The first syllable, "Is", is primarily the sound of the in-drawing of the breath, and hence acquires the significance of the Life-Principle in general, and more particularly of the individual Life. This recognition of the individualization of the Life-Principle formed the basis of Assyrian worship. The syllable "Is" was also rendered "As", "Ish", and "Ash", and gave rise to the worship of the Life-Principle under the plural name "Ashur", which thus represented the male and female elements, the former being worshipped as Ashr, or Asr, and the latter as Ashre, Ashira, Astarte, Iastara or Ishtar, a lunar goddess of Babylon, and the same idea of femininity is found in the Egyptian "Isis".

Hence the general conception conveyed by the syllable "Is" is that of a feminine spiritual principle manifesting itself in individuality — that is to say, the "Soul" or formative element — and it is thus indicative of all that we mean when we speak of the psychic side of nature. How completely the Assyrians identified themselves with the cultus of this principle is shown by the name of their country, which is derived from "Ashur".

The second syllable, "Ra", is the name of the great Egyptian sun-god and is thus the complementary of everything that is signified by "Is". It is primarily indicative of physical life rather than psychic life, and in general represents the Universal Life-giving power as distinguished from its manifestation in particular individuality. Ra symbolizes the Sun, while Is is symbolized by the Moon, and represents the masculine element as emphatically as Is represents the feminine.

The third syllable, "El", has the significance of Universal Being. It is "THE" — i.e. the nameless Principle, which includes in itself both the masculine and feminine elements, both the physical and the psychic, and is greater than them and gives rise to them. It is another form of the word Al, Ale, or Ala, which means "High", and is indicative of the Supreme Principle before it passes into any differentiated mode. It is pure Spirit in the universal.

Now, if Man is to attain liberty, it can only be by the realization of these Three Modes of Being — the physical, the psychic, and the spiritual; or, as the Bible expresses it, Body, Soul, and Spirit. He must know what these three are in himself and must also recognize the Source from which they spring, and he must at least have some moderately definite idea of their genesis into individuality. Therefore the man "instructed unto the kingdom of heaven" combines a threefold recognition of himself and of God which is accurately represented by the combination of the three syllables Is, Ra, and El. Unless these three are joined into a single unity, a single word, the recognition is incomplete and the full knowledge of truth has not been attained. "Ra" by itself implies only the knowledge of the physical world, and results in Materialism. "Is" by itself realizes only the psychic world, and results in sorcery. "El" by itself corresponds only with a vague apprehension of some overruling power, capricious and devoid of the element of Law, and thus results in idolatry.

It is only in the combination of all three elements that the true Reality is to be found, whether we study it in its physical, psychic, or spiritual aspect. We may for particular purposes give special prominence to one aspect over the two others, but this is for a time only, and even while we do so, we realize that the particular mode of Life-Power with which we are dealing derives its efficiency only from the fact of its being permeated by the other two.

We cannot too firmly impress upon our minds that, though there are three modes, there is only ONE LIFE; and in all our studies, and in their practical application, we must never forget the great truth that the Living Power which we use is a Synthesis, and that whenever we make an analysis we theoretically destroy the synthesis. The only purpose of making an analysis is to learn how to build up the synthesis; and it is for this reason that the Bible equally condemns the opposite extremes of materialism and sorcery. It tells us that "dogs and sorcerers" are excluded from the heavenly city, and when we understand what is meant by these terms, it becomes self-evident that it cannot be otherwise.

It is for this reason, also, that we find the Israelites so often warned both against the Babylonian and the Egyptian idolatries, not because there was no great underlying truth in the worship of those nations, but because it was a worship that excluded the idea of WHOLENESS. "Wilt thou be made whole?" is the Divine invitation to us all; and the Egyptian and Assyrian worships were eminently calculated to lead their votaries away from this Wholeness in opposite directions.

But that both the Assyrian and the Egyptian worship had a solid basis of truth is a fact to which the Bible itself bears this remarkable testimony: "In that day shall Israel be the third with Egypt and with Assyria, even a blessing in the midst of the land; whom the Lord of Hosts shall bless, saying, Blessed be Egypt my people, and Assyria the work of my hands, and Israel mine inheritance" (Isaiah 19:24,25). The Israelite worship was as essentially that of the principle represented by "El" as those of Egypt and Assyria were of the two others, and it needed the blessing of those two extremes by the recognition of their relation to the central, or spiritual, principle to constitute the realization of the true Divine Sonship of Man in which no element of this threefold being — body, soul, or spirit — is alien from unity with "the Father".

This, then, was the significance of the New Name given to Jacob. He had wrestled with the Divine until the light had begun to dawn upon him, and he thus acquired the right to a name which should correctly describe what he had now become. Formerly he had been Jacob — i.e. Yakub, a name derived from the root "Yak" or "One". This signifies the third stage of apprehension of the Divine problem which immediately precedes the final discovery of the great secret of the Trinity-in-Unity of Being. We realize the ONE-ness of the Universal Divine Principle, though we have not yet realized its Threefold nature both in ourselves and in the Universal.

But there are two other stages before this, the first of which is represented by Abraham and the second by Isaac. It should be noticed that the two syllables "Ra" and "Is" reappear in these names, the former indicative, as we have seen, of the masculine element of Spirit, and the latter of the feminine, while Jacob, or simple unity is indicative of the neuter.

If we look through the history of Abraham we find the masculine element especially predominant in it. He is the father of the nations that are to spring from him, he receives the covenant of circumcision, he is a warrior and goes forth to victorious battle, and the change of his name from Abram to Abraham is the substitution of a masculine for a neuter element.

In Isaac's history the feminine element is equally predominant. His name is connected with the laughter of his mother (Genesis 18), and his marriage with Rebekah is the pivot round which all the events of his life center; and again, his acquiescence in his own sacrifice marks the predominance of the passive element in his character. To him there comes no change of name; he is neither leader, warrior, nor spiritual wrestler, but the calm, contemplative man who "went out to meditate in the field at eventide"; he is typical of the purely receptive attitude of mind, and therefore the syllable "Is" is as indicative of his nature as the masculine syllable "Ra" is of his father's, or the neutral and purely mathematical conception indicated by the syllable "Yak" of his son's.

This affords a good instance of the way in which the deepest truths are often concealed in Bible names, and it should lead us to see that the value of the record does not turn on its literal accuracy at every point, but on its correct representation of the great principles to the knowledge of which it seeks to lead us.

It is of little moment at the present date how much of the book of Genesis is legendary and how much historical, and we can afford to view calmly such little inaccuracies on the face of the document as when we are told, in Exodus 6:3, that God was not known to Abraham by the name Jehovah, and in Genesis 22:14, that Abraham called the place where he was delivered from sacrificing Isaac "Jehovah-jireh". There are two typical schools of Biblical interpretation, one of which is historically represented by St Augustine and the other by St Jerome. Augustine, who was not an Orientalist and had not studied the original Hebrew, took his stand upon the textual accuracy of the Bible and urged that if once any inaccuracy were admitted to exist in it, we could not be certain of anything in the whole book. Jerome, who had made an accurate study of the original Hebrew, admitted the existence of inaccuracies in the text from the operation of the same natural causes which affect other ancient literature, such as errors of copyists, variations of oral tradition, and even possible adaptation to the requirements of something which the transcriber believed to be an essential doctrine.

These two representative men were not separated by an interval of centuries but were contemporary and actually in communication with each other, and we may therefore see from how early a date Christendom had been divided into blind reverence for the letter and intelligent enquiry into the history of its documents. St Jerome was the father of the Higher Criticism, and with such a respectable authority to back us, we need not be afraid to attribute any such casual errors as the one now in question to those natural causes which render all ancient documents liable to variation, and the point to which I would draw attention is that merely superficial contradictions which can be reasonably accounted for on purely natural grounds in no way affect the general inspiration of the Bible.

And by "inspiration" I mean an inner illumination on the part of the writers leading them to the immediate perception of Truth, which illumination is itself a fact in the regular order of Nature, the reason of which I hope to make clear in a subsequent volume. The books of the Pentateuch, as we possess them, were written by Ezra and his scribes after the return from the Babylonian captivity — those writers whom the Jews call "the men of the Great Synagogue", and whose writings were separated from the time of Moses by exactly the same interval that separates Tennyson's Idylls of the King from the date of the actual King Arthur.

This alone leaves a sufficiently wide margin for errors to creep into such earlier documents as these writers may have availed themselves of; and we must next reflect that another interval of several centuries separated them from the copies conveyed to Egypt in the second century before Christ for Ptolemy Soter's Greek translation, commonly known as the Septuagint. The "Temple Standard" Pentateuch, preserved at Jerusalem at the time of Jesus, can hardly have been the original document written by Ezra; but even supposing it to have been so, what became of it at the destruction of Jerusalem? Tradition says it was sent by Josephus to the Emperor of Rome; and written, as it is said to have been, on bulls' hides, we may well imagine that it perished by damp or other agencies, neglected as a barbarous relic in a city whose energies were concentrated on maintaining its position as arbitress of the world by conquest and diplomacy; at any rate, the document was never heard of again, and the oldest Jewish versions of the Pentateuch now extant are not older than the tenth century.

Under these circumstances we need not be surprised if variations have found their way into the text nor need we trouble ourselves much about them if we reflect that the real place where Truth exists is in Nature, and not in books, and that the book is merely a record of what others have learnt without book; and, moreover, owing to the deep reverence with which both Jewish and Christian Scriptures have been preserved, we may say that any errors or contradictions discovered in the text no more affect the body of the Truth contained in the Bible as a whole than the dust on the outside of an orange affects the value of the fruit. It is this inner truth that we are seeking, and if we at all realize the Master's statement that the Kingdom is within, superficial discrepancies will not present any difficulties to us.

We see, then, in the typical history of the three Patriarchs the announcement of the three great principles into which all forms of manifestation may be analyzed: the Masculine, Positive, or generating principle; the Feminine, Receptive, or formative principle; and the Neuter or Mathematical principle which, by determining the proportional relations between the other two, gives rise to the principle of variety and multiplicity.

Their successive statement in the symbolical history indicates the need for the preparatory study of each in detail if we would arrive at the True Light; and it is precisely the discovery that this separate study is by itself insufficient that brings us to the point where we have to wrestle in the darkness with the Divine Angel until the day dawns. We must unite the three principles into a single Unity, and thus learn to form the name "Israel"; and in so doing we discover that it has now become our own name, for we find that the kingdom of heaven — the realm of eternal principles — is within us, and that therefore whatever we discover there is that which we ourselves are.

Our wrestling ceases: the Divine Wrestler has put his name upon us, and the day is beginning to dawn; but as yet it is only the earliest hour of daybreak; it is the true sunlight, but it is still low on the horizon, and we must not make the mistake of supposing that this early morning hour is the same as the mid-day glory — in other words, we must not suppose that because we have once and forever finished wrestling with an unknown antagonist in darkness, therefore we have nothing more to do.

Life is a perpetual doing, though, thank God, not a perpetual wrestling. Our doing is the measure of our living, although the plane on which our doing is carried on may not be immediately patent to all observers; and it is exactly in proportion as we expand our doing that we expand our livingness. No one can grow for us, and it all depends upon ourselves how rapidly and how strongly we shall grow.

Chapter 4
The Mission of Moses

Having now gathered up in the briefest possible fashion the general gist of the history of the Patriarchs, we must pass on to the mission of Moses. And here let me impress upon the reader that the Bible repeats its few grand principles over and over again, only with greater detail as it proceeds, so that we shall find precisely the same principles involved in the history of the march of Israel into Canaan as in that of the three Patriarchs. It is the same statement as is contained in the story of Eden and in the tradition of the Flood, and we shall find it repeated throughout the Bible under other varieties of form which admit of more and more specific application of these principles to individual cases. I mention this to explain why we may sometimes appear to go over old ground: there is only ONE Truth, and more detailed acquaintance with it will not change its fundamentals.

We have seen that the Bible teaching regarding Man starts with two great facts: first, that he is the image of God, reproducing in individuality the same Universal Mind which is the Origin of all things, and thus reproducing also its creative process of Thought; and, secondly, that he is ignorant of this truth, and so brings upon himself all sorts of trouble and limitation; and it is the purpose of the Bible to lead us step by step out of this ignorance into this knowledge — step by step, for it is a process of growth, first in the individual, then in the race, and this growth depends on certain clear and ascertainable Laws inherent in the constitution of Man. Now the peculiarity of inherent Law is that it always acts uniformly, making no exception in favour of anyone, and it does this as well positively as negatively.

Our ignorance of any Law of Nature will never exempt us from its operation, and this is as true of ignorant obedience as of ignorant disobedience: the natural reward of ignorant obedience is no less certain than the natural punishment of ignorant disobedience; and it is on this principle that the great leaders of the race have always worked. They themselves knew the Law; but to impart the understanding of the Law to people in general was not the work of a day, nor of a generation, nor of many generations — in fact it is a work which is still only in its infancy — and therefore if people were to be saved from the consequences of disobedience to the Law, it could only be by some method of training which would lead them into ignorant obedience to it.

But this was not to be done by making any false statement of the Law, for Truth can never come out of falsehood; it must be done by presenting the Truth under such figures as would indicate the real relations of things, though not explaining how these relations arise, because to undeveloped minds such an explanation would be worse than useless. Hence came the whole system of the Mosaic Law.

On one occasion, when the Master was asked which was the greatest commandment of the Law, he replied by quoting the fourth verse of the sixth chapter of Deuteronomy, "Hear, O Israel: the Lord our God is one Lord", or, as the Revised version has it in Mark 12:29, "the Lord is ONE". This, he says, is the first of all the commandments; and we may therefore expect to find in this statement of Divine Unity the foundation on which everything else rests. Nor need we look far to find the reason of it, for we have already seen in the opening words of Genesis that in principio — that is, as the originating principle in all things — there can be nothing else but God or Spirit.

That is a conclusion which becomes unavoidable if we simply follow up the chain of cause and effect until we reach a Universal First Cause. We may call it by what name we choose: that will make no difference so long as we realize what must be its inherent nature and what must be our necessary relation to it.

Whatever name we give it, it is always the ONE Self-existent and Self-transforming Power of which everything is some mode of manifestation, simply because there is no other source from which anything could come. This ultimate deduction of reason is the recognition of the Unity of God and could not be more clearly stated than in the words which Isaiah puts into the mouth of the Divine Being, repeating the phrase in two consecutive sentences as though to lay additional stress upon it: "there is none beside Me ... I am God, and there is none else" (Isaiah 45:21,22). That is to say, "God" — or as we have learnt from the instructions to the woman of Samaria, Universal Spirit — is all that is.

This is the great Truth on which the mission of Moses was founded, and therefore that mission starts with the announcement of the Divine Name at the Burning Bush. "Moses said unto God, Behold, when I come into the children of Israel, and shall say unto them, The God of your fathers hath sent me unto you; and they shall say to me, What is his name? what shall I say unto them? And God said unto Moses, I AM THAT I AM; and He said, Thus shalt thou say unto the children of Israel, I AM hath sent me unto you".

So the name after which Moses inquired turned out to be no name, but the first person singular of the present tense of the verb TO BE, in its indicative mood. It is the announcement of BEING in the Absolute, in that first originating plane of Pure Spirit where, because the Material does not yet exist, there can be no extension in space, and consequently no sequence in time, and where therefore the only possible mode of being is the consciousness of Self-existence without limitation either of space or time, the realisation of the "universal Here and the everlasting Now", the concentration of the All into the Point and the expansion of the Point into the All. (see also Lecture 3 in The Edinburgh Lectures on Mental Science).

But though this may have been a new announcement to the masses of the Hebrew people, it could have been no new announcement for Moses, for we are told in the Acts that Moses was learned in all the wisdom of the Egyptians, a circumstance which is fully accounted for by his education at the court of Pharaoh, where he would be as a matter of course initiated into the deepest mysteries of the Egyptian religion. He must therefore have been familiar from boyhood with the words, "I AM that I AM", which as the inscription "Nuk pu Nuk" appeared on the walls of every temple; and having received the highest instruction in the land, brought up as the son of Pharaoh's daughter, he must have been well aware of their significance. But this instruction had hitherto been confined to those who had been initiated into the great mysteries of Osiris.

In whatever way we may interpret the story of Moses' meeting with the Divine Being at the burning bush, one thing is evident: it indicates the point in his career when it became plain to him that the only possible way for the Liberation of mankind was through the universal recognition of that Truth which till now had been the exclusive secret of the sanctuaries. What, then, was the great central Truth which was thus announced in this proclamation of the Divine Name? It has two sides to it. First, that Pure Spirit is the ultimate essence of all that is, and as a consequence the All-presence, the All-knowledge, the All-livingness, and the All-lovingness of "God". Then as the corollary of the proposition that "Spirit is all that is", there must be the converse proposition that "all that is is Spirit"; and since Man is included in the "all", we are again brought back to the original description of him as the image and likeness of God.

But in those days people had to be educated up to these two great truths, and they have not advanced very far in this education yet; so from the time when Moses' eyes were opened to see in these truths not a secret to be guarded for his private benefit, but the power which was to expand to the renovation of the world, he realized that it was his mission to set men free by educating them gradually into the true knowledge of the Divine Name. Then he conceived a great scheme.

Modern research has shown us that the knowledge of this great fundamental truth was not confined to Egypt, but formed the ultimate center of all the religions of antiquity; it was that secret in which the supreme initiation of all the highest mysteries culminated. It could not be otherwise, for it was the only ultimate conclusion to which generations of clear-headed thinkers could come. But these were sages, priests, philosophers, men of education and leisure; and this final deduction was beyond the reach of the toiling multitudes, whose whole energies had to be devoted to the earning of their daily bread.

Still it was impossible for these thinkers who had arrived at the great knowledge to pass over the multitudes without allowing them at least a few crumbs from their table. The true recognition of the "Self" must always carry with it the purpose of helping others to acquire it also; but it does not necessarily imply the immediate perception of the best means of doing so, and hence throughout antiquity we find an inner religion, the Supreme Mysteries, for the initiated few; and an outer religion, for the most part idolatrous, for the people. The people were not to be left without any religion, but they were given a religion which was deemed suited to their gross apprehension of things; and in the hands of lower orders of priests — themselves little, if at all, better instructed than the worshippers, these conceptions often became very gross indeed. Nevertheless, in their first intention, the "idols" were not without meaning.

The cultured Greeks laughed at the Egyptian temples as places where, in the midst of a magnificent edifice, when the sacred curtain of the innermost sanctuary was withdrawn, there was revealed an onion or a cat. Yet here was surely enough to prompt an intelligent person to enquiry. Why did the innermost sanctuary contain no Apollo Belvedere or other marvel unique and worthy to be enshrined, but only one of those wretched animals which disturbed the rest of the Greek traveler, newly arrived in Egypt, by nocturnal caterwaulings which must have been a marked feature in cities where pussy held undisputed sway? Or why was the odoriferous onion that lay by tons for sale in the markets here set upon a pedestal as an object of reverence? Surely there must be some deep significance in elevating such common objects to the central place of mystery. Yes: because in these commonest of common things there appeared the Great Central Mystery of LIFE more than in the sculptured marble of Phidias or Praxiteles.

Thus the Egyptian religion signified, to all who had the "nous" to penetrate it, the All-presence of the Eternal Living Spirit as the ONE true object of worship, to be found not only in temples, but in streets and fields, in all places alike. It signified this to those who had the intelligence to lift the veil, and this meant, perhaps, one in ten thousand of the population; and as soon as he had penetrated the real meaning, his lips were sealed, for he was admitted to the Mysteries. For the rest, the priests had such trivial superficial explanations as those which, ages later, they sought to palm off upon Herodotus; it was no part of their business to lift the veil of Isis.

And so Moses saw the generations toiling on and on in an ignorance which could not but have disastrous consequences sooner or later. Under the paternal rule of a truly illuminated priesthood, such a relation between the inner and the outer religion might be employed to maintain a condition of peaceful well-being for the masses during their intellectual infancy; but he saw that this state of things could not go on indefinitely.

With a general advance in intelligence must come a general disposition to question the outward forms of religion, while yet this general advance fell very far short of that fuller development which in solitary instances led the individual to grasp the meaning of the inner Truth. Then, when to any nation comes the ridicule of all it has hitherto held sacred, because it has never learnt the

Eternal truth itself but has placed its faith in forms and ceremonies and traditions which, useful in their day and generation, should have been unfolded to meet growing intelligence — when this condition of the national mind supervenes, woe to that nation, for it is left without God and without hope, and by the inevitable Law of nature on the plane of the MIND, it cannot but bring upon itself dire calamity.

From the standpoint of the governed, this benign, paternal government could not go on forever, and equally so from that of the rulers. What guarantee was there of a perpetual succession of priests illuminated not only in head but also in heart? Egypt was old when Moses was a youth, and the signs of decadence were not wanting; for the cruel oppression of the Israelites, whom four centuries of naturalization should have placed on equality with their fellow-subjects, was the very reverse of all that was truest in the inner teaching of the Egyptian temples. It was the index of practical atheism. The Science of the temples continued, but it had reached the bifurcation of the Way, and it had taken the Left-hand Path.

And if this was the case in Egypt, which led the van of civilization, what was to be expected from the rest of the world? What was the outlook into the future with an intellectual development expanding only on the material side, without any knowledge of those spiritual truths in which lies the real livingness of Life? Surely nothing but the ultimate destruction of mankind in internecine strife, led up to by long ages of that awful spiritual condition in which the outward polish of materialized intellectuality only serves to place additional resources at the disposal of the unmitigated savage within.

The system then in vogue had once been a valuable system, perhaps the only one possible, but Egypt was no longer young, and the day of that system had palpably gone by. What was to be done? That great central Truth which the old system had handed down from hoary antiquity must be made the common appanage of mankind. "Nuk pu Nuk" must no longer be the mysterious legend of the temples, but it must become the household word of every family throughout the world.

This is the work of generation upon generation, very far from being accomplished yet; and the only way to inaugurate it was by a new departure in which the great announcement that had hitherto been reserved as the last and final teaching must become the first and initial teaching. The supreme secret of the Mysteries must be made the starting-point of the child's education; and therefore the mission to Israel must open with the declaration of the I AM as the All-embracing ONE.

A sentence consists of a subject, copula, and predicate, but in the announcement of the Divine Name made to Moses, there is no predicate. The reason is that to predicate anything of a subject implies some special aspect of it, and thus by implication limits it, however extensive the predicate may be; and it is impossible to apply this mode of statement to the Universal Living Spirit. There can be nothing outside it. Itself is the Substance and the Life of all that is or ever can be. That is an ultimate conception from which it is impossible to get away.

Therefore, the only predicate corresponding to the Universal Subject must be the enumeration of the innumerable — the statement of all that is contained in infinite possibility — and, consequently, the place of the predicate must be left apparently unfilled, because it is the fullness which includes all. The only possible statement of the Divine is that of Present Subjective Being, the Universal "I" and the ever-present "AM". Therefore I AM is the Name of God; and the First of all the Commandments is the announcement of the Divine Being as the Infinite ONE.

I have discussed the subject of the Unity of Spirit in my Edinburgh Lectures on Mental Science, but I may repeat here the truth that, mathematically, the Infinite must be Unity. We cannot think of two Infinites, for as soon as duality appears, each member of it is limited by the other, else there would be no duality. Therefore we cannot multiply the Infinite. Similarly, we cannot divide it, for division again implies multiplicity or Numbers, and though these may be conceived of as existing relatively to each other within the Infinite, the very relation between them establishes limits where one begins and the other ends, and thus we are no longer dealing with the Infinite.

Of course all this is self-evident to the mathematician, who at once sees the absurdity of attempting to multiply or divide Infinity; but the non-mathematical reader should endeavour to realize the full meaning of the word "Infinite" as that which, being without limits, necessarily occupies all space and therefore includes all that is. The announcement that God is ONE is, therefore, the mathematical statement of the Universal Presence of Spirit, and the phrase "I AM" is the grammatical statement of the same thing.

And because the Universal Spirit is the Universal Life Itself, "over all, through all, and in all", there is yet a third statement of it, which is its Living statement: the reproduction of it in the man himself; and these three statements are one and cannot be separated. Each implies the two others, like the three sides of an equilateral triangle, and therefore the First of all the Commandments is that we shall recognize THE ONE. As numerically all other numbers are developed from unity, so all the possibilities of ever-expanding Life are developed from the All-including UNIT of Being, and therefore in this Commandment we find the root of our future growth to all eternity. This is why both Moses and Jesus assign to it the supreme place.

And here let me point out the intimate relation between the teaching of Jesus and the teaching of Moses. They are the two great figures of the Bible. As the Old Testament centers round the one, so the New Testament centers round the other. Each appeals to the other. Moses says, "Of thy brethren, shall the Lord thy God raise up a prophet like unto me" — the prophet that was to come should duplicate Moses; and when the prophet came, he said, "If they hear not Moses and the prophets, neither will they be persuaded though one rose from the dead". Each is the complement of the other. We shall never understand Jesus until we understand Moses, and we shall never understand Moses until we understand Jesus. Yet this is not a paradox, for to grasp the meaning of either we must find the key to their utterances in our own hearts and on our own lips in the words "I AM"; that is, we must go back to that Divine Universal Law of Being which is written within us, and of which both Moses and Jesus were the inspired exponents.

The mission of Moses, then, was to build up a nationality which should be independent both of time and country, and which should derive its solidarity from its recognition of the principle of THE ONE. Its national being must be based upon its expanding realization of the great central Truth, and to the guarding and development of that Truth this nation must be consecrated; and in the enslaved but not subdued children of the desert — the children of Israel — Moses found ready to hand the material which he needed. For these erstwhile wanderers had brought with them a simple monotheistic creed, a belief in the God of Abraham, Isaac, and Jacob, which, vaguely though it might be, already touched the threshold of the sacred mystery; and four hundred years of residence in Egypt had not extinguished, however it may have obscured, the great tradition. Here, then, Moses found the nucleus for the nationality he designed to found, and so he led forth the people in that great symbolic march through the wilderness whose story is told in the Exodus.

To the details of that history we may turn more intelligently after we have gained a clearer idea of what the great work really was which Moses inaugurated on the night of the first Passover. Perhaps some of my readers may be surprised to learn that it is still going on and that they are called upon to take a personal part in continuing the work of Moses, which has now so expanded as to reach themselves. But all this is contained in the commission which Moses first announced to those he was to deliver and grows naturally out of its unfoldment. The people he was to lead into liberty were "the people of God", and since "God" is the I AM, they were "THE PEOPLE OF THE I AM". This was the true name of this nation, which was to be founded upon an Eternal Ideal instead of on the historical conditions of time and the geographical conditions of place; and this essential name of the New Nation has been as accurately translated into its equivalent of "Israel" as we shall later see the essential Name of God has been translated by the word "Jehovah". "The People of God" led forth by Moses were proclaimed by the very terms of his commission to be "The People of the I AM".

Now the history of this people is dignified by a succession of Prophets such as no other nation lays claim to; yet the great Prophet who first consolidated their scattered tribes into a compact community, in prophesying the future of the people he had founded, passes over all these and, looking down the long centuries, points only to one other Prophet "like unto me". We constantly miss those little indications of Scripture on which the fuller understanding of it so greatly depends; and just as we miss the point when we are told that Man is created in the likeness of God, so we miss the point when we are told that this other prophet, Jesus, is a prophet of the same type as Moses.

The whole line of intervening prophets were not of that type. They had their own special work, but it was not a work like that of Moses. Isaiah, Jeremiah, Ezekiel, and the rest sink out of sight, and the only Prophet whom Moses sees in the future is brought into his field of vision by his likeness to himself. Any child in a Sunday school, if asked what it knew about Moses, would answer that he brought the children of Israel out of Egypt. No one would question that this was the distinctive fact regarding him, and therefore if we are to find a Prophet of the same type as Moses, we should expect to find in him the founder of a New Nationality of the same order as that founded by Moses — that is to say, a nationality subsisting independently of time and place and cohering by reason of its recognition of an Eternal Ideal.

To make Jesus a Prophet like unto Moses, he must in some way repeat the Exodus and re-establish "the people of the I AM". Now turning to the teaching of Jesus, we find that this is exactly what he did. There was nothing on which he laid greater stress than the I AM. "Except ye believe that I AM, ye shall perish in your sins" was the emphatic summary of his whole teaching. And here read carefully. Distinguish between what Jesus said and what the translators of our English Bible say that he said, for it makes all the difference. Our English version runs, "If ye believe not that I am He, ye shall die in your sins" (John 8:24), thus, by the introduction of a single word, assuming all sorts of theological doctrines having their origin in Persian and Neoplatonic speculations, the discussion of which would require a volume to itself. Not false doctrines, but great truths are presented in such infantine notions as to convey the most limiting conception of ideals whose vitality consists in their transcending all limitations. Thus both as theologians and grammarians the translators of the Authorized Version felt the want of a predicate to complete the words I AM, and so they added the word "he"; but, faithful according to their light, they were careful to draw attention to the fact that there was no "he" in the original, and therefore that word is printed in italics to show that it was supplied by the translators; and the Revised Version carefully notes this fact in the margin.

In the parallel case of the announcement to Moses at the burning bush, the translators did not attempt to introduce any predicate; they felt what I have pointed out: that no predicate could be sufficiently extensive to define Infinite Being; but here, supposing that Jesus was speaking of himself personally, they thought it necessary to introduce a word which should limit his statement accordingly. Now the only comment to be made on this passage of the English Bible is to note carefully that it is exactly what Jesus never said. In this connection he made no personal application of the verb "to be". What he said was, "Except ye believe that I AM, ye shall die in your sins" (R.V.). Now, if the criterion by which we are to recognize him as the Prophet predicted by Moses is his reproduction of the doings of Moses, then we cannot be wrong in supposing that his use of the I AM was as complete a generalization as was employed by Moses.

On the same principle on which theologians or grammarians would particularize the words to the individuality of Jesus, they might particularize them to Moses also. But going back to that generalized statement of Man which is the very first intimation the Bible gives of him, we find that if I AM is the generalized statement of "God", it must also be the generalized statement of "Man", for man is the image and likeness of God. Whatever is true of one is true of the other, only conversely and, as it were, by reflection; so that whatever is universal in God becomes individual in man.

If, then, Jesus was to duplicate the work of Moses, it could only be by taking as the foundation of his teaching the same statement of essential Being that Moses took as the foundation of his; and therefore we must look for a generic, and not for a specific, application of the I AM in his teaching also. And as soon as we do this, the veil is lifted and a power streams forth from all his instructions which shows us that it was no mere figure of speech when he said that the water which he should give would become, in each one who drank it, a well of water springing up into everlasting life. He came not to proclaim himself, but Man; not to tell us of his own Divinity separating him from the race and making him the Great Exception, but to tell us of our Divinity and to show in himself the Great Example of the I AM reaching its full personal expression in Man.

This Prophet is raised up "of our brethren", he is one of ourselves, and therefore he said, "The disciple when he is perfected shall be as his Master". It is the Universal I AM reproducing itself in the individuality of Man that Jesus would have us believe in. He is preaching nothing but the same old Truth with which the Bible begins, that Man is the image and likeness of God. He says, in effect, Make this recognition the center of your life and you have tapped the source of everlasting life; but refuse to believe it and you will die in your sins. Why? As a Divine vengeance upon you for daring to question a theological formulary to which some narrow-minded ecclesiastic applies the words of the Vincentian canon, "Quod semper, quod ubique, quod ab omnibus", when his formulary has never even been heard outside such limits as both historically and geographically give the lie direct to his assertion of "always", "everywhere", and "by all men"? Certainly not. Truth has a surer foundation than forms of words; it is deep down in the foundations of Being; and it is the failure to realize this Truth of Being in ourselves that is the refusal to believe in the I AM which must necessarily cause us to perish in our sins. It is not a theological vengeance, but the Law of Nature. Let us inquire, then, what this Law is.

It is the great Law that, to live at all, we must primarily live in ourselves. No one can live for us. We can never get away from being the center of our own world; or, in scientific language, our life is essentially subjective. There could be no objective life without a subjective entity to receive the perceptions which the objective faculties convey to it; and since the receiving entity is ourselves, the only life possible to us is that of living in our own perceptions. Whatever we believe does, for us, in very fact exist. Our beliefs may be erroneous from the point of view of a happier belief, but this does not alter the fact that for ourselves our beliefs are our realities, and these realities must continue until some ground is found for a change in belief.

And in turn, the subjective entity reacts upon the objective life, for if there is one fact which the advance of modern psychological science is making more clear than another it is that the subjective entity is "the builder of the body". And this is precisely what, on the information we have already gleaned from the Bible, it ought to be; for we have seen that the statement that man is the image of God can only be interpreted as a statement of his having in himself the same creative process of Thought to which alone it is possible to attribute the origin of anything. He is the image of God because he is the individualization of the Universal Mind at that stage of self-evolution in which the individual attains the capacity for reasoning from the seen to the unseen, and thus for penetrating behind the veil of outward appearances; so that, because of the reproduction of the Divine creative faculty in himself, the man's mental states or modes of Thought are bound to externalize themselves in his body and his circumstances.

This, then, is the Law of Man's Being. I do not stop to discuss it in detail as, writing for New Thought readers, I assume at least an elementary knowledge of these things on their part; and accordingly, this being the Law, we see that the more closely our conception of ourselves approximates to a broad generalization of the factors which go to make human personality, rather than that narrow conception which limits our notion of ourselves to certain particular relations that have gathered around us, the more fully we shall externalize this idea of ourselves. And because the idea is a generalization independent of any particular circumstance, it must necessarily externalize as a corresponding independence of circumstances; in other words, it must result in a control over conditions, whether of body or environment, proportioned to the completeness of our generalization.

The more perfect the generalization, the more perfect the corresponding control over conditions; and therefore to attain the most complete control, which means the most perfect Liberty, we need to conceive of ourselves as embodying the idea of the most perfect generalization. But complete generalization is only another expression for infinitude, and therefore we have again reached the point where it becomes impossible to attach any predicate to the verb "to Be"; and so the only statement which contains the whole Law of Man's Being is identical with the only statement which contains the whole of God's Being, and consequently I AM is as much the correct formula for Man as for God.

But if we do not believe this and make it the center of our life, we must perish in our sins. The Bible defines "sin" as "the transgression of the Law", and Jesus' warning is that by transgressing the Law of our own Being, we shall die. It would carry me beyond the general lines of this book to discuss the question of what is here meant by "Death"; but that it is not the everlasting damnation of the Western creeds is obvious from the single statement of the Bible, that the Master employed the interval between his death and resurrection in teaching those souls who had passed out of physical life in the catastrophe of the Deluge, persons who most assuredly had perished on account of their transgression of the Law. For further study of this subject I would refer the reader to the works of two orthodox divines, Farrar's Eternal Hope and Plumptre's Spirits in Prison.

The transgression of which Jesus speaks is the transgression of the Law of the I AM in ourselves, the non-recognition of the fact that we are the image and likeness of God. This is the old original sin of Eve. It is the belief in Evil as a substantive self-originating power. We believe ourselves under the control of all sorts of evils having their climax in Death; but whence does the evil get its power? Not from God, for no diminution of Life can come from the Fountain of Life. And if not from God, then from where else? God is the ONLY BEING — that is the teaching of the First Commandment — and therefore whatever is is some mode of God; and if this be so, then however evil may have a relative existence, it can have no substantive existence of its own. It is not a Living Originating Power. God, the Good, alone is that; and it is for this reason that in the doctrine of THE ONE and in the statement of the I AM is the foundation of eternal individual Life and Liberty.

So then the transgression is in supposing that there is, or can be, any Living Originating Power outside the I AM. Let us once see that this is impossible, and it follows that evil has no more dominion over us and we are free. But so long as we limit the I AM in ourselves to the narrow boundaries of the relative and conditioned and do not realize that, personified in ourselves, it must by its very nature still be as unfettered as when acting in the first creation of the universe, we shall never pass beyond the Law of Death which we thus impose upon ourselves.

In this way, then, Jesus proved himself to be the Prophet of whom Moses had spoken. He made the recognition of the I AM the sole foundation of his work; in other words, he placed before men the same radical and ultimate conception of Being that Moses had done — but with a difference. Moses elaborated this conception from the standpoint of the Universal; Jesus elaborated it from that of the Individual. The work of Moses must necessarily precede that of Jesus, for if the Universal Mind is not in some measure apprehended first, the individual mind cannot be apprehended as its image and reflection.

But it takes the teaching of both Moses and Jesus to make the complete teaching, for each is the complement to the other, and it is for this reason that Jesus said he came not to destroy the Law but to fulfill. Jesus took up the work where Moses left off, and expanded Moses' initial conception of a people founded on the recognition of the Unity of God into its proper outcome of the conception of a people founded on the recognition of the unity of Man as the expression of the Unity of God. How can we doubt that this latter conception also was in the mind of Moses? Had it not been, he would not have spoken of the Prophet like unto himself that should come hereafter. But he saw the ages during which his great idea must germinate within the limits of a single nationality before it could expand to humanity at large; and therefore before Jesus could gather into one the "People of the I AM" from every nation under heaven, it was necessary that one exclusive nation should be the official custodian of the great secret and mature it till the time was ripe for the formation of that great international nationality which is only now beginning to show forth its earliest blossoms.

Chapter 5

The Mission of Jesus

Hitherto, our interpretation of the Bible has worked along the lines of great Universal Laws naturally inherent in the constitution of Man and thus applicable to all men alike; but now we must turn to that other line of an Exclusive Selection to which I referred in the opening chapter. This is not an arbitrary selection — for that would contradict the very conception of the unchangeable Universal Law on which the whole Bible is founded — but it is a process of "natural selection" arising out of the Law itself and results not from any change in the Law but from the attainment of an exalted realization of what the Law really is.

The first suggestion of this process of separation is contained in the promise that the deliverance of the race should come through "the Seed of the Woman", for in contradistinction to this "Seed" there is the seed of the Serpent; "I will put enmity between thy seed and her seed". Again we see the process of selection coming out in the preference given to the offering of Abel over that of Cain, and again the selection is repeated in the intimation that Seth took the place of Abel, while it is to be remarked that the New Testament genealogy traces the ancestry of Jesus to Seth; so that the line of Seth is clearly indicated as carrying on the selection originally made in favour of Abel. In this line we find Noah who, with his family, was alone exempted from the universal overthrow of the Deluge; and many centuries later we find one man, Abraham, selected by means of a special covenant to be the progenitor of a chosen race from which in process of time the Messiah, the Promised Seed of the Woman, was to be born.

Now was there in these things any arbitrary selection? After due consideration, we shall find that there was not and that they arose out of the perfectly natural operation of mental laws working on the higher levels of Individualism, and the indications of this operation are given in the story of Cain and Abel. Abel was a keeper of sheep and Cain was a tiller of the earth, and if the reader will bear in mind what I said regarding the symbolic character of Bible personages and the metaphorical use of words, the meaning of the story will become clear.

There is a great difference between animal and vegetable life: the one is cold and devoid of any apparent element of volition, the other is full of warmth and adumbrates the quality of Will; so that as symbols, the animal represents the emotional qualities in Man, while the vegetable, following a mere law of sequence without the exercise of individual choice, more fitly represents the purely logical processes of reasoning.

Now we all know that the first spring of action in any chain of cause and effect which we set going starts with some emotion, some manner of feeling, and not with a mere argument. Argument, a reasoning process, may cause us to change the standpoint of our feeling and to conceive that as desirable which at first we did not consider so; but at the end it is the recognition of a desire which is the one and only spring of action. It is, therefore, the feelings and desires that give the true key to our life, and not mere logical statements; and so if the feelings and desires are going in the right direction, we may be very sure that the logic will not be wrong in its conclusions, even though it may be blundering in its method. Take care of the heart, and the head will take care of itself.

This, then, is the meaning of the story of Cain and Abel. If we realize that the Universal Mind, as the All-pervading undistributed Creative Power, must be subjective mind, we shall see that it can only respond in accordance with the Law of subjective mind; that is to say, its relation to the individual mind must always be in exact correspondence to what the individual mind conceives of it. This is unequivocally stated in a passage which is twice repeated in Scripture: "With the pure Thou wilt show Thyself pure; and with the froward Thou wilt show Thyself froward" (Psalm 18:26 and 2 Sam. 22:27), where the context makes it clear that these words are addressed to the Divine Being.

If, therefore, we grasp this Law of Correspondence, we shall see that the only conception of the Divine Mind which will really vivify our souls with living and life-giving power is to realize it not merely as a tremendous force to be mapped out intellectually according to its successive stages of sequence — though it is this also — but above all things as the Universal Heart with which our own must beat in sympathetic vibration if we would attain the true development of that power the possession of which constitutes "the glorious liberty of the sons of God" (Rom. 8:21).

In all our operations we must always remember that the Creative Power is a process of feeling and not of reasoning. Reasoning analyzes and dissects; feeling evolves and builds up. The relation between them is that reasoning explains how it is that feeling has this power; and the more plainly we see why it should be so, the more completely we are delivered from those negative feelings which act destructively by the same law by which affirmative feelings work constructively.

The first requisite, therefore, for drawing to ourselves that creative action of the Universal Spirit, which alone can set us free from the bondage of Limitation, is to call up its response on the side of feeling; and unless this is done first, no amount of argument, mere intellectuality, can have the desired effect, and this is what is symbolically represented in the statement that God accepted Abel's offering and rejected Cain's. It is the veiled statement of the truth that the action of the intellect alone, however powerful, is not sufficient to move the Creative Power. This does not in the least mean that the intellectual process is hurtful in itself or unacceptable before God, but it must come in its proper order as joining with feeling instead of taking its place. When a mere cold ratiocination is substituted for hearty warmth of volition, then Abel is symbolically slain by Cain.

But the allegory goes further. It tells us that the particular animal which Abel offered was the sheep; and from this point onward we find the metaphor of the shepherd and the sheep recurring throughout Scripture, and the reason is that the relation between the Shepherd and the Sheep is peculiarly one of Guidance and Protection.

Now this brings us to the point which we may call the "Severance of the Way". When we realize the Unity of the I AM — the identity, that is, of the Self-recognizing Principle in the Universal and in the Individual — we may form three conceptions of it: one according to which the Universal I AM is reduced to a mere unconscious force, which the individual mind can manipulate without any sort of responsibility; another, the converse of this, in which Volition remains entirely on the side of the Universal Mind, and the individual becomes a mere automaton; and the third, in which each phase of Mind is the reciprocal of the other, and consequently the inceptive action may commence on either side.

Now it is this reciprocal action that the Bible all along puts before us as the true Way. From the center of his own smaller circle of perception the individual is free to make any selection that he will, and if he acts from a clear recognition of the true relations of things, the first use he will make of this power will be to guard himself against any possible misuse of it by recognizing that his own circle revolves within the greater circle of that Whole of which he is an infinitesimal part; and therefore he will always seek to conform his individual action to the movement of the Universal Spirit.

His sense of the Wholeness of that Universal Life which finds Individual center in himself, and his consciousness of his identity with it, will lead him to see that there must be, above his own individual view of things derived from a merely partial knowledge, a higher and more far-seeing Wisdom which, because it is the Life-in-itself, cannot be in any way adverse to him; and he will therefore seek to maintain such a mental attitude as will draw towards himself the response of the Universal Mind as a Power of unfailing Guidance, Provision, and Protection. But to do this means the curbing of that self-will which is guided only by the narrow perception of expediency derived from past experiences; in other words, it requires us to act from trust in the Universal Mind, thus investing it with a Personal character, rather than from calculations based on our own objective view, which is necessarily limited to secondary causes. In a word, we must learn to walk by faith and not by sight.

Now the institution of Sacrifice is the most effective way for impressing this mental attitude. Viewed merely superficially, it implies the desire of the worshipper to submit himself to the Divine Guidance by reconciliation through a propitiatory offering, and thus the required mental attitude is maintained. If we see that the blood of bulls and goats and the ashes of a heifer can have no power in themselves to effect reconciliation, and yet cannot see any more intelligible reason, then, if we will to accept the principle of sacrifice in the light of a mere mystery, we hereby still submit our individual will to the conception of a Higher Guidance, and so in this view also the desired mental attitude is maintained.

And at last when we reach the point where we see that the Universal Mind, which is also the Universal LAW, cannot have a retrospective vindictive character any more than any of the Laws of nature which emanate from it, we see that the true sacrifice is the willingness to give up smaller personal aims for the purpose of bringing into concrete manifestation those great principles of universal harmony which are the foundations of the Kingdom of God; and when we reach this point, we see the philosophical reasons why the maintenance of this attitude of the individual towards the Universal Mind is the one and only basis on which the individuality can expand or, indeed, continue to exist at all.

It is in correspondence with these three stages that the Bible first puts before us the patriarchal and Levitical sacrifices, next explains these as symbols of the Great Sacrifice of the Suffering Messiah, and finally tells us that God does not require the death of any victim and that the true offering is that of the heart and the will; and so the Psalms sum up the whole matter by saying, "Sacrifice and burnt-offering thou wouldest not" (Ps. 40:6), and instead of these, "Lo, I come to do Thy will, O my God; yea, Thy Law is within my heart" (Ps. 40:8).

But the idea of Sacrifice has the idea of Covenant for its correlative. If the acceptance of the principle of Sacrifice brings the worshipper into a peculiarly close relation to the Divine Mind, it equally brings the Divine Mind into a peculiarly close relation to the worshipper; and since the Divine Mind is the Life-in-itself, the very Essence-of-Being which is the root of all conscious individuality, this identification of the Divine with the Individual results in his continual expansion, or, to use the Master's words, in his having Life and having it more abundantly (John 10:10); and consequently, his powers steadily increase, and he is led by the most unlooked-for sequences of cause and effect into continually improving conditions which enable him to do more and more effectual work, so as to make him a center of power, not only to himself, but to all with whom he comes in contact.

This continual progress is the result of the natural law of the relation between himself and the Universal Mind when he does not invert its action, and because it works with the same unchangeableness as all other Natural Laws, it constitutes an Everlasting Covenant which can no more be broken than those astronomical laws which keep the planets in their orbits, the smallest infraction of which would destroy the entire cosmic system; and it is for this reason that we find in the Bible such frequent allusions to the Laws of Nature as typical of the certainty of the relation between God and His people. "Gather My saints (separated ones) together unto Me; those that have made a covenant with Me by sacrifice" (Psalm 50:5); the two principles of Sacrifice and Covenant rightly understood will always be found to go hand in hand.

The idea of Guidance and Protection which is thus set forth recurs throughout the Bible under the emblem of the Shepherd and the Sheep, and it is in a peculiar manner appropriated to "the People of the I AM": "From thence is the Shepherd, the Stone of Israel" (Gen. 49:24); "Give ear, O Shepherd of Israel, Thou that leadest Joseph like a flock" (Psalm 80:1); "The Lord is my Shepherd; I shall not want" (Psalm 23:1); "I am the Good Shepherd"; and similarly in many other passages. If, then, this conception of the Shepherd and the Sheep represents the mental attitude of "Israel", we may reasonably expect it to be precisely opposite to all that is symbolically meant by "Egypt". If "Israel" takes for its Stone of Foundation the principle of Guidance by the Supreme Power, then "Egypt" must base itself on the contrary principle of making its own choice without any guidance — that is to say, determined self-will. And hence we find it written that "every Shepherd is an abomination to the Egyptian" (Gen. 46:34).

Now it is a very remarkable thing that tradition points to the Great Pyramid as having been erected by a "Shepherd" power which dominated Egypt, not by force of arms, but by a mysterious influence which, although they detested it, the Egyptians found it impossible to resist. These "Shepherds" built the Great Pyramid and then, having accomplished their work, returned to the land from whence they came. So says the tradition. The Pyramid remains to this day, and the researches of modern science show that it is a monumental statement of all the great measures of the cosmic system wrought out with an accuracy which can only be accounted for by more than human knowledge.

And where should we find this knowledge except in the Universal Mind, of which the cosmic system is the visible manifestation? If, as it appears to me, this mind is primarily subconscious, then, by the general law of relation between subjective and objective mind, it could reproduce its inherent knowledge of all cosmic facts in any individual mind that had systematically trained itself into sympathy with the Universal Mind in that particular direction. But such training is impossible unless the individual mind first recognizes the Universal Mind as an Intelligence capable of giving the highest instruction, and to which, therefore, the individual mind is bound to look for guidance.

We must carefully avoid the mistake of supposing that subconsciousness means unconsciousness. That idea is clearly negatived by the fact of hypnotism. Whatever unconsciousness there may be is on the part of the objective mind, which is unconscious of the action of the subjective mind. But a careful study of the subject shows that the subjective mind, so far from knowing less than the objective mind, knows infinitely more; and if this be true of the individual subjective mind, how much more must it be true of the Universal Subjective Mind, of which all individual consciousness is a particular mode of manifestation.

For these reasons, the only people who could build such a monument as a Great Pyramid must be those who realized the principles of Divine Guidance or the Power which is set forth under the emblem of the Shepherd and the Sheep; and therefore we can see how it is that tradition associates the building of the Pyramid with a Shepherd Power.

Nor is this all. Having first demonstrated its trustworthiness by the refined accuracy of its astronomical and geodetic measurements, the Pyramid challenges our attention with a series of time-measurements, all of which were prophetic at the date of its erection, and some of which have already become historic, while the period of others is now rapidly running out. The central point of these time-measurements is the date of the birth of Christ, and if we think of him in his character of "the Good Shepherd", we have yet another testimony to the supreme importance which Scripture attaches to the relation between the Shepherd and the Sheep. For the Great Pyramid is a Bible in stone, and there can be no doubt that it is this marvel of the ages which is referred to in the nineteenth chapter of Isaiah, where it says, "In that day there shall be an altar to the Lord in the midst of the land of Egypt".

And so we find that the central fact to which the Great Pyramid leads up is the coming of "the Good Shepherd"; and Jesus explains the reason for this title in the fact that "the Good Shepherd giveth his life for the Sheep". That is what distinguishes him from the hireling who is not a true shepherd; so that here we find ourselves back again at the idea of Sacrifice, only now it is not the Sheep that are sacrificed but the Shepherd. Could anything be plainer? The sacrifice is not an offering of blood to a sanguinary Deity, but it is the Chief Shepherd sacrificing himself to the necessities of the case.

And what are the necessities of the case? The student of Mental Science should see here the grandest application of the Law of Suggestion in a supreme act of self-devotion logically proceeding from the knowledge of the fundamental truths regarding Subjective and Objective Mind. Jesus stands before us as the Grand Master of Mental Science. It is written that "he knew what was in man" (John 2:25), and in his mission we have the practical fruits of that knowledge.

The Great Sacrifice is also the Great Suggestion. If we realize that the Creative Power of our Thought is the root from which all our experiences, whether subjective or objective, arise, we shall see that everything depends on the nature of the suggestions which give colour to our Thought. If from our consciousness of guilt they are suggestions of retribution, then, in accordance with the predominating tone of our Thought, we shall externalize the evil that we fear; and if we carry this terrible suggestion with us through the gate of death into that other life which is purely subjective, then assuredly it will work itself out in our realizations, and so we must continue to suffer until we believe that we have paid the uttermost farthing. This is not a judicial sentence, but the inexorable working of Natural Law. But if we can find a counter-suggestion of such paramount magnitude as to obliterate all sense of liability to punishment, then, by the same Law, our fears are removed; and whether in the body or out of the body, we rejoice in the sense of pardon and reconciliation to our Father which is in heaven.

Now we can well imagine that one who has attained the supreme knowledge of all Laws, and as a consequence has developed the powers which the knowledge must necessarily carry with it, would find in the conveying of such an incalculably valuable suggestion to the race an object worthy of his exalted capacities. For such a one, ordinary ambitions would have no meaning; he has already left them far behind. But if he elects to devote himself to this great work, he must count the cost, for nothing short of delivering himself to death can accomplish it. The Master said, "Greater love hath no man than this, that a man lay down his life for his friends" (John 15:13), and if the Law of Suggestion was to be employed in such a way as to appeal to the whole race, it could only be by so deeply impressing them with the realization of the Divine Love that all fear should be forever cast out; therefore the suggestion must be that of a Love which nothing can exceed, and so it must consist in him who undertakes the mission giving himself to Voluntary Death.

For herein is the difference between the crucifixion of Jesus and those thousands of other crucifixions which disgraced the annals of Rome: it was entirely voluntary. This also places it above all other acts of heroism. Many have died for the sake of others, but to them death was a necessity, and their devotion consisted in accepting it when and how they did. But with Jesus the case was entirely different. He was beyond the necessity of death, and no man could take his life from him. He himself had power to lay it down and to take it up again (John 10:17), but he was under no compulsion to do so; therefore his yielding himself to a death of excruciating agony was the master-stroke of Love and the supreme practical application of Mental Science.

When he said, "It is finished", he had accomplished a work which is aptly represented by The Cubical Stone which is The Figure of the New Jerusalem, of which it is written that "the length and the breadth and the height thereof are equal" (Rev. 21:16). For turn it which way you will, it still always serves its great purpose of impressing the suggestions of superlative Love which can be trusted to the uttermost. Even the crude conception of the Father's "justice" being satisfied by the sacrifice of "the Son", however faulty both as Law and as Theology, in no way misses the mark from the metaphysical standpoint of Suggestion; and those who have not yet got beyond this stage in their conception of the Divine Being receive the assurance of the Divine Love towards themselves as completely as those who are able to grasp most clearly the sequence of cause and effect really involved; and for these latter it resolves itself into the simple argument a fortiori (with still greater reason - Ed.) that if the Universal Spirit could thus inspire one to die for us who was already beyond the necessity of death, then It cannot be less loving in the bulk than It has shown Itself in the sample.

It is an axiom that the Universal cannot act on the plane of the Particular except by becoming individualized upon that plane, and therefore we may argue that so far as it was possible for the Universal Spirit to give Itself to death for us, It did so in the person of Jesus Christ; and so we may say that to all intents and purposes God died for us upon the Cross to prove to us the Love of God.

Let us, then, no longer doubt the fact of this Love but, realizing it to the full, let us make the Cross of Christ not the mysterious end of an unintelligent religion, but the beginning of a bright, practical, and glorious New Life, taking for our starting-point the apostolic words, "there is now no condemnation to them that are in Christ Jesus" (Rom. 8:1). We have now consciously left all condemnation behind us, and we set forward on our New Life with the self-obvious maxim that "if God be for us, who can be against us?" (Rom. 8:31) We may meet with opposition, but there is with us a Power and an Intelligence which no opposition can overcome, and so we become "more than conquerors through Him that loved us" (Rom. 8:37).

This is the nature of the Great Suggestion wrought out by Jesus; so that here again we find that the acceptance of the Great Sacrifice gives rise to the consciousness of a peculiarly close and endearing relation between the Individual and the Universal Mind, which may well be described as an Everlasting Covenant because it is founded not on any favoritism on the part of God, neither on any deeds of merit on the part of Man, but on the accurate working of Universal Law when realized in the higher manifestations of Individualism; and so it is truly written, "by his Knowledge shall My righteous servant justify many" (Is. 53:11). Thus it is that Jesus completes the work of Moses in building up into a peculiar people, a chosen generation, "the People of the I AM" (1 Peter 2:9).

It was this conception of themselves as a chosen nation, separate from all others and united to God by a special covenant based upon sacrifice, that did in effect operate to produce the reality of this ideal in the people of Israel. Here again we see the Law of Suggestion at work. All their institutions, whether religious or political, were based upon the assumption of a covenant with Abraham forever ratified to his descendants, and centering round the promised Messiah; and so, whether looking at the past, the present, or the future, an Israelite was perpetually met by the most powerful suggestion of his peculiar position in the Divine favour.

If we recognize in Abraham one whose deep realization of the truth concerning the promised "Seed" had specially placed him in touch with the Universal Mind in that particular direction, we may naturally suppose a special illumination on this subject which would lead him to impress this idea upon his son Isaac as the foundation-fact of his life; and so from generation to generation, the supreme realization to all his descendants would be that of their covenant relation to God. And besides the impression conveyed by personal teaching, the law of heredity would cause each member of this race to be born with a prenatal subjective consciousness of this great Suggestion, which would carry its effect into the building up of his life, quite independently of any objectively conscious knowledge of the subject. This involves intricate psychological problems which I cannot stop to discuss here, but all New Thought readers are sufficiently acquainted with the potency of "race-beliefs" to realize how powerful a factor this subjective transmission of a hereditary suggestion would be in forming "the people of the I AM".

And there is yet another aspect of this subject which is of peculiar interest to the British and American nations, into which, however, I shall not enter in this book; but it will be sufficient for me to say that when a suggestion has once been implanted by the Divine Mind, as the Bible tells us that God did to Abraham in the most emphatic manner, taking oath by His Own Being because He could swear by none greater (Heb. 6:13), that suggestion is bound to grow to the most magnificent fulfillment: "My word that goeth forth out of My mouth shall not return unto Me void, but shall accomplish that which I please, and it shall prosper in the thing whereunto I sent it" (Isaiah 55:11).

For the reasons which I have now endeavoured to explain, the principle of "the Shepherd" is "the Stone of Israel"; it is that great ideal by which the nationality of the "People of the I AM" coheres, and it is, therefore, at once the Foundation Stone and the Crowning Stone of the whole edifice. To those who cannot realize the great universal truths which are summed up in the two-fold ideal of Sacrifice and Covenant, it must always be the Stone of stumbling and the Rock of offence; but to "the People of the I AM", whether individually or collectively, it must forever be "the Stone of Israel" (Gen 49:24) and "the Rock of our Salvation" (e.g. Ps. 95:1). To lay in Zion this Chief Corner Stone was the mission of Jesus Christ.

Chapter 6

The Building of the Temple

In our study of the Bible, we must always remember that what it is seeking to teach us is the knowledge of the grand Universal principles which are at the root of all modes of living activity, whether in that world of environment which we commonly speak of as Nature, or in those human relations which we call the World of Man, or in those innermost springs of being which we speak of as the Divine World. The Bible is throughout dealing with those three factors, which I have spoken of in the commencement of this book as "God", "Man", and "the Universe", and is explaining the Law of Evolution by which "God" or Universal Undifferentiated Spirit continually passes into more and more perfect forms of Self-expression culminating in Perfected Man.

However deep the mysteries we may encounter, there is nothing unnatural anywhere. Everything has its place in the due order of the Great Whole. A mistaken conception of this Order may lead us to invert it, and by so doing we provide those negative conditions whose presence calls forth the Power of the Negative with all its disastrous consequences; but even this inverted action is perfectly natural, for it is all according to recognizable Law, whether on the side of calculation or of feeling.

These Laws of the Universe, whether within us or without or around us, are always the same, and the only question is whether through our ignorance we shall use them in that inverted sense which sums them all up in the Law of Death, or in that true and harmonious order which sums them up in the Law of Life. These are the things which under a variety of figures the Bible presents to us, and it is for us by reverent, yet intelligent, inquiry to penetrate the successive veils which hide them from the eyes of those who will not take the trouble to investigate for themselves. It is this Grand Order of the Universe that is symbolized by Solomon's Temple.

We have seen that it was the mission of Moses to mould into definite form the material which ages of unnoticed growth had prepared, to consolidate into national being "the People of the I AM", and to lead them out of Egypt. This work, with which the truly national history of Israel commenced, had its completion in the reign of Solomon, when all enemies had been extirpated from the Promised Land, and the state founded by Moses out of wandering tribes had culminated in a powerful monarchy, ruled over by a king whose name has ever since become both in East and West the synonym for the supreme attainment of wisdom, power, and glory.

If the purpose of Moses had been only that of a national lawgiver and founder of a political state, a Lycurgus or a Rollo, it would have found its perfect attainment in the reign of Solomon; but Moses had a far grander end in view, and looking down the long vista of the ages he saw, not Solomon, but the carpenter who said, "a greater than Solomon is here" (Matt. 12:42; Luke 11:31). And the way for the carpenter could only be prepared by that long period of decadence which set in with the first days of Solomon's successor. "The People of the I AM" are concealed among all nations and must be brought forth by the Prophet, who should realize the work of Moses not only in a national, but also in a universal, significance.

These are the three typical figures of Hebrew history; the beginning, the middle, and the end — Moses, Solomon, Jesus; and the three are distinguished by one common characteristic: they are all Builders of the Temple. Moses erected the tabernacle, that portable temple which accompanied the Israelites in their journeyings. Solomon reproduced it in an edifice of wood and stone fixed firmly upon its rocky foundation. Jesus said, "Destroy this temple, and in three days I will raise it up again" (John 2:19); but "he spoke of the temple of his body" (John 2:21).

Thus they stand before us the Three Great Builders, each building with a perfect knowledge according to a Divine pattern; and if the Divine is that in which there is no variableness of shadow of turning (James 1:17), how can we suppose that the pattern was other than one and the same? We may, therefore, expect to find in the work of the three Builders the same principles, however differently expressed; for they each in different ways proclaimed the same all-embracing truth that God, Man, and the Universe, however varied may be the multiplicity of outward forms, are ONE.

St Paul gives us an important key to the interpretation of Scripture when he tells us that its leading characters also represent great universal principles, and this is pre-eminently the case with Solomon. His name, in common with the names Salem and Jerusalem, is derived from a word signifying Wholeness (Sálim, the Whole), and therefore means the man who has realized "the Wholeness", or in other words the Universal Unity. This is the secret of his greatness.

He who has found the Unity of the Whole has obtained "the Key of Knowledge", and it is now in his power to enter intelligently upon the study of his own being and of the relations which arise out of it, and to help others as he himself advances into greater light. This is the man who is able to become a Builder.

But such a man cannot come of any parentage; he must be the "Son of David"; and it was to test their knowledge in this respect that the Master posed the carping scribes with the question as to how the Son of David could also be his Lord (Matt. 22:43-46). As rulers in Israel, they should have known these things and instructed the people in them, but they would not come, as did Nicodemus (John 3:1-2), to him who would teach them; and so, like Hiram (1 Kings 5), the architect of Solomon's Temple, the Master was murdered by those who should have been his scholars and helpers.

The Builder of the Temple, then, must be "the Son of David"; and again we find that much of the significance of this saying is concealed in the names. David is the English form of the Oriental "Daud", which means "Beloved", and the Builder is therefore the Son of the Beloved. David is called in Scripture "the man after God's own heart", a description exactly answering to the name; and we therefore find that Solomon the Builder is the son of the man who has entered into that reciprocal relation with "God", or the Universal Spirit, which can only be described as Love.

To define what is primarily feeling is to attempt the impossible; but the essence of the feeling consists in the recognition of such a reciprocity of nature that each supplies what the other wants, and that neither is complete without the other. In the last analysis, the reason for this feeling is to be discovered in the relation of the Individual to the Universal Mind as each being the necessary correlative of the other, and it is the recognition of this truth that makes David the father of Solomon.

When this recognition by the individual mind of its own nature and of its relation to the Universal Mind takes place, it gives birth to a new being in the man; for he now finds not that he has ceased to be the self he was before, but that that self includes a far greater self, which is none other than the reproduction of the Universal Self in his individual consciousness. Thenceforward he works more and more of set purpose by means of this greater self, the self within the self, as he grows into fuller understanding of the Law by which this greater self has become developed within him.

He learns that it is this greater self within the self that is the true Builder, because it is none other than the reproduction of the Infinite Creative Power of the Universe. He realizes that the working of this power must always be a continual building up. It is the Universal Life-Principle, and to suppose that to have any other action than continual expansion into more and more perfect forms of self-expression would be to suppose it acting in contradiction to its own nature which, whether on the colossal scale of a solar system or on the miniature scale of a man, must be that of a self-inherent activity which is forever building up.

When anyone is thus intellectually enlightened, he has reached that stage of development which is signified by the name David: he is "beloved" — that is to say, he is exercising a specific individual attraction towards the Spirit in its universal and undifferentiated mode.

We are here dealing with the Principle of Evolution in its highest phases, and if we keep this in mind it becomes clear that the intellectual man who perceives this is himself the evolving principle manifesting at that stage where it becomes an individuality capable of understanding its own identity with the Spiritual Force which, by Self-evolution, produces all things. He thus realizes himself to be the Reciprocal of the Universal Mind, which is the Divine Spirit, and he sees that his reciprocity consists in Evolution having reached in him the point where that factor is developed which cannot have a place in the Universal Mind as such, but without which the continuation of Evolution in its highest phases is impossible — the factor, namely, of individual will.

We lose the key to the whole teaching of the Bible if we lose sight of the truth that the Universal cannot, as such, initiate a course of action on the plane of the particular. It can do so only by becoming the individual, which is precisely the production of the intellectually enlightened man we are speaking about. The failure to see this very obvious Law is the root of all the theological discordances that have retarded the work of true religion to the present time, and therefore the sooner we see through the error, the better.

Anyone who has advanced to the perception of this Law necessarily becomes a center of attraction to Undifferentiated Spirit in its highest modes, the modes of Intelligence and Feeling, as well as in its lower modes of Vital Energy. This results from the very nature of the evolutionary hypothesis. All creation commences with the primary movement of the Spirit, and since the Spirit is Life-in-itself, this movement must be forever going on.

To take an analogy from chemistry, it is perpetually in the nascent state — that is, continually pressing forward to find the most suitable affinities with which to coalesce into self-expression. This is exactly what Jesus said to the woman of Samaria: "The Father (Universal Spirit) seeketh such to worship Him (John 4:23); and it is because of this mutual attraction between the individual mind that has come to the knowledge of its own true nature and the Universal Mind that the person who is thus enlightened is called "the Beloved"; he is beginning to understand what is meant by Man being the image of God and to grasp the significance of the old-world saying that "Spirit is the power that knows itself".

As this intellectual comprehension of the great Truth matures, it gives rise to the recognition of an interior power which is something beyond the intellect but not yet independent of it, something regarding which we can make intellectual statements that clear the way for its recognition, but which is itself a Living Power and not a mere statement about such a power.

It may seem a truism to say that no statement about a thing is the thing, yet we are apt to miss this in practice. The Master pointed this out very clearly when he said to the Jews, "Search the Scriptures, for in them ye think ye have everlasting life, and they are they which testify of Me" (John 5:39). He said in effect, "You make a mistake by supposing that the reading of a book can in itself confer Life. What your Scriptures do is to make statements regarding that which I am. Realize what those statements mean, and then you will see in me the living example of the Living Truth; and seeing this, you will seek for the development of the same thing in yourselves. The disciple, when perfected, shall be as his Master".

The Building-Power is that innermost spiritual faculty which is the reproduction in the individual of the same Universal Building-Power by which the whole Creation exists, and the purpose of intellectual statements regarding it is to remove mental obstacles and to induce the mental state which will enable this supreme innermost power to work in accordance with conscious selection on the part of the individual. It is the same power which has brought the race up to where it is, and which has evolved the individual as part of the race.

All further evolution must result from the conscious employment of the Evolutionary Law by the intelligence of the individual himself. Now it is this recognized innermost creative power that is signified by Solomon — it must be preceded by the purified and enlightened intellect — and therefore it is called the Son of David and becomes the Builder of the Temple. For the Master's statement shows that, in its true significance, the Temple is that of Man's individuality; and if this is so with the individual, equally it must be so in the totality of manifested being, and thus it is also true that the whole Universe is none other than the Temple of the Living God.

This great truth of the Divine Presence is what the instructed builders sought to symbolize in Solomon's Temple, whether that Presence be considered on the scale of the Universe or of an individual man. If the Universal Divine Presence is a fact, then the Individual Divine Presence is a fact also, because the individual is included in the Universal; it is the working of a general Law in a particular instance, and thus we are brought to one of the great statements of the ancient wisdom, that Man is the Microcosm — that is to say, the reproduction of all the principles which give rise to the manifestation of the Universe, or the Macrocosm; and therefore, to serve its proper emblematical purpose, the Temple must represent both the Macrocosm and the Microcosm.

It would be far too elaborate a work for the present volume to enter in detail into the symbolical statements of both physical and supraphysical nature contained first in the Tabernacle and afterwards in the Temple; but as the Universal Mind inspired the builders of the Pyramid with the correct knowledge of the cosmic measures, so the Bible tells us that Moses was inspired to produce in the Tabernacle the symbolic representation of great universal truths; he was bidden to make all things accurately according to the pattern showed him on the Mount, and the same truths received a more permanent symbolization in Solomon's Temple.

An excellent example of this symbolism is afforded by the two pillars set up by Solomon at the entrance to the Temple: the one on the right hand, called Jachin, and the one on the left, called Boaz (1 Kings 7:21). They seemed to have had no structural connection with the building but merely to have stood at its entrance for the purpose of bearing these symbolic names. What, then, do they signify? The English J often stands for the Oriental Y, and the name Jachin is therefore Yakhin, which is an intensified form of the word YAK or ONE, thus signifying first the principle of Unity as the Foundation of all things, and then the Mathematical element throughout the Universe, since all numbers are evolved from the ONE, and under certain methods of treatment will always resolve themselves again into it.

But the mathematical element is the element of Measurement, Proportion, and Relation. It is not the Living Life, but only the recognition of the proportional adjustments which the Life gives rise to. To balance the Mathematical element we require the Vital element, and this element finds its most perfect expression in that wonderful complex of Thought, Feeling, and Volition which we call Personality. The pillar Jachin is therefore balanced by the pillar Boaz, a name connected with the root of the word "awaz", or Voice.

Speech is the distinguishing characteristic of Personality. To clothe a conception in adequate language is to give it definition and thus make it clear to ourselves and to others. A distinct statement of our idea is the first step in the operation of consciously building it up into concrete existence, and therefore we find that in all the great religions of the race, the Divine Creative

Power is spoken of as "the Word".

Let us get away from all confused mysticism regarding this term. The formulated Word is the expression of a definite Purpose, and therefore it stands for the action of Intelligent Volition; and it is as showing the place which this factor holds in the evolutionary process that the pillar Boaz stands opposite the pillar Jachin as its necessary complement and equilibration. The union of the two signifies Intelligent Purpose working by means of Necessary Law, and the only way of entering into "the Temple", whether of the cosmos or of the individual, is by passing between these Two Pillars of the Universe and realizing the combined action of Law and Volition.

This is the Narrow Way that leads us into the building not made with hands (2 Cor. 5:1), within which all the mysteries shall be unfolded before us in a regular order and succession. He who climbs up some other way is a thief and a robber (John 10:8) and brings punishment upon himself as the natural effect of his own rashness; for, knowing nothing of the true Order of the Inner Life, he plunges prematurely into the midst of things of whose real nature he is ignorant, and sooner or later learns to his cost the truth of the Scriptural warning, "whoso breaketh an hedge, a serpent shall bite him" (Eccl. 10:8).

We may not enter the Temple save by passing between the pillars, and we cannot pass between them till we can tell their meaning. It is the purpose of the Bible to give us the Key to this Knowledge. It is not the only instruction it has to give, but it is its initial course, and when this has been mastered, it will open out into deeper things, the inner secrets of the sanctuary. But the first thing is to pass between Jachin and Boaz, and then the Divine Interpreter will meet us on the threshold and will unfold the mysteries of the Temple in their due order, so that as each one is opened to us in succession, we are prepared for its reception and thus need fear no danger, because at each step we always know that we are dealing with and have attained the spiritual, intellectual, and physical development qualifying us to employ each new revelation in the right way.

For the opening of the inner mysteries is not for the gratification of mere idle curiosity; it is for the increasing of our Livingness; and the highest quality of Livingness is Life-givingness; and every measure of Life-givingness, be it only the giving of a cup of cold water (Matt. 10:42) means use of the powers and knowledge which we possess. The Temple instruction is therefore intended to qualify us as workers, and the value to ourselves of what we receive within is seen in the measure of intelligence and love with which we transmute our Temple gold into the current coin of daily life.

The building-up process is that of Evolution, whether in the material world or in the human individuality or in the race as a whole, and the Bible presents the analogy to us very forcibly under the metaphor of "the Stone". Speaking of the rejection of his own teaching, the Master said, "What is this, then, that is written, 'The Stone which the builders rejected, the same is become the head of the corner'?" referring to the 118th Psalm (Luke 20:17). A careful perusal of the Master's history as given in the Gospel will show us very clearly what "the Stone" is; it is the material out of which the Temple of the Spirit is to be built up, which we now see is nothing else than Perfected Humanity.

Each individual is a temple himself, as St Paul tells us, and at the same time a single stone in the construction of the Great Temple which is the regenerated race, that "People of the I AM" which was inaugurated when Moses first pitched the tabernacle in the wilderness. But the process must always be an individual one, for a nation is nothing but an aggregation of individuals, and therefore in considering the metaphor of "the Stone" as applied to the individual, we shall realize its wider application also.

Now the Master was executed on the charge of blasphemy for asserting the identity of his own nature with that of God. The subjection of the Jews to the Roman rule placed the power of life and death in the hands of a tribunal which could not take cognizance of such an offence — "Take ye him and judge him according to your law" (John 18:31), said Pilate when the charge of blasphemy was preferred before him; and in order to bring him to execution it became necessary to substitute for the original charge of blasphemy one of high treason, so as to bring it within the jurisdiction of the court. "Whosoever maketh himself a king speaketh against Caesar" (John 19:12) — and so the inscription fastened to the cross was "Jesus of Nazareth, the King of the Jews" (John 19:19). But the true reason why Jesus was hunted to death was expressed by the scribes, who mocked the sufferer with the words "He trusted in God; let Him deliver him now if He will have him, for he said 'I am the son of God'." (Matt. 27:43)

The teaching of Jesus was the inversion of all that was taught by the official priesthood. Their whole teaching rested on the hypothesis that God and Man are absolutely distinct in nature, thus directly contradicting the earliest statement of their own Scriptures regarding Man, that he is the image and likeness of God. As a consequence of this false assumption, they supposed that the whole Mosaic Law and Ritual was intended to pacify God and make him favourable to the worshipper, and so in their minds the entire system tended only to emphasize the gulf that separated Man from God.

What the nexus of cause and effect was by which this system operated to produce the result of reconciling God to the worshipper was a question which they never attempted to face; for had they, after the example of their patriarch, determinedly wrestled with the problem of why their Law was what it was, that Law would have shone forth with a self-illuminating light which would have made clear to them that all the teaching of Moses and the Prophets and the Psalms was concerning that grand ideal of a Divine Humanity which it was the mission of Jesus to proclaim and exemplify.

But they would not face the question of the reason of these things. They had received a certain traditional interpretation of their Scriptures and their Ritual and, as Jesus said, made the real commands of God void by their traditions. They were tied by "authorities", and this at second hand. They did not inquire what Moses meant, but only followed on the lines of what somebody else said he meant; in other words, they would not think for themselves. They were content to say, "Our Law and Ritual are what they are because God has so ordered them"; but they would not go further and inquire why God ordered them so.

With them, the whole question of revelation became the question whether Moses had or had not made such an announcement of the Divine Will, and so their religion rested ultimately only on historical evidences. But they did not face the question, "How am I to know that the so-called prophet ever received any communication from the Divine at all?" In the last resort, there can be only one criterion by which to judge the truth of any claim to a Divine communication, which is that the message should present an intelligible sequence of cause and effect.

No man can prove that God has spoken to him; the only possible proof is the inherent truth of the message, making it appeal to our feelings and our reason with a power that carries conviction with it. "The Spirit of Truth shall convince you", said the Master; and when this inner conviction of Truth is felt, it will invariably be found that, by thinking it over carefully, the reason of the feeling will manifest itself in an intelligible sequence of cause and effect. Short of realizing such a sequence, we have not realized the Truth. The only other proof is that of practical results, and to this test the Master tells us to bring the teaching that we hear; and the teaching he bade us judge by this standard was his own.

It is a principle that no great system can endure for ages, exercising a widespread and permanent influence over large masses of mankind, without any element of Truth in it. There have been, and still are, great systems influencing mankind which contain many and serious errors, but what has given them their power is the Truth that is in them and not the error; and careful inquiry into the secret of their vitality will enable us to detect and remove the error.

Now had the leaders of the Jews investigated their national system with intelligence and moral courage, they would have argued that its manifest vitality and elevating spiritual tone showed that it contained a great and living Truth. This Truth could not be in the mere external observances and the promised results, and therefore the vitalising Truth must be in some principle which supplied the connection that was apparently wanting. They would have argued that God could not have arbitrarily commanded a set of meaningless observances, and that therefore these observances must be the expression of some LAW inherent in the very nature of Man's being.

In a word, they would have realized that, to be true at all, a thing must be within the All-embracing Law of Cause and Effect, and that religion itself could be no exception to the rule — it must, in short, be natural because, if God be ONE, He cannot introduce anywhere an arbitrary and meaningless caprice subversive of the principle of Order throughout the Universe. To suppose the introduction of anything by a mere act of Divine Volition, without a foundation in the sequence of the Universal Order, would be to deny the Unity of God, and thus to deny the Divine Being altogether.

Had the rulers of Israel, therefore, understood the meaning of the first two Commandments, they would have realized that their first duty, as instructors of the people, was to probe the whole Mosaic system until they reached the bedrock of cause and effect on which it rested. But this is just what they did not do. Their reverence for names was greater than their reverence for Truth and, assuming that Moses taught what he never did, they put to death the teacher of whom Moses had prophesied as the one who should complete his word in building up "the people of the I AM".

Thus they rejected "the Stone of Israel", and in so doing they fought against God — that is, against the Law of Spirit in Self-evolution. For it was this Law, and this only, that the Carpenter of Nazareth taught. He came not to destroy the teachings of Moses and of the Prophets, but to fulfill by showing what it was that, under various veils and coverings, had been handed down through the generations. It was his mission to complete the Building of the Temple by exhibiting Perfected Man as the apex of the Pyramid of Evolution.

Broad and strong and deep was laid the foundation of this Pyramid in that first movement of the ONE which the Bible tells of in its opening words; and thenceforward the building has progressed through countless ages till Man, now sufficiently developed intellectually, requires only the final step of recognizing that the Universal Spirit reaches, in him, the reproduction of Itself in individuality to take his proper place as the crown and completion of the whole evolutionary process. He has to realize that the opening statement of Scripture concerning himself is not a mere figure of speech but a practical fact, and that he really is the image and likeness of the Universal Spirit.

This was the teaching of Jesus. When the Jews sought to stone him for saying that God was his Father (John 10:31), he replied by quoting the 82nd Psalm, "I said ye are gods", and laid stress on this as "Scripture that cannot be broken" — that is, as written in the very nature of things, that signatura rerum (signature of things) by which each thing has its proper place in the universal order. He replied in effect, "I am only saying of myself what your own Law says of every one of you. I do not set myself forth as an exception, but as the example of what the nature of every man truly is". The same mistake has been perpetuated to the present day; but gradually people are beginning to see what the great truth is which Jesus taught and which Moses and the Prophets and the Psalms had proclaimed before him.

Perfected Man is the apex of the Evolutionary Pyramid, and this by a necessary sequence. First comes the Mineral Kingdom, lying inert and motionless, without any sort of individual recognition. Then comes the Vegetable Kingdom, capable of assimilating food, with individual life, but with only the most rudimentary intelligence, and rooted to one spot. Next comes the Animal Kingdom, where intelligence is manifestly on the increase, and the individual is no longer rooted to a single spot physically, yet is so intellectually, for its round of ideas is limited only to the supply of its bodily wants. Then comes the fourth or Human kingdom, where the individual is not rooted to one spot either physically or intellectually, for his thought can penetrate all space. But even he has not yet reached Liberty, for he is still the slave of "circumstances over which he has no control": his thoughts are unlimited, but they remain mere dreams until he can attain the power of giving them realization. Unlimited power of conception is his, but to complete his evolution he must acquire a corresponding power of creation. With that he will arrive at perfect Liberty.

Throughout the Four Kingdoms which have yet been developed, the progress from the lower to the higher is always towards greater liberty and therefore, in accordance with that principle of Continuity which Science recognizes as nowhere broken in Nature, Perfect Liberty must be the goal towards which the evolutionary process is tending. One state more is necessary to complete the Pyramid of Manifested nature: the addition of a Fifth Kingdom, which shall complete the work for which the four lower Kingdoms are the preparation — the Kingdom in which Spirit shall be the ruling factor, and thus the Kingdom of Spirit which is the Kingdom of God.

These considerations bring out into a very clear light one meaning of Daniel's prophecy of "the Stone", cut out without hands, which grew until it filled the whole earth (Daniel 2:34,35). It is that same "Stone" of which Jesus spoke and is bound by the inevitable sequence of Evolution to become the Chief Cornerstone — that is, the angular or five-pointed stone in which all four sides of the Pyramid find their completion. It is that headstone capping the whole, of which it is written that it shall be brought forth with shouts of "Grace, grace unto it" (Zech. 4:7).

The Fifth Kingdom, the Kingdom of spiritually developed Man, is that which is now slowly growing, as one individual after another awakes to the recognition of his own spiritual nature, seeing in it not a mere vague religious sentiment but an actual working principle to be consciously used in everything that concerns himself. This "Kingdom of God", or of Spirit, was compared by the Master to leaven hidden in meal, which spread by a silent process until the whole was leavened.

The establishment of this Fifth Kingdom is a natural process of growth, a great silent revolution which will gradually change the face of society by first changing its spirit; and for this reason the Master said, "The Kingdom of God cometh not with observation". Outward forms of government will perhaps always vary in different countries, but the recognition of Man as the true Temple must produce the same effects of "justice, mercy, and truth" in every land, so that war and crime, ignorance and want, sickness and fear shall be known no more, and sorrow and sighing shall flee away (Isaiah 35:10).

This is the meaning of the Building of the Temple, and in studying it we must remember that the sacred symbols apply not only to Man but also to his environment. The Tabernacle of Moses and the Temple of Solomon not only represent the Microcosm but also the Macrocosm. And this leads us to the threshold of a very deep mystery: the effect of the spiritual condition of the human race upon Nature as a whole, regarding which St Paul tells us that the entire creation is waiting in anxious expectation for the revealing of the sons of God (Rom. 8:19).

The Building of the Temple is thus a threefold process, commencing with the individual man, spreading from the individual to the race, and from the race to the whole environment in which we live. This is the return to Eden, where there is nothing hurtful or destructive.

The expulsion from the spiritual "Garden of the Lord" led man into a world that brought forth thorns and thistles, and the earth was "cursed for his sake"; that is to say, the mental attitude resulting from "the Fall" induced a corresponding condition in Nature; and by the same Law, the mental attitude which is restoration from "the Fall" will produce a corresponding renovation of the material world, a state of things which is described with poetic imagery in the eleventh chapter of Isaiah.

This influence of the human race upon their surroundings, whether for good or for evil, is only the natural result of carrying out to its final consequences the initial proposition of the Bible that Man is the image of God. This is the affirmation of the inherently creative power of his Thought; and if this be true, then the collective Thought of the race must be the subtle power which determines the prevailing conditions of the natural world.

The uncertain mixed conditions among which we live very accurately represent our uncertain and mixed modes of Thought. We think from the standpoint of a mixture of good and evil and have no certainty as to which is really the controlling power. Good, we say, works "within certain limits"; but who or what fixes those limits we cannot guess. In short, if we analyze the average belief of mankind as represented in Christian countries at the present day, it resolves itself into belief in a sort of rough-and-tumble between God and Devil, in which sometimes one is uppermost and sometimes the other; and so we entirely lose the conception of a definite control by the Power of Good steadily acting in accordance with its own character and not subject to the dictation of some Evil Power which prescribes "certain limits" for it.

This balance between good and evil is undoubtedly the present state of things, but it is the reflection of our own Thought, and the remedy for it is therefore that knowledge of the inner Law which shows us that we ourselves are producing the evils we deplore. It is for this reason that the Apostle warns us against emulations, wrath, and strife (Gal. 5:20). They all proceed from a denial of the Creative Power of our Thought — in other words, the denial that Man is the "image of God". They proceed from the hypothesis that good can exist only "within certain limits", and that therefore our work must not be directed towards the producing of more good, but to scrambling for a larger share of the limited quantity of good that has been doled out to the world by a bankrupt Deity.

Whether this scramble be between individuals in the commercial wotld, or between classes in social life, or between nations in the glorious name of murder with the best modern appliances, the underlying principle is always that of competition based on the idea that the gain of one can only accrue by another's loss; and therefore what prevents us today from "entering into rest" (Psalm 95:11; Heb. 4:3) is the same cause that produced the same effect in the time of the Psalmist: "they could not enter in because of unbelief" and "they limited the Holy ONE of Israel". So long as we persist in the belief that the truly originating causes of things are to be found anywhere but in our own mental attitude, we condemn ourselves to interminable toil and strife.

But if, instead of looking at conditions, we endeavoured to realize First Cause as that which acts independently of all conditions, because the conditions flow from it and not vice versa, we should see that the whole teaching of the Bible is to lead us to understand that, because man is the image of God, he can never divest his Thought of its inherent creative power; and for this reason it sets before us the limitless goodness of the Heavenly Father as the model which in our own use of this power we are to follow. "He maketh His sun to rise on the evil and on the good, and sendeth his rain on the just and on the unjust" (Matt. 5:45). In other words, the Universal First Cause is not concerned with pre-existing conditions but continually radiates forth its creative energy, transmuting the evil into the good and the good into something still better; and since it is the prerogative of Man to use the same creative power from the standpoint of the individual, he must use it in the same manner if he would produce effects of Life and not of Death.

He cannot divest his Thought of its creative power, but it rests with him to choose between Life and Death according to the way in which he employs it. As each one realizes that conditions are created from within and not from without, he begins to see the force of the Master's invitation: "Come unto me all ye that labour and are heavy laden, and I will give you rest" (Matt. 11:28). He sees that the only thing that has prevented him from entering into rest has been unbelief in the limitless power of drawing from that inexhaustible storehouse; and when we thus realize the true nature of the Divine Law of Supply, we see that it depends not on taking from others without giving a fair equivalent, but rather on giving good measure pressed down and shaken together (Luke 6:38) (a Biblical expression of abundance, originally referring to grain).

The Creative Law is that the quality of the Thought which starts any particular chain of cause and effect continues through every link of the chain, and therefore if the originating Thought be that of the absolute goodness-in-itself of the intended creation, irrespective of all circumstances, then this quality will be inherent not only in the thing immediately created, but also in the whole incalculable series of results flowing from it.

Therefore, to make our work good for its own sake is the surest way to make it return to us in a rich harvest, which it will do by a natural Law of Growth if we only allow it time to grow. By degrees, one after another finds this out for himself, and the eventual recognition of these truths by the mass of mankind must make "the desert rejoice and blossom as the rose" (Isaiah 35:1). Let each one therefore take part joyfully in the Building of the Temple, in which shall be offered, forever, the twofold worship of Glory to God and Goodwill to Man.

Chapter 7

The Sacred Name

A point that can hardly fail to strike the Bible student is the frequency with which we are directed to the Name of the Lord as the source of strength and protection instead of to God Himself; and the steady uniformity of this practice, both in the Old and New Testaments, clearly indicates the intention to put us upon some special line of inquiry with regard to the Sacred Name. Not only is this suggested by the frequency of the expression, but the Bible gives a very remarkable instance which shows that the Sacred Name must be considered as a formula containing a summary of all wisdom.

The Master tells us that the Queen of the South came to hear the wisdom of Solomon, and if we turn to 1 Kings 10:1, we find that the fame of Solomon's wisdom, which induced the Queen of Sheba to come to prove him with hard questions, was "concerning the Name of the Lord". This accords with the immemorial tradition of the Jews, that the knowledge of the secret Name of God enables him who possesses it to perform the most stupendous miracles.

This Hidden Name — the "Schem-hammaphoraseh" — was revealed, they say, to Moses and taught by him to Aaron and handed on by him to his successors. It was the secret enshrined in the Holy of Holies and was scrupulously guarded by the successive High Priests. It is the supreme secret, and its knowledge is the supreme object of attainment. Thus tradition and Scripture alike point to "The NAME" as the source of Light and Life, and Deliverance from all evil.

May we not therefore suppose that this must be the veiled statement of some great Truth? The purpose of a name is to call up, by a single word, the complete idea of the thing named, with all those qualities and relations that make it what it is, instead of having to describe all this in detail every time we want to suggest the conception of it. The correct name of a thing thus conveys the idea of its whole nature, and accordingly the correct Name of God should, in some manner, be a concise statement of the Divine Nature as the Source of all Life, Wisdom, Power, and Goodness, and the Origin of all manifested being.

For this reason the Bible puts before us "the Name of the Lord" not only as the object of supreme veneration, but also as the grand subject of study, by means of which we may command the Power that will provide us with all good and protect us from all ill. Let us, then, see what we can learn regarding this marvelous Name.

The Bible calls the Divine Being by a variety of Names, but when we have once got the general clue to the Sacred name, we shall find that each of them implies all the others, since each suggests some particular aspect of THAT which is the All-embracing UNIT, the everlasting ONE, which cannot be divided, and any one aspect of which must therefore convey to the instructed mind the suggestion of all the others. We will therefore seek first this general clue which will throw light on more particular appellations.

I think most people will agree that the especially personal Name by which the Divine Being is called in the Bible is Jehovah. If any Name, throughout the entire range of Scriptures, seems to invest the Divine Being with a distinct individuality, it is this one; and yet when we come to inquire into its meaning, we find that it is precisely the most emphatic statement of a universality which is the very antithesis of all that we understand by the word "individual".

The clue to this discovery is contained in the statement that God revealed Himself to Moses by the Name Jehovah (Ex. 6:3); for since the Bible contains no statement of any other revelation of the Divine Name to Moses, except that made at the burning bush, we are at once put upon the track of some connection between the Name Jehovah and the command received by Moses to tell the children of Israel that I AM had commissioned him to deliver them.

Now, the Name which in English is rendered "Jehovah" is composed of four Hebrew letters — Yod, Hé, Vau, Hé — thus spelling "Yevé", and this is the word which we have to analyze. And this brings us to the fact that the whole Hebrew alphabet is invested with a certain symbolical character because, in the estimation of learned Jews, it exemplifies the great principle of Evolution; for they rightly consider that Evolution is nothing else than the working of the Divine Spirit through all worlds, whether visible or invisible.

It would require a long study to take the reader through the detailed examination of every letter, but the general idea may be stated as follows: The letter Yod is a minute mark of a definite shape, though little more than a point, and a careful inspection of the Hebrew alphabet shows that all the other letters are combinations of this initial form. It is thus the "generating point" from which all the other letters proceed, each letter being in some way or other a reproduction of the Yod; and accordingly, it has not inaptly been regarded as a symbol of the All-originating First Principle.

If, therefore, a Name was to be devised which should represent the mystery of the Divine Being as at once the Unity which includes all Multiplicity, and the Multiplicity which is included in the Unity, the logical sequence of ideas required that the Hebrew form of such a word should commence with the letter Yod. The name of the letter is suggested by the sound of the indrawing of the breath and thus indicates self-containedness. The opposite conception is that of the sending forth of the breath, which is represented by the sound Hé, and this letter indicates that which is not self-contained, but which emanates from the Source of Life. Yod thus represents essential Life, while Hé represents Derived Life.

The letter Vau, taken alone, signifies "and" and thus conveys the idea of a "Link". This is followed by a repetition of the "Hé", so that the second portion of the Sacred name conveys the idea of a plurality of derived lives connected together by some common link and is, therefore, the symbol of the Unity passing into manifestation as the Multiplicity of all individual beings.

The whole name thus constitutes a most perfect statement of the Divine Being as that Universal Life which, to use the apostolic words, is "over all, and through all, and in all" (Eph. 4:6); so that once more we are brought back to what the Master said was the fundamental statement of all Truth, namely, that God is THE ONE, this indicating that Unity of Spirit from which all individualities proceed and in which they are included.

But the second portion of the Divine name is EVE (the Hebrew Hé corresponds with the English E), which we have found to be the individualized Life-Principle or the Soul, and thus this portion of the Sacred Name not only denotes Multiplicity, but also indicates the fact that the derived life stands towards the Originating Life in the relation of the feminine to the masculine. If this feminine nature of the Soul relatively to the Universal Spirit be steadily kept in mind, it will be found to contain the key not only to many passages of Scripture but also to many facts of Nature both in the inner and outer worlds. The words of Isaiah 54:5, "Thy Maker is thine husband" are not a mere figure of speech, but a statement of the great fundamental law of human personality; and this relative femininity of the Soul, which in this passage is pronounced so unequivocally, will be found on investigation to be assumed as a general principle throughout Scripture.

We have already seen from the story of "the Fall" that Eve represents the soul as distinguished from the body; and just as the Bible opens with this assertion of the feminine nature of the Soul, so it closes with it, and a large portion of the magnificent symbolism of Revelation is occupied in depicting, under the form of two mystical "Women", the generalized history of the adulterous soul and of the faithful soul which, as "the Bride", joins with "the Spirit" in the Universal invitation to all who will, to drink of the water of Life and live forever.

It is, then, this mystery of the femininity of the soul as a general principle of Nature, and its necessary relation to the corresponding Masculine principle, that is the great truth enshrined in the Sacred Name Jehovah. The first letter of the name implies "self-containedness", the statement in the universal of all that we mean individually when we speak of ourselves as "I"; and the remaining portion is the form of a verb expressing continuous Being; and the whole Name therefore is the exact statement of "I AM" which was made to Moses at the burning bush.

The Name "Jehovah" is thus the concealed statement of the great doctrine of Evolution seen in its spiritual aspect. It is the statement that every form of manifestation is an unfolding of the ONE original principle, and that beside this original ONE reappearing under infinite variety of forms there is no other.

But further, this Name is a statement that the passing of the Unity into that infinite galaxy of Life which, though now sometimes sorrowing, is destined to become one glorious rose of myriad petals, each of which is a rejoicing creative being, can take place only through Duality. Is this a mystery? Yes, the greatest of mysteries, including all others, for it is that Universal mystery of Attraction upon which all research, even in physical science, eventually abuts; and yet, that Duality must be established before Unity can pass into all the powers and beauties of external manifestation is a proposition so self-evident as to be almost absurd in its simplicity; indeed, the very simplicity of the great universal truths is a stumbling-block to many who, like Naaman (2 Kings 5), expect something sensational.

Now this very simple proposition is that, in order to do any kind of work, there must not only be something that works but also something that is worked upon; in other words, there must be both an active and a passive factor. The scope of this book will not allow me to discuss the process by which the Duality is evolved from Unity, though physical science supplies us with very clear analogies. But in general terms, the Universal Passive is evolved by the Universal Active as its necessary complement and provides all those conditions which are required to enable the Active Principle to manifest itself in the varied forms that constitute the successive stages of Evolution; and the interaction of these two reciprocal principles throughout Nature is as clearly indicated by the Sacred Name as the principle of Unity itself.

And the Threefold nature of all defined being at once follows from the recognition of these two interacting principles, for whatever is produced by their interaction can be neither a simple reproduction of the Active principle alone nor of the Passive alone, but must be an intermingling of the two, combining in itself the nature of both, and thus possessing an independent nature of its own, which is not exactly that of either of the originating principles.

Other and very important deductions again follow from this one, but they cannot be adequately entered upon in an introductory book like the present; still, enough has now been said to show that the Name "Jehovah" contains in itself the Three Fundamental Principles of the Universe — the Unity, the Duality, and the Trinity — and by their inclusion in a single word affirms that no contradiction exists between them, but that they are all necessary phases of the Universal Truth, which is only ONE.

Much search has been made by many for what the Cabalists call "the Lost Word", that "Word of Power" the possession of which makes all things possible to him who discovers it. Great students of bygone days devoted their lives to this search, such as Reuchlin in Germany and Pico della Mirandola in Italy and, so far as the outside world judges, without any result; while later centuries discredited their studies by comparison with the practical nature of the Baconian philosophy, not wotting that Bacon (Sir Francis Bacon, 1561-1626) himself was a leader in the school to which these men belonged. (Essays of Francis Bacon)

But now the tide is beginning to turn, and improved methods of scientific research are approaching, from the physical side, that One Great Center in which all lines of truth eventually converge; and so the fast-spreading recognition of Man's spiritual nature is leading once more to the search for "the Word of Power". And rightly did the old Hebrew builders and their followers in the fifteenth, sixteenth, and seventeenth centuries connect this "Lost Word" with the Sacred name; but whether because they purposely surrounded it with mystery, or because the simplicity of the truth proved a stumbling-block to them, their open writings only indicate a search through endless mazes, while the clue to the labyrinth lay in the Word itself.

Are we any nearer its discovery now? The answer is at once Yes and No. The "Lost Word" was as close to those old thinkers as it is to us, but to those whose eyes and ears are sealed by prejudice, it will always remain as far off as though it belonged to another planet. The Bible, however, is most explicit upon this subject; and as in the children's game the hidden thimble is concealed from the seekers by its very conspicuousness, so the concealment of the "Lost Word" lies in its absolute simplicity.

Nothing so commonplace could possibly be it, and yet the Scripture plainly tells us that its intimate familiarity is the token by which we shall know it. We need not say, "Who shall go up for us to heaven and bring it unto us, that we may hear it and do it? Neither is it beyond the sea that thou shouldst say, Who shall go over the sea for us and bring it unto us, that we hear it and do it? But the Word is very nigh unto thee, in thy mouth and in thy heart, that thou mayest do it" (Deut. 30: 12-14). Realize that the only "Word of Power" is the Divine Name, and the mystery at once flashes into light.

The "Lost Word" which we have been seeking to discover with pain and cost and infinite study has been all the time in our heart and in our mouth. It is nothing else than that familiar expression which we use so many times a day: I AM. This is the Divine Name revealed to Moses at the burning bush, and it is the Word that is enshrined in the Name Jehovah; and if we believe that the Bible means what it says when it tells us that Man is the image and likeness of God, then we shall see that the same statement of Being, which in the Universal applies to God, must in the individual and particular apply to Man also.

This "Word" is always in our hearts, for the consciousness of our own individuality consists only in the recognition that I AM, and the assertion of our own being as one of the necessities of ordinary speech is upon our lips continually. Thus the "Word of Power" is close at hand to everyone, and it continues to be the "Lost Word" only because of our ignorance of all that is enfolded in it.

A comparison of the teaching of Moses and Jesus will show that they are two complementary statements of the one fundamental truth of the "I AM". Moses views this truth from the standpoint of Universal being and sees man evolving from the Infinite Mind and subject to it as the Great Law-giver. Jesus views it from the standpoint of the individual and sees Man comprehending the Infinite by limitless expansion of his own mind, and thus returning to the Universal Mind as a son coming back to his natural place in the house of his father.

Each is necessary to the correct understanding of the other, and thus Jesus came not to abrogate the work of Moses, but to complete it. The "I AM" is ever in the forefront of his teaching: "I AM the Way, the Truth, and the Life" (John 14:6); "I AM the Resurrection and the Life" (John 11:25); "Except ye believe I AM ye shall perish in your sins" (John 8:24). These and similar sayings shine forth with marvelous radiance when once we see that he was not speaking of himself personally, but of the Individualized Principle of Being in the generic sense which is applicable to all mankind.

What is wanted is our recognition of that innermost self which is pure Spirit, and therefore not subject to any conditions whatever. All conditions arise from one combination or another of the two original conditions, Time and Space; and since these two primary conditions can have no place in essential being and are only created by its Thought, the true recognition of the "I AM" is a recognition of the Self, which sees it as eternally subsisting in its own Being, sending forth all forms at its will and withdrawing them again at its pleasure.

To know this is to know Life-in-itself; and any knowledge short of this is only to know the appearance of Life, to recognize merely the activity of the vehicles through which it functions, while failing to recognize the motive power itself. It is recognizing only "EVE" without "YOD". The "Word of Power" which sets us free is the whole Divine Name, and not one part of it without the other. It is the separation of its two portions, the Masculine and the Feminine, that has caused the long and weary pilgrimage of mankind through the ages.

The separation of the two elements of the Divine Name is not true in the Heart of Being, but Man, by reasoning only from the testimony of the outward senses, forcibly puts asunder what God forever joins together; and it is because the Bridegroom has thus been taken away that the children of the bride-chamber have been starved upon meager fare, coarse and hardly earned, when they ought to have feasted with continual joy.

But the Great Marriage of Heaven and Earth at last takes place, and all nature joins in the song of exultation, a glorious epithalamium (a song celebrating the joining together in marriage) whose cadences roll on through the ages, ever spreading into fresh harmonies as new themes evolve from the first grand wedding march which celebrates the eternal union of the Mystical Marriage.

When this union is realized by the individual as subsisting in himself, then the I AM becomes to him personally all that the Master said it would. He realizes that it is in him a deathless principle and that though its mode of self-expression may alter, its essential Beingness, which is the I Myself consciousness in each of us, never can; and so this principle is found to be in us both Life and Resurrection. As Life, it never ceases; and as Resurrection, it is continually providing higher and higher forms for its expression of Itself, which is ourself.

No matter what may be our particular theory of the specific modus operandi (method of operation) by which this renewal takes place, there can be no mistake about the principle; our physical theory of the Resurrection may be wrong, but the Law that Life will always provide a suitable form, for its self-expression is unchangeable and universal and must, therefore, be as true of the Life-Principle manifesting itself as the individuality which I AM, as in all its other modes of manifestation.

When we thus realize the true nature of the I AM that I AM — that is, the Beingness that I Myself AM — we discover that the whole principle of Being is in ourselves — not "Eve" only, but "YOD" also; and this being the case, we no longer have to go with our pitcher to draw temporary draughts from a well outside, for now we discover that the exhaustless spring of Living Water is within ourselves.

Now we can see why it is that except we believe in the I AM, we must perish in our sins, for "sin is the transgression of the Law" (1 John 3:4), and ignorant infraction of the Law will bring its penalty as certainly as willful infraction. "Ignorantia legis nominem excusat" (Ignorance of the law is no excuse) is a legal maxim which obtains throughout Nature, and the innocent child who ignorantly applies a light to a barrel of gunpowder will be as ruthlessly blown up as the anarchist who perishes in the perpetration of some hideous outrage. If, therefore, we ignorantly controvert the Law of our own Being, we must suffer the inevitable consequences by our failure to rise into that Life of Liberty and Joy which the full knowledge of the power of our I AM-ness must necessarily carry with it.

Let us remember that Perfect Liberty is our goal. The perfect Law is the Law of Liberty. The Tree of Life is the Tree of Liberty, and it is not a plant of spontaneous growth; but as the center of the Mystical Garden, it is its chief glory and therefore deserves the most assiduous cultivation. But it yields its produce as it grows and does not keep us waiting till it reaches maturity before giving us any reward for work; for if maturity means a point at which it will grow no more, then it will never reach maturity, for since the ground in which this Tree has its root is the Eternal Life-in-itself, there is nowhere in the Universe any power to limit its growth and so, under intelligent cultivation, it will go on expanding into increasing strength, beauty, and fruitfulness forever.

This is the meaning of the Scriptural saying, "His reward is with him and his work before him" (Isaiah 40:10 and 62:11). Ordinarily, we should suppose it would be the other way; but when we see that the possibilities of self-expansion are endless and depend on our intelligent study and work, and that at every step of the way we are bound to derive all present benefit from the degree of knowledge we are working up to, it becomes clear that the sacred text has kept the right order, and that always our reward is with us and our work before us; for the reward is the continually increasing joy and glory of perpetually unfolding Life.

All along the line our progress depends on working up to the knowledge we possess, for what we do not act up to we do not really believe; and the power which will overcome all difficulties is confidence in the Eternal Life-in-ourself, which is the individualized expression of the ONE I AM that spoke to Moses at the burning bush.

For what is meant by the burning bush? Surely, as we see the refugee feeding Jethro's flock in the solitude of the desert and gazing on the Fire enveloping the bush without consuming it, we realize that here again we are turning over the pages of a sacred picture-book which first attracts the little child with its vivid scenes painted in glowing colours of a wonderful Eastern life in the dim far-back ages, which prompts him as he grows older to ask the meaning of the pictures, and which at last reveals it to him in the discovery that they are pictures neither of the East nor of the West, not of this century nor of that, but of all time and of all place, and that he himself is the central figure of them all.

The Bible is the picture-book of the evolution of Man, and this particular picture of the "burning bush" is that of human individuality in its unity with the all-enveloping Fire of the Universal Spirit of Life. The "bush" represents "Wood", which under its Greek name of "hulé", we recognize as the generic term for "Matter"; and the "burning bush" thus signifies the union of Spirit and Matter into a single whole, that perfectness of manifested Being in which the lower principles of the individual are recognized as forming the vehicle for the concentrating of the All-originating Spirit. The "bush" still remains a bush, but it is a glorified bush sending forth a glorious aura of warmth and light, from the midst of which proceeds the creative voice of the I AM. This is the great truth symbolized by the revelation to Moses as he fed his father-in-law's flock in the wilderness and, as the same revelation comes to each of us now, the words of that other Prophet of whom Moses spoke become clear to us, and we see that by realizing the true being of the I AM in ourselves, we grasp that principle which will put an end to our infraction of the Law, because it is the very Law itself forever becoming personal with our own personality.

This, then is the great truth we learn from the Name "Jehovah". As the Name is infinite, so also will be the expansions of its meaning; but this book not being infinite, I have been able only to touch on the broad outlines of its vastness; still, enough has been said to give the clue we were seeking, to elucidate the meaning of other forms of the Sacred Name.

Naturally, the reader will think of that other Name, of which it is written that there is none other under heaven whereby we may be saved, which statement at once confronts us with the assertion that we are saved by a Name. "What's in a name?" asks Shakespeare — or Bacon (an allusion to the suspicion that William Shakespeare was a pseudonym for Francis Bacon or a co-operative of writers led by Bacon.). A good deal, we suppose, when we meet with such a statement as this, or its Old Testament equivalent, "the Name of the Lord is a strong tower; the righteous runneth into it and is safe" (Prov. 18:10).

But we have already found that the Great Name of the Old Testament is something very different from a merely personal appellation, and the same is true of the Great Name of the New Testament also. It is, indeed, the name of that Prophet of the I AM whom Moses predicted as completing the work which he had begun; but precisely because he is the Representative Man of all ages, his Name must represent all that constitutes Perfected Humanity.

And it is so with a Divine simplicity. It is the combination of the earthly name with the heavenly: Jesus, at the time a very common name among the Jews, and Christ, which is not a name but a description, "the Anointed One". Each name is the proper complement of the other, and together they indicate the sublime truth that the anointing of the Divine Spirit is the birthright of every human being, only awaiting our recognition of our true nature to show Itself with power. The carpenter — the workman with his everyday name — is the Christ; and the lesson to be learned is that the ONE I AM is in every man, and that that forming of Christ in us which St Paul speaks of is a personal development in accordance with recognizable laws inherent in every human being. If Christ is the Great Example, it must be as the Example of that which we have it in us to become, and not of something entirely foreign to our nature; and it is because of this community of nature that he is "the first-born among many brethren" (Rom. 8:29).

The space at my disposal will not allow me to enter here into the deeply important questions of the Nativity and the Resurrection. The Bible affirms them both, and they are necessary and logical results of that specialized and selective line of Evolution of which I have spoken (see Involution and Evolution); but to show the sequence of cause and effect by which this is brought about, and its dependence upon the initial Impersonal nature of the Universal Mind, is not to be done in a few pages.

If, however, I should meet with sufficient encouragement from the readers of the present volume, I hope to follow it up with another in which these topics will be discussed (see The Creative Process in the Individual), and in the meanwhile we may learn from the generalization contained in the Great Name of the New Testament that lesson of the Brotherhood of Humanity which the Master has impressed upon us in the words, "The King shall answer and say unto them, Verily I say unto you, inasmuch as ye have done it unto one of the least of these My brethren, ye have done it unto Me" (Matt. 25:40). The Name of Jesus Christ is, therefore, the proclamation of the inherent Divine nature of Man, with all its limitless possibilities, and is thus once more the statement of the Bible's initial proposition that Man is made in the image and likeness of God.

And these thoughts recall yet another of the Divine Names which teaches the same lesson: Immanuel, "God with us", or, as it might perhaps be rendered, "God in us", "Immanent God", the finding of God in ourselves, which is in exact accordance with the Master's teaching that the Kingdom of Heaven is within us. This Name, which occurs in Isaiah 7:14, speaks for itself, and should be compared with the description given in Isaiah 9:6-7, which is the old familiar Christmas text, "Unto us a child is born", etc. Now, whoever the "us" may be, the prophet clearly speaks of the Wonderful Child as being born to them. They are the parents and He is their child. But in the description which follows, we are told equally clearly that He is "the Everlasting Father"; and the teaching of Jesus leaves us in no doubt that "the Father" is the Divine All-creating Spirit, which is therefore "the Father" of the "us" who are the parents of the child.

This lands us in a curious paradox. There can be no reasonable doubt that the word "us" is here spoken of human personalities, and that in the same breath the Divine Being who is spoken of as their Father is announced to them as their Child. We have therefore here a sequence of three generations: the Father of the parents, the "us" who are the parents, and the Child who is born to them; and since the Father of the parents and the Child of the parents is said to be the same Being, there is no avoiding the conclusion that the wonderful Child is his own Grandfather, and vice versa.

This is one of those sacred puzzles of which many instances occur in the Bible, and whose meaning is clear enough when we know the answer, and the purpose of which is to lead us to look for an answer which will put us in possession of the great truth which it is the purpose of all Scripture to teach us. The riddle propounded by Isaiah, "What is it which becomes its own grandson?" is substantially the same with which the Master posed the scribes when he asked them how David's son could at the same time be his Lord (Luke 20:41); and the identity of the question is apparent from the fact that in the passage in Isaiah we are told that this wonderful child shall sit on the throne of David.

A further description of him occurs in Isaiah 11:1, where we again find the same three stages — first Jesse, next the stem proceeding out of Jesse, and lastly the Rod or Branch growing out of the stem. Now Jesse is the father of David, and therefore "the Branch" is the same person regarding whom Isaiah and Jesus propounded their conundrums. Placing these four remarkable passages together, we get the following description of the wonderful child:

> His name is Immanuel.
> His father's name is David.
> His grandfather's name is Jesse.
> And He is His own grandfather and Lord over His father.

What is it that answers to this description? Again we find the solution of the enigma in the names. "Jesse" means "to be" or "he that is", which at once brings us back to all we have learned concerning the Universal I AM — the ONE Eternal Spirit which is "the Everlasting Father".

"David" means "the Beloved", or the man who realizes his true relation to the Infinite Spirit; and the description of Daniel as a man greatly beloved and who had set his heart to understand (Daniel 10:11) shows that it is this set purpose of seeking to understand the nature of the Universal Spirit and the mode of our own relation to it that raises the individual to the position of David or "the Beloved".

This is in strict agreement with the Master's teaching to the woman of Samaria (John 4), that the Eternal Spirit, which is "the Father", seeks those who will worship, not according to this or that form, but in spirit and in truth, having a real knowledge of what it is they worship and of the true nature of the mental act they perform. "We know what we worship" is the mark by which Jesus distinguishes the worship of the "Israelites indeed", the "People of the I AM", from that of the Samaritans, though fully recognizing the right intention of their worship of the "unknown God" (Compare John 4:22 with Acts 17:23).

It was after his successful wrestling with the Divine Being, and in consequence of his determination not to let go until it had been fully revealed, that Jacob obtained the name of "Israel" (Jacob and Personal Struggle).

Then from the individual's illuminated recognition of the Truth of Being — the discovery that he himself is the concentration of the Universal Spirit into particular personality — there necessarily arises the reproduction of the Universal Spirit in the Individual Mind. This is re-generation; that is to say, the second generating of the Divine UNIT as another Unity or manifestation of itself in the form of the Individual, in no way differing in nature from the original All-embracing

Unit, but only in the mode of expression, having now become individual personality with all the attributes of personality.

On the plane of the Universal, the place of these more highly specialized attributes was held by a generic tendency towards life-givingness, increase, and beauty; and this generic tendency the reproduced Unit now follows up with the additional powers it has evolved by the attainment of self-recognizing individuality.

The new personality thus generated may be considered as the child of the individual soul which gives birth to it; and since there is only ONE Spirit anywhere and everywhere, it can be only another mode of the original ONE. Consequently, the "Son" who is thus born to David, "the Beloved", is himself "the Everlasting Father", and thus the answer to the sacred puzzle is that the man who has really learned the inner meaning of the words "know thyself" discovers that the true I AM in himself is one with the Universal I AM, which is the root of all individualized being.

It is in the light of these sublime truths that the Name of "the Son" is equally with that of "the Father" the Sacred name, in the true knowledge of which salvation is alone to be found. For what do we mean by "Salvation"? "That we might be saved from the hand of all that hate us" (Luke 1:71) is the answer; that is, from the power of everything that militates against our enjoyment of the fullest life. That we might attain to continually increasing degrees of Life was the declared object of the Master's mission, and therefore salvation means the power to ask and receive that our joy may be full; and the only way this power can ever come to us is by the recognition of our own possibilities as being each of us the image and likeness of God.

Therefore it is written, "to them gave He power to become the Sons of God, even to them that believe in His Name" (John 1:12) and the word rendered "power" may also be rendered as "right", so that this passage assures us both of our power and right to take possession of our inheritance as sons and daughters of the Almighty. Now mark well that this promise is not held forth as a reward for the acceptance of some theological speculation which conveys no real meaning to us and which by its very terms must be incapable of proof; but it is the natural and logical outcome of the initial proposition with which the Bible opens, that Spirit is the ONE and Only Source, Origin, and Substance of all things, a self-evident truth the contrary of which it is impossible to conceive.

What I here call "Spirit" you may, if you please, call "the Unknowable", or x, or denote it by a single stroke; the name or symbol we choose is quite immaterial, so long as we grasp the fact that the initial Originating Power must of necessity reproduce Itself all the way down the scale, no matter how different the forms under which it does so. In whatever way we may denote It, It is always the Great Expressor; and all that is, we ourselves included, is Its Expression of Itself, so that the whole teaching of Truth may be summed up in the words, "The Expressor and the Expressed are ONE".

Work out the problem in any way you will and you will never arrive at any other final result than this; and so we always come back to that fundamental axiom which Jesus announced as the supreme statement of the LAW. This is the great truth enshrined in every form of the Sacred Name; and therefore it is that every form of the Great Name, when rightly understood, is found to be "the Word of Power".

But we must never forget that the opening description of Man, as made in the image and likeness of God, has added to it the words "male and female created He them" (Gen 1:27) and if we grasp the full significance of this statement, we shall see that the recognition of Truth is not complete unless we realize the place of the Passive or Feminine element in Being. It is for this reason that in ancient times initiation could be entered upon either along the Doric or Ionic line (i.e. in the tradition of the Greek Mysteries), the former being more especially for males and the latter for females; but by whichever line it was commenced, a perfect initiation implied a return along the opposite line, in accordance with St Paul's dictum that "neither is the man without the woman, neither the woman without the man, in the Lord" (1 Cor. 11:2), and therefore there are not wanting in Scripture statements of the Sacred Name answering to this fact.

One of the most remarkable of these is found in Hosea 2:16: "And it shall be at that day, saith the Lord, that thou shalt call Me Ishi, and shalt call me no more Baali". What is the meaning of this change of Name? Realize that a name has a meaning, and it becomes clear that some radical change must be intended. But this cannot be any change in the Divine Being, for from first to last the Scripture bears emphatic testimony to the unchangeableness of "God". "I AM the Lord, I change not; therefore ye sons of Jacob are not consumed", says the Old Testament (Malachi 3:6); "The Father of light with whom there is no variableness, neither shadow of turning", says the New (James 1:17).

The change cannot, then, be in the nature of "God", and therefore cannot be a change in the Law by which that nature expresses itself; consequently, it can only be a change in the conditions under which the Law is working. Now this is precisely the sort of change that is spoken of. "Baali" means Lord, the master of a servant, the proprietor of a slave. "Ishi", on the other hand, means "Husband", and the change of name therefore indicates a change in the condition of some feminine element towards its correlative masculine element.

This corresponding change is stated in Isaiah 62:4: "Thou shalt no more be termed Forsaken, neither shall thy land any more be termed Desolate, but thou shalt be called Hephzibah, and thy land Beulah; for the Lord delighteth in thee, and thy land shall be married". The word "Hephzibah" is rendered in the margin "my delight", which is sufficiently significant, but its derivation is from the Semitic root "hafz", which in all its combinations always carries the idea of protection or guarding; and the name Hephzibah may therefore be more accurately rendered "a guarded one", thus at once recalling the words in which the New Testament describes those "who by the power of God are guarded through faith unto salvation" (1 Peter 1:5, R.V.).

Now the change indicated by these names is that of a female slave who is set free by her master and then married by him, and I think it would be impossible to hit upon a more accurate analogy for describing the emancipation of the soul from bondage and its establishment in a relation of confidence and love towards the Divine Universal Mind.

We must never forget the feminine nature of the soul relatively to the Universal Mind. Their Union produces the Wonderful Child who shall rule all things, and who is the Essential Male called in the Bible "the Son"; but the soul itself is, and always must be, feminine. Until she becomes illumined, the soul can only conceive of God as a master whom she is bound to obey, and hence she strives to keep in His good graces by sacrifices, ceremonies, and observances of all sorts — He is "Baali" and must be propitiated. But when the liberating light breaks upon her, she discovers that the Universal Principle has hitherto held this relation to her because she had conceived of It only in this way and had thus provided It only with such conditions as compelled It to exhibit Itself in this form.

Now she learns that these conditions are not imposed by the Universal Principle Itself, but that it must of necessity follow that line of expression which each particular individuality opens up for It; and when this is clearly perceived, with all the consequences that flow from it, the soul finds that she is no longer a slave but is in perfect Liberty, and that her relation to the Great Mind is that of a beloved wife, guarded, honoured, and treated on terms of equality.

This is the truth illustrated, as St Paul tells us, in the allegory of Sarah and Hagar. Hagar, the slave, is expelled, and Sarah, the Princess, takes her place. These two symbolical women, like the two "women" of Revelation, indicate two opposite conditions of the soul; and similarly their "sons", like the offspring of those two other "women", represent the respective powers which these two conditions of soul generate — the one living in the wilderness of secondary causes and becoming an archer — that is, relying upon the use of external means, not understanding the true nature of causation, and therefore dependent for his results upon just happening to make a good shot, and often making very bad ones — the other, like Isaac, the acknowledged heir of all the Father's possessions, assuming gradually more and more of his powers and responsibilities until, by the combined influence of natural growth and careful training, he at last attains that mature development which qualifies him to participate in the administration of the paternal authority.

The true relation of the individual soul to the Universal Principle could not be more perfectly depicted than by the names Ishi and Hephzibah. We have only to turn to any well-ordered family to see the force of the illustration. The respective spheres of the husband and wife as the heads of such a household are clearly defined. The husband provides the supplies and the wife distributes them, and each has that confidence in the other which renders any interference with one another's action quite unnecessary.

This is the precise analogue of the relation between the individual and the Universal Mind. The individual mind is not the creator of power, but the distributor of it, just as in physical science we realize that we do not create energy, but only change its form and direction. But exactly as the Universal store of Nature from which we draw physical energy does not dictate to us in what form, in what quantities, or for what purpose we shall use it, so in like manner the Universal principle does not dictate the specific conditions under which it is to be employed, but will manifest itself according to any conditions that we may provide for it by our own mental attitude; and therefore the only limitations to be laid upon our use of it are those arising from the Law of Love. Liberty without Love is Destruction, and Love without Liberty is Despair.

Just as in photography we need for the production of a perfect image the combined action of an accelerator and a restrainer (i.e. of the chemical reactions), so to produce perfect images of the Divine strength, beauty, and gladness, we require a self-projecting force which is the full liberty of Creative Power, combined with a directing and restraining force which is the tenderness of wisdom and love; and so in the description of the Perfect Woman we read that in her mouth is the Law of Kindness. Hephzibah, the Perfect Woman, rules her household wisely in love and so applies the raw material, which she can draw from her husband's storehouse without stint, that, by her diligence and understanding, she converts it into all those varied forms of use and beauty which are indicated under the similitudes of domestic provision and merchandise in the thirty-first chapter of Proverbs.

We find, then, two aspects of the Sacred name: one which presents it as the Universal I AM, the All-productive Power which is the root of all manifestation, and thus includes all individualities within Itself, involving them in the circulus of Its own movement; and the other indicative of the reciprocal relation between this Power and the individual soul. But there is yet a third aspect under which this Power may be viewed, and that is as working through the individual who has become conscious of his own relation to it and of his consequent direction and instruction by it. In this sense the Old Testament enumerates its Names in the text I have already quoted: "His Name shall be called Wonderful, Counselor, the Mighty God, the Everlasting Father, and the Prince of Peace" (Isaiah 9:6). In the Book of Job this is called "the Interpreter" (3:23), and in the New Testament this Name is called "The Word".

What may be the nature of the Divine Self-consciousness in itself is a matter on which we can in no way profitably speculate; to do so is trying to analyze that which, as the starting-point of all else, must necessarily be incapable of analysis for the simple reason that there can be nothing before the First. But what we can realize is the mode in which we experience our own relation to the Originating Spirit, and this will be found to form a threefold recognition of it, corresponding with what I have said above. Our primary recognition of the Spirit is that of an All-embracing Universal Principle, a simple Unity; but gradually we shall come to find that our perception of this Unity contains enfolded in It a threefold relation to our personality which implies the existence of a corresponding threefold aspect in the Unity. We must always recollect that all we can know of God is our own consciousness of our relation to Him, and eventually we shall find that this relation is, first, generic, as to the Creating Spirit; secondly, specific, as forming a particular class of individuals holding a special relation to the Spirit; and thirdly, individual, as differentiated units of this particular class. Thus by a Law of Reciprocity, we realize "the Father" or Parent Spirit, "the Son" or Divine Ideal of Human Personality, and "the Holy Spirit" as the operation of the Original Spirit upon the individual, resulting from the individual's recognition of his relation to the Father in a Divine Sonship. Seen in this light, the doctrine of the Trinity in Unity ceases to be either a contradiction in terms or the conception of a limiting anthropomorphism, but on the contrary it is found to be the statement of the highest experiences of the human soul.

With these preliminary remarks, I would lay particular stress upon the Name given to the Universal Principle in its Third aspect, that of manifestation through the individual mind. In this sense it is emphatically called "The Word", and a study of comparative religions shows that this conception of the Universal Mind, manifesting Itself as Speech, has been reached by all the great race-religions in their deeper significances. The "Logos" of Greek philosophy, the "Vach" of the Sanskrit, are typical instances, and the reason is to be found, as in all statements of truth, in the nature of the thing itself.

The Biblical account of creation represents the work as completed by the appearing of Man; that is to say, the evolutionary process culminates in the Creative Principle expressing Itself in a form differing from all lower ones in its capacity for reasoning. Now reasoning implies the use of words either spoken or employed mentally, for whether we wish to make the stages of an argument plain to another or to ourselves, it can only be done by putting the sequence of cause and effect into words.

The first idea suggested by the principle of Speech is, therefore, that of individual intelligence, and next, as following from this, we get the idea of expressing individual will; then, as we begin to realize the reciprocal relation between the Universal Mind and the individual mind, which necessarily results from the latter being an evolution from the former, our conception of intelligence and volition becomes extended from the individual to the Universal, and we see that because these qualities exist in human personality, they must exist in some more generalized mode in that Universal Mind, of which the individual mind is a more specialized reproduction; and so we arrive at the result that the Speech-principle is the highest expression of the Divine Wisdom, Power, and Love, whose combined action produces what we call Creation.

In this sense, then, the Bible attributes the creation of the world to the Divine Word, and it therefore rightly says that "In the beginning was The Word, and The Word was with God, and The Word was God", and that without The Word "was not anything made that was made"; and from this commencement, the natural sequence of evolution brings us to the crowning result in the manifestation of The Word as Man, at first ignorant of his Divine origin, but nevertheless containing all the potentialities which the recognition of his true nature as the image of God will enable him to develop. And when at length this recognition comes to anyone, he arises and returns to "The Father", and in the discovery of his true relation to the Divine Mind finds that he also is a child of the Almighty and can speak "the Word of Power".

He may have been the prodigal who has wasted his substance, or the respectable brother who thought that only limited supplies were doled out to him; but as soon as the truth dawns upon him, he realizes the meaning of the words, "Son, thou art always with Me, and all that I have is thine" (Luke 15:31). In Its Third aspect as "the Word", the Universal Principle becomes specialized. In its earlier modes it is the Life-Principle working by a Law of Averages, and thus maintaining the race as a whole, but not providing special accommodation for the individual. And it is inconceivable that the Cosmic Power, as such, should ever pass beyond what we may call the administration of the world in globo (i.e. in a global sense), for to suppose It doing so would involve the self-contradiction of the Universal acting on the plane of the Particular without becoming the particular; and it is precisely by becoming the particular, or by evolution into individual minds, that it carries on the work beyond the stage at which things are governed by a mere Law of Averages.

It is thus that we become "fellow-workers with God" and that "the Father" is represented as inviting His sons to work in His vineyard. By recognition of his own true place in the scheme of evolution, Man learns that his function is to carry on the work which has been begun in the Universal to still further applications in the Particular, thus affording the key to the Master's words, "My Father worketh hitherto, and I work" (John 5:17); and the instrument by which the instructed man does this is his knowledge of the Sacred Name in its Threefold significance.

The study of the sacred name is the study of the Livingness of Being and of the Law of Expression in all its phases, and no book or library of books is sufficient to cope with such a vast idea. All any writer can do is to point out the broad lines of the subject, and each reader must make his own personal application of it. But the Law remains forever that the sincere desire for Truth produces a corresponding unfoldment of Truth, and the supreme Truth is reached in that final recognition of the Divine Name, "God is Love".

Chapter 8

The Devil

It is impossible to read the Bible and ignore the important part which it assigns to the Devil. The Devil first appears as the Serpent in the story of "the Fall" and figures throughout Scripture till the final scene in Revelation, where "the old Serpent, which is the Devil and Satan", is cast into the lake of fire. What, then, is meant by the Devil? We may start with the self-obvious proposition that "God" and the "Devil" must be the exact opposites of each other. Whatever God is, the Devil is not. Since God is Being, the Devil is Not-Being. And so we are met by the paradox that though the Bible says so much about the Devil, yet the Devil does not exist. It is precisely this fact of non-existence that makes up the Devil; it is that power which in appearance is, and in reality is not; in a word, it is the Power of the Negative.

We are put upon this track by the statement in 2 Corinthians 1:20 that in Christ, all the promises of God are Yea and Amen — that is, essentially Affirmative; in other words, that all our growth towards Perfected Humanity must be by recognition of the Positive and not by recognition of the Negative. The prime fact of Negation is its Nothingness; but owing to the impossibility of ever divesting our Thought of its Creative Power, our conception of the Negative as something having a substantive existence of its own becomes a very real power indeed, and it is this power that the Bible calls "the Devil and Satan", the same old Serpent which we find beguiling Eve in the Book of Genesis. It is equally a mistake to say that there is an Evil Power or that there is not. Let us examine this paradox.

A little consideration will show us that it is impossible for there to be an Infinite and Universal Power of Evil, for unless the Infinite and Universal Power were Creative, nothing could exist. If it be creative, then it is the Life-Principle working always for self-expression, and to suppose the undifferentiated principle of Life acting otherwise than life-givingly would contradict the very idea of its livingness.

Whatever tends to expand and improve life is the Good, and therefore it is a primary intuition from which we cannot get away that the Infinite, Originating, and Maintaining Power can only be Good. But to find this absolute and unchangeable "Good", we require to get to the very bedrock of Being, to that as yet undifferentiated Life-in-itself inherent in, and forming one with, Universal Primordial Substance, of which I have spoken in a former chapter (The Creative Power of Thought). This All-underlying Life is forever expressing itself through Form; but the Form is not the Life, and it is from not seeing this that so much confusion arises.

The Universal Life-Principle, simply as such, finds expression as much in one form as another, and is just as active in the scattered particles which once made a human body as it was in those particles when they cohered together in the living man; this is merely the well-recognized scientific truth of the Conservation of Energy.

On the other hand, we cannot help perceiving that there is something in the individual which exercises a greater power than the perpetual energy residing in the ultimate atoms; for otherwise what is it that maintains in our bodies for perhaps a century the unstable equilibrium of atomic forces which, when that something is withdrawn, cannot continue for twenty-four hours? Is this something another something than that which is at work as the perpetual energy within the atoms? No, for otherwise there would be two originating powers in the Universe, and if our study of the Bible teaches us anything, it is that the Originating Power is only ONE; and we must therefore conceive of the Power we are examining as the same Power that resides in the ultimate atoms, only now working at a higher level. It has welded the atoms into a distinct organism, however lowly, and so to distinguish this mode of power from the mere atomic energies, we may call it the Integrating Power, or the Power that Builds Up.

Now evolution is a continuous process of building up, and what makes the world of today a different world from that of the ichthyosaurus and the pterodactyl is the successive building up of more and more complex organisms, culminating at last in the production of Man as an organism both physically and mentally capable of expressing the Life of the Supreme Intelligence by means of the Individual Consciousness. Why, then, should not the Power, which is able to carry on the race as a perpetually improving expression of itself, do the same thing in the individual? That is the question with which we have to deal; in other words, why need the individual die? Why should he not go on in a perpetual expansion?

This question may seem absurd in the light of past experience. Those who believe only in blind forces answer that death is the law of Nature, and those who believe in the Divine Wisdom answer that it is the appointment of God. But strange as it may seem, both these answers are wrong. That death should be the ultimate law of Nature contradicts the principle of continuity as exemplified in the Lifeward tendency of evolution; and that it is the will of God is most emphatically denied by the Bible, for that tells us that he that has the power of death is the Devil (Hebrews 2:14). There is no beating about the bush; not God but the Devil sends death. There is no getting out of the plain words. Let us examine this statement.

We have seen that whatever God is, the Devil must be the opposite, and therefore if God is the Power that builds up, the Integrating power, the Devil must be the power that pulls down, or the disintegrating power. Now what is disintegration? It is the breaking up of what was previously an "integer" or perfect Whole, the separation of its component parts. But what is it that causes the separation? It is still the Building-up Power, only the Law of Affinity by which it works is now acting from other centers, so as to build up other organisms.

The Universal Power is still at its building work, only it seems to have lost sight of its original motive and to have taken up fresh motives in other directions. And this is precisely the state of the case; it is just the want of continuous motive that causes disintegration. The only possible motive of the All-originating Life-Principle must be the expression of Life, and therefore we may almost picture it as continually seeking to embody itself in intelligences which shall be able to grasp its motive and co-operate with it by keeping that motive constantly in mind.

Granted that this individualization of motive could take place, there appears no reason why it should not continue to work on indefinitely. A tree is an organized center of life, but without the intelligence which would enable it to individualize the motive of the Universal Life-Principle. It individualizes a certain measure of the Universal Vital Energy, but it does not individualize the Universal Intelligence, and therefore when the measure of energy which it has individualized is exhausted, it dies; and the same thing happens with animals and men.

But as the particular intelligence advances in the recognition of itself as the individualization of the Universal Intelligence, it becomes more and more capable of seizing upon the initial motive of the Universal Mind and giving it permanence. And supposing this recognition to be complete, the logical result would be never-ceasing and perpetually expanding individual life, thus bringing us back to those promises which I have quoted in the opening pages of this book, and reminding us of the Master's statement to the woman of Samaria that "the Father" is always "seeking" those who will worship Him in spirit and in truth; that is, those who can enter into the spirit of what "the Father" is aiming at.

But what happens in the absence of a perfect recognition of the Universal Motive is that sooner or later the machinery runs down, and the "motive" is transferred to other centers where the same process is repeated, and so Life and Death alternate with each other in a ceaseless round. The disintegrating process is the Universal Builder taking the materials for fresh constructions from a tenement without a tenant; that is, from an organism which has not reached the measure of intelligence necessary to perpetuate the Universal Motive in itself or, as the Master put it in the parable of the ten virgins, such as have not a supply of oil to keep their lamps burning (Matt. 25).

This Negative disintegrating force is the Integrating Power working, so to say, at a lower level relatively to that at which it had been working in the organism that is being dissolved. It is not another power. Both the Bible and common sense tell us that ultimately there can be only ONE power in the Universe which must, therefore, be the Building-power, so that there can be no such thing as a power which is negative in itself; but it shows itself negatively in relation to the particular individual, if through want of recognition he fails to provide the requisite conditions for it to work positively.

Work it always will, for its very being is ceaseless activity; but whether it will act positively or negatively towards any particular individual depends entirely on whether he provides positive or negative conditions for its manifestation, just as we may produce a positive or negative current according to the electrical conditions which we supply.

We see, then, that what gives the Positive Power a negative action is the failure to intelligently recognize our own individualization of it. In the lower forms of life this failure is inevitable, because they are not provided with an organism capable of such a recognition. In Man, the suitable organism is present, but he seeks knowledge only from past experiences which have necessarily been of the negative order, and does not, by the combined action of reason and faith, look into the Infinite for the unfoldment of limitless possibilities; and so he employs his intelligence to deny that which, if he affirmed it, would be in him the spring of perpetual renovation.

The Power of the Negative, therefore, has its root in the denial of the Affirmative; and so we die because we have not yet learned to understand the Principle of Life; we have yet to learn the great Law, that "the higher mode of intelligence controls the lower". In consequence of our ignorance, we attribute an affirmative power to the Negative — that is to say, the power of taking an initiative on its own account, not seeing that it is a condition resulting from the absence of something more positive; and so the power of the Negative consists in affirming that to be true which is not true, and for this reason it is called in scripture the father of lies, or that principle from which all false statements are generated.

The word "Devil" means "false accuser" or "false affirmer", and this name is therefore in itself sufficient to show us that what is meant is the creative principle of Affirmation used in the wrong direction, a truth which has been handed down to us from old times in the saying "Diabolus est Deus inversus" (The Devil is God inverted). This is how it is that "the Devil" can be a vast impersonal power while at the same time having no existence, and so the paradox with which we started is solved. And now it becomes clear why we are told that "the Devil" has the power of death. It is not held by a personal individual, but results quite naturally from that ignorant and inverted Thought which is "the Spirit that denies".

This is the exact opposite to "the Son of God", in whom all things are only "Yea and Amen". That is the Spirit of the Affirmative and, therefore, the Spirit of Life; and so it is that the Son of God was manifested that "he might destroy him that had the power of death, that is, the Devil, and deliver them who, through fear of death, were all in their lifetime subject to bondage" (Hebrews 2:14-15).

Again, we are told that the Devil is Satan. This name appears to be another form of "Saturn" and may also be connected with the root "sat" or "seven", Saturn being in the old symbolical astronomy the outermost or seventh planet. In that system the center is occupied by Sol or the Sun, which represents the Life-giving Principle, and Saturn represents the opposite extreme, or Matter at the point furthest removed from Pure Spirit.

Now, taken in due order, Matter or Concrete Form is as necessary as Spirit itself, for without it there could be no manifestation of Spirit; in other words, there could be no existence at all. Seen from this point of view, there is nothing evil in it, but on the contrary, it may be compared to the lamp which concentrates the light and gives it a particular direction, and in this respects Matter is called "Lucifer" or the Light-bearer. This is Matter taking its proper place in the order of the Kingdom of Heaven. But if "Lucifer" falls from Heaven, becomes rebellious, and endeavours to usurp the place of "Sol", then it is the fallen Archangel and becomes "Satan", or that outermost planet which moves in an orbit whose remoteness from the warmth and light of the Sun renders all human life and joy impossible, a symbolism which we retain in our common speech when we say that a man has a saturnine aspect.

Thus "Satan" is the same old Serpent that deceived Eve; it is the wrong belief that sets merely secondary causes, which are only conditions, in the place of First Cause or that originating power of Thought which makes enlightened Man the image of his Maker and the Son of God. (For the all-important distinction between Causes and Conditions, see Chapter 9 of my Edinburgh Lectures on Mental Science.)

But we must not make the mistake of supposing that because there is no Universal Devil in the same sense as there is Universal God, therefore there are no individual devils. The Bible frequently speaks of them, and one of the commissions given by the Master to his followers was to cast out devils.

The words used for the Devil are, in the Greek, "Diabolos", and in the Hebrew, "Satan", both having the same general meaning of the Principle of Negation; but individual devils are called in the Hebrew, "sair", a hairy one, and in the Greek, "daimon", a spirit or shade, and these terms indicate evil spirits having personal identity.

Now without stopping to discuss the question whether there are orders of spiritual individuals which have never been human, let us confine our attention to the immense multitudes of disembodied human spirits which, under any hypothesis, must crowd the realms of the unseen. Can we suppose them all to be good? Certainly not, for we have no reason to suppose that mere severance from its physical instrument either changes the moral quality or expands the intelligence of the mind, and therefore if there is such a thing as survival after death at all, we cannot conceive of the other world otherwise than as containing millions upon millions of spirits in various stages of ignorance and ill-will, and consequently ready to make the most unscrupulous use of their powers where opportunity offers.

The time is fast passing away when it will be possible to regard such a conception as fantastic, and taking our stand simply upon the well-ascertained ground of thought-transference and telepathy, we may well ask, if such powers as these can be exercised by the spiritual entity while still clothed in flesh, why should they not be equally, or even more powerfully, employed by spirits out of the flesh?

This opens an immense field of inquiry which we cannot stop to investigate; but setting aside all other classes of evidence on this subject, the experimentally ascertained facts of telepathy bring to light possibilities which would explain all that the Bible says regarding the malefic influence of evil spirits. But the inference to be drawn from this is not that we should go in continual terror of obsession or other injury, but that we should realize that our position as "sons and daughters of the Almighty" places us beyond the reach of such malignant entities.

Our familiar principle, the Law of Attraction, is at work here also. Like attracts like; and if we would keep these undesirable entities at a distance, we can do so most effectually by centering our thoughts on those things which we know from their nature cannot invite evil influences. Let us follow the apostolic advice, and "whatsoever things are true, whatsoever things are honest, whatsoever things are just, whatsoever things are pure, whatsoever things are lovely, whatsoever things are of good report; if there be any virtue and if there be any praise, think on these things" (Philippians 4:8). Then, however far the Law of Attraction may extend from us into the other world, we may rest assured that it will only act to bring us in touch with that innumerable company of angels and spirits of just men made perfect, of whom we are told in the twelfth chapter of Hebrews, and who, because they are joined in the same worship of the ONE Divine Spirit as ourselves, can only act in accordance with the principles of harmony and love.

I will not attempt the analysis of so important a subject in the short space at my disposal, but I would caution all students against tampering with anything that savours of ceremonial magic. However little acknowledged in public, it is by no means infrequently practiced at the present day and, if on no other grounds, it should be resolutely shunned as a powerful system of autosuggestion capable of producing the most disastrous effects on those who employ it. No New Thought reader can be ignorant of the power of autosuggestion, and I would therefore ask each one to think out for himself what the tendency of autosuggestion conducted on such lines as these must be. "I speak as unto wise men, judge what I say (1 Cor. 10:15).

The Bible is by no means silent on this subject, but I may sum up its teaching in a few lines. It assumes, throughout, the possibility of intercourse (i.e. exchange of thoughts or feelings) between men and spirits but, with the exception of the Master's temptation, where I understand a symbolic representation of the general principle of evil — the Power of the Negative which we have already considered — it should be remarked that all its record is of appearances of good angels as ministering spirits to heirs of salvation.

Nor were these visitants sought after by those who received them; their appearance was always spontaneous; and the solitary instance which the Bible records of a spirit appearing whom it was sought to raise by incantation is of the appearance of Samuel to Saul, announcing that his rebellion had culminated in this act of witchcraft, and this was followed by the suicide of Saul on the next day (1 Sam. 28).

If, then, our study of the Bible has led us to the conclusion that it is the statement of the Law of the inevitable sequences of cause and effect, this uniform direction of its teachings must indicate the presence of certain sequences in this connection also, although we may not yet understand them. This knowledge will come to us by degrees with the natural expansion of our powers, and when it arrives in its proper order, we shall be qualified to use it; and if we realize that there is a Universal Mind capable of guiding us at all, we may trust it not to keep back from us anything that it is necessary we should know at each stage of our onward journey. Do we want knowledge? The Master has promised that the Spirit of Truth shall guide us into all truth. "Should not a people seek unto their God instead of unto them that have familiar spirits?" (Isaiah 8:19). There is a reason at the back of all these things.

We thus see that the whole question of the power of evil turns on the two fundamental Laws which I spoke of in the opening pages of this book as forming the basis of Bible teaching: the Law of Suggestion and the Law of the Creative Power of Thought. The conception of an abstract principle of evil, the Devil, receives its power from our own autosuggestion of its existence; and the power of evil spirits results from a mental attitude which allows us to receive their suggestions.

Then in both cases, the suggestion having been accepted, our own creative power of Thought does the rest and so prepares the way for receiving still further suggestions of the same sort. Now the antidote to all this is a right conception of God or the Universal Spirit of Life as the ONE and only originating Power. If we realize that relatively to us this Power manifests itself through the medium of our own Thought, and that in so doing it in no way changes its inherent quality of Life-givingness, this recognition must constitute such a supremely powerful and all-embracing Suggestion as must necessarily eradicate all suggestions of a contrary description; and so our Thought, being based on this Supreme Suggestion of Good, is certain to have a correspondingly life-giving character.

To recognize the essential One-ness of this Power is to recognize it as God, and to recognize its essential Life-givingness is to recognize it as Love, and so we shall realize in ourselves the truth that "God is Love". Then "if God be for us, who can be against us?" (Romans 8:31) and so we realize the further truth that "perfect love casteth out fear" (1 John 4:18), with the result that in our own world there can be no devil.

Chapter 9

The Law of Liberty

Nothing is more indicative of our ignorance regarding the purpose and meaning of the Bible than the distinction which it is often sought to draw between the Law and the Gospel. We are told of different "dispensations", as though the Divine method of conducting the world changed after the fashion of political constitutions. If this were the case, we should never know under what system of administration we were living, for we could only be informed of these alterations by persons who were "in the know" with the Divine Power, and we should have nothing but their bare assertion to justify their claims.

This is the logical outcome of any system which is based upon the allegation of specific determination by a Divine Autocrat. It cannot be otherwise, and therefore all such systems are destined sooner or later to fall to pieces, because their foundation of so-called "authority" crumbles away under the scrutiny of intelligent investigation. The Divine orderings can only be known by the Divine workings, and the intelligent study of the Divine working is the only criterion which the Bible, rightly understood, anywhere sets up for the recognition of Truth.

All of the Psalms are based entirely on this principle, and the Master claimed their testimony to his mission. He himself spoke of tradition as rendering void the true Law of God; and so far from claiming to introduce any new dispensation, he emphatically declared that his special business was to fulfill the Law — that is, to demonstrate it in all its completeness. If the Law taught by Moses is true, and the Gospel preached by Jesus is true, then they are both true together and are simply statements of the same Truth from different standpoints; and the proofs of their truth will be found in their agreement with one another and with the universal principles of Natural Law which we can learn by the study of ourselves and of our environment.

If the Old and New Testaments are right in saying that the foundation of all other knowledge is that God is ONE, then we may be certain that we are on the wrong track if we think that Divine Truth can be different at one time to what it is at another. We realize the principle of "continuity" throughout physical nature, and if we see that the physical must originate in the spiritual, we cannot deny the extension of "continuity" throughout the entire system; and therefore, if the messages of the Old and New Testaments are both true, we may expect to find the same principle of "continuity" running through both. On investigation this will be found to be the case, and no truer definition can be given of the Gospel than that it is the Law worked out to its logical conclusions.

The Law which the Bible sets forth from first to last is the Law of Human Individuality. The Bible is the spiritual Natural History Book of Man. It begins with his creation by evolution from the kingdoms which had preceded him, and it terminates with his apotheosis. The line is long, but it is straight, and reaches its glorious destination by an orderly sequence of cause and effect. It is the statement of the evolution of the individual as the result of his recognition of the Law by which he came to be a human being at all. When he sees that this happened neither by chance nor by arbitrary command, then, and not till then, will he wake up to the fact that he is what he is by reason of a Law inherent in himself, the action of which he can therefore carry on indefinitely by correctly understanding and cheerfully following it.

His first general perception that there is such a Law at all is followed by the realization that it must be the Law of his own individuality, for he has only discovered the existence of the Law by recognizing himself as the Expression of it; and therefore he finds that, before all else, the Law is that he shall be himself. But a Law which allows us to be ourselves is Perfect Liberty, and thus we get back to St James' statement that the Perfect Law is the Law of Liberty.

Obviously it is not Liberty to allow ourselves to be depressed into such a mental attitude of submission to every form and degree of misery as coming to us "by the will of God" that we at last reach a condition of apathy in which one blow more or less makes very little difference. Such teaching is based on the Devil's beatitude — "Blessed are they that expect nothing, for they shall not be disappointed" — but that is not the Gospel of Deliverance which Jesus preached in his first discourse in the synagogue of Nazareth. Jesus' teaching was not the deification of suffering, but the fullness of Joy; and he emphatically declared that all bondage — everything which keeps us from enjoying our life to the full — is the working of that Power of the Negative which the Bible calls the Devil. To give up hope and regard ourselves as the sport of an inexorable fate is not Liberty. It is not obedience to a higher power, but abject submission to a lower — the power of ignorance, unintelligence, and negation.

Perfect Liberty is the consciousness that we are not thus bound by any power of evil but that, on the contrary, we are centers in which the Creative Spirit of the Universe finds particular expression. Then we are in harmony with its continual progressive movement towards still more perfect modes of expression, and therefore its thought and our thought, its action and our action, become identical, so that in expressing the Spirit we express ourselves. When we reach this unity of consciousness, we cannot but find it to be perfect Liberty; for our own self-expression, being also that of the All-creating Spirit as it manifests in our individuality, is no longer bound by antecedent conditions, but starts afresh from the standpoint of Original Creative Energy.

This is Liberty according to Law, the Law of the All-creating Harmony, in which God's way and our way coincide. The idea of Liberty, without a unifying Harmony as its basis, is inconceivable, for with everyone struggling to get their own way at somebody else's expense, you create a pandemonium, and that is just why there is so much of that element in the world at the present time. But such an inverted idea of liberty is based on the assumption that Man does not possess the power of controlling his conditions by his Thought; in other words, the flat denial of the initial statement of Scripture regarding him that he is made "in the image and likeness of God".

Once grant the creative power of our Thought and there is an end of struggling for our own way, and an end of gaining it at someone else's expense; for, since by the terms of the hypothesis we can create what we like, the simplest way of getting what we want is not to snatch it from somebody else, but to make it for ourselves; and since there is no limit to Thought, there can be no need for straining; and for everyone to have his own way in this manner would be to banish all strife, want, sickness, and sorrow from the earth.

Now it is precisely on this assumption of the creative power of our Thought that the whole Bible rests. If not, what is the meaning of being saved by Faith? Faith is essentially Thought; and therefore every call to have Faith in God is a call to trust in the power of our own Thought about God. "According to your faith be it unto you" (Matt. 15:28?), says the New Testament. "As a man thinketh in his heart, so is he" (Prov. 23:7), says the Old Testament. The entire Book is nothing but one continuous statement of the Creative Power of Thought.

The whole Bible is a commentary on the text, "Man is the image and likeness of God". And it comments on this text sometimes by explaining why, by reason of the ONE-ness of the Spirit, this must necessarily be so; sometimes by incitements to emotional states calculated to call this power into activity; sometimes by precepts warning us against those emotions which would produce its inverse action; sometimes by the example of those who have successfully demonstrated this power, and conversely by examples of those who have perverted it; sometimes by statements of the terrible consequences that must inevitably follow such perversion; and sometimes by glorious promises of the illimitable possibilities residing in this wonderful power if used in the right way; and thus it is that "All Scripture is profitable for doctrine, for reproof, for correction, for instruction in righteousness" (2 Tim. 3:16).

All this proceeds from the initial assumption with which the Bible starts regarding man, that he is the reproduction in individuality of that which God is in Universality. Start with this assumption, and the whole Bible works out logically. Deny it, and the Book becomes nothing but a mass of inconsistencies and contradictions. The value of the Bible as a storehouse of knowledge and a guide into Life depends entirely on our attitude with regard to its fundamental proposition.

But this proposition contains in itself the Affirmation of our Liberty; and the Gospel preached by Jesus amounts simply to this, that if anyone realizes himself as the reproduction, in conscious individuality, of the same principles which the Law of the Old Testament bids us recognize in the Divine Mind, he will thereby enter upon an unlimited inheritance of Life and Liberty. But to do this we must realize the Divine image in ourselves on all lines.

We cannot enter upon a full life of Joy and Liberty by trying to realize the Divine image along one line only. If we seek to reproduce the Creative Power without its correlatives of Wisdom and Love, we shall do so only to our own injury; for there is one thing which is impossible alike to God and man, and that is to plant a seed of one sort and make it yield fruit of another. We can never get beyond the Law that the effect must be of the same nature as the cause. To abrogate this Law would be to destroy the very foundation of the Creative Power of Thought, for then we could never reckon upon what our Thought might produce; so that the very same Law which places creative power at our disposal necessarily provides punishment for its misuse and reward for its right employment.

And this is equally the case along the two other lines. To seek development only on the line of Knowledge is to contemplate a store of wealth while remaining ignorant of the one fact which gives it any value: that it is our own; and, in like manner, to cultivate only Love makes our great motive power evaporate in a weak sentimentality which accomplishes nothing, because it does not know how and does not feel able. So here we see the force of the Master's words when he bids us aim at a perfection like that of our "Father" in heaven, a perfection based on the knowledge that all being is threefold in essence and one in expression; and that therefore we can attain Liberty only be recognizing this universal Law in ourselves also; and that, accordingly, the Thought that sets us free must be a simultaneous movement along all three lines of our nature.

The Divine Mind may be represented by a large circle and the individual mind by a small one, but that is no reason why the smaller circle should not be as perfect for its own area as the larger; and therefore the initial statement of the Bible that Man is the image of God is the charter of Individual Liberty for each one, provided we realize that this likeness must extend to the whole threefold unity that is ourself, and not to a part only. Our Liberty, therefore, consists in being ourselves in our Wholeness, and this means the conscious exercise of all our powers, whether of our visible or invisible personality. It means being ourselves, not trying to be somebody else.

The principles by which anyone ever attains to self-expression, whether in the humblest or the most exalted degree, are always the same, for they are Universals and apply to everyone alike, and therefore we may advantageously study their working in the lives of others; but to suppose that the expression of these principles is bound to take the same form in us that it did in the individual who is the object of our hero-worship, is to deny the first principle of manifested being, which is Individuality.

If someone towers above the crowd, it is because he has grown to that height, and I cannot permanently attain the same elevation by climbing on his shoulders but only by growing to the same height myself. Therefore, the attempt to copy a particular individual, however beautiful his character, is bondage and a relinquishing of our birthright of Selfhood.

What we have to do in studying those lives which we admire is to discover the Universal principles which those persons embodied in their way, and then set to work to embody them in ours. To do this is to realize the Universal I AM manifesting itself in every Individuality; and when we see this, we find that the statement of the Law of Individual Liberty is the declaration that was made to Moses at the burning bush and is the truth that Jesus proclaimed when he said that it was the recognition of the I AM that would set us free from the Law of bondage and death.

In speaking of the I AM as the Principle of Life, neither Jesus nor Moses used the words personally, and Jesus especially avoids any such misconstruction by saying, "If I bear witness of myself, my witness is not true" (John 5:31); in other words, he came to set forth not himself personally, but those great principles common to all mankind, of which he exemplified the full development.

When a little child is first told that God made the world, it accepts the statement without doubting, but immediately and logically follows it up with the question, then who made God? And the unsophisticated mother very often gives the correct answer, God made Himself. There is the whole secret, and when we come down — or rather when we rise — to the level of these souls whose pure intuitions have not been warped by arguments drawn only from the outside of things, we see that the principle of continual self-creation into all varieties of individuality affords the true clue to all that we are and to all that is around us; and when we see this, the teaching regarding the I AM in ourselves becomes clear, logical, and simple.

Then we understand that the Law of our Whole Being — that which is Cause as well as Effect — is the reproduction in Individuality of the same Power which makes the worlds; and when this is understood in its Wholeness, we see that this principle cannot, as manifested in us, be in opposition to its manifestation of itself in other forms. The Whole must be homogeneous; that which is homogeneous cannot act in opposition to itself; and consequently this homogeneous principle, which underlies all individuality and is the I AM in each, can never act contrary to the Law of Life. Therefore, to know ourselves as the concentration of this principle into a focus of self-recognition is to be at one with the Life-Principle which is in all worlds and under all forms.

It is this recognition of our own Individuality as being a reproduction of the Universal Principle in the whole personality that constitutes belief in "the Son", or the principle of spiritual sonship, which brings us out of bondage into the liberty of knowledge and power.

But the reader who is still within the trammels of the traditional exegesis will probably say, if this be so, what is meant by such texts as that contained in the fifty-third chapter of Isaiah, "He was wounded for our transgressions", etc.? and the answer is that the personality here spoken of is still the same typical man — the Divine Son — who is described by Isaiah as "the Wonderful Child", only seen from another point of view. This is the description of him in his prenatal stage, that is, before his manifestation as the Son whose name is Wonderful, Counselor, etc.

And this brings us to the consideration of a very recondite subject, the question whether "Spirit" ever does pass into unconsciousness. Whether from the physiological or the psychological side, there is important evidence tending to the conclusion that "Spirit" is never in a condition of unconsciousness; and if this is the case with that concentration of pure Spirit which is the individualized I AM in each of us, how can we conceive its suffering from those transgressions of the Law of our own being which result in all the misery, pain, and death that the world has witnessed?

If the Spirit in us is the very Impersonation (i.e. individualized in a person; no suggestion of fraud is intended!) of the Law of Life, what woundings, what bruisings it must suffer in the course of educating the lower principles into self-recognition and spontaneous compliance with the true Law of the Individuality in its Wholeness!

Then we see that it is only by the infinite persistence of the Spirit in its struggle towards perfecting the vehicles of its Self-expression that the Individuality in all its completeness can ever be brought to maturity and the crown set to the work of Evolution which commenced far back in the dim unfathomable past. We realize St Paul's meaning in saying that the Spirit groans with unutterable groanings, for it is that principle which St John tells us cannot sin (1 John 3:9 and 5:18), that is, cannot act contrary to the true Law of Being; and thus a peculiar emphasis is set on the injunctions "Grieve not the Spirit" (Eph. 4:30), "Quench not the Spirit" (1 Thess. 5:19), for the Individualized Spirit is the intensely Living Center of ourselves — the I AM that I Myself AM in every one of us.

The question of the ultimate consciousness of the individuality under the outward semblance of unconsciousness, as in trance, or under the conditions induced by hypnotism or anaesthetics, involves problems of a scientific character which I hope to have an opportunity of discussing on another occasion; but even supposing there is no such latent consciousness of suffering as I have suggested, we may well transfer the whole description of Isaiah 53 to the conscious sufferings of the outer man. That, at any rate, is a "man of sorrows and acquainted with grief", and the reason of these sufferings is the want of Wholeness; they are the result of trying to live only in one portion of our nature — and that the lower — instead of in the Whole, and consequently these sufferings will continue until we realize that even balance of all parts of our nature which alone constitutes true individuality, or that which is without division.

By the buffeting of experience, the lower personality is being continually driven to inquire more and more into the reason of its sufferings, and as it grows in intelligence, it sees that they always result from some willful or ignorant infraction of the Law of Things-as-they-are, as distinguished from Things-as-they-look; and so by degrees the lower personality grows into union with the higher personality, which itself is the Law of Things-as-they-are become Personal, until at last the two are found to be ONE, and the Perfected Man stands forth Whole.

This is the process to which the writer of the Epistle to the Hebrews refers when he says that "though he were a son, yet learned he obedience by the things which he suffered" (Heb. 5:8), thus indicating a course of education which can only apply to a personality whose evolution is not yet completed. But by these sufferings of the lower personality the salvation of the entire individuality is at length accomplished for, being thus led to study the Law of the Whole, the lower or simply intellectual mentality at last discovers its relation to the Intuitive and Creative Principle and realizes that nothing short of harmonious union of the two makes a Complete Man. Until this recognition takes place, the real meaning of suffering is not understood.

To talk about "the Mystery of Pain" is like talking of the mystery of broken glass if we throw a stone at a window — it is of our own making. We attribute our sufferings to "the will of God" simply because we can think of nothing else to attribute them to, being ignorant alike of ourselves as centers of causation and of God as the Universal Life-Principle, which cannot will evil against anyone. So long as we are at this stage of intelligence, we esteem the lower personality (the only self we yet know) to be "stricken and smitten of God" — we put it all down to God's account — while all the time the cause of our wounding and bruising was not the will of God, but our own transgressions and iniquities; transgression: the infraction of the Law of causation; and iniquity: unequalness, or the want of even balance between all portions of our Individuality, without which the liberating recognition of our own I AM-ness can never take place.

This reading of this wonderful chapter (Is. 53) takes it out of the region of merely speculative theology and brings it into a region where we can understand its statements as links in a chain of cause and effect connecting the promised redemption with facts that we know, and starting from causes whose working is obvious to us.

This reading in no way detracts from the value of this passage as a prophecy of the great work of the Master, for it is a generic description applicable to each, in his degree, who in any way labours or suffers for the good of others; and the description is therefore supremely applicable to Jesus, in whom that perfect Individualization of the Divine of which we speak was fully accomplished.

The Law of Man's Individuality is therefore the Law of Liberty, and equally it is the Gospel of Peace; for when we truly understand the Law of our own individuality, we see that the same Law finds its expression in everyone else, and consequently we shall reverence the Law in others exactly in proportion as we value it in ourselves. To do this is to follow the Golden Rule of doing to others what we would they should do unto us; and because we know that the Law of Liberty in ourselves must include the free use of our own creative power, there is no longer any inducement to infringe the rights of others, for we can satisfy all our desires by the exercise of our knowledge of the Law.

As this comes to be understood, co-operation will take the place of competition with the result of removing all ground of enmity, whether between individuals, classes, or nations; and thus the continual recognition of the Divine or "highest" principles in ourselves brings "peace on earth and good-will among men" naturally in its train, and it is for this reason that the Bible everywhere couples the reign of peace on earth with the Knowledge of God.

The whole object of the Bible is to teach us to be ourselves and yet more ourselves. It does not trouble itself with political or social questions, or even with those of religious organization, but it goes to the root of all, which is the Individual. First set people right individually, and they will naturally set themselves right collectively. It is only by applying to mankind the old proverb "take care of the pence and the pounds will take care of themselves"; and therefore the Bible deals only with the two extremes of the scale, the Universal Mind and the Individual Mind. Let the relation between these two be clearly understood, and all other relations will settle themselves on lines which, however varied in form, will always be characterized by individual Liberty working to the expression of perfect social harmony.

Chapter 10

The Teaching of Jesus

In this chapter I shall endeavour to give a connected idea of the general scope and purpose of the Master's teachings, the point of which we in great measure miss by taking particular sayings separately, and so losing the force which pertains to them by reason of the place they hold in his system as a whole. For, be it remembered, Jesus was teaching a definite system — not a creed, nor a ritual, nor a code of speculative ethics, but a system resulting from the threefold source of spiritual inspiration, intellectual reasoning, and experimental observation, which are the three modes in which the Universal Mind manifests itself as Conscious Reasoning Power or "the Word". And therefore this system combines the religious, philosophical, and scientific characters, because it is a statement of the action of universal principles at the level where they find expression through the human mind.

As we proceed, we shall find that the basis of this system is the same perception of the unity between the Expressor and the Expressed which is also the basis of the teaching of Moses, and which is summed up in the significant phrase I AM. Jesus brings out the consequences of this Unity in their relation to the Individual and therefore presupposes the teaching of Moses regarding the Universal Unity as the necessary foundation for its reflection in the individual.

The great point to be noted in the teaching of Jesus is his statement of the absolute liberty of the individual. That was the subject of his first discourse in the synagogue of Nazareth (Luke 4:16); he continued his teaching with the statement, "the truth shall make you free" (John 8:32); and he finished it with the final declaration before Pilate the he had come into the world to the end that he should bear witness to the Truth (John 18:37). Thus to teach the knowledge of Liberating Truth was the beginning, the middle, and the end of the great work which the Master set before him.

Now there are two facts about this teaching that deserve our special attention. The first is that the perfect liberty of the individual must be in accordance with the will of God; for on any other supposition Jesus would have been teaching rebellion against the Divine will; and therefore any system of religion which inculcates blind submission to the will of God must do so at the cost of branding Jesus as a leader of rebellion against the Divine authority.

The other point is that this freedom is represented simply as the result of coming to know the Truth. If words mean anything, this means that Liberty in truth exists at the present moment, and that what keeps us from enjoying it is simply our ignorance of the fact. In other words, the Master's teaching is that the essential and therefore ever-present Law of each individual human life is absolute Liberty; it is so in the very nature of Being, and it is only our ingrained belief to the contrary that keeps us in bondage to all sorts of limitation.

Of course, it is easy to explain away all that the Master said by interpreting it in the light of our past experiences; but these experiences themselves constitute the very bondage from which he came to deliver us, and therefore to do this is to destroy his whole work. We do not require his teaching to go back to the belittling and narrowing influence of past experiences; we do that naturally enough so long as we remain ignorant of any other possibilities. It is just this being tied up that we want to get loose from, and he came to tell us that, when we know the Truth, we shall find we are not tied up at all. If we hold fast to the initial teaching of Genesis, that the Divine Principle makes things by itself becoming them, then it follows that when it becomes the individual man, it cannot have any other than its own natural movement in him — that is, a continual pushing forward into fuller and fuller expression of itself, which therefore becomes fuller and fuller life in the individual; and consequently, anything that tends to limit the full expression of the individual life must be abhorrent to the Universal Mind expressing itself in that individuality.

Then comes the question as to the way in which this truth is to be realized; and the practical way inculcated by the Master is very simple. It is only that we are to take this truth for granted. That is all. We may be ready to exclaim that this is a large demand upon our faith; but after all, it is the only way in which we ever do anything. We take all the operations of the Life-Principle in our physical body for granted, and what is wanted is a similar confidence in the working of our spiritual faculties.

We trust our bodily powers because we assume their action as the natural Law of our being; and in just the same way we can only use our interior powers by tacitly assuming them to be as natural to us as any others. We must bear in mind that from first to last the Master's teaching was never other than a veiled statement of Truth: he spoke "the word" to the people in parables, and "without a parable spoke he not unto them" (Matt. 13:34). It is indeed added "and when they were alone he expounded all things to his disciples"; but if we take the interpretation of the parable of the sower as a sample (Matt. 13:3-9), we can see how very far these expositions were from being a full and detailed explanation.

The thickest and outermost veil is removed, but we are still very far from plain speaking among "the full-grown" which St Paul tells us was equally distant from his own writing to the Corinthians. I say this on the best authority, that of the Master himself. We might have supposed that in that last discourse, which commences with the fourteenth chapter of St John's Gospel, he had withdrawn the final veil from his teaching; but no, we have his own words for it that even this is a veiled statement of the Truth. He tell his disciples that the time when he shall show them plainly of "the Father" is still future (John 16:25).

He left the final interpretation to be given by the only possible interpreter, the Spirit of Truth, as the real significance of his words should in time dawn upon each of his hearers with an inner meaning that would be none other than the revelation of The Sacred Name. As this meaning dawns upon us, we find that Jesus no longer speaks to us in proverbs, but that his parables tell us plainly of "the Father", and our only wonder is that we did not discern his true meaning long ago.

He is telling us of great universal principles which are reproduced everywhere and in everything with special reference to their reproduction on the plane of Personality. He is not telling us of rules which God has laid down in one way and could, had He chosen, have laid down in another, but of universal Laws which are therefore inherent in the constitution of Man. Let us, then, examine some of his sayings in this light.

The thread on which the pearls of the Master's teaching are strung together is that Perfect Liberty is the natural result of knowing the Truth. "When you find what the Truth really is, you will find it to be that you are perfectly free" (John 8:32) is the center from which all His other statements radiate. But the final discovery cannot be made for you; you must each make it for yourself. Therefore, "he that hath ears to hear, let him hear" (Luke 14:35).

This is nowhere brought out more clearly than in the parable of the Prodigal Son (Luke 15:11-32). The fact of sonship had never altered for either of the two brothers, but in different ways they each missed the point of their position as sons. The one limited himself by separating off a particular share of the Father's goods for himself, which, just because of being a limited share, was speedily exhausted, leaving him in misery and want.

The other brother equally limited himself by supposing that he had no power to draw from his Father's stores, but must wait till he in some way acquired a specific permission to do so, not realizing his inherent right, as his Father's son, to take whatever he wanted.

The one son took up a false idea of independence, thinking it consisted in separating himself and, to use an expressive vulgarism, in being entirely "on his own hook", while the other, in his recoil from this conception, went to the opposite extreme and believed himself to have no independence at all.

The younger son's return, so far from extinguishing the instinct for Liberty, gratified it to the full by placing him in a position of honour and command in his Father's house; and the elder son is rebuked with the simple words, "Why wait for me to give you what is yours already? All that I have is thine". It would be impossible to state the relation between the Individual Mind and the Universal Mind more clearly than in this parable, or the two classes of error which prevent us from understanding and utilizing this relation.

The younger brother is the man who, not realizing his own spiritual nature, lives on the resources of the lower personality till their failure to meet his needs drives him to look for something which cannot thus be exhausted, and eventually he finds it in the recognition of his own spiritual being as his inalienable birthright, because he was made in the image and likeness of God and could not by any possibility have been created otherwise.

Gradually, as he becomes more and more conscious of the full effects of this recognition, he finds that "the Father" advances to meet him, until at last they are folded in each other's arms, and he realizes the true meaning of the words, "I and my father are ONE". Then he learns that Liberty is in union and not in separation, and realizing his identity with the Infinite, he finds that all its inexhaustible stores are open to him.

This is not rhapsody but simple fact, which becomes clear if we see that the only possible action of the undifferentiated Life-Principle must be to always press forward into fuller and fuller expression of itself, in particular forms of life, in strict accordance with the conditions which each form provides for its manifestation. And when anyone thoroughly grasps this principle of the differentiation, through form, of an entirely undistributed universal potential, then he will see that the mode of differentiation depends on the direction in which the specializing entity is reaching out.

If he further gets some insight into the boundless possibilities which must result from this, he will realize the necessity, before all things, of seeking to reproduce in individuality that Harmonious Order which is the foundation of the universal system.

And since he cannot particularize the whole Infinite at a single stroke, which would be a mathematical impossibility, he utilizes its boundless stores by particularizing, from moment to moment, the specific desires, powers, and attractions which at that moment he requires to employ.

And, since the Energy from which he draws is infinite in quantity and unspecialized in quality, there is no limit either of extent or of kind to the purposes for which he may employ it. But he can only do this by abiding in "the Father's" house, and by conforming to the rule of the house, which is the Law of Love.

This is the only restriction, if it can be called a restriction, to avoid using our powers injuriously; and this restriction becomes self-obvious when we consider that the very thing which puts us in possession of this limitless power of drawing from the Infinite is the recognition of our identity with the Universal ONE, and that any employment of our powers to the intentional injury of others is in itself a direct denial of that "unity of the Spirit which is the bond of peace".

The binding power (religio) of Universal Love is thus seen to be inherent in the very nature of the Liberty which we attain by the Knowledge of the Truth; but except this, there is no other restriction. Why? Because, by the very hypothesis of the case, we are employing First cause when we consciously use our creative power with the knowledge that our Thought is the individual action of the same Spirit which, in its Universal action, is both the Cause and the Being of every mode of manifestation; for the great fact which distinguishes First Cause from secondary causation is its entire independence of all conditions, because it is not the outcome of conditions but itself creates them — it produces its own conditions step by step as it goes along. (For fuller explanation regarding the use of First Cause, see my Edinburgh Lectures on Mental Science.)

If, therefore, the Law of Love be taken as the foundation, any line of action can be worked out successfully and profitably; but this does not alter the fact that a higher degree of intelligence will see a much wider field of action than a lower one, and therefore if our field of activity is to grow, it can only be as a result of the growth of our intelligence; and consequently, the first use we should make of our power of drawing from the Infinite should be for steady growth in understanding.

Life is the capacity for action and enjoyment, and therefore any extension of the field for the exercise of our capacities is an increase of our own livingness and enjoyment; and so the continual companionship of the Spirit of Truth, leading us into continually expanding perception of the limitless possibilities that are open to ourselves and to the whole race, is the supreme Vivifying Influence; and thus we find that the Spirit of Truth is identical with the Spirit of Life. It is this consciousness of companionship that is the Presence of the Father; and it is in returning to this Presence and dwelling in it that we get back to the Source of our own spiritual nature and so find ourselves in possession of boundless possibilities without any fear of misusing them, because we do not seek to be possessors of the Divine Power without being possessors of the Divine Love and Wisdom also.

And the elder brother is the man who has not thrown off the Divine guidance as the younger had done, but who has realized it only in the light of a restriction. Always his question is, "Within what limits may I act?" and consequently, starting with the idea of limitation, he finds limitation everywhere; and thus, though he does not go into a far country like his brother, he relegates himself to a position no better than that of a servant; his wages are measured by his work, his creeds, his orthodoxies, his limitations of all sorts and descriptions, which he imagines to be of Divine appointment, while all the time he has imported them himself.

But him also "the Father" meets with the gracious words, "Son, thou art ever with me, and all that I have is thine"; and therefore as soon as this elder brother becomes sufficiently enlightened to perceive that all the elements of restriction in his beliefs, save only the Law of Love, have no place in the ultimate reality of Life, he too re-enters the house, now no longer as a servant but as a son, and joins in the festival of everlasting joy.

We find the same lesson on the parable of the Talents (Matt. 25:14-30). The use of the powers and opportunities we have, just where we are now, naturally opens up sequences by which still further opportunities, and consequently higher development of our powers, become possible; and these higher developments in their turn open the way to yet further expansion, so that there is no limit to the process of growth other than what we set it to by denying or doubting the principle of growth in ourselves, which is what is meant by the servant burying his talent in the earth.

"The lord" is the Living Principle of Evolution which obtains equally on all planes, and nothing has been more fully established by science than the Law that as soon as progress stops, retrogression begins; so that it is only by continual advance we can escape the penalty with which Professor threatens us in his humorous verse, that we shall

> "Return to the monad from which we all sprang,
> Which nobody can deny."

But on the other hand, the employment of our faculties and opportunities, so far as we realize them, is, by the same Law, certain to produce its own reward. By being faithful over a few things, we shall become rulers over many things, for God is not unmindful to forget your labour of love, and so day by day we shall enter more and more fully into the joy of our Lord.

The same idea is repeated in the parable of the man who contrived to get into the wedding feast without the wedding garment (Matt. 22:2-14). The Divine Marriage is the attainment by the individual mind of conscious union with the Universal Mind or "the Spirit"; and the feast, as in the parable of the Prodigal Son, signifies the joy which results from the attainment of Perfect Liberty, which means power over all the resources of the Universe, whether within us or around us.

Now, as I have already pointed out, the only way in which this power can be used safely and profitably is through that recognition of its Source which makes it in all points subservient to the Law of Love, and this was precisely what the intruder did not realize. He is the type of the man who fails in exactly the opposite way to the servant who buries his Lord's talent in the earth. This man has cultivated his powers to the uttermost, and so is able to enter along with the other guests. He has attained that Knowledge of the Laws of the spiritual side of Nature which is the storehouse of the Infinite; but he has missed the essential point of all his Knowledge, the recognition that the Law of Power is one with the Law of Love, and so, desiring to separate the Divine Power from the Divine Love, and to grasp the one while rejecting the other, he finds that the very Laws of which he has made himself master by his Knowledge overwhelm him with their own tremendousness and by their reflex action become the servants who bind him hand and foot and cast him into the outer darkness. The Divine Power can never be separated with impunity from the Divine Love and Guidance.

The parable of the unjust steward (Luke 16:1-13) is based upon the Law of the subjective nature of individual life. As in all the parables, "the lord" is the supreme Self-evolving Principle of the Universe which, relatively to us, is purely subjective because it acts in and through ourselves. As such, it follows the invariable Law of subjective mind, which is that of response to any suggestion that is impressed upon it with sufficient power. (I have discussed this subject at greater length in lectures 4 and 5 in my Edinburgh Lectures on Mental Science).

Consequently, "the lord" does not dispute the correctness of the accounts rendered by the steward but, on the contrary, commends him for his wisdom in recognizing the true principle by which to escape the results of his past maladministration of the estate.

St. Paul tells us that he is truly approved "whom the Lord commendeth", and the commendation of the steward is unequivocally stated by Jesus; and therefore we must realize that we have here the statement of some principle which harmonizes with the Life-giving tendency of the Universal Spirit. And this principle is not far to seek. It is the acceptance by "the Lord" of less than the full amount due to Him.

It is the statement of Ezekiel 18:21-22 that if the wicked man forsake his way, "he shall surely live and not die. All his transgressions that he hath committed shall not be mentioned unto him; in his righteousness that he hath done he shall live". It is what the Master speaks of as agreeing with the adversary while we are still in the way with him; in other words, it is the recognition that because the Laws of the Universe are not vindictive but simply causal, therefore the reversal of our former misemployment of First Cause, which in our case is our Thought demonstrated in a particular line of action, must necessarily result in the reversal of all those evil consequences which would otherwise have flowed from our previous wrongdoing.

I have enlarged in a previous chapter on the operation of the Law of Suggestion with regard to the question of sacrifice; and when we either see that the Law of Sacrifice culminates in No Sacrifice or reach the place where we realize that a Great and Sufficient Sacrifice has been offered up once for all, then we have that solid ground of suggestion which results in the summing-up of the whole Gospel in the simple words "Don't do it again".

If we once realize the great truth stated in Psalm 18:26 and 2 Samuel 22:27, that the Divine Universal Spirit always becomes to us exactly the correlative of our own principle of action, and that it does so naturally by the Law of Subjective Mind, then it must become clear that it can have no vindictive power in it or, as the Bible expresses it, "Fury is not in Me" (Isaiah 27:4).

But for the very same reason, we cannot trifle with the Great Mind by trying to impress one character upon it by our thought while we are impressing another upon it by our actions. This is to show our ignorance of the nature of the Law with which we are dealing; for a little consideration will show us that we cannot impress two opposite suggestions at the same time. The man who tried to do so is described in the parable of the servant who threw his fellow-servant into prison after his own debt had been cancelled (Matt. 18:23-35). The previous pardon availed him nothing, and he was cast into prison till he should pay the uttermost farthing.

The meaning becomes evident when we see that what we are dealing with is the supreme Law of our own being. We do not really believe what we do not act up to; if, therefore, we cast our fellow-servant into prison, no amount of philosophical speculation in an opposite direction will set us at liberty. Why? Because our action demonstrates that our real belief is in limitation. Such compulsion can only proceed from the idea that we shall be the poorer if we do not screw the money out of our fellow-servant, and this is to deny our own power of drawing from the Infinite in the most emphatic manner, and so to destroy the whole edifice of Liberty.

We cannot impress upon ourselves too strongly the impossibility of living by two contradictory principles at the same time. And the same argument holds good when we conceive that the debt is due to our injured feelings, our pride, and the like — the principle is always the same; it is that perfect Liberty places us above the reach of all such considerations, because by the very hypothesis of being absolute freedom, it can create far more rapidly than any of our fellow-servants can run up debts; and our attitude towards those who are thus running up scores should be to endeavour to lead them into that region of fullness where the relation of debtor and creditor cannot exist, because it becomes merged in the radiation of creative power.

But perhaps the most impressive of all the parables is that in which, on the night when he was betrayed, the Master expressed the great mystery of God and Man by symbolic action rather than by words, girding himself with a towel and washing the disciples' feet (John 13:3-15). He assured Peter that though the meaning of this symbolic act was not apparent at the time, it should become clear later on.

A wonderful light is thrown on this dramatization of a great principle by comparing it with the Master's utterance in Luke 12:35-37. The idea of girding is very conspicuous in that parable. First, we are bidden to have our loins girded and our lights burning, like unto men that wait for their Lord. Then we are told that if the servants are found thus prepared, when the Lord does come the positions will be reversed, and he will make them sit down and will gird himself and serve them.

Now what Jesus in this parable taught in words, he taught on the night of the Last Supper in acts. There is a strict parallel: in both cases the Master, the Lord, girds himself and serves those who had hitherto accounted themselves as his servants. The emphatic reduplication of this parable shows that here we have something of the very highest importance presented to us; and undoubtedly it is the veiled statement of the supreme mystery of individual being. And this mystery is the raising to the highest spiritual levels of the old maxim that Nature will obey us in proportion as we first obey Nature. The universal principles can never act contrary to themselves, whether on the spiritual or the physical level, and therefore unless we are prepared by study of the Law and obedience to it, we cannot make use of these principles at any level; but granted such preparation on our part and the Law becomes our humble servant, obeying us in every particular on the one condition that we first obey it.

It is thus that modern science has made us masters of a world of power which, for all practical purposes, did not exist in the times of the Tudors; and, transferring this truth to the highest and innermost, to the very principle of Life itself, the meaning becomes plain. Because the Life-Principle is not something separate from ourselves, but is the Supporter of our individuality, therefore the more we understand and obey its great generic Law, the more fully shall we be able to make any specific applications of it that we like — but on one condition: we must be washed. "If I wash thee not, thou hast no part with me", were the words of the Master. He spoke as the conscious mouthpiece of the Universal Spirit, and this must therefore be taken as the personal utterance of the Spirit itself; and seen in this light, the meaning becomes clear: we must first be cleansed by the Spirit.

And here we meet with another symbolical fact of the highest importance. The dramatization of the final truth of spiritual knowledge took place after the supper was ended. Now as we all know, the supper was itself of supreme symbolical significance. It was the Jewish Passover and the Christian Commemoration, and tradition tells us it was also the symbolic act by which, throughout antiquity, the highest initiates signified their identical realization of Truth, however apparently separated by outward forms or nationality.

We find these mystical emblems of bread and wine presented to Abraham by Melchizedek, himself the type of the man who has realized the supreme truth of the birth which is "without father, without mother, without beginning of days or end of years" (Hebrews 7:3); and therefore if we would grasp the full meaning of the Master's action on that last night, we must understand the meaning of the symbolic meal of which he and his followers had just partaken. Briefly stated, it is the recognition by the participant of his unity with, and power of appropriating, the Divine in its twofold mode of Spirit and Substance.

Science and Religion are not two separate things. They both have the same object: to bring us nearer and nearer to the point where we shall find ourselves in touch with the ONE Universal Cause. Therefore the two were never dissociated by the greatest thinkers of antiquity, and the inseparableness of energy and matter, which is now recognized by the most advanced science as the starting-point of all its speculations, is none other than the old, old doctrine of the identity of Spirit and ultimate Substance.

Now it is this twofold nature of the Universal First cause that is symbolized by the bread and wine. The fluid and the solid, or Spirit and Substance, as the two Universal supports of all manifested Forms — these are the Universal principles which the two typical elements signify. But in order that the individual may be consciously benefited by them, he must recognize his own participation in them, and he denotes his Knowledge on this point by eating the bread and drinking the wine; and his intention in doing so is to signify his recognition of two great facts: one, that he lives by continually drawing from the Infinite Spirit in its twofold unity; and the other, that he not only does this automatically but also has the power to consciously differentiate the Universal Energy for any purpose that he will.

Now this combination of dependence and control could not be more perfectly symbolized than by the acts of eating and drinking. We cannot do without food, but it is at our own discretion to select what and when we shall eat. And if we realize the true meaning of "the Christ", we shall see that it is that principle of Perfected Humanity which is the highest expression of the Universal Spirit-Substance; and taken in this sense, the bread and wine are fitting emblems of the flesh and blood, or Substance and Spirit, of the "Son of Man", the ideal Type of all Humanity.

And so it is that we cannot realize the Eternal Life except by consciously partaking of the inner-most Life-Principle, with due recognition of its true nature — not meaning the mere observance of a ceremonial rite, however august in its associations and however useful as a powerful sugges-tion; but meaning personal recognition of the Supreme Truth which that rite signifies.

This, then, was the meaning of the symbolic meal which had just concluded. It indicated the participant's recognition of his union with the Universal Spirit as being the supreme fact on which his individual life was based, the ultimate of all Truth. Now the word rendered "washed" in John 13:10 is more correctly given in the Revised Version as "bathed", a word that signifies total immersion. But no "bathing" had taken place on this occasion; to what, then, did Jesus allude when he spoke to his disciples as men who had been "bathed"? It is precisely that which, in Ephesians 5:26, is spoken of as "the washing of water by the word", "water" being, as we have seen, the Universal Substance, and "the word" the synonym for that Intelligence which is the very essence of Spirit. The meaning, then, is that by partaking of this symbolic meal they had signified their recognition of their own total immersion in the ONE Universal Divine Being, which is at once both Spirit and Substance; and since they could not conceive of It otherwise than as Most Holy, this recognition must thenceforward have a purifying influence upon the whole man.

This great recognition does not need to be repeated. Seen once, it is seen forever; and therefore "he that is washed needeth not save to wash his feet, but is clean every whit" (John 13:10). But though the principle is grasped — which, of course, is the substantial foundation for the new life — immediate perfection does not follow. Very far from it. And so we have to come day by day to the Spirit for the washing away of those stains which we contract in our daily walk through life. "If we say that we have no sin, the truth is not in us; but if we confess our sin, He is faithful and just to forgive us our sin and to cleanse us from all unrighteousness" (1 John 1:8-9).

It is this daily confession, not to man but to the Divine Spirit Itself, which produces the daily cleansing, and thus Its first service to us is to wash our feet. If we thus receive the daily wash-ing, we shall, day by day, put away from us that sense of separation from the Divine Universal Mind which only the conscious retention of guilt in the heart can produce, after once we have been "bathed" by the recognition of our individual relation to It; and if our study of the Bible has taught us anything, it has taught us that the very Essence of Life is in its identity and unity throughout all forms of manifestation.

To allow ourselves, therefore, to remain conscious of separation from the Spirit of the Whole is to accept the idea of Disintegration, which is the very principle of death; and if we thus accept death at the fountainhead, it must necessarily spread through the whole stream of our individual existence and poison the waters. But it is inconceivable that anyone who has once realized the Great Unity should ever again willingly remain in conscious separation from it, and therefore immediate open-hearted approach to the Divine Spirit is the ever-ready remedy as soon as any consciousness of separation makes itself felt.

And the symbol includes yet another meaning. If the bathing or total immersion signifies our unity with the Spirit of the Whole, then the washing of the feet must signify the same thing in a lesser degree, and the meaning implied is the ever-present attendance of the Infinite Undif-ferentiated Spirit ready to be differentiated by us to any daily service, no matter how lowly. Seen in this light, this acted parable is not a mere reminder of our imperfection — which, unless cor-rected by a sense of power, could only be a perpetual suggestion of weakness that would inca-pacitate us from doing anything — but indicates our continual command over all the resources of the Infinite for every object that all the endless succession of days can ever bring before us. We may draw from this what we like, when we like, and for what purpose we like; nothing can prevent us but ignorance or consciousness of separation.

The idea thus graphically set forth was expanded throughout that marvellous discourse (John 15) with which the Master's ministry in his mortal body terminated. As ever, his theme was the perfect Liberty of the individual resulting from recognition of our true relation to the Universal Mind. The ONE great I AM is the Vine, the lesser ones are the branches. We cannot bear fruit except we abide in the Vine; but abiding in it there is no limit to the developments we may attain.

The Spirit of Truth will guide us into all Truth, and the possession of all Truth must carry the possession of all Power along with it; and since the Spirit of Truth can be none other than the Spirit of Life, to be guided into all Truth must be to be guided into the Power of an endless life.

This does not need our removal from the world: "I pray not that Thou shouldest take them out of the world, but that Thou shouldest keep them from evil (John 17:15). What is needed is ceasing to eat of that poisonous fruit the tasting of which expelled Man from the Paradise he is designed to inhabit. The true recognition of the ONE leaves no place for any other; and if we follow the Master's direction not to estimate things by their superficial appearance, but by their central principle of being, then we shall find that nothing is evil in essence, and that the origin of evil is always a wrong application of what is good in itself, thus bringing us back to the declaration of the first chapter of Genesis, that God saw all that He had created, "and behold it was very good".

If, then, we realize that our Liberty resides in the creative power of our Thought, we shall see the immense importance of recognizing the essence of things as distinguished from the misplaced order in which we often first become acquainted with them. If we let our Thought dwell on an inverted order, we perpetuate that order; but if, going below the surface, we fix our Thought upon the essential nature of things and see that it is logically impossible for anything to be essentially bad which is a specific expression of the Universal Good, then we shall in our Thought call all things good, and so help to bring about that golden age when the old inverted order shall have passed away, and a new world of joy and liberty shall take its place.

This, then, is briefly the line followed by the Master's teaching, and his miracles were simply the natural outcome of his perfect recognition of his own principles. Already the unfolding recognition of these principles is beginning to produce the same results at the present day, and the number of well-authenticated cures effected by mental means increases every year. And this is precisely in accordance with Jesus' own prediction. He enumerated the signs which should follow those who really believed what he really taught, and in so saying he was simply making a statement of cause and effect. He never set up his power as proof of a nature different from our own; on the contrary, he said that those who learned what he taught should eventually be able to do still greater miracles, and he summed up the whole position in the words "the disciple when he is perfected shall be as his Master" (Luke 6:40).

Again he laid special stress on the perfect naturalness of all that he taught by guarding us against the error of supposing that the intervention of any intermediary was required between us and "the Father". If we could assign such a position to any being, it would be to himself, but he emphatically disclaims it. "In that day ye shall ask in my name; and I say not unto you that I will pray the Father for you, for the Father Himself loveth you, because ye have loved me and believed that I came forth from the Father (John 16:26-7). If the student has realized what has been said in the chapter on "the Sacred Name", he will see that the opening words of this utterance can be nothing else than a statement of universal Truth, and that the love and belief in himself, spoken of in the concluding clause, are the love of this Truth exhibited in its highest form as Man evolved to perfection, and belief in the power of the Spirit to produce such an evolution.

I do not say that there is nothing personal in the statement; on the contrary, it is eminently personal to "the man Christ Jesus", but as the Type of Perfected Humanity — the first-fruit of the further evolution which is to complete the pyramid of manifested being upon earth by the introduction of the Fifth Kingdom, which is that of the Spirit. When we realize what is accomplished in him, we see what is potential in ourselves; and since we have now reached the point beyond which any further evolution can only result from our conscious co-operation with the evolutionary principle, all our future progress depends on the extent to which we do recognize the potentialities contained in our own individuality.

Therefore to realize the manifestation of the Divine which Jesus stands for, and to love it, is the indispensable condition for attaining that access to "the Father" which means the full development in ourselves of all the powers of the Spirit.

The point which rivets our attention in this utterance of the Master's is the fact that we do not need the intervention of any third party to beseech "the Father" for us, because "the Father" Himself loves us. This statement (i.e. John 16:26-7), which we may well call the greatest of all the teachings of Jesus, setting us free, as it does, from the cramping influences of a limited and imperfect theology, he has bracketed together with the recognition of himself; and therefore if we would follow his teaching, we cannot separate these two things which he has joined; but if we realize in him the embodiment of the Divine Ideal of Humanity, his meaning becomes clear — it is that our recognition of this idea is itself the very thing that places us in immediate touch with "the Father".

By accepting the Divine Ideal as our own, we provide the conditions under which the Undifferentiated Universal Subconscious Mind becomes able to differentiate Itself into the particular and concrete expression of that Potential of Personality which is eternally inherent in It; and thus in each one who realizes the Truth which the Master taught, the Universal Mind attains an individualization capable of consciously recognizing Itself.

To attain this is the great end of Evolution, and in thus gaining Its end the ONE becomes the MANY, and the MANY return into the ONE — not by an absorption depriving them of individual identity, which would be to stultify the entire operation of the Spirit in Evolution by simply ending where it had begun, but by impressing upon innumerable individualities the perfect and completed likeness of that Original in the potential image of which they were first created.

The entire Bible is the unfolding of its initial statement that Man is made in the image of God, and the teaching of Jesus is the proclamation and demonstration of this Truth in its complete development, the Individual rejoicing in perfect Life and Liberty because of his conscious ONEness with the Universal.

The teaching of Jesus, whether by word or deed, may therefore be summed up as follows. He says in effect to each of us: What you really are in essence is a concentration of the ONE Universal Life-Spirit into conscious Individuality. If you live from the recognition of this Truth as your starting-point, it makes you Free. You cannot do this as long as you imagine that you have one center and the Infinite another. You can only do it by recognizing that the two centers coincide and that That which, being Infinite, is incapable of centralization in Itself, finds center in you. (see Lecture 3 in The Doré Lectures on Mental Science)

Think of these things until you see that it is impossible for them to be otherwise, and then step forward in perfect confidence, knowing that the Universal principles must necessarily act with the same mathematical precision in yourself that they do in the attractions of matter or in the vibrations of ether. His teaching is identical with the teaching of Moses, that there is only ONE Being manifested anywhere, and that the various degrees of its manifested consciousness are to be measured by one standard — the recognition of the meaning of the words I AM.

I have endeavoured to show that the Bible is neither a collection of traditions belonging only to a petty tribe, nor yet a statement of dogmas which can give no account of themselves beyond the protestation that they are mysteries which must be accepted by faith — which faith, when we come to analyze it, consists only in accepting the bare assertion of those very persons who, when we ask them for the explanation of the things they bid us believe, are unable to give any explanation beyond the word "MYSTERY".

The true element of Mystery we shall never get rid of, for it is inherent in the ultimate nature of all things; but it is an element that perpetually unfolds, inviting us at each step to still further inquiry by satisfactorily and intelligently answering every question that we put in really logical succession, and thus the Mystery continually opens out into Meaning and never pulls us up short with an anathema for our irreverence in daring to inquire into Divine secrets.

When the interrogated is driven to the fulmination of anathemas, it is very plain that he has reached the end of his tether. As Byron says in "Don Juan":

"He Knew not what to say, and so he swore",

and therefore this mode of answering a question always indicated one of two things: ignorance of the subject or the intention to conceal facts. On either alternative, any "authority" which thus only tells us to "shut up" thereby at once loses all claim to our regard. Every undiscovered fact in the great Universal Order is a Divine Secret until we find the key that unlocks it; but the Psalmist tells us that the secret of the Lord is with them that fear Him, and the Master says that there is nothing hidden that shall not be revealed.

To seek, therefore, to understand the great principles on which the Bible is written, so far from being an act of presumption, is the most practical proof we can give of our reverence for it; and if the foregoing pages have in any way helped the reader to see in the Bible a statement of the working of the Laws which are inherent in the nature of things and follow an intelligible sequence of cause and effect, my purpose in writing will be answered.

The limited space at my disposal has allowed me only to treat the whole subject in an introductory manner, and in particular I have not yet shown the method by which the ONE Universal Principle follows out an exclusive line of unfoldment, building up a "Chosen people" by a process of natural selection culminating in the Great Central Figure of the Gospels. It does this without in any way departing from its Universal character, for it is that Power which cannot deny itself; but it does it as a consequence of this very Universality; and upon the importance of this specialized action of the Universal Principle to the future development of the race it is impossible to lay too much stress.

The Bible tells us that there is such a special selection, and if we have found truth in its more general statements, we may reasonably expect to find the same truth in its more specialized statements also.

Chapter 11
The Forgiveness of Sin

In the preceding chapters I have dealt principally with the teaching of the Bible regarding the reciprocity of being between God and man — that ultimate spiritual nature of man which affords the generic basis in all men upon which the Spirit of God can work to produce further specific development of the individual. But if we stop short at the recognition of this merely generic similarity, we are liable to be led into an erroneous course of reasoning resulting in logical conclusions the very opposite of all that the Bible is seeking to teach us; in a word, we shall be led into an atheism far deeper than that of the mere materialist, in that it is on the spiritual plane — the inverted development of the supreme principle of our nature.

Such a dire result comes from a one-sided view of things, a knowledge of certain truths without the knowledge of their counterbalancing truths; and the counterbalancing truth which will preserve us from so great a calamity is contained in the Bible teaching regarding the forgiveness of sin.

Once grant that there is such a thing as the forgiveness of sin, and the root of all possible spiritual inversion is logically cut away, for there must be One who is able and willing to forgive and who is therefore the object of worship and is capable of entering into a specific, conscious, personal relation to us. It is therefore important to realize what the Bible teaching on this subject is.

The logic of it is sufficiently simple if we grant the premise on which it starts. It is that man, by his essential and true innermost nature, is a being fitted and intended to live in uninterrupted intercourse with the All-creating spirit, thus continually receiving a ceaseless inflow of life from this infinite source. At the same time, it is impossible for a being capable of thus partaking of the infinite life of the Originating Spirit to be a mere piece of mechanism, mechanically incapable of moving in more than one direction; for if he is to reproduce in his individuality that power of origination and initiative which must be the very essence of the Creative Spirit's recognition of itself, he must possess a corresponding liberty of choice as to the way in which he will use his powers; and if he chooses wrongly, the inevitable law of cause and effect must produce the natural consequences of his choice.

The nature of this wrong choice is told us in the allegorical story of "the Fall". It is mistaking the sequence of laws which necessarily proceeds from any creative act for the creative power itself — the error of looking upon secondary causes as the originating cause and not seeing that they are themselves effects of something antecedent which works through them to the production of the ultimate effect. This is the fundamental error, and the opposite truth consists in connecting the ultimate effect directly with the intention of the originating intelligence and (from this point of view) excluding all consideration of the chain of intermediary causes which link these two extremes together.

The exact weighing and balancing of the action of secondary causes, or particular laws of relation, has its proper place; it is the necessary basis of our work when we are constructing anything from without, just as an architect could not build a safe house without carefully calculating the strains and thrusts to which his materials would be subjected. But when we are considering an act of creation, we are dealing with an exactly opposite process, one that works from within by a vital growth which naturally assimilates to itself all that is necessary for its completion.

In the latter case we do not have to consider the mechanism through which the vital energy brings forth its ultimate fruition, for by the very fact of its being inherent energy working for manifestation in a certain direction, it must necessarily produce all those relations, visible or invisible, which go to make the completed whole.

The fundamental error consists in ignoring this distinction between direct creation and external construction — in entirely losing sight of the former and consequently attempting to accomplish by knowledge of particular laws, which are applicable only to construction from without, what can only be accomplished by a direct creation which produces laws instead of being restricted by them.

The temptation then is to substitute our intellectual knowledge of the relations between various existing laws with which we are acquainted for that Creative Power which is not subject to any antecedent conditions and can produce what it will, while conforming always to its own recognition of itself as perfectly harmonious Being. (See my Creative Process in the Individual) This temptation is a very subtle one. It appeals to all that we can gather from secondary causes, whether in the seen or the unseen, and to all the deductions we can make from these observations. To all appearances it is entirely reasonable, only its reasoning is restricted to the circle of secondary causation and contemplates the great First Cause as a mere force whose action is limited by certain particular laws.

Looked at superficially, it does appear as if this course of reasoning was correct. But in truth it does not take into account the originating power of the Creative Spirit and is in reality a course of reasoning which is only applicable to construction from without and not to growth from within.

Now so long as we do not recognize a Power which can transcend all our past experiences, we naturally look to a more extended knowledge of particular laws as a means by which we can attain to a power of control which will at last place us beyond subjection to any control, the general principle involved being that by our knowledge we can balance the positive and negative aspects of law against each other in any proportion we like and become masters of the situation by this method.

Is this not a correct description of much of the teaching we meet with at the present day? And does it not exactly agree with the words of the old allegory, "ye shall be as gods knowing good and evil? (Gen 3:5)

The ultimate desire of every human being is for more fullness of life — to thoroughly enjoy living — and the more we enjoy living, the more we shall naturally desire to live and enjoy still more. In a word, our true desire under whatever guises we may try to conceal it is to "have life and to have it more abundantly" (John 10:10). This desire is innate in us because of our generic relation to the Spirit of Life, and therefore, so far from being condemned by Scripture, its fulfillment is placed before us as the one object of attainment, and the professed purpose of the Bible is to lead us to seek it in the right way instead of in the wrong one. To seek it in the right way is Righteousness or Rightness. To seek it in the wrong way is the Inversion of Rightness and is what is meant by Sin.

Those grosser forms of sin which we all recognize as such are only the one original transgression — of seeking from without what can only come by growth from within — when assuming its crudest aspect, but the underlying principle is the same; and so the allegory of the Fall is typical of all sin, of that inverted conception of life which, because it is inverted, must necessarily lead us away from the Spiritual Source of Life instead of towards it. The story is, so to say, a sort of algebraic generalization of the factors concerned.

When this becomes clear to us, we begin to see the necessity for the removal of sin. We see that hitherto we have been trying to live by an inverted conception of the principle of Life, whether this wrong conception has shown itself in crude and gross forms or more subtly in the purely intellectual region.

In either case the result is the same — the consciousness that we have not free intercourse with the Spiritual Source of Life; and as this dawns upon us, we instinctively feel the need of some other way than the one we have been hitherto pursuing. We find that what we want is not Knowledge but Love. And this is logical, for in the last analysis we shall find that Love is the only Creative Power. (See The Creative Process in the Individual)

Then we perceive that what we require for the perpetuation and continual increase of our individual life is a mental attitude which renders us perpetually and increasingly receptive of the Creative Love — the consciousness of a personal and individual relation to it beyond and in addition to our merely generic relation as items in the cosmic whole.

Then something must be done to assure us of this specific relation, to assure us that neither our erroneous thoughts in the past, nor yet the erroneous action to which they have given rise, can separate us from this Love, either by making it turn away from us or by a law of cause and effect proceeding from our wrong thoughts and acts themselves. And to give us such a confidence we require to be assured that the initiative movement proceeds from the side of the Divine Spirit; for if we suppose that the initiative starts from our side, then we can have no assurance that it has been accepted, or that the law of "Karma" is not dogging our steps.

It is this misconception of pacifying the Almighty by an initiative originating on our side that shows itself in penances, sacrifices, and various rites and ceremonies at the end of which we do not know whether our operations have been successful, or whether through deficiency in quantity or quality they have failed of the desired result.

All such performances are vitiated by the inherent defect of making the first move towards reconciliation come from our side. It is nothing else than carrying into our highest spiritual yearnings the old error of trying to produce by working from without what can only be produced by growth from within. We are still substituting the constructive process for the creative.

Accordingly, the Bible tells us that the fundamental proposition that there is such a thing as forgiveness of sin is enunciated by God Himself; and so we find that the story of the Fall includes the promise of the One by whom man shall be redeemed and released from sin and brought into conscious realization of that reciprocal intercourse with the Source of Life which is the essence of his innermost being. Man is told to look to the Divine promise of forgiveness, and from this point onwards belief in this promise is set forth as the way by which sin and its consequences are effectually removed.

I sometimes meet with those who object to the teaching that there is forgiveness. To such I would say, Why do you object to this teaching? Of course, if you are entirely without sin, you have no need of it for yourself; but then you are a very rare exception and at the same time beastly selfish not to consider all the rest of us who are of the more ordinary sort. Or if you put it that everybody is without sin, then the newspapers of all countries flatly contradict you with their daily details of thefts, murders, swindles, and the like.

But perhaps you will say that sin must be punished. Why must? What is the object of punishment? Its purpose is to rub it well in, so that the offender may not do it again for fear of consequences. But supposing he has become convinced of the true nature of his offence so as to hate it for its own sake and to shrink from it with abhorrence, what then is to be gained by going on whacking him? The change in his own view of things has already accomplished all, and more than all, that any amount of whacking could do, and this is the teaching of the Bible. Its purpose is to see sin in its true light as severance from the Source of Life, and if this has been accomplished why should punishment be prolonged?

Again, the conception of a God who will not forgive sin when repented of is the conception of a monstrosity. It is the conception of the Spirit of Life determining to deal death, when by its very nature it must be seeking to express Life to the fullest extent that the expressing vehicle will admit of; and repentance is turning away from something that had previously hindered this fuller expression. Therefore such a conception is illogical, for it implies the Spirit of Life acting in opposition to itself. Also such a God ceases to be the object of worship, for there is nothing to be gained by worshipping Him. He can only be the object of fear and hatred.

On the other hand, the conception of a God who cannot forgive sin is the conception of no God at all. It is the conception of a mere Force, and you cannot enter into a personal relation with unintelligent forces — you can only study them scientifically and utilize them so far as your knowledge of their law admits; and this logically brings you back to your own knowledge and power as your only source of life, so that in this case also there is nothing to worship.

If, then, there is such a mental attitude as that of worship, the looking to an Infinite Source of life and joy and strength, it can only be based upon the recognition that this All-creating Spirit is able to forgive sin and desires to do so.

We may therefore say that the conception of Itself as pardoning all who ask for pardon is necessarily an integral portion of the Spirit's Self-recognition in Its relation to the human race, and the inherentness of this idea is set forth in Scripture in such phrases as "the lamb of God that taketh away the sin of the world" (John 1:29) and "the lamb slain from the foundation of the world" (Rev 13:8?), thus pointing to an aspect of the Spirit's Self-contemplation exactly reciprocal to the need of all who desire to be set free from that inversion of their true nature which, while it continues, must necessarily prevent their unimpeded access to the Spirit of Life.

Then, since the Divine Self-conception is bound to work out into realization, a supreme manifestation of this eternal principle is the legitimate outcome of all that we can conceive of the creative working of the Spirit when viewed from the particular standpoint of the existence of sin in the world, and so the appearing of One who should give complete expression in space and time to the Spirit's recognition of human needs by a supreme act of self-sacrificing Love reasonably forms the grand center of the whole teaching of the Bible.

The Great Sacrifice is the Self-offering of Love to meet the requirements of the soul of man. Our psychological constitution requires it, and it is adequately adapted to fit in with every aspect of our mental nature, whether in the least or the most advanced members of the race. It is the supreme manifestation of that Love which is the Original Creative Power, and the Bible presents it to us as such.

Hear Christ's own description of it: "Greater love hath no man than this, that a man lay down his life for his friends" (John 15:13); "God so loved the world that He sent His only begotten Son into the world, that whosoever believeth on Him should not perish but have everlasting life" (John 3:16). All is attributed to Love on the one hand and Belief on the other — the Creating Spirit and the simple recognition of it — thus meeting exactly those conditions which we found to constitute the conditions for vital growth from within as distinguished from mechanical construction from without, and therefore not depending on our knowledge but on our faith.

Nor is this conception of the forgiveness of the All-originating Love to be found in the New Testament only. If we turn to the Old Testament we find such statements as the following: "And the Lord descended in a cloud and stood with him (Moses) there, and proclaimed the Name of the Lord. And the Lord passed by and proclaimed, The Lord, the Lord God, merciful and gracious, long-suffering and abundant in goodness and truth, keeping mercy for thousands, forgiving iniquity, transgression, and sin" (Ex. 34:5-7); "I, even I, am he that blotteth out thy transgressions for my own sake, and will not remember thy sins" (Isaiah 43:25); "I have blotted out as a thick cloud thy transgressions, and as a cloud thy sins; return unto me, for I have redeemed thee" (Isaiah 44:22); "If the wicked will turn from all his sins that he hath committed, and keep all my statutes, and do that which is lawful and right, he shall surely live, he shall not die. All his transgressions that he hath committed, they shall not be mentioned unto him; in his righteousness that he hath done he shall live" (Ezek. 18:21-2).

No doubt on the other hand there are threatenings against sin; but the whole tenor of the Bible is clear, that these threatenings apply only so long as we continue to do evil. Both the promises and the threatenings are nothing else than the statement of that Law of Correspondence with which my readers are no doubt sufficiently familiar — the great creative law by which spiritual causes produce their analogues in the outer world, and which is identically the same law whether it works positively or negatively.

The phrase "for my own sake" in Isaiah 43:25 should be noted, as it exactly bears out what I have said about the inherent quality of forgiveness as forming a necessary part of the Creating Spirit's conception of Itself in Its relation to the human race. This is the fundamental basis of the whole matter, and this truth has been dimly perceived by all the great religions of the world; in fact, it is just the perception of this truth that distinguishes a religion from a mere philosophy on the one hand and from magical rites on the other; and I think I cannot end this chapter more suitably than by a quotation which shows how, ages before Christianity was known to them, our rude Norse ancestors had at least some adumbration that the supreme offering must be that of the Divine Love to itself. The passage occurs in the Elder Edda, where O-din, the Supreme God, addresses himself while hanging in self-sacrifice in Ygdrasil, the Cosmic Tree:

> I knew that I hung
> In the wind-rocked tree
> Nine whole nights,
> Wounded with a spear,
> And to O-din offered
> Myself to myself,
> On that tree
> Of which no one knows
> From what root it springs.
> (From Strange Survivals,
> by Sabine Baring-Gould)

Chapter 12

Forgiveness, Its Relation to Healing and to The State of the Departed in the Other World

If we have now grasped some conception of forgiveness as one of the essential qualities of the All-creating Spirit, it will throw some light on several occasions when Jesus accompanied his miracles of healing with the words "Thy sins are forgiven".

There must have been some intimate connection between the forgiveness and the healing, and though the exact nature of this connection may be beyond our present perception, involving relations of cause and effect too deep for our imperfect powers of analysis, still we can see in a general way that it is in accordance with the teaching of the Bible on the subject.

The Bible is a book about man in his relation to God, and it therefore starts with certain fundamental statements regarding this relation. These are to the effect that death, and consequently disease and decrepitude, are not laws of man's innermost being. How could they be? How could the negative be the law of the positive? How could death be the law of Life? Therefore we are told that in the true order of things this is not the case.

The first thing we are told about man is that he is made in the image and likeness of God, the Spirit of Life, therefore capable of manifesting a similar equality of Life. But we must note the words "image" and "likeness". They do not impart identity but resemblance. An "image" implies an original to which it conforms, and so does a "likeness". These words remind us of the passage in which St. Paul speaks of our "reflecting as a mirror the glory of the Lord" and being thus "transformed into the same image from glory to glory (2 Cor. 3:18, RV). It is this same idea as in the first chapter of Genesis, only expanded so as to show the method by which the image and likeness are produced. It is by reflection. Our mind is, as it were, a mirror reflecting that towards which it is turned. This is the nature of Mind.

We become like what we contemplate. We cannot avoid it, for we are made that way, and therefore everything depends on what we are in the habit of contemplating. Then if we realize that growth, or the manifestation of the spiritual principle, always proceeds from the innermost to the outermost, by a creative process from within as distinguished from a constructive process from without, we shall see that the working of the mind upon the body, and the effect it will produce upon it, depends entirely on what form the mind itself is taking; and what form it will take depends on what it is reflecting.

This is the key to the great enigma. In proportion as we reflect the Pure Spirit of Life, we live; and in proportion as we reflect the Material, contemplating it as a power in itself instead of as the plastic vehicle of the Spirit, we bring ourselves under a law of limitation which culminates in death. It is the same law of Mind in both cases, only in the one case it is employed positively and in the other negatively.

Something like this seems to be St Paul's idea when he says that the Law of the Spirit of Life makes him free from the law of sin and death (Rom. 8:2). It is always this law of mental reflection that is at work within us, producing its logical effects, positively or negatively, according to the image which it mirrors forth.

At the risk of appearing tedious, I may dwell for a while on the word "image". It is the substantive corresponding to the verb "to image" — that is, to fashion an "image" or "thought-form" by our mental power of imagery. Now as I have endeavoured to make clear in my book The Creative Process in the Individual, the life and substance of all things must first subsist as images in the Divine Mind before they can come into manifestation in the world of time and space, much as in Plato's conception of archetypal ideas; therefore we may read the text in Genesis as indicating that Man exists primarily in the Divine conception of him. The real, true Man subsists eternally in the Divine Imagination as the necessary correlative to the Spirit's Self-recognition as all that constitutes Personality.

If the Universal Spirit is to realize in itself the consciousness of Will, the perception of Beauty, and the reciprocity of Love — all, in fact, that makes life intelligently living — it can do so only by projecting a mental image which will give rise to the corresponding consciousness; and so we may read the text as meaning that man thus subsists in the Divine image, or creating thought, of him. If the reader grasps this idea, he will find it throws light upon many otherwise perplexing problems.

This, then, is the real nature of sin. Whatever shape it may take, its essence is always the same: it is turning our mental mirror the wrong way and so reflecting the limited and negative, that which is not Life-in-itself, and correspondingly forming ourselves into a corresponding image and likeness. The story of the Fall typifies the essential qualities of all sin. It is seeking the Living among the dead — trying to build up the skill and power of the worker out of the atoms of the material in which he works; just as though, when you wanted a carpenter, you went into his workshop and tried to make him out of sawdust.

Now if we grasp the great fundamental law that our mind, meaning by this our spiritual creative power, attracts conditions which correspond to its own conception of itself, and that its conception of itself must always be the exact reflection of its own dominant thought, then we can in some measure understand why Christ announced forgiveness of sin as the accompaniment of physical healing.

By sin, in the sense we have now seen, death and all lesser evils enter into the world. Sin is the cause and they are the effect. Then if the cause is removed, the effect must cease — the root of the plant has been cut away, and so the fruit must wither. It is a simple working of cause and effect.

It is true that Jesus is not recorded to have announced forgiveness in every case in which he bestowed healing, and no doubt he had as good reasons for not making the announcement in some cases as for making it in others.

I cannot pretend to analyze those reasons, for that would imply a knowledge on my part equal to his own; but from what we do know of psychological laws and of the power of mind over body, I might hazard the conjecture that in those cases where he pronounced forgiveness, the sufferer apprehended that his sickness was in some way the consequence of his sins, and therefore it was necessary to his bodily healing that he should be assured of their pardon.

In other cases there may not have been such a conviction, and to speak of forgiveness would only withdraw the mind of the sufferer from that immediately receptive attitude which was necessary for the working of the spiritual power.

But who shall say that the principle of the removal of the root of suffering by the forgiveness of sin was not always present in the mind of the august healer? Rather we may suppose that it always was. On one occasion he very pointedly put this forward. The proof, he said, that the Son of Man has power on earth to forgive sins is this: I can say to the palsied man, "Arise and walk", and it is accomplished (Luke 5:24). This was what was in the mind of the Great Healer, and comparing it with the general teaching of Scripture on the subject, we may reasonably suppose that he always worked from this basic principle, whether the exigencies of the particular case made it, or not, desirable to impress the fact of forgiveness upon the person to be healed.

If we start with the assumption that sickness and death of the body result from imperfect realization of life by the soul, and that the extent and mode of the soul's realization of life is the result and mode its realization of union with its Divine Source, then it follows that the logical root of healing must be in the removal of the sense of separation — the removal, that is, of that inverted conception of our relation to the Spirit of Life which is "sin" — and the replacing of it by the right conception in accordance with which we shall more and more fully reflect the true image of "the Father" or Parent Spirit.

When we see this, we begin to apprehend more clearly the meaning of St Paul's words, "There is now no condemnation to them that are in Christ Jesus, which walk not after the flesh but after the Spirit" (Rom. 8:1).

Again, there is another phase of this subject which we cannot afford to neglect. Although, as it appears to me, there are grounds for supposing that the present resurrection of the body — its transmutation while in the present life into a body of another order, like to the resurrection body of Christ, is not beyond the bounds of possibility, still this supreme victory of the Life-Principle is not a thing of general realization; and so we are confronted by the question, What happens on the other side when we get there? I have treated this question at some length in my The Creative Process in the Individual, but I would here refer to it chiefly in connection with the subject of the forgiveness of sin.

Now if, as I apprehend, the condition of consciousness when we pass out of the body is in the majority of cases purely subjective, then from what we know of the laws of subjective mind we may infer that we live there in the consciousness of whatever was our dominant mode of thought during Earth life. We have brought this over with us on parting with our objective mentality as it operates through its physical instrument, the brain; and if this is the case, then the nature of our experiences in the other world will depend on the nature of the dominant thought with which we have left this one, the idea which was most deeply impressed upon our subjective mind.

If this be so, what a stupendous importance it gives to the question whether we do or do not believe in the forgiveness of sin. If we pass into the unseen with the fixed idea that no such thing is possible, then what can our subjective experience be but the bearing of a burden of which we can find no way to rid ourselves; for by the conditions of the case, all these objective things with which we can now distract our attention will be beyond our reach.

When the loss of our objective mentality deprives us of the power of inaugurating fresh trains of ideas, which practically means new outlooks on life, we shall find ourselves bound within the memories of our past life on earth, and since the outward conditions which then coloured our view of things will no longer exist, we shall see the motives and feelings which led to our actions in their true light, making us see what it was in ourselves rather than in our circumstances which led us to do as we did.

The mode of thought which gave the key to our past life will still be there, and no doubt the memory of particular facts also, for this is what has been most deeply impressed upon our subjective mind; and since by the conditions of the case the consciousness is entirely subjective, these memories will appear to be the re-enacting of past things, only now seen in their true nature, stripped of all the accessories which gave a false colouring to them.

Of course what the pain of such a compulsory re-enacting of the past life may amount to must depend on what the past life has been; but even in the most blameless life we can well suppose that there have been passages which we would rather not repeat when we saw the mental conditions in ourselves which gave rise to them — not necessarily crimes or grave moral delinquencies, but the shortcomings of the everyday respectable life, the unkind words we thought so little of but which cut so deep, the selfishness which perhaps ran on for years and which, because of that very self-centeredness, we did not see dimming the happiness of those around us. These and the like things of even the most blameless life we should not like to be compelled to repeat when seen in their true light, and how much less the episodes of a life which has not been blameless.

That there should be a re-enacting of past memories is what we might infer from our knowledge of the law of subjective mind, but there are not wanting certain facts of experience which go to support the a priori argument (argument from self-evident).

Many of my readers, I daresay, will smile at the mention of ghosts, but I can assure them that there is a good deal of reality in ghosts, especially to the ghosts themselves. Remember that if there are such things as ghosts, they were once people such as you and I are today; and the practical point is that the reader may be a ghost himself before very long. Therefore one of my objects in the present chapter is to show how to avoid becoming a ghost.

I used to laugh at ghosts when I was a young man and thought it all bunkum, but an experience which I went through many years ago entirely changed my ideas on the subject and indeed was the starting-point of my giving consideration to the laws of the unseen side of things. If it had not been for that ghost, you would not be reading this book. However, I will not go into details here, for the story has already been published both in French and English magazines. (Cahapter 2 in The Law and the Word)

Of course, I don't believe everything I hear, nor do I think that because a thing is in print it is necessarily true — heaven forbid, for then how could I read the daily newspapers? — but applying to each case the rules of evidence as strictly as though I were trying a man for his life, I find a residuum of instances in which it is impossible to come to any other conclusion than that a haunting spirit has actually been seen.

We are often told that you never meet persons who have themselves seen a ghost but only those who know somebody else who has; in other words, you can never get at the actual witness to cross-examine him, but only at hearsay evidence. But I can contradict this entirely. Since I began to investigate the subject seriously, I am surprised at the number of persons of both sexes who have circumstantially related to me their personal experiences of this sort and have stood the test of careful cross-examination in which I held a brief for the standpoint of "scientific doubt". Therefore when I say a few words about ghosts, I am talking on a subject that I have investigated.

In a large majority of cases it will be found that the spirit appears to be bound to a particular spot and to go on repeating certain actions, and the inference is that the subjective dreaming, so to say, of the departed is in these cases so intense as to create a thought-form of their conception to themselves sufficiently vivid to impress itself upon the etheric atmosphere of the locality and so become visible to those who are sufficiently sensitive.

Now, that this is not always the consequence of some great crime or other terrible happening is shown by a case in which the former owners of a house, husband and wife, after having long been habitually seen about the premises, were at last questioned by a lady who was sufficiently sensitive to communicate with them. They stated that the only thing that bound them to the house was their inordinate love of it during life. They had so centered their minds upon it that now they could not get away though they longed to do so; and, judging by their appearance and the confirmation of their identity subsequently obtained from some old documents, it would seem that they had been tied up like this for several generations.

This is an instance of having too much of a "pied a terre" (a temporary or second lodging, literally 'a foot to the ground'), and I don't think any of us would like it to become our own cases; and a fortiori (with greater reason or more convincing force) the same must hold good where the recollections of the departed are of a darker kind.

What, then, is the way out of the dilemma? It must be by some working of the law of cause and effect, and this working must take place somewhere within our own mind — we must in some way get a state of consciousness which will set us free from all troubling memories and keep before us, even in the unseen world, the prospect of happier developments.

Then the only mental attitude which can produce this effect is belief in forgiveness, the assurance that all the transgressions and shortcomings of the past have been blotted out forever. If we attain this realization in this present life, if this assurance is our dominant idea — the idea upon which all our other ideas are based — then by all the laws of mind we are bound to carry this consciousness with us into the other world and thus find ourselves free from all that would make our existence there unhappy.

Or even if we have not yet attained such a vivid assurance as to be able to say "I know", and can as yet only say "I hope", still the fact that we recognize that the principle of forgiveness exists will cause us to lay hold of it as our dominant idea in the subjective state and so place us in a position to gain clearer and clearer perception of the truth that there is forgiveness, and that it is for us.

Perhaps the critical reader may here remark that I am attributing to the subjective mind the power of starting a new train of ideas, and so contradicting what I have just said about the departed being shut up within the circle of those ideas which they have brought over with them from this world. It looks as if I had made a slip, but I haven't; for if we have carried over with us — not, perhaps, the full assurance of actual pardon but even the belief that forgiveness is possible — we have brought along with us a root idea whose very essence is that of making a new start.

It is the fundamental conception of a new order and as such carries with it the conception of ourselves as entering upon new trains of thought and new fields of action — in a word, the dominant idea of the subjective mind is that of having brought the objective mental faculties along with it. If this the mode of self-consciousness then it becomes an actual fact, and the whole mentality is brought over in its entirety; so that those who are thus in the light are liberated from imprisonment in the circulus of past memories by the very same law which binds those fast who refuse to admit the liberating principle of forgiveness. It is the same law of our mental constitution in both cases, only acting affirmatively in the one and negatively in the other, just as an iron ship floats by the identical law by which a solid lump or iron sinks.

Of course we may conceive of degrees in these things. We may well suppose that some may recognize the actual working of forgiveness in their own case less clearly than others; but whatever may be the degree of recognition of the personal fact, the realization of the principle is the same for all; and this principle must assuredly bear fruit in due time in the complete deliverance of the soul from all that would otherwise hold it in bondage.

Far be it from me to say that the case of those who pass over convinced in their denial of the principle of forgiveness is forever hopeless; but by the nature of mental law they must remain bound until they see it. Moreover by their denial of this principle they must fail to bring over their objective mentality, and so they must remain shut up in the world of their subjective memories until some of those who have brought over their whole mentality are able to penetrate the spheres of their subjective mind and impress upon it a new conception, that of forgiveness, and so plant in them the seed for the new growth of their objective mental powers.

And perhaps we may even go so far as to suppose that the power of those who are thus in wholeness of mind to aid those who are not is not confined to such as have passed over; it may be the privilege also of those who are still in the body, for the action of mind upon mind is not a thing of physical substances. If so, then we can see a reason for prayers for the departed, to say nothing of the many instances in which ghosts are reported to have besought the intercession of the living for their liberation. There is, however, in certain quarters, a lamentable inversion of this principle where prayers for the departed are turned into an article of traffic and a means for making money. I may have something to say about this in another book, and meanwhile I would only say, Beware of spurious imitations.

Of course this picture of the condition of souls in the other world does not profess to be drawn from actual knowledge, but it appears to me to be a reasonable deduction from all that we know of the laws of our mental constitution; and if the experiences of the departed logically result from the working of those laws, then what greater action of the Divine Love and Wisdom can we conceive than such an expression of itself as must utilize these laws affirmatively for our liberation instead of negatively for our bondage? The Law of Cause and Effect cannot be broken, but it can be applied with intelligence and love instead of being left to work itself out negatively for want of guidance.

So it is, then, that the doctrine of the forgiveness of sins is the mainspring of the Bible — the promise of a Messiah in the Old Testament and the fulfillment of that promise in the New — and the realization, whether in or out of the body, that God is both able and desiring to forgive, freely and without any offering save that of His own providing, and requiring nothing in return except this: that "to whom much hath been forgiven, the same loveth much".

Chapter 13

The Divine Giving

In the last two chapters we have considered the principle of the forgiveness of sin; and having laid this foundation, I would now direct attention to the working of the same principle in other directions. In its essence it is the quality of givingness — Free Giving, having Simple Accepting for its correlative, for the clear reason that you cannot put a man in possession of a gift if he will not take it. Now a little consideration will show us that Free Giving is a necessity of the very being of the All-originating Spirit. By the very fact that it is All-originating we have nothing to give to it, nothing except that reciprocity of feeling which, as we have seen, is fundamental to the Divine ideal of Man, that ideal which has called the human race into existence.

If, then, we have nothing to give but our love and worship, why not take up the position of grateful and expectant receivers? It simplifies matters and relieves us of a great deal of worry, and moreover it is undoubtedly scriptural. The reason we don't do so is because we don't believe in the free giving, and consequently we cannot adopt a mental attitude of receiving, and so the Spirit cannot make the gift.

If we seek the reason why this is so, we shall find it in our materialism, our inability to see beyond secondary causes. We get things through certain visible channels, and we mistake these for the source.

"The things I possess I got with my money, and my money I got by work". Of course you did. God doesn't put dollar bills or banknotes into your cash box by a conjuring trick. God makes things generically, whether it be iron or brains, and then we have to use them. But the iron or brains, or whatever else it may be, ultimately proceeds from the All-creating Spirit; and the more clearly we see this, the easier we shall find it to go direct to the Spirit for all we want.

Then we shall argue that, just as the Spirit can create the thing we desire, so it can also create the way by which that thing shall come to us, and so we shall not be bothered about the way. We shall work according to the sort of abilities God has bestowed upon us and according to the opportunities provided; but we shall not try to force circumstances or to do something out of our line.

Then we shall find circumstances open out and our abilities increase, and this without putting any undue strain upon ourselves, but on the contrary with a great sense of restfulness.

And the secret is this: we are not bearing the burden ourselves. We are not trying to force things on the external plane by our objective powers, nor yet on the subjective plane by trying to compel the Spirit; therefore, though diligent in our calling, we are at rest. And the foundation of this rest is that we believe in a Divine Promise, and the Promise is in the nature of the Divine Being.

This is why the Bible lays so much stress upon the idea of Promise. Promise is the law of Creative Power simplified to the utmost simplicity. Faith in a Divine Promise is the strongest attitude of mental Affirmation. It is the affirmation of the desire of the Creative Spirit to create the gift, and of its power and willingness to do so, and therefore of the production also of all the means by which the gift is to be brought to us. Also it fixes no limits and so does not restrict the mode of operation, and thus it conforms exactly to the principles of the original cosmic creation, so that the whole Universe around us becomes a testimony to the stability of the foundation on which our hope is based. This reference to the cosmic creation as bearing witness to the ground of our faith is of constant recurrence in the Bible, and its purpose is to impress upon us that the Power to which we look is that Power which in the beginning made the heavens and the earth.

The reason why this is made the starting-point of faith is that we start with an undoubted fact: the Universe exists. Then a little consideration will show us that it must have had its origin in the Thought of the Universal Spirit before its manifestation in time and space, so that here we start with another self-evident fact; and these two obvious and incontrovertible facts supply us with premises from which to reason; so that knowing our premises to be true, we know that our conclusion must be true also, if we only reason correctly from the premises. This is the logic of it.

Then the reasoning proceeds as follows: in the beginning there were no antecedent conditions, and the whole creation came out of the desire of the Spirit for Self-expression. By the nature of the case, the conception of the existence of any antecedent conditions is impossible; and so we see that creation from within (as distinguished from construction from without) has the entire absence of pre-determining and limiting conditions as its distinguishing characteristic.

Then our thought, inspired by the promise, is, so to say, reflected back into the Mind of the Universal Spirit in direct relation to ourselves and thus becomes part and parcel of the Self-realization of the Spirit in connection with ourselves personally, thus bringing about a working of the creative Law of Reciprocity from the standpoint of our own individuality; and because the activity thus called forth is that of the Original Creative Energy, the First Cause itself, it is as unhampered by antecedent conditions as was the original cosmic creation itself.

I have gone more fully into this subject in my Creative Process in the Individual, but I hope I have now said sufficient to make the general principle clear and to show that the Bible promises are nothing else than the statement of the essential creativeness of the All-originating Spirit when operating in reciprocity with the individual mind. If we believe in the power of Affirmation, then trust in the Divine promise is the strongest affirmation we can make. And if we believe in the power of Denials, then such a simple trust is also the strongest denial we can make for, being absolute confidence, it constitutes an emphatic denial of any power, whether in the visible or the invisible, to prevent the fulfillment of the promise.

It is for this reason that the Bible lays such stress on belief in the Divine promises as the way to receive the blessing. The Bible was written for the benefit of any reader, whether learned or unlearned, and takes into consideration the fact that the latter are by far the more numerous; therefore it reduces the matter to its simplest elements: Hear the promise, Believe it, and Receive its fulfillment.

The fact that the statement of any truth has been reduced to its simplest terms does not imply that it cannot stand the test of investigation; all that it implies is that it has been put into the best shape for immediate use alike for those who are able, and for those who are unable, to investigate the underlying principle. We press the button and the electric bell rings, whether we are trained electricians or not; but the fact that the bell rings for those who know nothing about electricity does not hinder the investigator from learning why it rings. On the other hand, the greatest electrician does not have to go through the whole theory of the working of the current when he rings at the door of your house, which would be inconvenient to say the least of it; and still less does he have to solve the ultimate problem of what electricity actually is in itself, for he knows no more about that than anybody else.

And so in the end he has to come back to the same simple faith in electricity as the man who does not know the difference between the positive and negative poles of a battery. His greater knowledge ought to extend his faith in electricity, because he knows it can do much greater things than ringing a bell; and in like manner any clearer insight we may gain into the modus operandi (method of operation) of the Divine promises should increase our trust in them, while at the same time it leaves us on just the same level with the most ignorant as to what the Divine Spirit actually is in itself.

We all alike have to come back to the standpoint of a simple faith in the vitalizing working of the energizing power, whether God or electricity, and therefore the Bible simplifies matters by bidding us take this ultimate position as our starting-point, and not say, "I am confident because I know the law", but "I am confident because I know in whom I have believed".

I think some such considerations as these must have been at the back of St Paul's mind, making him draw that distinction between Law and Faith which runs through all his Epistles. It is true he is, in the first instance, speaking of the ceremonial law of the Mosaic ritual, for he was addressing Jews for the most part; but if we reflect that reliance on that ceremonial was only one particular mode of relying upon knowledge of laws, we shall see that the principle is applicable to all laws; and moreover the original Greek word used by St Paul implies law in general, thus giving a scope to his argument which makes it as applicable to ourselves as to Jews.

And the point is this: laws are statements of the relations of certain things to certain other things under certain conditions. Given the same things and the same conditions, the same laws will come into play because the same relation has been established between the things; but this is exactly the sphere which excludes the idea of original creation.

It is the sphere of science, of analysis, of measurement; it is the proper domain of all merely constructive work; but that is just what original creation is not. Original creation is not troubled about antecedent conditions; it creates new conditions, and by so doing establishes new relations and therefore new laws; and since the declared purpose of the Bible is to bring us into a new order, in which all that is meant by "the Fall" shall be obliterated, this is nothing else than a New Creation, which indeed the Bible calls it.

Therefore our knowledge of particular laws, whether mental or material, is of no avail for this purpose, and we have to come back to the stand-point of simple faith.

I do not wish to say anything against the knowledge of particular laws, either mental or material, which is useful in its way; but what I do want to emphasize is that this knowledge is not the Creative Power. If we get hold of this distinction, we shall see what is meant by the promises contained in the Bible. They are statements of the original creating power of the Spirit as it works from the standpoint of a specific personal relation to the individual, which relation is brought about by the expectant attitude of the individual mind, which renders it receptive to the anticipated creative action of the Spirit; and it is this mental attitude that the Bible calls Faith.

Seen in this light, faith in the promise is not a mere unreasoning belief, neither is it in opposition to law; but on the contrary, it is the most all-embracing conclusion to which reasoning can lead us and the channel through which the Supreme Law of the Universe — the Law of the creative activity of the All-originating Spirit — operates to make new conditions for the individual. It is not trying to make yourself believe what you know is not true, but it is the exercise of the highest reason based upon the knowledge of the highest truth.

The Divine promise and the individual faith are thus the correlatives of each other and together constitute a creative power to which we can assign no limits. When we begin to apprehend this connection of Cause and Effect, we see the force of the statements made by the Master: "All things are possible to him that believeth" (Mark 9:23); "Have faith in God and nothing shall be impossible unto you" (Matt. 17:20); and the like. If we attribute any authority whatever to his sayings, we are justified by them in affirming that there is no limit to the power of faith and that his declarations on this subject are not mere figures of speech, but statements of the special and individual working of the Creative Law of the Universe.

Viewed in this light, the Bible promises assume a practical aspect and a personal application, and we see what is meant by being Children of Promise. We are no longer under bondage to Law — that is, to those laws of sequences which arise from the relations of existing things to one another — but have risen into what the Bible tells us is the Perfect Law, the Law of Liberty; and so according to the symbolism of the two representative mothers, Hagar and Sarah, we are no longer children of the bond-woman but of the free (Gal. 4:31).

Only, to be "heirs according to promise" we must be descendants of Abraham. I am not prepared to say that the majority of readers of this book are not so literally, though they may not be aware of the fact; but that is another branch of the subject with which I deal elsewhere ("Salvation is of the Jews" in The Doré Lectures).

Setting aside this historical question, let us here consider the question of spiritual principles. On this point the teaching of the Bible is very plain. It is that they are children of Abraham who are of the faith of Abraham; they are his seed according to promise — that is, they are living by the same principle which is set forth as forming the groundwork of Abraham's life: "Abraham believed God, and it was counted unto him for righteousness" (Rom. 4:3).

Now what will be the fruit of such a root? It must necessarily produce two results in our inner life: Restfulness and Enthusiasm. At first sight these two might appear opposed to one another: but it is not so, for Enthusiasm is born of confidence and so also is Restfulness. Both are necessary for the work we have to do. Without Enthusiasm there can be no vigorous work; even if attempted, it would only be done as task-work, something which we had to grind at compulsorily, and though I would not deny that a certain amount of good and useful work may be done from a mere sense of obligation, still it will be of a very inferior quality to what is done spontaneously for love of the work itself.

Take the case of the poor artist who is the slave of the dealer and has to labour from morning to night to turn out scores of little pot-boilers by a more or less mechanical process. If he be a born artist, the fact will assert itself in spite of the conditions, and even the pot-boilers will have some degree of merit. But put the same man in more favourable circumstances where he is no longer restricted by trade requirements but is allowed to give full scope to his genius, then the artist in him rises up, he creates his own vision of nature, and masterpieces come from his brush.

This is because he is now working from enthusiasm and not from Compulsion. It is also because he is working with a sense of Restfulness; he is no longer obliged to turn out so many pot-boilers per week to meet the demands of the petty dealer but can take his own time and choose his own subject and treat it in his own way.

Then the business side of his work will be negotiated for him by the big dealer, the man who also is an artist in his own way and knows the difference between the productions of spontaneous feeling and mere mechanical dexterity, and who finds his own profit in helping the artist to maintain that freedom from anxiety and the sense of compulsion without which such high-class works as the big dealer's business depends on cannot be produced.

Now this is a parable. God is the big dealer, and his best work through man is done for love and not by compulsion; and the more we realize this, the better work we shall do. Am I irreverent in comparing God to some great picture-dealer of world-wide reputation and saying that he too gains his profits in the transaction? I think not; for Christ himself tells us of the master who looked to receive a profit out of his servants' work, and I have only clothed the old parable in modern garb and coloured it with a familiar colouring.

And we may carry the simile yet further. The great dealer knows how to place the masterpieces in which he deals, he is in touch with connoisseurs with whom the artist cannot come in contact;

and if the artist had to attend to all this, what would become of his creative vision?

"How do you manage to paint such exquisite pictures?" it was once asked of Corot; and he replied "Je reve mon tableau, et plus tard je peindrai mon reve". There spoke the true artist: "I dream my picture, and afterwards I paint my dream". The true artist dreams with his eyes open, looking at nature, and it is because he thus sees the inner spirit of her beauty through its external veil of form that he can show others what they could nor see, unaided, for themselves. This is his function, and the large-minded dealer enables him to perform it by taking the business side of the matter in hand in a generous spirit combined with a shrewd knowledge of the market, and so leaves the painter to his proper work by seeing his vision of nature and interpreting it by his individual method of interpretation.

So with the Divine Healer. He knows the ropes, He has command of the market, and He will deal in a liberal spirit with all who place their work in His hands. Let us, then, do diligently, honestly, and cheerfully the work of today, not as serving a hard taskmaster, but in happy confidence, and day by day hand it over to the Loving Creating Spirit who will bring out connections we had never dreamt of, and open up fresh avenues for us where we saw no way. You are the artist, and God is your honest, appreciative, and powerful Dealer.

But what else is this except exchanging the burden of Law for the peaceful liberty of Faith in the Divine Goodness, the All-givingness of the Heavenly Father? To attain this is far better than puzzling our brains over abstruse questions of theology and metaphysics. The whole thing is summed up in this: if you take your own knowledge of law as the starting-point of the creative action in your personal life, you have inverted the true order, and the logical result from your premises will be to bring the whole burden upon yourself like a thousand of bricks; but if you take the All-givingness of the Creating Spirit as your starting-point, then everything else will fall into a harmonious order, and all you will have to do is to receive and use what you receive, asking the Divine guidance to use it rightly.

You throw the burden on whichever side you regard as taking the initiative in your personal creative series. If you take it, you make God a mere impersonal force, and ultimately you have nothing to depend on but your own unaided knowledge and power. If on the other hand you regard God as taking the initiative by an All-givingness peculiarly connected with yourself, then the action is reversed and you will find yourself backed up by the Infinite Love, Wisdom, and Power.

Of course there is a reason for these things, and I have endeavoured to suggest a few thoughts as to the reason; but the practical advice I give to each reader is: stop arguing about it. Try it, my boy; try it, my dear girl — for the promise is: "Let him take hold of My strength that he may be at peace with Me, and he shall make peace with Me" (Isaiah 27:5).

Chapter 14

The Spirit of Antichrist

When we have realized the essential nature of any principle, we can form a pretty fair guess as to the general lines on which it will show itself in action, whether in individuals, or institutions, or nations, or events. The evolution of principles is the key to all history in the past, and similarly it is the key to all the history that is to come; therefore, if we grasp the significance of any principle, though we may not be able to prophesy particular events, we shall be able to form some general idea of the sort of developments its prevalence must give rise to.

Now all through the Bible we find the statement of two leading principles which are diametrically opposed to one another: the principle of Sonship or reliance upon God, and its opposite or the denial of God; and it is this latter that is called the spirit of Antichrist.

This spirit, or mode of thought, is described in the second chapter of the second epistle to the Thessalonians and the fourth chapter of the first epistle to Timothy; and its distinctive note is that it sets itself up in the temple of God, placing itself above all that is worshipped, and a similar description is given in Daniel 11:36-39.

The widespread development of this inverted principle, the Bible tells us, is the key to the history of "the latter days", those times in which we now live, and the prophetic Scriptures are largely occupied with the struggle which must take place between these opposing principles. It is impossible for the two to amalgamate, for they are in direct antagonism; and the Bible tells us that, though the struggle may be severe, the victory must at last remain with those who worship God.

The reason for this becomes evident if we look at the fundamental nature of the principles themselves. One is the principle of the Affirmative, and the other is the principle of the Negative. One is that which builds up, and the other is that which pulls down. One consents to the initiative being taken by that Spirit which has brought all creation into existence, and the other bids this Spirit take a back seat and denies that it has any power of initiative. This is the essence of the opposition between the two principles. Whatever one affirms, the other denies; and so, since no agreement is possible, the conflict between them must continue until one or the other gets the final victory.

Now if the spirit of Antichrist is what the Bible describes it, we cannot shut our eyes to the fact that it is now present among us. St Paul tells us that it was already beginning to work in his day, only that at that time there was a hindrance to its fuller development; but he adds that when that hindrance should be removed, the development of the spirit of Antichrist would be phenomenal.

Various commentators on this text have explained the hindrance alluded to by St Paul to have been the existence of the Roman Empire, and no doubt this is true as far as it goes. In this passage (2 Thess. 2:1) St. Paul reminds the Thessalonians of something he had told them on the subject — that is, something he had communicated verbally, and not in writing — regarding the falling away which would take place before the resurrection. He says, "Remember ye not, when I was yet with you, I told you of these things? And now ye know what withholdeth that he might be revealed in his time".

The very earliest traditions tell us that what St. Paul had then verbally explained to the Thessalonians was that the Roman Empire as then existing must pass away before these further developments could take place; but he was careful not to put this in writing lest it should expose the Christians to additional persecution on the charge of being enemies to the state.

This tradition is by no means a vague one. We first find it mentioned by Irenaeus (St. Irenaeus, 140-203 CE, Bishop of Lugdunum (Lyon)), the disciple of Polycarp (St. Polycarp, fl. 2nd century CE, Greek Bishop of Smyrna), who was himself the disciple of St. John; so that we get it on the authority of one who had been instructed by a personal friend and acquaintance of the apostles, and we may therefore feel assured that in this tradition we have a correct statement of what St. Paul had said regarding the nature of the hindrance to which he alludes in this epistle.

The existence of the Roman Empire, then, was doubtless the outward and immediate cause of this hindrance to the coming of Antichrist; but we must remember that at the back of the external and visible circumstances which are instrumental in the history of the world there are mental and spiritual causes, and so the matter goes further and deeper than any existing political conditions. It is a question of spiritual principles, a question of causes; and so long as any given cause is at work, its effects will continue to show themselves, though the particular form they will assume will vary with the conditions under which the manifestation takes place.

Therefore we may look deeper than the political conditions of St Paul's time to find the spiritual and causal nature of the hindrance to which he alludes. He tells us that at the time when he wrote, the spirit of Antichrist was already working, but that its complete manifestation was delayed till a later period by reason of a certain impediment which would be removed in due time; and a comparison of his statement with that of St Peter in the third chapter of the second epistle shows that the removal of this impediment and the full manifestation of the spirit of Antichrist were to be looked for in the time of the end.

Now Daniel says the very same thing (Dan. 12:1-4), and he points out the marks by which the time of the end is to be recognized. They are two: "Many shall run to and fro, and knowledge shall be increased"; and if this is not an accurate description of things at the present time, well — I leave the reader to fill in the blank. We may say, then, that the time when the hindrance to the manifestation of Antichrist is to be removed is a time when knowledge has been increased; and if we reflect that the whole matter is one of spiritual powers, is it not reasonable to suppose that the hindrance which in St Paul's time prevented the fuller development of the spiritual power of Antichrist was ignorance of the nature of spiritual power in general?

Now this knowledge is becoming more and more widely diffused, and consequently the danger of its inverted application is today far greater than in St Paul's time; and therefore the more we realize what potentialities open before us, the more it behoves us to be on our guard lest we regard them in such a way as to take the place of God in the temple of God.

It may, or may not, be that "the Man of Sin" exhibiting himself as God in the Temple of God is to be understood as an actual ceremony taking place in an actual building; though even this is not altogether inconceivable if we recollect that during the French Revolution a notorious actress was enthroned upon the high altar in the cathedral of Notre Dame as the Goddess of Reason and received the public adoration of the official representative of France. What has been may be again, and we know that history repeats itself; but I think we have to look for something more personal and powerful than any theatrical exhibition of this kind.

If we search the Scriptures, we shall find that the real Temple of God is Man. When Christ said, "'Destroy this temple, and in three days I will raise it up' he spoke of the temple of his body" (John 2:19-21); and again St Paul says, "Know ye not that ye are the temple of God?" (1 Cor. 3:16). Moreover, the promise is, "I will dwell in them, and walk in them; and I will be their God, and they shall be My people" (2 Cor. 6:16), and so on in many similar passages, a careful consideration of which leaves no doubt but that the true significance of "the temple" in Scripture is that of human individuality.

The meaning then becomes clear. The temple which is profaned is the innermost sanctuary of our heart, out of which come all the issues of our individual life: "as he thinketh in his heart so is he" (Prov. 23:7); and if this be true, then it is of the utmost importance who is enthroned there. Is it the All-originating Creative Spirit with its infinite love, wisdom, and power, or is it our personal knowledge and will? It must be one of the two. Which is it?

The difference is immense, and it consists in this: if our personal knowledge, wisdom, and will-power are the highest things we know, then we are left exactly where we were and are making no advance. We may, indeed, accumulate a certain amount of knowledge of the hidden laws of physical and psychic forces not commonly known to our fellow-men, which knowledge must necessarily carry a corresponding power along with it; but this only places us in a position where we more urgently need a higher knowledge and a higher wisdom to guide us.

The greater the power you put into anyone's hands, the more mischief will result if through ignorance of its true uses he misapplies it. He may understand the mere mechanism, so to say, of this power perfectly, so that he will know how to make it work. It is not on the mechanical side that the mistake will occur. But the mistake will be in the purpose to which the power is applied; and if that be wrong, the greater the power, the worse will be the results. You may teach a child to drive a motor-car, but unless you can at the same time invest him with powers of observation and caution and promptness in emergency beyond his years, his driving will end in a smash.

Now it is just this inspiration beyond our natural acuteness, of foresight beyond our unaided vision, that we require for the really useful employment of any enhanced powers that may come to us as the result of our increasing knowledge; and this is not to be drawn from the knowledge of what we may call the merely mechanical working of the Law of Cause and Effect, whether on the side of the visible or of the invisible. That knowledge, taken by itself, is only the lower knowledge — learning, so to say, how to do the particular trick. But to make it of real value, we need to know not only how to do it, but why to do it. And since the only true why is the building up of a harmonious whole both in ourselves and in the race — a whole which, by an organic connection between the causes sown today and the results produced tomorrow, shall continually germinate into greater and greater fullness of joyous life — and since the production of such a continuously growing and rejoicing wholeness is the only reasonable purpose to which our knowledge and our powers, whether great or small, can be applied, how are we to get such an outlook into the unending future and into our present relations in all their ultimate consequences by our own personal knowledge however extended?

We are sowing causes all the time with only a very limited outlook as to what they will produce; but if we are conscious that we have submitted our action to the guidance of the Supreme Wisdom and Love, we know that we must be importing into it an adjustment with the great purpose of the Universe.

We cannot grasp that purpose in all its details and infinite extent, but we can see that it must be an unending growth into ever increasing manifestation of the Life, Love, and Beauty which the All-originating Spirit is in itself.

That Spirit is in itself Unity, and its Self-expression is through its manifestation in Multiplicity; and the more clearly we see this, the more clearly we shall see that the way to co-operate with it is by seeking to make our own thought the channel of its Thought. But to do this is to recognize the presence of a Divine Intelligence guiding our thought and a Divine Power working through our actions; and this recognition, coupled with the desire that our thought should be thus guided and our actions thus vivified, is the very essence of Worship. It is the very opposite to the mental attitude which sets itself up as needing no guidance and no help from a higher source, and which denies the working of any higher power; and so worship becomes the foundation principle of the life. This does not mean a specific ceremonial observance, but the adoption of the principle of worship, which is the recognition of the true relation of the individual mind to the Parent Mind from which it springs.

If anyone finds that a particular ceremonial conduces towards this end, then that ceremonial is useful to him, but it does not follow that the same ceremonial is necessary for somebody else. It is just like water-colour painting. One man requires to keep his paper dry through the progress of the work, while another paints entirely in the wet; yet if they are both artists, each will record his vision in a way that will unfold to the spectator some secret of nature's beauty. Each must use the means which at his present stage he finds most conducive to the end, only let him remember that it is the end alone which really counts.

Therefore it is that the Great Teacher laid down only one rule for worship — that it should be "in spirit and in truth". The essence and not the form is what counts, because the whole thing is a question of mental attitude. It is that attitude of constant Receptiveness which is the only possible conscious correlative to the infinite Divine Givingness. To attain this is conscious union with the All-creating Spirit.

The logic of it may be briefly put thus: we want to come into touch with the Power which originates the Universe; but we cannot do this and at the same time disqualify it by denying that it continues to be originative when it comes in touch with ourselves. Therefore to be really in touch with it as the originating Power, we must let It lead us and not try to compel It; and to do this is to worship.

The mark of the opposite mental attitude is to take no heed of such a Guiding Power, and then the only alternative is to set one's self in its place. When we realize that spiritual causes are always at the back of external phenomena, and the more we come to see that particular causes can be resolved into variations of an ultimate cause, the more our intent to rule that ultimate cause must result in self-deification.

But the bad logic comes in not seeing that the real ultimate cause must be entirely originative — that this is just what makes it worth seeking — and trying to deprive it of this power by attempting to compel it instead of looking to it for leading.

It is just here that those who realize the nature of spiritual causation are in greater danger than the mere materialist. There really is an unseen Force which can be controlled in the manner they contemplate, and their mistake is in supposing that this Force is the ultimate Creating Power.

I daresay some readers will smile at this, and I am well aware that it is quite possible to build up an apparently logical argument to show that what I am now speaking of is a merely fanciful idea; but to these I will not make any reply — the matter is one requiring careful development, and a partial and inadequate explanation would be worse than useless. I must therefore leave its discussion to some other occasion and in the meanwhile ask my readers to assume the existence of this Force simply as a working hypothesis. In asking this I am not asking more than they are ready to concede in the case of physical science, where it is necessary to assume the existence of purely speculative conditions of energy and matter if we would co-ordinate the observed phenomena of Nature into an intelligible whole; and in like manner I would ask the critical reader to assume as a working hypothesis the existence of an Essence intermediate between the Originating Spirit and the world of external manifestation.

The existence of such an intermediary is a conclusion which has been arrived at by some of the deepest thinkers who have ever lived, and it has been called by various names in different countries and ages; but for the purpose of the present book I think I cannot do better than adopt the name given to it by the European writers of the fifteenth, sixteenth, and seventeenth centuries.

They called it "Anima Mundi", or the Soul of the World, as distinguished from "Animus Dei", or the Divine Spirit, and they were careful to discriminate between the two.

If you look in a Latin dictionary, you will find that this word, which means life, mind, or soul, is given in a twofold form, masculine and feminine, Animus and Anima. Now it is in the dual nature thus indicated that the action of spiritual causation consists, and we cannot eliminate either of the two factors without involving a confusion of ideas which the recognition of their interaction would prevent us falling into.

When once we recognize the nature and function of Amina Mundi, we shall find that, under a variety of symbols, it is referred to throughout the Bible and indeed forms one of the principal subjects of its teaching; but to explain these Bible references would require a book to itself. In general terms, however, we may say that Anima Mundi is "the Eternal Feminine" and the necessary correlative to Animus Dei, the true Originating Spirit. It is what the medieval writers called "the Universal Medium" and is that principle which, as I pointed out in the opening chapters of this book, is esoterically called "Water".

It is not the Originating Principle itself, but it is that principle through which the Originating Principle operates. It is not originative but receptive, not the seed but the ground, formative of that with which it is impregnated, as is indicated by the old French expression for it, "ventre saint gris", the "holy blue womb" — the innermost maturing place of Nature; and its power is that of attracting the conditions necessary for the full maturing of that seed with which it is impregnated and thus bringing about the growth which ultimately culminates in completed manifestation.

Perhaps the idea may be put into terms of modern Western thought by calling it the Subconscious Mind of the Universe; and if we regard it in this light, we may apply to it all those laws of the interaction between conscious and subconscious mentality with which I conclude most of my readers are familiar. (On this subject I would refer the reader to my Edinburgh Lectures on Mental Science.)

Now the chief characteristics of subconscious mind are its amenability to suggestion and its power of working out into material conditions the logical consequences of the suggestion impressed upon it. It is not originative, but formative. It does not provide the seed, but it causes it to grow; and the seed is the suggestion impressed upon it by the objective mind.

If, then, we credit the Universal Subjective Mind with these same qualities, we find ourselves face to face with a stupendous power which by its nature affords the matrix for the germination of all the seeds of thought that are planted in it.

Looking at the totality of Nature as we see it — the various types of life, vegetable, animal, and human, and the evolution of these types from earlier ones — we can only come to the conclusion that the Originating Mind, Animus Dei as distinguished from Anima Mundi, must in the first instance see things generically — the type rather than the individual — much as Plato puts it in his doctrine of archetypal ideas; and so the world, as we know it, is governed by a Law of Averages which maintains and advances the race whatever may become of the individual.

We may call this a generic or type creation as distinguished from the conception of a specific creation of particular individuals; but, as I have explained more fully in The Creative Process in the Individual, the culminating point of such a generic creation must be the production of individual minds which are capable of realizing the general principle at work and therefore of giving it individual application.

Now it is the imperfect apprehension of this principle that causes its inversion. It is recognizing Anima Mundi without Animus Dei. And the more a man sees of the immense possibilities of his own thought and volition working upon Anima Mundi while at the same time ignoring Animus Dei, the more likely he is to grow too big for his boots. He then logically has nothing to guide him but his own personal will; and with all the resources of Anima Mundi at his disposal, there is no saying to what extremes he may not go. "L' appetit vient en mangeant" (appetite comes from eating), and the more power he gets, the more he will want; and the more his desires are gratified, the more he will become satiated and require fresh stimulus to his jaded appetites.

This is no fancy picture. History tells us of the Emperor Tiberius offering a great reward to anyone who would discover a new pleasure, and Nero burning Rome for a sensation. Picture such men in possession of a knowledge of psychic laws which would place all the powers of Anima Mundi at their disposal, and then imagine not one such, but hundreds or thousands combining in some common enterprise under the leadership of some pre-eminently gifted individual, and recollect in this connection the accumulated power of massed mental action — and what must the result be? Surely just what the Bible tells us: the working of all sorts of prodigies which to the uninstructed multitude must appear to be nothing else than miracles.

The knowledge, then, of the enormous possibilities stored up in the Anima Mundi, or the Soul of Nature, is the great instrument through which the power of the Antichrist will work. It is, indeed, the acquisition of this power that will more and more confirm him in his idea of self-deification; and note that though for convenience I use the singular pronoun, I am speaking of a class — that is, of all who do not offer to God the sincere worship of trust in the Divine Love, Wisdom, and Power. I use the name Antichrist as that of a class, and one which seems likely to be widespread before long, though this in no way excludes the possibility of some phenomenally powerful leader of this class attaining to a pre-eminence which will make him the typical manifestation of the principal of self-deification.

Antichrist, whether as class or as individual, has attained to the recognition of a great universal principle which I have endeavoured to set forth in this and other books: the principle of the introduction of "the Personal Factor" into the realm of unseen causes. He has laid hold of a great truth.

All progress beyond the merely generic working of the Law of Averages is to be made by the introduction of the Personal Factor; but the mistake which Antichrist makes is that he cannot see any personality but his own. He sees the Soul of Nature and the power of its responsiveness to the Personal elements in the mind of man, and he sees no further. Therefore, after his own fashion, he recognizes a spiritual power of mere forces, but he does not recognize beyond this the presence of "the God of gods" (Dan. 11:36-38). Logically, therefore, he becomes to himself the Person. He rightly says that the Law of Cause and Effect is Universal and that the expansion of this law to the production of hitherto unknown effects depends upon the introduction of the personal factor; but he does not understand the reinforcement of the individual human personality by a Divine Personality, the recognition of which would bring in that principle of Worship which, from the standpoint of this imperfect assumption of premises, he logically denies.

To this power based upon self-deification is opposed the power based upon the worship of God; and the fact to be noted is that they are both using the same instrument. Both work by the power of the personal factor acting upon the impersonal Soul of Nature. The Anima Mundi itself is simply neutral. It is responsive to impression and generative of the conditions corresponding to the seed sown in it; but being entirely impersonal, it is without any sort of moral consciousness and will therefore respond equally to the impress of good or of evil.

Therefore in estimating the final result, Anima Mundi may be entirely eliminated from our calculations. To put it mathematically, if Anima Mundi be represented by the same quantity on either side of the equation, it may be struck out from both sides, and then the real calculation will involve only the remaining factors. In the case we are considering, the only other factor is that of Personality, and consequently the ultimate question at issue is: on which side is the greater force of Personality.

The answer to this question is to be found in the Cosmic Creation. We are part of that creation; our personality is part of it. Our personality proceeds by derivation from the All-originating Spirit and therefore, logically, that Spirit must be the Infinite of Personality.

It is true we cannot analyze or fathom the profundities of that Spirit, and from this point of view we may speak of it as "the Unknowable"; and so we may not be able to define what the All-creating Spirit's consciousness of Personality may be to Itself; but unless we entirely deny our derivation from it, must it not be clear that it must contain the infinite potential of all that can ever constitute personality in ourselves? And if this be so, then the growth of our own personality must be proportioned to the extent to which this potential flows into us; and to adopt the receptive mental attitude towards our Creator which will allow of such an inflowing is to take that attitude of Worship which Antichrist denies. Therefore the greater power of Personality is on the side of the worshippers of God.

Then, if this be so, their control over the powers of the unseen is greater than that of the Antichrist, but they do not seek to control those powers in the same way that he does. He knows no personality but his own, and so he seeks to gain this control by his own knowledge of particular laws and by his own force of will and is thus limited by the capacities of his own personality, however extensive they may be. His method is to consciously control Anima Mundi for his own purposes by his own strength.

Those on the opposite side do not thus seek to subject Anima Mundi to their personal will. Many, perhaps the majority of them, do not even know that there is any such thing as Anima Mundi, and so they rely on a simple trust in "the Father". And those among them who do know it know also that the worshipper of God may entirely eliminate it from consideration, as I have already said, and so they also rely upon simple trust in "the Father"; the only difference is that, knowing something of the nature of the medium through which the unseen powers are working on both sides, and that the ultimate question is only that of Personality, they should have a yet stronger faith than their less instructed brethren, though in kind it is still the same faith — that of the Son in the Father.

Whether, then, instructed in these matters or not, the worshippers of God will by their very faith and worship be exercising a constant influence upon Anima Mundi, attracting all those conditions which must tend to their final victory over the opposing force.

Their worship enshrines the All-creating Spirit in their hearts, and their thoughts of Him and desires towards Him go forth into the Soul of Nature, impregnating it with the seed of the good, the beautiful, and the life-giving, which must assuredly bring forth fruit in its own likeness in due time.

Their method may not produce the sensational effects which may, perhaps, be produced by their opponents when the development of psychic forces reaches its climax, but in the end all such temporary wonders will be swept away by the overflowing of power which must result when Anima Mundi becomes permeated by Animus Dei, not merely as now in the generic sense of the maintenance of the world, but also in the specific sense of the introduction of the Personal factor in its complete Divine manifestation.

Thus it will be seen that in its grand delineations of the closing scenes of the present age, the Bible nowhere departs from the Universal Law of Cause and Effect. There is a reason for everything if we can only penetrate deep enough to find it; and the laws of causation with which we are gradually gaining a better acquaintance in the realm of our own mentality are the same laws which in their wider scope embrace nations and make history.

When we see this, the why and wherefore of even that great climax of the present age which the Bible sets before us becomes intelligible. We may not be able to predict specific events, but we can recognize the development of principles, and so we see more clearly the meaning of those inspired prophecies which would otherwise be enigmatic to us.

Then when we see that these prophecies are in no way isolated from the natural laws of the Universe, but rather are based upon them and are in fact the description of those very laws operating in their widest field of action on the human plane, we shall feel the more confidence in those hints of definite measures of time which they afford us.

This is a very important part of their message, and though we may not be able to reckon the precise day or year, we may yet come to a very close approximation of our present whereabouts in the chronological calendar, and there are many indications to show that we are very rapidly approaching that climax which the Bible calls the end of the age.

This, however, is far too large a question for me to open up in these concluding pages, and perhaps it may be my privilege to treat of it at some future time; but I have endeavoured here to offer some suggestions of the general lines on which the Bible student may intelligently approach the subject, realizing the close connection that exists between the Bible teachings regarding the forgiveness of sin, the spirituality of worship, the development of personality, and the originative action of the All-creating Spirit. These are all parts of one great whole and cannot be dissociated. To dissociate them is to pull down the edifice of the Divine Temple; to realize their unity is to build up — that true Temple of God which is the Individuality of Man made perfect by the indwelling of the Holy Spirit.

It shall come to pass that whosoever shall call on the Name of the Lord shall be saved. (Acts 2:21)

Him that cometh to Me I will in no wise cast out. (John 6:37)

MARANATHA.

Collected Essays of Thomas Troward

Foreword
An Appreciation
by Paul Derrick

How is one to know a friend? Certainly not by the duration of an acquaintance. Neither can friendship be bought or sold by service rendered. Nor can it be coined into acts of gallantry or phrases of flattery. It has no part in the small change of courtesy. It is outside all these, containing them all and superior to them all.

To some is given the great privilege of a day set apart to mark the arrival of a total stranger panoplied with all the insignia of friendship. He comes unannounced. He bears no letter of introduction. No mutual friend can vouch for him. Suddenly and silently he steps unexpectedly out of the shadow of material concern and spiritual obscurity into the radiance of intimate friendship, as a picture is projected upon a lighted screen. But unlike the phantom picture, he is an instant reality that one's whole being immediately recognizes, and the radiance of fellowship that pervades his word, thought, and action holds all the essence of long companionship.

Unfortunately there are too few of these bright messengers of God to be met with in life's pilgrimage, but that Judge Thomas Troward was one of them will never be doubted by the thousands who are now mourning his departure from among us. Those whose closest touch with him has been the reading of his books will mourn him as a friend only less than those who listened to him on the platform. For no books ever written more clearly expressed the author. The same simple lucidity and gentle humanity, the same effort to discard complicated non-essentials, mark both the man and his books.

Although the spirit of benign friendliness pervades his writings and illuminated his public life, yet much of his capacity for friendship was denied those who were not privileged to clasp hands with him and to sit beside him in familiar confidence. Only in the intimacy of the fireside did he wholly reveal his innate modesty and simplicity of character. Here alone, glamoured with his radiating friendship, was shown the wealth of his richly stored mind equipped by nature and long training to deal logically with the most profound and abstruse questions of life. Here indeed was proof of his greatness, his unassuming superiority, his humanity, his keen sense of honour, his wit and humour, his generosity and all the characteristics of a rare gentleman, a kindly philosopher, and a true friend.

To Judge Troward was given the logician's power to strip a subject bare of all superfluous and concealing verbiage and to exhibit the gleaming jewels of truth and reality in splendid simplicity. This supreme quality, this ability to make the complex simple, the power to subordinate the non-essential, gave to his conversation, to his lectures, to his writings, and in no less degree to his personality, a direct and charming naïveté that at once challenged attention and compelled confidence and affection.

His sincerity was beyond question. However much one might differ from him in opinion, at least one never doubted his profound faith and complete devotion to truth. His guileless nature was beyond ungenerous suspicions and selfish ambitions. He walked calmly upon his way wrapped in the majesty of his great thoughts, oblivious to the vexations of the world's cynicism. Charity and reverence for the indwelling spirit marked all his relations. Tolerance of the opinions of others, benevolence, and tenderness dwelt in his every word and act. Yet his careful consideration of others did not paralyze the strength of his firm will or his power to strike hard blows at wrong and error. The search for truth, to which his life was devoted, was to him a holy quest. That he could and would lay a lance in defense of his opinions is evidenced in his writings, and has many times been demonstrated to the discomfiture of assailing critics. But his urbanity was a part of himself and never departed from him.

Not to destroy but to create was his part in the world. In developing his philosophy he built upon the foundations of his predecessors. No good and true stone to be found among the ruins of the past, but was carefully worked into hus superstructure of modern thought, radiant with spirituality, to the building of which the enthusiasm of his life was devoted.

To one who has studied Judge Troward, and grasped the significance of his theory of the "Universal Subconscious Mind", and who also has attained to an appreciation of Henri Bergson's [Henri Louis Bergson, 1859-1941, French philosopher who produced a philosophy of 'creative evolution'.] theory of a "Universal Livingness", superior to and outside the material Universe, there must appear a distinct correlation of ideas. That intricate and ponderously irrefutable argument that Bergson has so patiently built up by deep scientific research and unsurpassed profundity of thought and crystal-clear reason, that leads to the substantial conclusion that man has leapt the barrier of materiality only by the urge of some external pressure superior to himself, but which, by reason of infinite effort, he alone of all terrestrial beings has succeeded in utilizing in a superior manner and to his advantage: this well-rounded and exhaustively demonstrated argument in favour of a super-livingness in the Universe, which finds it highest terrestrial expression in man, appears to be the scientific demonstration of Judge Troward's basic principle of the "Universal Subconscious Mind". This Universal and infinite God-consciousness which Judge Troward postulates as man's subconsciousness, and from which man was created and maintained, and of which all physical, mental, and spiritual manifestation is a form of expression, appears to be a corollary of Bergson's demonstrated "Universal Livingness". What Bergson has so brilliantly proven by patient and exhaustive processes of science, Judge Troward arrived at by intuition, and postulated as the basis of his argument, which he proceeded to develop by deductive reasoning.

The writer was struck by the apparent parallelism of these two distinctly dissimilar philosophies, and mentioned the discovery to Judge Troward who naturally expressed a wish to read Bergson, with whose writings he was wholly unacquainted. A loan of Bergson's "Creative Evolution" produced no comment for several weeks, when it was returned with the characteristic remark, "I've tried my best to get hold of him, but I don't know what he is talking about". I mention the remark as being characteristic only because it indicates his extreme modesty and disregard of exhaustive scientific research.

The Bergson method of scientific expression was unintelligible to his mind, trained to intuitive reasoning. The very elaborateness and microscopic detail that makes Bergson great is opposed to Judge Troward's method of simplicity. He cared not for complexities, and the intricate minutiae of the process of creation, but was only concerned with its motive power — the spiritual principles upon which it was organized and upon which it proceeds.

Although the conservator of truth of every form and degree wherever found, Judge Troward was a ruthless destroyer of sham and pretense. To those submissive minds that placidly accept everything indiscriminately, and also those who prefer to follow along paths of well-beaten opinion because the beaten path is popular, to all such he would perhaps appear to be an irreverent iconoclast seeking to uproot long accepted dogma and to overturn existing faiths. Such an opinion of Judge Troward's work could not prevail with anyone who has studied his teachings.

His reverence for the fundamental truths of religious faith was profound, and every student of his writings will testify to the great constructive value of his work. He builded upon an ancient foundation a new and nobler structure of human destiny, solid in its simplicity and beautiful in its innate grandeur.

But to the wide circle of Judge Troward's friends he will best and most gloriously be remembered as a teacher. In his magic mind the unfathomable revealed its depths and the illimitable its boundaries; metaphysics took on the simplicity of the ponderable, and man himself occupied a new and more dignified place in the cosmos. Not only did he perceive clearly, but he also possessed that quality of mind even more rare than deep and clear perception, that clarity of expression and exposition that can carry another and less-informed mind along with it, on the current of its understanding, to a logical and comprehended conclusion.

In his books, his lectures, and his personality, he was always ready to take the student by the hand, and in perfect simplicity and friendliness to walk and talk with him about the deeper mysteries of life — the life that includes death — and to shed the brilliant light of his wisdom upon the obscure and difficult problems that torment sincere but rebellious minds.

His artistic nature found expression in brush and canvas, and his great love for the sea is reflected in many beautiful marine sketches. But if painting was his recreation, his work was the pursuit of Truth wherever to be found, and in whatever disguise.

His life has enriched and enlarged the lives of many, and all those who knew him will understand that in helping others he was accomplishing exactly what he most desired. Knowledge, to him, was worth only what it yielded in uplifting humanity to a higher spiritual appreciation, and to a deeper understanding of God's purpose and man's destiny.

> A man, indeed! He strove not for a place,
> Nor rest, nor rule. He daily walked with God.
> His willing feet with service swift were shod—
> An eager soul to serve the human race,
> Illume the mind, and fill the heart with grace—
> Hope blooms afresh where'er those feet have trod.

Chapter 1
The Principle of Guidance

If I were asked which of all the spiritual principles I ranked first, I should feel inclined to say the Principle of Guidance, not in the sense of being more essential that the others — for every portion is equally essential to the completeness of a perfect whole — but in the sense of being first in order of sequence and giving value to all our other powers by placing them in their due relation to one another. "Giving value to our other powers", I say, because this also is one of our powers. It is that which, judged from the standpoint of personal self-consciousness, is above us; but which, realized from the point of view of the unity of all Spirit, is part and parcel of ourselves, because it is that Infinite Mind which is of necessity identified with all its manifestations.

Looking to this Infinite Mind as a Superior Intelligence from which we may receive guidance does not therefore imply looking to an external source. On the contrary, it is looking to the innermost spring of our own being, with a confidence in its action which enables us to proceed to the execution of our plans with a firmness and assurance that are in themselves the very guarantee of our success.

The action of the spiritual principles in us follows the order which we impose upon them by our thought; therefore the order of realization will reproduce the order of desire; and if we neglect this first principle of right order and guidance, we shall find ourselves beginning to put forth other great powers, which are at present latent within us, without knowing how to find suitable employment for them. This would be a very perilous condition: for without having before us objects worthy of the powers to which we awaken, we should waste them on petty purposes dictated only by the narrow range of our unilluminated intellect. Therefore the ancient wisdom says, "With all thy getting, get understanding".

The awakening to consciousness of our mysterious interior powers will sooner or later take place, and will result in our using them whether or not we understand the law of their development. The interior powers are natural powers as much as the exterior ones. We can direct their use by a knowledge of their laws; and it is therefore of the highest importance to have some sound principles of guidance in the use of these higher faculties as they begin to manifest themselves.

If, therefore, we would safely and profitably enter upon the possession of the great inheritance of power that is opening out before us, we must before all things seek to realize in ourselves that Superior Intelligence which will become an unfailing principle of guidance if we will only recognize it as such. Everything depends on our recognition. Thoughts are things, and therefore as we will our thoughts to be, so we will the thing to be. If, then, we will to use the Infinite Spirit as a spirit of guidance, we shall find that the fact is as we have willed it, and in doing this we are still making use of our own supreme principle. And this is the true "understanding" which, by placing all the other powers in their correct order, creates one grand unity of power directed to clearly defined and worthy aims, in place of the dispersion of our powers, by which they only neutralize each other and effect nothing.

This is that Spirit of Truth which shall guide us into all Truth. It is the sincere Desire in us to reach out after Truth. Truth first and Power afterwards is the reasonable order, which we cannot invert without injury to ourselves and others; but if we follow this order we shall always find scope for our powers in developing into present realities the continually growing glory of our vision of the ideal.

The ideal is the true real, but it must be brought into manifestation before it can be shown to be so, and it is in this that the *practical* nature of our mental studies consists. It is the *practical* mystic who is the man of power: the man who, realizing the mystical powers within, fits his outward action to this knowledge, and so shows his faith by his works; and assuredly the first step is to make use of that power of infallible guidance which he can call to his aid simply by desiring to be led by it.

Chapter 2
The "I Am"

We often do not sufficiently recognize the truth of Walt Whitman's pithy saying, "I am not all contained between my hat and my boots". We forget the twofold nature of the "I Am", that it is at once both the manifested and the unmanifested, the Universal and the individual. By losing sight of this truth we surround ourselves with limitations; we see only part of the self, and then we are surprised that the part fails to do the work of the whole. Factors crop up on which we had not reckoned, we wonder where they come from, and we do not understand that they necessarily arise from that great Unity in which we are all included.

It is the grand intelligence and liveliness of the Universal Spirit continually pressing forward to manifestation of itself in a glorious humanity.

This must be effected by each individual's recognition of his power to co-operate with the Supreme Principle through an intelligent conception of its purpose and of the natural laws by which that purpose is accomplished — a recognition which can proceed only from the realization that he himself is none other than the same Universal principle in particular manifestation.

When he sees this, he sees that Walt Whitman's saying is true and that his source of intelligence, power, and purpose is in that Universal Self, which is his as well as another's just because it is Universal, and which is therefore as completely and entirely identified with himself as though there were no other expression of it in the world.

The understanding which alone gives value to knowledge is the understanding that, when we employ the formula "I am, therefore I can, therefore I will", the "I AM" with which the series starts is a Being Who, so to speak, has His head in heaven and His feet upon the Earth, a perfect Unity, and with a range of ideas far transcending the little ideas which are limited by the requirements of a day or an hour.

On the other hand, the requirements of the day and the hour are real while they last, and since the manifested life can be lived only in the moment that now is, whether it be today or ten thousand years hence, our need is to harmonize the life of expression with the life of purpose and, by realizing in ourselves the source of the highest purposes, to realize also the life of the fullest expression.

This is the meaning of prayer. Prayer is not a foolish seeking to change the Mind of Supreme Wisdom. It is rather an intelligent seeking to embody that wisdom in our thoughts so as more and more perfectly to express it in expressing ourselves. Thus, as we gradually grow into the habit of finding this inspiring Presence within ourselves, and of realizing its forward movement as the ultimate determining factor in all true healthful mental action, it will become second nature to us to have all our plans, down to the apparently most trivial, so floating upon the undercurrent of this Universal Intelligence that a great harmony will come into our lives, every discordant manifestation will disappear, and we shall find ourselves more and more controlling all things into the forms that we desire.

Why? Because we have attained to commanding the Spirit and making it obey us? Certainly not, for "if the blind lead the blind, both shall fall into the ditch"; but because we are companions of the Spirit, and by a continuous and growing intimacy have changed, not "the Mind of the Spirit", but our own. We have learned to think from a higher standpoint, where we see that the old-world saying "Know thyself" includes the knowledge of all that we mean when we speak of God.

I AM IS ONE

This may seem a very elementary proposition, but it is one of which we are too apt to lose sight. What does it mean? It means everything; but we are most concerned with what it means in regard to ourselves, and to each of us personally it means this. It means that there are not two Spirits, one which is myself and one which is another. It means that there is not some great unknown power external to myself which may be actuated by perfectly different motives to my own and which will, therefore, oppose me with its irresistible force and pass over me, leaving me crushed and broken like the devotee over whom the Car of Jagannath has rolled. It means that there is only one Mind, one motive, one power — not two opposing each other — and that my conscious mind in all its movements is only the One Mind expressing Itself as (not merely through) my own particular individuality.

There are not two I AMs, but one I AM. Whatever, therefore, I can conceive the Great Universal Life Principle to be, that I am.

Let us try to fully realize what this means. Can you conceive the Great Originating and Sustaining Life-Principle of the whole Universe as poor, weak, sordid, miserable, jealous, angry, anxious, uncertain, or in any other way limited? We know that this is impossible. Then because the I AM is One, it is equally untrue of ourselves. Learn first to distinguish the true self that you are from the mental and physical processes which it throws forth as instruments of its expression, and then learn that this self controls these instruments, and not vice versa. As we advance in this knowledge we know ourselves to be unlimited. We realize that, in the miniature world whose center we are, we ourselves are the very same overflowing of joyous liveliness that the Great Life Spirit is in the Great All.

The I AM is One.

Chapter 3

Yourself

I want to talk to you about the liveliness there is in being yourself. It has at least the merit of simplicity, for it must surely be easier to be oneself than pretend to be something or somebody else. Yet that is what so many are constantly trying to do; the self that is their own is not good enough for them, and so they are always trying to go one better than what God has made them, with endless strain and struggle as the consequence.

Of course they are right to put before them an ideal infinitely grander than anything they have yet attained — the only possible way of progress is by following an ideal that is always a stage ahead of us — but the mistake is in not seeing that its attainment is a matter of growth, and that growth must be the expansion of something that already exists in us, and therefore implies our being what we are as its starting point. This growth is a continuous process, and we cannot do next month's growth without first doing this month's; but we are always wanting to jump into some ideal of the future, not seeing that we can reach it only by steadily going on from where we are now.

These considerations should make us more confident and more comfortable. We are employing a force which is much greater than we believe ourselves to be, yet it is not separate from us and needing to be persuaded or compelled or inveigled into doing what we want; it is the substratum of our own being which is continually passing up into manifestation on the visible plane and becoming that personal self to which we often limit our attention without considering whence it proceeds. But in truth the outer self is the surface growth of that individuality which lies concealed far down in the deeps below, and which is none other than the Spirit-of-Life which underlies all forms of manifestation.

Endeavour to realize what this Spirit must be in itself — that is to say, apart from any of the conditions that arise from the various relations which necessarily establish themselves between its various forms of individualization. In its homogeneous Self what else can it be but pure Life — Essence-of-Life, if you like so to call it? Then realize that as Essence-of-Life it exists in the innermost of every one of its forms of manifestation in as perfect simplicity as any we can attribute to it in our most abstract conceptions. In this light we see it to be the eternally Self-generating Power which, to express itself, flows into form.

This Universal Essence-of-Life is a continual becoming (into form), and since we are a part of Nature we do not need to go further than ourselves to find the Life-giving Energy at work with all its powers. Hence all we have to do is to allow it to rise to the surface. We do not have to make it rise any more than the engineer who sinks the bore-pipe for an artesian well has to make the water rise in it; the water does that by its own energy, springing as a fountain a hundred feet into the air. Just so we shall find a fountain of Essence-of-Life ready to spring up in ourselves, inexhaustible and continually increasing in its flow, as Jesus taught long ago to a woman at a wayside well.

This up-springing of Life-Essence is not another's — it is our own. It does not require deep studies, hard labours, weary journeys to attain it; it is not the monopoly of this teacher or that writer, whose lectures we must attend or whose books we must read to get it. It is the innermost of ourselves, and a little common-sense thought as to how anything comes to be anything will soon convince us that the great inexhaustible Life must be the very root and substance of us, permeating every fiber of our being.

Surely to be this vast infinitude of Living Power must be enough to satisfy all our desires, and yet this wonderful ideal is nothing else but what we already are in principio — it is all there is in ourselves now, only awaiting our recognition for its manifestation. It is not the Essence-of-Life which has to grow, for that is eternally present in itself; but it is our recognition of it that has to grow, and this growth cannot be forced. It must come by a natural process, the first necessity of which is to abstain from all straining after being something which at the present time we cannot naturally be. The Law of our Evolution has put us in possession of certain powers and opportunities, and our further development depends on our doing just what these powers and opportunities make it possible for us to do, here and now.

If we do what we are able to do today, it will open the way for us to do something better tomorrow, and in this manner the growing process will proceed healthily and happily in a rapidly increasing ratio. This is so much easier than striving to compel things to be what they are not, and it is also so much more fruitful in good results. It is not sitting still doing nothing, and there is plenty of room for the exercise of all our mental faculties, but these faculties are themselves the outcome of the Essence-of-Life, and are not the creating power but only give direction to it. Now it is this moving power at the back of the various faculties that is the true innermost self; and if we realize the identity between the innermost and the outermost, we shall see that we therefore have at our present disposal all that is necessary for our unlimited development in the future.

Thus our liveliness consists simply in being ourselves, only more so, and in recognizing this we get rid of a great burden of unnecessary straining and striving, and the place of the old *Sturm und Drang* will be taken, not by inertia, but by a joyous activity which knows that it always has the requisite power to manifest itself in forms of good and beauty. What does it matter whither this leads us? If we are following the line of the beautiful and good, then we shall produce the beautiful and good, and thus bring increasing joy into the world, whatever particular form it may assume.

We limit ourselves when we try to fix accurately beforehand the particular form of good that we shall produce. We should aim not so much at having or making some particular thing as at expressing all that we are. The expressing will grow out of realizing the treasures that are ours already, and contemplating the beauty, the affirmative side, of all that we are now, apart from the negative conceptions and detractions which veil this positive good from us. When we do this we shall be astonished to see what possibilities reside in ourselves as we are and with our present surroundings, all unlovely as we may deem them: and commencing to work at once upon whatever we find affirmative in these, and withdrawing our thought from what we have hitherto seen as negative in them, the right road will open up before us, leading us in wonderful ways to the development of powers that we never suspected, and the enjoyment of happiness that we never anticipated.

We have never been out of our right path, only we have been walking in it backwards instead of forwards. Now that we have begun to follow the path in the right direction, we find that it is none other than the way of peace, the path of joy, and the road to eternal life. These things we may attain by simply living naturally with ourselves. It is because we are trying to be or do something which is not natural to us that we experience weariness and labour where we should find all our activities joyously concentrated on objects which lead to their own accomplishment by the force of the love that we have for them.

When we make the grand discovery of how to live naturally, we shall find it to be all, and more than all, that we had ever desired; our daily life will become a perpetual joy to ourselves, and we shall radiate light and life wherever we go.

Chapter 4

Desire as the Motive Power

There are certain Oriental schools of thought, together with various Western offshoots from them, which are entirely founded on the principle of annihilating all desire. "Reach that point at which you have no wish for anything and you will find yourself free", is the sum and substance of their teaching; and in support of this they put forward a great deal of very specious argument which is all the more likely to entangle the unwary because it contains a recognition of many of the profoundest truths of Nature.

But we must bear in mind that it is possible to have a very deep knowledge of psychological facts, and at the same time to vitiate the results of our knowledge by an entirely wrong assumption in regard to the law which binds these facts together in the Universal system; and the injurious results of misapprehension upon such a vital question are so radical and far-reaching that we cannot too forcibly urge the necessity of clearly understanding the true nature of the point at issue. Stripped of all accessories and embellishments, the question resolves itself into this: Which shall we choose for our portion — Life or Death? There can be no accommodation between the two; and whichever we select as our guiding principle must produce results of a kind proper to itself.

The whole of this momentous question turns on the place that we assign to desire in our system of thought. Is it the Tree of Life in the midst of the Garden of the Soul? Or is it the Upas Tree creating a wilderness of death all around? This is the issue on which we have to form a judgment, and this judgment must colour all our perception of life and determine the entire range of possibilities.

Let us, then, try to picture to ourselves the ideal proposed by the systems to which I have alluded — a man who has succeeded in entirely eliminating all desire. To him all things must be alike. The good and the evil must be as one, for nothing has any longer the power to raise any desire in him; he has no longer any feeling which will prompt him to say, "This is good, therefore I choose it; that is evil, therefore I reject it"; for all choice implies the perception of something more desirable in what is chosen than in what is rejected, and consequently the existence of that feeling of desire which has been entirely eliminated from the ideal we are contemplating.

Then, if the perception of all that makes one thing preferable to another has been obliterated, there can be no motive for any sort of action whatever. Endue a being who has thus extinguished his faculty of desire with the power to create a Universe, and he has no motive for employing it. Endue him with all knowledge, and it will be useless to him; for, since desire has no place in him, he is without any purpose for which to turn his knowledge to account. And with Love we cannot endue him, for that is desire in its supreme degree.

But if all this be excluded, what is left of the man? Nothing, except the mere outward form. If he has actually obtained this ideal, he has practically ceased to be. Nothing can by any means interest him, for there is nothing to attract or repel in one thing more than in another. He must be dead alike to all feeling and to all motive of action, for both feeling and action imply the preference for one condition rather than another; and where desire is utterly extinguished, no such preference can exist.

No doubt someone may object that it is only evil desires which are thus to be suppressed;

but a perusal of the writings of the schools in question will show that this is not the case. The foundation of the whole system is that all desire must be obliterated, the desire for the good just as much as the desire for the evil. The good is as much "illusion" as the evil, and until we have reached absolute indifference to both we have not attained freedom. When we have utterly crushed out all desire we are free. And the practical results of such a philosophy are shown in the case of Indian devotees who, in pursuance of their resolve to crush out all desire, both for good and evil alike, become nothing more than outward images of men, from which all power of perception and action have long since fled.

The mergence in the Universal, at which they thus aim, becomes nothing more than a self-induced hypnotism which, if maintained for a sufficient length of time, saps away every power of mental and bodily activity, leaving nothing but the outside husk of an attenuated human form — the hopeless wreck of what was once a living man. This is the logical result of a system which assumes for its starting point that desire is evil in itself, that every desire is *per se* a form of bondage, independently of the nature of its object. The majority of the followers of this philosophy may lack sufficient resolution to carry it out rigorously to its practical conclusions; but whether their ideal is to be realized in this world or in some other, the utter extinction of desire means nothing else than absolute apathy, without feeling and without action.

How entirely false such an ideal is — not only from the standpoint of our daily life, but also from that of the most transcendental conception of the Universal Principle — is evidenced by the mere fact that anything exists at all. If the highest ideal is that of utter apathy, then the Creative Power of the Universe must be extremely low-minded; and all that we have hitherto been accustomed to look upon as the marvelous order and beauty of creation is nothing but a display of vulgarity and ignorance of sound philosophy.

But the fact that creation exists proves that the Universal Mind thinks differently, and we have only to look around us to see that the true ideal is the exercise of creative power. Hence, so far from desire being a thing to be annihilated, it is the very root of every conceivable mode of Life. Without it, Life could not be. Every form of expression implies the selection of all that goes to make up the form, and the passing-by of whatever is not required for that purpose; hence a desire for that which is selected in preference to what is laid aside. And this selective desire is none other than the Universal Law of Attraction.

Whether this law acts as the chemical affinity of apparently unconscious atoms, or in the instinctive, if unreasoned, attractions of the vegetable and animal worlds, it is still the principle of selective affinity; and it continues to be the same when it passes on into the higher kingdoms which are ruled by reason and conscious purpose. The modes of activity in each of these kingdoms are dictated by the nature of the kingdom, but the activity itself always results from the preference of a certain subject for a certain object to the exclusion of all others; and all action consists in the reciprocal movement of the two towards each other in obedience to the law of their affinity.

When this takes place in the kingdom of conscious individuality, the affinities exhibit themselves as mental action; but the principle of selection prevails without exception throughout the Universe. In the conscious mind this attraction towards its affinity becomes desire — the desire to create some condition of things better than that now existing. Our want of knowledge may cause us to make mistakes as to what this better thing really is, and so in seeking to carry out our desire we may give it a wrong direction; but the fault is not in the desire itself, but in our mistaken notion of what it requires for its satisfaction. Hence unrest and dissatisfaction until its true affinity is found; but, as soon as this is discovered, the law of attraction at once asserts itself and produces that better condition, the dream of which first gave direction to out thoughts.

Thus it is eternally true that desire is the cause of all feeling and all action: in other words, of all Life. The whole liveliness of Life consists in receiving or in radiating forth the vibrations produced by the Law of Attraction; and in the kingdom of mind these vibrations necessarily become conscious out-reachings of the mind in the direction in which it feels attraction; that is to say, they become desires. Desire is therefore the mind seeking to manifest itself in some form which as yet exists only in its thought. It is the principle of creation, whether the thing created be a world or a wooden spoon; both have their origin in the desire to bring something into existence which does not yet exist. Whatever may be the scale on which we exercise our creative ability, the motive power must always be desire.

Desire is the force behind all things; it is the moving principle of the Universe and the innermost center of all Life. Hence, to take the negation of desire for our primal principle is to endeavour to stamp out Life itself; but what we have to do is to acquire the requisite knowledge by which to guide our desires to their true objects of satisfaction. To do this is the whole end of knowledge; and any knowledge applied otherwise is only a partial knowledge which, having failed in its purpose, is nothing but ignorance. Desire is thus the sum-total of the liveliness of Life, for it is that in which all movement originates, whether on the physical level or the spiritual. In a word, desire is the creative power, and must be carefully guarded, trained, and directed accordingly; but thus to seek to develop it to the highest perfection is the very opposite of trying to kill it outright.

And desire has fulfillment for its correlative. The desire and its fulfillment are bound together as cause and effect; and when we realize the law of their sequence, we shall be more than ever impressed with the supreme importance of Desire as the great center of Life.

Chapter 5
The Central Control

In contemplating the relations between body, soul, and spirit, between Universal Mind and individual mind, the methodized study of which constitutes Mental Science, we must never forget that these relations indicate not the separateness, but the unity, of these principles. We must learn not to attribute one part of our action to one part of our being, and another to another. Neither the action nor the functions are split up into separate parts. The action is a whole, and the being that does it is a whole; and in the healthy organism the reciprocal movements of the principles are so harmonious as never to suggest any feeling other than that of a perfectly whole and undivided self. If there is any other feeling we may be sure that there is abnormal action somewhere, and we should set ourselves to discover and remove the cause of it.

The reason for this is that in any perfect organism there cannot be more than one center of control. A rivalry of controlling principles would be the destruction of the organic wholeness; for either the elements would separate and group themselves round one or other of the centers, according to their respective affinities, or else they would be reduced to a condition of merely chaotic confusion; in either case the original organism would cease to exist. Seen in this light, therefore, it is a self-evident truth that, if we are to retain our individuality — in other words, if we are to continue to exist — it can be only by retaining our hold upon the central controlling principle in ourselves; and if this be the charter of our being, it follows that all our future development depends on our recognizing and accepting this central controlling principle. To this end, therefore, all our endeavours should be directed; for otherwise all our studies in Mental Science will lead us into a confused labyrinth of principles and counter-principles, which will be considerably worse than the state of ignorant simplicity from which we started.

The central controlling principle is the Will, and we must never lose sight of the fact that all the other principles about which we have learnt in our studies exist only as its instruments. The Will is the true self, of which they are all functions, and all our progress consists of our increased recognition of the fact. It is the Will that says "I AM"; and therefore, however exalted, or even in their higher developments apparently miraculous, our powers may be, they are all subject to the central controlling power of the Will. When the enlightened Will shall have learnt to identify itself perfectly with the limitless powers of knowledge, judgment, and creative thought which are at its disposal, then the individual will have attained to perfect wholeness, and all limitations will have passed away forever.

And nothing short of this consciousness of Perfect Wholeness can satisfy us. Everything that falls short of it is in that degree an embodiment of the principle of Death, that great enemy against which the principle of Life must continue to wage unceasing war, in whatever form or measure it may show itself, until "death is swallowed up in victory". There can be no compromise. Either we are affirming Life as a principle, or we are denying it, no matter on how great or how small a scale; and the criterion by which to determine our attitude is our realization of our own Wholeness. Death is the principle of disintegration; and whenever we admit the power of any portion of our organism, whether spiritual or bodily, to induce any condition independently of the intention of the Will, we admit that the force of disintegration is superior to the controlling center in ourselves, and we conceive of ourselves as held in bondage by an adversary, from which bondage the only way of release is by the attainment of a truer way of thinking.

And the reason is that, either through ignorance or carelessness, we have surrendered our position of control over the system as a whole, and have lost the element of Purpose, around which the consciousness of individuality must always center. Every state of our consciousness, whether active or passive, should be the result of a distinct purpose adopted by our own free will; for the passive states should be quite as much under the control of the Will as the active. It is the lack of purpose that deprives us of power. The higher and more clearly defined our purpose, the greater stimulus we have for realizing our control over all our faculties for its attainment; and since the grandest of all purposes is the strengthening and ennobling of Life, in proportion as we make this our aim, we shall find ourselves in unison with the Supreme Universal Mind, acting each in our individual sphere for the furtherance of the same purpose which animates the ruling principle of the Great Whole and, as a consequence, shall find that its intelligence and powers are at our disposal.

But in all this there must be no strain. The true exercise of the Will is not an exercise of unnatural force. It is simply the leading of our powers into their natural channels by intelligently recognizing the direction in which those channels go. However various in detail, they have one clearly defined common tendency towards the increasing of Life — whether in ourselves or in others — and if we keep this steadily in view, all our powers, whether interior or exterior, will be found to work so harmoniously together that there will be no sense of independent action on the part of any one of them. The distinctions drawn for purposes of study will be laid aside, and the Self in us will be found to be the realization of a grand ideal being, at once individual and Universal, consciously free in its individual wholeness and in its joyous participation in the Life of the Universal Whole.

Chapter 6

Completeness

A point on which students of Mental Science often fail to lay sufficient stress is the completeness of man — not a completeness to be attained hereafter, but here and now. We have been so accustomed to have the imperfection of man drummed into us in books, sermons, and hymns, and above all in a mistaken interpretation of the Bible, that at first the idea of his completeness altogether staggers us. Yet until we see this we must remain shut out from the highest and best that Mental Science has to offer, from a thorough understanding of its philosophy, and from its greatest practical achievements.

To do any work successfully you must believe yourself to be a *whole* man in respect of it. The completed work is the outward image of a corresponding completeness in yourself. And if this is true in respect of one work it is true of all; the difference in the importance of the work does not matter; we cannot successfully attempt any work until, for some reason or other, we believe ourselves able to accomplish it; in other words, until we believe that none of the conditions for its completion is wanting in us, and that we are therefore complete in respect of it. Our recognition of our completeness is thus the measure of what we are able to do, and hence the great importance of knowing the fact of our own completeness.

But it may be asked, do we not see imperfection all around? Is there not sorrow, sickness, and trouble? Yes; but why? Just for the very reason that we do not realize our completeness. If we realized that in its fullness, these things would not be; and in the degree in which we come to realize it we shall find them steadily diminish. Now if we really grasp the two fundamental truths that Spirit is Life pure and simple, and that external things are the result of interior forces, then it ought not to be difficult to see why we should be complete; for to suppose otherwise is to suppose the creative power of the Universe to be either unable or unwilling to produce the complete expression of its own intention in the creation of man.

That it should be unable to do so would be to depose it from its place as the creative principle, and that it should be unwilling to fulfill its own intention is a contradiction in terms; so that on either supposition we come to a *reductio ad absurdum*. In forming man the creative principle therefore must have produced a perfect work, and our conception of ourselves as imperfect can only be the result of our own ignorance of what we really are; and our advance, therefore, does not consist in having something new added to us, but in learning to bring into action powers which already exist in us, but which we have never tried to use, and therefore have not developed, simply because we have always taken it for granted that we are by nature defective in some of the most important faculties necessary to fit us to our environment.

If we wish to attain to these great powers, the question is, Where are we to seek them. And the answer is in *ourselves*. That is the great secret. We are not to go outside ourselves to look for power. As soon as we do so we find, not power, but weakness. To seek strength from any outside source is to make affirmation of our weakness, and all know what the natural result of such an affirmation must be.

We are complete in ourselves; and the reason why we fail to realize this is that we do not understand how far the "self" of ourselves extends. We know that the whole of anything consists of all its parts and not only of some of them; yet this is just what we do not seem to know about ourselves. We say rightly that every person is a concentration of the Universal Spirit into individual consciousness; but if so, then each individual consciousness must find the Universal Spirit to be the infinite expression of itself. It is this part of the "Self" that we so often leave out in our estimate of what we are; and consequently we look upon ourselves as crawling pigmies when we might think of ourselves as archangels. We try to work with the mere shadows of ourselves instead of with the glorious substance, and then wonder at our failures. If we only understood that our "better half" is the whole infinite of Spirit — that which creates and sustains the Universe — then we should know how complete our completeness is.

As we approach this conception, our completeness becomes a reality to us, and we find that we need not go outside ourselves for anything. We have only to draw on that part of ourselves which is infinite to carry out any intention we may form in our individual consciousness; for there is no barrier between the two parts, otherwise they would not be a whole. Each belongs perfectly to the other, and the two are one. There is no antagonism between them, for the Infinite Life can have no interest against its individualization of itself. If there is any feeling of tension it proceeds from our not fully realizing this conception of our own wholeness; we are placing a barrier somewhere when in truth there is none; and the tension will continue until we find out where and how we are setting up this barrier and remove it.

This feeling of tension is the feeling that we are *not using our Whole Being.* We are trying to make half do the work of the whole; but we cannot rid ourselves of our wholeness, and therefore the whole protests against our attempts to set one half against the other. But when we realize that our concentration out of the Infinite also implies our expansion into it, we shall see that our whole "self" includes both the concentration and the expansion; and seeing this first intellectually, we shall gradually learn to use our knowledge practically and bring our whole man to bear upon whatever we take in hand. We shall find that there is in us a constant action and reaction between the infinite and the individual, like the circulation of the blood from the heart to the extremities and back again, a constant pulsation of vital energy quite natural and free from all strain and exertion.

This is the great secret of the liveliness of Life, and it is called by many names and set forth under many symbols in various religions and philosophies, each of which has its value in proportion as it brings us nearer to the realization of this perfect wholeness. But the thing itself is Life, and therefore can only be suggested but not described by any words or symbols; it is a matter of personal experience which no one can convey to another. All we can do is point out the direction in which this experience is to be sought, and to tell others the intellectual arguments which have helped us to find it; but the experience itself is the operation of definite vital functions of the inner being, and no one but ourselves can do our living for us.

But, so far as it is possible to express these things in words, what must be the result of realizing that the "self" in us includes the Infinite as well as the individual? All the resources of the Infinite must be at our disposal; we may draw on them as we will, and there is no limit save that imposed by the Law of Kindness, a self-imposed limitation which, because of being self-imposed, is not bondage but only another expression of our liberty. Thus we are free and all limitations are removed.

We are also no longer ignorant, for since the "self" in us includes the Infinite, we can draw thence all needed knowledge, and though we may not always be able to formulate this knowledge in the mentality, we shall feel its guidance, and eventually the mentality will learn to put this also into form of words; and thus by combining thought and experience, theory and practice, we shall by degrees come more and more into the knowledge of the Law of our Being, and find that there is no place in it for fear, because it is the law of perfect liberty. And knowing what our whole self really is, we shall walk erect as free men and women radiating Light and Life all round, so that our very presence will carry a vivifying influence with it, because we realize ourselves to be an Affirmative Whole, and not a mere negative disintegration of parts.

We know that our whole self includes the Greater Man which is back of and causes the phenomenal man, and this Greater Man is the true human principle in us. It is, therefore, Universal in its sympathies, but at the same time not less individually ourself, and thus the true man in us, being at once both Universal and individual, can be trusted as a sure guide. It is that "Thinker" which is behind the conscious mentality and which, if we will accept it as our center, and realize that it is not a separate entity but ourself, will be found equal to every occasion, and will lead us out of a condition of servitude into "the glorious liberty of the sons of God".

Chapter 7

Submission

There are two kinds of submission: submission to superior force and submission to superior truth. The one is weakness and the other is strength. It is an exceedingly important part of our training to learn to distinguish between these two, and the more so because the wrong kind is extolled by nearly all schools of popular religious teaching at the present day as constituting the highest degree of human attainment. By some this is pressed so far as to make it an instrument of actual oppression; and with all it is a source of weakness and a bar to progress. We are forbidden to question what is called the wise dispensation of Providence. We are told that pain and sorrow are to be accepted because they are the will of God; and there is much eloquent speaking and writing concerning the beauty of quiet resignation, all of which appeals to a certain class of gentle minds who have not yet learnt that gentleness does not consist in the absence of power but in the kindly and beneficent use of it.

Minds cast in this mould are peculiarly apt to be misled. They perceive a certain beauty in the picture of weakness leaning upon strength, but they attribute its soothing influence to the wrong element of the combination. A thoughtful analysis would show them that their feelings consisted of pity for the weak figure and admiration for the strong one, and that the suggestiveness of the whole arose from its satisfying the artistic sense of balance which requires a combination of this sort.

But which of the two figures in the picture would they themselves prefer to be? Surely not the weak one needing help, but the strong one giving it. By itself the weak figure only stirs our pity and not our admiration. Its form may be beautiful, but its very beauty only serves to enhance the sense of something lacking — and the something lacking is strength. The attraction which the doctrine of passive resignation possesses for certain minds is based upon an appeal to sentiment, which is accepted without any suspicion that the sentiment appealed to is a false one.

Now the healthful influence of the movement known as "The Higher Thought" [or "New Thought" or "Mental Science" or just "Mentalism] consists precisely in this — that it sets itself rigorously to combat this debilitating doctrine of submission. It can see as well as others the beauty of weakness leaning upon strength; but it sees that the real source of the beauty lies in the strong element of the combination. The true beauty consists in the power to confer strength, and this power is not to be acquired by submission, but by exactly the opposite method of continually asserting our determination not to submit.

Of course, if we take it for granted that all the sorrow, sickness, pain, trouble, and other adversity in the world is the expression of the Will of God, then doubtless we must resign ourselves to the inevitable with all the submission we can muster, and comfort ourselves with the vague hope that somehow in some far-off future we shall find that "Good is the final goal of ill" — though even this vague hope is a protest against the very submission we are endeavouring to exercise. But to make the assumption that the evil of life is the Will of God is to assume what a careful and intelligent study of the laws of the Universe, both mental and physical, will show us is not the truth; and if we turn to that Book which contains the fullest delineation of these Universal laws, we shall find nothing taught more clearly than that submission to the evils of life is not submission to the Will of God.

Nothing that obscures life, or restricts it, can proceed from the same source as the Power which gives light to them that sit in darkness, and deliverance to them that are bound. Negation can never be Affirmation; and the error we have always to guard against is that of attributing positive power to the Negative. If we once grasp the truth that God is Life, and that Life in every mode of its expression can never be anything else than Affirmative, then it must become clear to us that nothing which is of the opposite tendency can be according to the Will of God. For God (the good) to will any of the "evil" that is in the world would be for Life to act with the purpose of diminishing itself, which contradicts the very idea of Life. God is Life, and Life is, by its very nature, Affirmative. The submission we have hitherto made has been to our own weakness, ignorance, and fear, and not to the supreme good.

But is no such thing as submission required of us in any circumstances? Are we always to have our own way in everything? Assuredly the whole secret of our progress to liberty is involved in acquiring the habit of submission, but it is submission to superior Truth, not to superior force. It sometimes happens that, when we attain a higher Truth, we find that its reception requires us to rearrange the truths which we possessed before: not, indeed, to lay any of them aside, for Truth once recognized cannot be again put out of sight, but to recognize a different relative proportion between them from that which we had seen previously. Then there comes a submitting of what has hitherto been our highest truth to one which we recognize as still higher, a process not always easy of attainment, but which must be gone through if our spiritual development is not to be arrested. The lesser degree of life must be swallowed up in the greater; and for this purpose it is necessary for us to learn that the smaller degree was only a partial and limited aspect of that which is more universal, stronger, and of greater significance in every way.

Now, in going through the processes of spiritual growth, there is ample scope for that training in self-knowledge and self-control which is commonly understood by the word "submission". But the character of the act is materially altered. It is no longer a half-despairing resignation to a superior force external to ourselves which we can only vaguely hope is acting kindly and wisely, but it is an intelligent recognition of the true nature of our own interior forces and of the laws by which a robust spiritual constitution is to be developed; and the submission is no longer to limitations which drain life of its liveliness and against which we instinctively rebel, but to the law of our own evolution which manifests itself in continually increasing degrees of life and strength.

The submission which we recognize is the price that has to be paid for increase in any direction. Even in the Money Market we must invest before we can realize profits. It is a Universal rule that nature obeys us exactly in proportion as we first obey Nature; and this is as true in regard to spiritual science as to physical. The only question is whether we will yield an ignorant submission to the principle of death, or a joyous and intelligent obedience to the principle of Life.

If we have clearly grasped the fact of our identity with the Universal Spirit, we shall find that, in the right direction, there is really no such thing as submission. Submission is to the power of another — a man cannot be said to submit to himself. When the "I AM" in us recognizes a greater degree of I AM-ness (if I may coin the word) than it has hitherto attained, then, by the very force of this recognition, it becomes what it sees, and therefore naturally puts off from itself whatever would limit its expression of its own completeness.

But this is a natural process of growth, and not an unnatural act of submission; it is not the pouring-out of ourselves in weakness, but the gathering of ourselves together in increasing strength. There is no weakness in Spirit, it is all strength; and we must therefore always be watchful against the insidious approaches of the Negative which would invert the true position. The Negative always points to some external source of strength. Its formula is "I AM NOT". It always seeks to fix a gulf between us and the Infinite Sufficiency. It would always have us believe that the sufficiency is not our own, but that by an act of uncertain favour we may have occasional spoonfuls of it doled out to us. Jesus' teaching is different. We do not need to come with our pitcher to the well to draw water, like the woman of Samaria, but we have in ourselves an inexhaustible supply of the living water springing up into everlasting life.

Let us then inscribe "No Surrender" in bold characters upon our banner, and advance undaunted to claim our rightful heritage of liberty and life.

Chapter 8

Mind and Hand

I have before me a curious piece of ancient Egyptian symbolism. It represents the sun sending down to the earth innumerable rays, with the peculiarity that each ray terminates in a hand. This method of representing the sun is so unusual that it suggests the presence in the designer's mind of some idea rather different from those generally associated with the sun as a spiritual emblem. If I interpret the symbol rightly, it sets forth the truth, not only of the Divine Being as the Great Source of all Life and all Illumination, but also the correlative truth of our individual relation to that center. Each ray is terminated by a hand, and a hand is the emblem of active working; and I think it would be difficult to give a better symbolical representation of innumerable individualities, each working separately, yet all deriving their activity from a common source. The hand is at work upon the earth, and the sun, from which it is a ray, is shining in the heavens; but the connecting line shows whence all the strength and skill of the hand are derived.

If we look at the microcosm of our own person we find this principle exactly reproduced. Our hand is the instrument by which all our work is done — literary, artistic, mechanical, or household — but we know that all this work is really the work of the mind, the will-power at the center of our system, which first determines what is to be done, and then sets the hand to work to do it; and in the doing of it the mind and hand become one, so that the hand is none other than the mind working. Now, transferring this analogy to the macrocosm, we see that we each stand in the same relation to the Universal Mind that our hand does to our individual mind — at least, that is our normal relation; and we shall never put forth our full strength except from this standpoint.

We rightly realize our will as the center of our individuality; but we should do better to picture our individuality as an ellipse rather than a circle, a figure having two "conjugate foci", two equilibrated centers of revolution rather than a single one, one of which is the will-power or faculty of doing, and the other the consciousness or perception of being. If we realize only one of these two centers we shall lose both mental and moral balance. If we lose sight of that center which is our personal will, we shall become flabby visionaries without any backbone. If, in our anxiety to develop backbone, we lose sight of the other center, we shall find that we have lost that which corresponds to the lungs and heart in the physical body, and that our backbone, however perfectly developed, is rapidly drying up for want of those functions which minister vitality to the whole system, and is only fit to be hung up in a museum to show what a rigid, lifeless thing the strongest vertebral column becomes when separated from the organization by which alone it can receive nourishment. We must realize the one focus of our individuality as clearly as the other, and bring both into equal balance, if we would develop all our powers and rise to that perfection of Life which has no limits to its glorious possibilities.

Keeping the ancient Egyptian symbol before us, and considering ourselves as the hand, we find that we derive all our power from an infinite center; and because it is infinite we need never fear that we shall fail to draw to ourselves all that we require for our work, whether it be the intelligence to lay hold of the proper tool, or the strength to use it. And, moreover, we learn from the symbol that this central power is generic. This is a most important truth. It is the center from which all the hands proceed, and is as fully open to any one hand as to any other. Each hand is doing its separate work, and the whole of the central energy is at its disposal for its own specific purpose. The work of the central energy, as such, is to supply vitality to the hands, and it is they that differentiate this universal power into all the varied forms of application which their different aptitudes and opportunities suggest.

We, as the hands, live and work because the Central Mind lives and works in us. We are one with it, and it is one with us; and so long as we keep this primal truth before us, we realize ourselves as beings of unlimited goodness and intelligence and power, and we work in the fullness of strength and confidence accordingly; but if we lose sight of this truth, we shall find that the strongest will must get exhausted at last in the unequal struggle of the individual against the Universe.

For if we do not recognize the Central Mind as the source of our vitality, we are literally "fighting for our own hand", and all the other hands are against us, for we have lost the principle of connection with them. This is what must infallibly happen if we rely on nothing but our individual will-power. But if we realize that the will is the power by which we give out, and that every giving out implies a corresponding taking in, then we shall find in the boundless ocean of central living Spirit the source from which we can go on taking in *ad infinitum*, and which thus enables us to give out to any extent we please.

But for the wise and effective giving out, a strong and enlightened will is an absolute necessity; and therefore we do well to cultivate the will, or the active side of our nature. But we must equally cultivate the receptive side also; and when we do this rightly by seeing in the Infinite Mind the one source of supply, our will-power becomes intensified by the knowledge that the whole power of the Infinite is present to back it up. With this continual sense of Infinite Power behind us we can go calmly and steadily to the accomplishment of any purpose, however difficult, without straining or effort, knowing that it shall be achieved — not by the hand only, but by the invincible Mind that works through it.

"Not by might, nor by power, but by My Spirit, saith the Lord of hosts".

Chapter 9

Entering into the Spirit of It

"Entering into the Spirit of It". What a common expression! And yet how much it really means, how absolutely everything! We enter into the spirit of an undertaking, into the spirit of a movement, into the spirit of an author, even into the spirit of a game; and it makes all the difference both to us and to that into which we enter.

A game without any spirit is a poor affair; an association in which there is no spirit falls to pieces, and a spiritless undertaking is sure to be a failure. On the other hand, the book which is meaningless to the unsympathetic reader is full of life and suggestion to the one who enters into the spirit of the writer; the man who enters into the spirit of the music finds a spring of refreshment in some fine recital which is entirely missed by the cold critic who comes only to judge according to the standard of a rigid rule; and so on in every case that we can think of. If we do not enter the spirit of the thing, it has no invigorating effect upon us, and we regard it as dull, insipid, and worthless.

This is our everyday experience, and these are the words in which we express it. And the words are well chosen. They show our intuitive recognition of the spirit as the fundamental reality in everything, however small or however great. Let us be right as to the spirit of a thing, and everything else will successfully follow.

By entering into the spirit of anything we establish a mutual vivifying action and reaction between it and ourselves; we vivify it with our own vitality, and it vivifies us with a living interest which we call its spirit; and therefore the more fully we enter into the spirit of all with which we are concerned, the more thoroughly do we become alive. The more completely we do this the more we shall find that we are penetrating into the great secret of Life. It may seem a truism, but the great secret of Life is its Liveliness, and it is just more of this quality of Liveliness that we want to get hold of; it is that good thing of which we can never have too much.

But every fact implies also its negative, and we never properly understand a thing until we not only know what it is, but also clearly understand what it is not. To a complete understanding the knowledge of the negative is as necessary as the knowledge of the affirmative, for the perfect knowledge consists in realizing the relation between the two. The perfect power grows out of this knowledge by enabling us to balance the affirmative and negative against each other in any proportion that we will, thus giving flexibility to what would otherwise be too rigid, and form to what would otherwise be too fluid. By uniting these two extremes, we produce any result we may desire. It is the old Hermetic saying, *"Coagula et solve"* — "Solidify the fluid and dissolve the solid"; and therefore, if we would discover the secret of "entering into the spirit of it", we must get some idea of the negative, which is the "not-spirit".

In various ages this negative phase has been expressed in different forms of words suitable to the spirit of the time. So, clothing this idea in the attire of the present day, I will sum up the opposite of Spirit in the word "Mechanism". Before all things this is a mechanical age, and it is astonishing how great a part of what we call our social advance has its root in the mechanical arts. Reduce the mechanical arts to what they were in the days of the Plantagenets and the greater part of our boasted civilization would recede through the centuries along with them.

We may not be conscious of all this, but the mechanical tendency of the age has a firm grip upon society at large. We habitually look at the mechanical side of things in preference to any other. Everything is done mechanically, from the carving on a piece of furniture to the arrangement of the social system. It has to be fitted to the mechanical exigencies. We enter into the mechanism of it instead of into the Spirit of it, and so limit the Spirit and refuse to let it have its own way; and then, as a consequence, we get entirely mechanical action, and complete our circle of ignorance by supposing that this is the only sort of action there is.

Yet this is not a necessary state of things even in regard to "physical science", for the men who have made the greatest advances in that direction are those who have most clearly seen the subordination of the mechanical to the spiritual. The man who can recognize a natural law only as it operates through certain forms of mechanism with which he is familiar will never rise to the construction of the highest forms of mechanism which might be built upon that law, for he fails to see that it is the law which determines the mechanism and not vice versa. This man will make no advance in science, either theoretical or applied, and the world will never owe any debt of gratitude to him. But the man who recognizes that the mechanism for the application of any principle grows out of the true apprehension of the principle studies the principle first, knowing that when that is properly grasped it will necessarily suggest all that is wanted for bringing it into practical use.

And if this is true in regard to so-called "physical" science, it is a fortiori true as regards the Science of Spirit. There is a mechanical attitude of mind which judges everything by the limitations of past experiences, allowing nothing for the fact that those experiences were for the most part the results of our ignorance of spiritual law. But if we realize the true law of Being we shall rise above these mechanical conceptions. We shall not deny the reality of the body or of the physical world as facts, knowing that they also are Spirit, but we shall learn to deny their power as causes. We shall learn to distinguish between the *causa causata* and the *causa causans*, the secondary or apparent physical cause and the primary or spiritual cause without which the secondary cause would not exist; and so we shall get a new standpoint of clear knowledge and certain power by stepping over the threshold of the mechanical and entering into the spirit of it.

What we have to do is to maintain our even balance between the two extremes, denying neither Spirit nor the mechanism which is its form and through which it works. The one is as necessary to a perfect whole as the other, for there must be an *outside* as well as an *inside*; only we must remember that the creative principle is always *inside*, and that the outside only exhibits what the inside creates. Hence, whatever external effect we would produce, we must first enter into the spirit of it and work upon the spiritual principle, whether in ourselves or in others. By so doing our insight will become greatly enlarged, for from without we can see only one small portion of the circumference, while from the center we can see the whole of it. If we fully grasp the truth that Spirit is Creator, we can dispense with painful investigations into the mechanical side of all our problems.

If we are constructing from without, then we have to calculate anxiously the strength of the materials and the force of every thrust and strain to which they may be subjected; and very possibly after all we may find that we have made a mistake somewhere in our elaborate calculations. But if we realize the power of creating from within, we shall find all these calculations correctly made for us; for the same Spirit which is Creator is also that which the Bible calls "the Wonderful Numberer". Construction from without is based upon analysis, and no analysis is complete without accurate quantitative knowledge; but creation is the very opposite of analysis, and carries its own mathematics with it.

To enter into the spirit of anything, then, is to make yourself one in thought with the creative principle that is at the center of it; and therefore why not go to the center of all things at once, and enter into the Spirit of Life?

Do you ask where to find it? *In yourself*, and in proportion as you find it there, you will find it everywhere else. Look at Life as the one thing that is, whether in or around you; try to realize the liveliness of it, and then seek to enter into the Spirit of it by affirming it to be the whole of what you are.

Affirm this continually in your thoughts, and by degrees the affirmation will grow into a real living force within you, so that it will become a second nature to you, and you will find it impossible and unnatural to think in any other way. The nearer you approach this point the greater you will find your control over both body and circumstances, until at last you shall so enter into the Spirit of it — into the Spirit of the Divine creative power which is the root of all things. In the words of Jesus, "nothing shall be impossible to you" because you have so entered into the Spirit of it that you discover yourself to be one with it. Then all the old limitations will have passed away, and you will be living in an entirely new world of Life, Liberty, and Love, of which you yourself are the radiating center.

You will realize the truth that your Thought is a limitless creative power, and that you yourself are behind your Thought, controlling and directing it with Knowledge for any purpose which Love motivates and Wisdom plans. Thus you will cease from your labours, your struggles, and your anxieties, and you will enter into that new order where perfect rest is one with ceaseless activity.

Chapter 10

Beauty

Do we sufficiently direct our thoughts to the subject of Beauty? I think not. We are too apt to regard Beauty as a merely superficial thing, and do not realize all that it implies. This was not the case with the great thinkers of the ancient world — see the place which no less a one than Plato gives to Beauty as the expression of all that is highest and greatest in the system of the Universe. These great men of old were no superficial thinkers and, therefore, would never have elevated to the supreme place anything that is only superficial.

Therefore, we shall do well to ask what it is that these great minds found in the idea of Beauty which made it thus appeal to them as the most perfect outward expression of all that lies deepest in the fundamental laws of Being. It is because, rightly apprehended, Beauty represents the supreme living quality of Thought. It is the glorious overflowing of fullness of Love which indicates the presence of infinite reserves of Power behind it. It is the joyous profusion that shows the possession of inexhaustible stores of wealth which can afford to be thus lavish and yet remain as exhaustless as before. Read aright, Beauty is the index to the whole nature of Being.

Beauty is the externalization of Harmony, and Harmony is the co-ordinated working of all the powers of being, both in the individual and in the relation of the individual to the Infinite from which it springs; and therefore this Harmony conducts us at once into the presence of the innermost undifferentiated Life. Thus Beauty is in most immediate touch with the very *arcanum* of Life; it is the brightness of glory spreading itself over the sanctuary of the Divine Spirit. For if, viewed from without, this is only because it speeds across the bridge of Reason with such quick feet that we pass from the outermost to the inmost and back again in the twinkling of an eye; but the bridge is still there and, retracing our steps more leisurely, we shall find that, viewed from within, Beauty is no less the province of the calm reasoner and analyst. What the poet and the artist seize upon intuitively, he elaborates gradually, but the result is the same in both cases; for no intuition is true which does not admit of being expanded into a rational sequence of intelligible factors, and no argument is true which does not admit of being condensed into that rapid suggestion which is intuition.

Thus the impassioned artist and the calm thinker both find that the only true Beauty proceeds naturally from the actual construction of that which it expresses. It is not something added on as an afterthought, but something pre-existing in the original idea, something to which that idea naturally leads up and which pre-supposes that idea as affording its *raison d'etre*.

The test of Beauty is, What does it express? Is it merely a veneer, a coat of paint laid on from without? Then it is indeed nothing but a whited sepulcher, a covering to hide the vacuity or deformity which needs to be removed. But is it the true and natural outcome of what is beneath the surface? Then it is the index to superabounding Life and Love and Intelligence which is not content with mere utilitarianism hastening to escape as early as possible from the labour of construction as though from an enforced and unwelcome task, but rather rejoicing over its work and unwilling to quit it until it has expressed this rejoicing in every fittest touch of form and colour and exquisite proportion that the material will admit of, and this without departing by a hairsbreadth from the original purpose of the design.

Wherever, therefore, we find Beauty, we may infer an enormous reserve of Power behind it; in fact we may look upon it as the visible expression of the great truth that Life-Power is infinite. And when the inner meaning of Beauty is thus revealed to us, and we learn to know it as the very fullness and overflowing of Power, we shall find that we have gained a new standard for the guidance of our own lives. We must begin to use this wonderful process which we have learnt from Nature. Having learnt how Nature works — how God works — we must begin to work in like manner, and never consider any work complete until we have carried it to some final outcome of Beauty, whether material, intellectual, or spiritual.

Is my intention good? That is the initial question, for the intention determines the nature of the essence in everything. What is the most beautiful form in which I can express the good I intend? That is the ultimate question: for the true Beauty which our work expresses is the measure of the Power, Intelligence, Love — in a word, of the quantity and quality of our own life — which we have put into it. True Beauty, mind you — that which is beautiful because it most perfectly expresses the original idea, not a mere ornamentation occupying our thoughts as a thing apart from the use intended.

Nothing is of so small account but it has its fullest power of expression in some form of Beauty peculiarly its own. Beauty is the law of perfect Thought, be the subject of our Thought some scheme affecting the welfare of millions or a word spoken to a little child. True Beauty and true Power are the correlatives one of the other. Kindly expression originates in kindly thought; and kindly expression is the essence of Beauty which, seeking to express itself ever more and more perfectly, becomes that fine touch of sympathy which is artistic skill, whether applied in working upon material substances or upon the emotions of the heart. But remember: first Use, then Beauty, and neither complete without the other. Use without Beauty is ungracious giving, and Beauty without Use is humbug. Never forget, however, that there is a region of the mind where the Use is found in the Beauty, where Beauty itself serves the direct purpose of raising us to see a higher ideal which will thenceforward permeate our lives, giving a more lively quality to all we think and say and do.

Seen thus, the Beautiful is the true expression of the Good. From whichever end of the scale we look, we shall find that they accurately measure each other. They are the same thing in the outermost and the innermost respectively. But in our search for a higher Beauty than we have yet found, we must beware of missing the Beauty that already exists. Perfect harmony with its environment and perfect expression of its own inward nature are what constitute Beauty; and our ignorance of the nature of the thing or its environment may shut our eyes to the Beauty it already has. It takes the genius of a Millet in paint, or a Whitman in words, to show us the beauty of those ordinary work-a-day figures with which our world is for the most part peopled, whose originals we pass by as having no form or comeliness.

Assuredly the mission of every thinking man and woman is to help build up everywhere forms of greater beauty, spiritual, intellectual, and material; but if we could make something grander than Watteau gardens or Dresden china shepherdesses, we must enter the great realistic school of Nature and learn to recognize the beauty that already surrounds us, although it may have a little dirt on the surface. Then, when we have learnt the great principles of Beauty from the All-Spirit which it is, we shall know how to develop the Beauty on its own proper lines without perpetuating the dirt; and we shall know that all Beauty is the expression of Living Power, and that we can measure our power by the degree of beauty into which we can transform it, rendering our lives

> "By loveliness of perfect deeds
> More strong than all poetic thought".

Chapter 11

Touching Lightly

What is our point of support? Is it in ourselves or outside us? Are we self-poised, or does our balance depend on something external? According to the actual belief in which our answer to these questions is embodied, so will our lives be. In everything there are two parts, the essential and the incidental — that which is the nucleus and *raison d'etre* of the whole thing, and that which gathers round this nucleus and takes form from it. The true knowledge always consists in distinguishing these two from each other, and error always consists in misplacing them.

In all our affairs there are two factors, ourselves and the matter to be dealt with, and since for us the nature of anything is always determined by our thought of it, it is entirely a question of our belief which of these two factors shall be the essential and which the accessory. Whichever we regard as essential, the other at once becomes the incidental. The incidental can never be absent. For any sort of action to take place there must be some conditions under which the activity passes out into visible results; but the same sort of activity may occur under a variety of different conditions, and may thus produce very different visible results. So in every matter we shall always find an essential or energizing factor, and an incidental factor which derives its quality from the nature of the energy.

We can therefore never escape from having to select our essential and our incidental factor, and whichever we select as the essential, we thereby place the other in the position of the incidental. If, then, we make the mistake of reversing the true position and suppose that the energizing force comes from the merely accessory circumstances, we make *them* our point of support and lean upon them, and stand or fall with them accordingly; and so we come into a condition of weakness and obsequious waiting on all sorts of external influences, which is the very reverse of that strength, wisdom, and opulence which are the only meaning of Liberty.

But if we would ask ourselves the common-sense question, Where can the center of a man's Life be except in himself? we should see that in all which pertains to us the energizing center must be in ourselves. We can never get away from ourselves as the center of our own universe, and the sooner we clearly understand this the better. There is really no energy in our universe but what emanates from ourselves in the first instance, and the power which appears to reside in our surroundings is derived entirely from our own mind.

If once we realize this, and consider that the Life which flows into us from the Universal Life-Principle is at every moment new Life entirely undifferentiated to any particular purpose besides that of supporting our own individuality, and that it is therefore ours to externalize in any form we will, then we find that this manifestation of the eternal Life-Principle in ourselves is the standpoint from which we can control our surroundings. We must lean firmly on the central point of our own being and not on anything else. Our mistake is in taking our surroundings too much 'au grand sérioux'. We should touch things more lightly. As soon as we feel that their weight impedes our free handling of them, they are mastering us and not we them.

Light handling does not mean weak handling. On the contrary, lightness of touch is incompatible with a weak grasp of the instrument, which implies that the weight of the tool is excessive relatively to the force that seeks to guide it. A light, even playful, handling therefore implies a firm grasp and perfect control over the instrument. It is only in the hands of a Grinling Gibbons that the carving tool can create miracles of aerial lightness from the solid wood. The light yet firm touch tells not of weakness, but of power held in reserve; and if we realize our own out-and-out spiritual nature we know that behind any measure of power we may put forth there is the whole reserve of the infinite to back us up.

As we come to know this we begin to handle things lightly, playing with them as a juggler does with his flying knives, which cannot make the slightest movement other than he has assigned to them, for we begin to see that our control over things is part of the necessary order of the Universe. The disorder we have met with in the past has resulted from our never having attempted consciously to introduce this element of our personal control as part of the system.

Of course, I speak of the whole man, and not merely of that part of him which Walt Whitman says is contained between his hat and his boots. The whole man is an infinitude, and the visible portion of him is the instrument through which he looks out upon and enjoys all that belongs to him, his own kingdom of the infinite. And when he learns that this is the meaning of his conscious individuality, he sees how it is that he is infinite, and finds that he is one with Infinite Mind, which is the innermost core of the Universe.

Having thus reached the true center of his own being, he can never give this central place to anything else, but will realize that relatively to this all other things are in the position of the incidental and accessory; and growing daily in this knowledge he will learn so to handle all things lightly, yet firmly, that grief, fear, and error will have less and less space in his world, until at last sorrow and sighing shall flee away, and everlasting joy shall take their place. We may as yet have taken only a few steps on the way, but they are in the right direction, and what we have to do now is go on.

Chapter 12

A lesson from Browning

Perhaps you know a little poem of Browning's called "An Epistle Containing the Strange Medical Experience of Karshish, the Arab Physician". The somewhat weird conception is that the Arab physician, travelling in Palestine soon after the date when the Gospel narrative closes, meets with Lazarus whom Jesus raised from the dead, and in this letter to a medical friend describes the strange effect which this vision of the other life has produced upon the resuscitated man.

The poem should be studied as a whole, but for the present a few lines selected here and there must do duty to indicate the character of the change which has come over Lazarus. After comparing him to a beggar who, having suddenly received boundless wealth, is unable to regulate its use to his requirements, Karshish continues:

> So here — we call the treasure knowledge, say,
> Increased beyond the fleshly faculty —
> Heaven opened to a soul while yet on earth,
> Earth forced on a soul's use while seeing   heaven:
> The man is witless of the size, the sum,
> The value in proportion of all things.

In fact he has become conscious of

> The spiritual life around the earthly life:
> The law of that is known to him as this,
> His heart and brain move there, his feet   stay here,

and the result is a loss of mental balance entirely unfitting him for the affairs of ordinary life.

Now there can be no doubt that Browning had a far more serious intention in writing this poem than just to record a fantastic notion that flitted through his brain. If we read between the lines, it must be clear from the general tenor of his writings that, however he may have acquired it, Browning had a very deep acquaintance with the inner region of spiritual causes which gave rise to all that we see of outward phenomenal manifestation. There are continual allusions in his works to the life behind the veil, and it is to this suggestion of some mystery underlying his words that we owe the many attempts to fathom his meaning expressed through Browning Societies and the like — attempts which fail or succeed according as they are made from "the without" or from "the within". No one was better qualified than the poet to realize the immense benefits of the inner knowledge, and for the same reason he is also qualified to warn us of the dangers on the way to its acquisition, for nowhere is it more true that "a little knowledge is a dangerous thing", and it is one of the greatest of these dangers that he points out in this poem.

Under the figure of Lazarus he describes the man who has practically grasped the reality of the inner side of things, for whom the veil has been removed, and who knows that the external and visible takes its rise from the internal and spiritual. But the description is that of one whose eyes have been so dazzled by the light that he has lost the power of accommodating his vision to the world of sense. He now commits the same error from the side of "the within" that he formerly committed from the side of "the without", the error of supposing that there is no vital reality in the aspect of things on which his thoughts are not immediately centered. This is want of mental balance, whether it shows itself by refusing reality to the inward or the outward. To be so absorbed in speculative ideas as to be unable to give them practical application in daily life is to allow our highest thoughts to evaporate in dreams.

There is a world of philosophy in the simple statement that there can be no inside without an outside; and the great secret in life is in learning to see things in their wholeness, and to realize the inside and the outside simultaneously. Each of them without the other is a mere abstraction having no real existence, and which we contemplate separately only for the purpose of reviewing the logical steps by which they are connected together as cause and effect. Nature does not separate them, for they are inseparable; and the law of nature is the law of life.

It is related of Pythagoras that, after he had led his scholars to the dizziest heights of the inner knowledge, he never failed to impress upon them the converse lesson of tracing out the steps by which these inner principles translate themselves into the familiar conditions of the outward things by which we are surrounded. The process of analysis is merely an expedient for discovering what springs in the realm of causes we are to touch in order to produce certain effects in the realm of manifestation. But this is not sufficient. We must also learn to calculate how those particular effects, when produced, will stand related to the world of already existing effects among which we propose to launch them, how they will modify these and be in turn modified by them; and this calculation of effects is as necessary as the knowledge of causes.

We cannot impress upon ourselves too strongly that reality consists of both an inside and an outside, a generating principle and a generated condition, and that anything short of the reality of wholeness is illusion on one side or the other. Nothing could have been further from Browning's intention than to deter seekers after truth from studying the principles of Being, for without the knowledge of them truth must always remain wrapped in mystery; but the lesson he would impress on us is that of guarding vigilantly the mental equilibrium which alone will enable us to develop those boundless powers whose infinite unfolding is the fullness of Life.

And we must remember above all that the soul of life is Love, and that Love shows itself by service, and service proceeds from sympathy, which is the capacity for seeing things from the point of view of those whom we would help, while at the same time seeing them also in their true relations; and therefore, if we would realize that Love which is the inmost vitalizing principle even of the most interior powers, it must be kept alive by maintaining our hold upon the exterior life as being equally real with the inward principles of which it is the manifestation.

Chapter 13
Present Truth

If Thought Power is good for anything, it is good for everything. If it can produce one thing, it can produce all things. For what is to hinder it? Nothing can stop us from thinking. We can think what we please, and if to think is to form, then we can form what we please. The whole question, therefore, resolves itself into this: Is it true that that to think is to form? If so, do we not see that our limitations are formed in precisely the same way as our expansions? We think that conditions outside our thought have power over us, and so we think power into them. So the great question of life is whether there is any creative power other than Thought. If so, where it it, and what is it?

Both philosophy and religion lead us to the truth that "in the beginning" there was no creative power other than Spirit, and the only mode of activity we can possibly attribute to Spirit is Thought, and so we find Thought as the root of all things. And if this was the case "in the beginning" it must be so still, for if all things originate in Thought, all things must be modes of Thought, and so it is impossible for Spirit ever to hand over its creations to some power which is not itself — that is to say, which is not Thought-power; and consequently all the forms and circumstances that surround us are manifestations of the creative power of Thought.

But it may be objected that this is God's Thought; and that the creative power is in God and not Man. But this goes away from the self-evident axiomatic truth that "in the beginning" nothing could have had any origin except in the Divine Mind, and Man himself is therefore a mode of the Divine Thought. Again, Man is self-conscious; therefore Man is the Divine Thought evolved into individual consciousness, and when he becomes sufficiently enlightened to realize this as his origin, then he sees that he is a reproduction in *individuality* of the *same* spirit which produces all things, and that his own thought in individuality has exactly the same quality as the Divine Thought in universality, just as fire is equally igneous whether burning round a large center of combustion or a small one, and thus we are logically brought to the conclusion that our thought must have creative power.

But people say, "We have not found it so. We are surrounded by all sorts of circumstances that we do not desire". Yes, you *fear* them, and in so doing you *think* them, and in this way you are constantly exercising this Divine prerogative of creation by Thought, only through ignorance you use it in a wrong direction. Therefore the Book of Divine Instructions so constantly repeats, "Fear not; doubt not", because we can never divest our Thought of its inherent creative quality, and the only question is whether we shall use it ignorantly to our injury or understandingly to our benefit.

The Master summed up his teaching in the aphorism that knowledge of the Truth would make us free. Here is no announcement of anything we have to do, or of anything that has to be done for us, in order to gain our liberty; neither is it a statement of anything future. Truth is what it is. He did not say, you must wait till something becomes true which is not true now. He said: "Know what is Truth now, and you will find that the Truth concerning yourself is Liberty". If the knowledge of Truth makes us free it can only be because in truth we are free already, only we do not know it.

Our liberty consists in our reproducing on the scale of the individual the same creative power of Thought which first brought the world into existence, "so that the things which are seen were not made of things which do appear". Let us, then, confidently claim our birthright as "sons and daughters of the Almighty", and by habitually thinking the good, the beautiful, and the true, surround ourselves with conditions corresponding to our thoughts, and by our teaching and example help others to do the same.

Chapter 14

Affirmative Power

Thoroughly to realize the true nature of affirmative power is to possess the key to the great secret. We feel its presence in all the innumerable forms of life by which we are surrounded and we feel it as the life in ourselves; and at last someday the truth bursts upon us like a revelation that we can wield this power, this life, by the process of Thought. And as soon as we see this, the importance of regulating our thinking begins to dawn upon us. We ask ourselves what this thought process is, and we then find that it is thinking affirmative force into forms which are the product of our own thought. We mentally conceive the form and then think life into it.

This must always be the nature of the creative process on whatever scale, whether on the grand scale of the Universal Cosmic Mind or on the miniature scale of the individual mind; the difference is only in degree and not in kind. We may picture the mental machinery by which this is done in a way that best satisfies our intellect — and the satisfying of the intellect on this point is a potent factor in giving us that confidence in our mental action without which we can effect nothing — but the actual externalization is the result of something more powerful than a merely intellectual apprehension. It is the result of that inner mental state which, for want of a better word, we may call our emotional conception of ourselves. It is the "self" which we feel ourselves to be which takes forms of our own creating. For this reason our thought must be so grounded upon knowledge that we shall feel the truth of it, and thus be able to produce in ourselves that mental attitude of feeling which corresponds to the condition which we desire to externalize.

We cannot think into manifestation a different sort of life to that which we realize in ourselves. As Horace says, "*Nemo dat quod non habet*", we cannot give what we have not got. And, on the other hand, we can never cease creating forms of some sort by our mental activity, thinking life into them. The point must be very carefully noted. We cannot sit still producing nothing: the mental machinery will keep on turning out work of some sort, and it rests with us to determine of what sort it shall be. In our entire ignorance or imperfect realization of this, we create negative forms and think life into them. We create forms of death, sickness, sorrow, trouble, and limitation of all sorts, and then think life into these forms, with the result that, however non-existent in themselves, to us they become realities and throw their shadow across the path which would otherwise be bright with the many-coloured beauties of innumerable flowers and the glory of the sunshine.

This need not be. It is giving to the negative an affirmative force which does not belong to it. Consider what is meant by the negative. It is the absence of something. It is not-being, and is the absence of all that constitutes being. Left to itself, it remains in its own nothingness, and it only assumes form and activity when we give these to it by our thought.

Here, then, is the great reason for practicing control over our thought. It is the one and only instrument we have to work with, but it is an instrument which works with the greatest certainty — for limitation if we think limitation, for enlargement if we think enlargement. Our thought as feeling is the magnet which draws to us those conditions which accurately correspond to itself. This is the meaning of the saying that "thoughts are things".

But, you say, how can I think differently from the circumstances? Certainly you are not required to say that the circumstances at the present moment are what they are not; to say so would be untrue; but what is wanted is not to think from the standpoint of the circumstances at all. Think from that interior standpoint where there are no circumstances, and from whence you can dictate what circumstances shall be, and then leave the circumstances to take care of themselves.

Do not think of this, that, or the other particular circumstances of health, peace, etc., but of health, peace, and prosperity themselves. Here is an advertisement from Pearson's Weekly: "Think money. Big money-makers think money." This is a perfectly sound statement of the power of thought, although it is only an advertisement; but we may make an advance beyond thinking "money". We can think "Life" in all its fullness, together with that perfect harmony of conditions which includes all that we need of money and a thousand other good things besides, for some of which money stands as the symbol of exchangeable value, while others cannot be estimated by so material a standard.

Therefore think Life, illumination, harmony, prosperity, happiness — think the things rather than this or that condition of them. And then by the sure operation of the Universal Law, these things will form themselves into the shapes best suited to your particular case, and will enter your life as active, living forces, which will never depart from you because you know them to be part and parcel of your own being.

Chapter 15

The Spirit of Opulence

It is quite a mistake to suppose that we must restrict and stint ourselves in order to develop greater power or usefulness. This is to form the conception of the Divine Power as so limited that the best use we can make of it is by a policy of self-starvation, whether material or mental. Of course, if we believe that some form of self-starvation is necessary to our producing good work, then so long as we entertain this belief the fact actually is so for us. "Whatsoever is not of faith" — that is, not in accordance with our honest belief — "is sin" (Rom. 14:23). By acting contrary to what we really believe, we bring a suggestion of opposition to the Divine Spirit, and this must necessarily paralyze our efforts and surround us with a murky atmosphere of distrust and want of joy.

But all this exists in, and is produced by, our belief; and when we come to examine the grounds of this belief we shall find that it rests upon an entire misapprehension of the nature of our own power. If we clearly realize that the creative power in ourselves is unlimited, then there is no reason for limiting the extent to which we may enjoy what we can create by means of it. Where we are drawing from the infinite, we need never be afraid of taking more than our share. That is not where the danger lies. The danger is in not sufficiently realizing our own richness and in looking upon the externalized products of our creative power as being the true riches instead of the creative power of Spirit Itself.

If we avoid this error, there is no need to limit ourselves in taking what we will from the infinite storehouse: "All things are yours" (1 Cor. 3:21). And the way to avoid this error is by realizing that the true wealth is in identifying ourselves with the spirit of opulence. We must be opulent in our thought. Do not "think money", as such, for it is only one means of opulence; but "think opulence" — that is, largely, generously, liberally — and you will find that the means of realizing this thought will flow to you from all quarters, whether as money or as a hundred other things not to be reckoned in cash.

We must not make ourselves dependent on any particular form of wealth, or insist on its coming to us through some particular channel. That is at once to impose a limitation, to shut out other forms of wealth, and to close other channels. Rather, we must enter into the spirit of it. Now the spirit is Life: and throughout the Universe, Life ultimately consists in circulation — whether within the physical body of the individual or on the scale of the entire solar system. Circulation means a continual flowing around, and the spirit of opulence is no exception to the Universal law of all life.

When once this principle becomes clear to us we shall see that our attention should be directed rather to the giving than to the receiving. We must look upon ourselves, not as misers' chests to be kept locked for our own benefit, but as centers of distribution. The better we fulfill our function as such centers, the greater will be the corresponding inflow. If we choke the outlet, the current must slacken, and a full and free flow can be obtained only by keeping it open. The spirit of opulence — that is, the opulent mode of thought — consists in cultivating the feeling that we possess all sorts of riches which we can bestow upon others, and which we can bestow liberally because by this very action we open the way for still greater supplies to flow in.

But you say, "I am short of money; I hardly know how to pay for necessaries. What have I to give?"

The answer is that we must always start from the point where we are. If your wealth at the present moment is not abundant on the material plane, you need not trouble to start on that plane. There are other sorts of wealth, still more valuable, on the spiritual and intellectual planes, with which you can begin. You can start from this point and practice the spirit of opulence even though your balance at the bank may be nil. And then the Universal Law of Attraction will begin to assert itself. You will not only begin to experience an inflow on the spiritual and intellectual planes, but it will extend itself to the material plane also.

If you have realized the spirit of opulence, you cannot help drawing to yourself material good as well as that higher wealth which is not to be measured by any monetary standard. When you truly understand the spirit of opulence, you will neither affect to despise this form of good, nor will you attribute to it a value that does not belong to it; but you will co-ordinate it with your other more interior forms of wealth so as to make it the material instrument in smoothing the way for their more perfect expression.

Used thus, with understanding of the relation which it bears to spiritual and intellectual wealth, material wealth becomes one with them, and is no more to be shunned and feared than it is to be sought for its own sake.

It is not money, but the love of money, that is the root of evil. The spirit of opulence is precisely the attitude of mind which is furthest removed from the love of money for its own sake. It does not believe in money. What it does believe in is the generous feeling which is the intuitive recognition of the great law of circulation, which does not in any undertaking make its first question, 'How much am I going to get by it?' but rather, 'How much am I going to do by it?' And making this the first question, the getting will flow in with a generous profusion, and with a spontaneity and rightness of direction that are absent when our first thought is of receiving only.

We are not called upon to give what we have not yet got and to run into debt; but we are to give liberally of what we have, with the knowledge that by so doing we are setting the law of circulation to work. As this law brings us greater and greater inflows of every kind of good, so our outgiving will increase — not by depriving ourselves of any expansion of our own life that we may desire, but by finding that every expansion makes us more powerful instruments for expanding the life of others. "Live and let live" is the motto of true opulence.

The Universal Spirit

Chapter 1

Consciousness of Spirit

To realize fully how much of our present daily life consists in symbols is to find the answer to the old, old question, 'What is Truth?'; and in the degree in which we begin to recognize this, we begin to approach Truth. The realization of Truth consists in the ability to translate symbols, whether natural or conventional, into their equivalents; and the root of all the errors of mankind consists in the inability to do this and consequently in maintaining that the symbol has nothing behind it. The great duty incumbent on all who have attained to this knowledge is to impress upon their fellow men that there is an inner side to things and that, until this inner side is known, the things themselves are not known.

There is an inner and an outer side to everything; and the quality of the superficial mind which causes it to fail in the attainment of Truth is its willingness to rest content with the outside only. So long as this is the case, it is impossible for a man to grasp the import of his own relation to the Universal: and it is this relation which constitutes all that is signified by the word "Truth".

So long as a man fixes his attention only on the superficial, it is impossible for him to make any progress in knowledge. He is denying that principle of "Growth" which is the root of all life, whether spiritual, intellectual, or material, for he does not stop to reflect that all which he sees as the outer side of things can result only from some germinal principle hidden deep in the center of their being.

Expansion from the center by growth according to a necessary order of sequence: this is the Law of Life of which the whole Universe is the outcome, alike in the one great solidarity of cosmic Being and in the separate individualities of its minutest organisms. This great principle is the key to the whole riddle of Life upon whatever plane we contemplate it; and without this key the door from the outer to the inner side of things can never be opened. It is therefore the duty of all to whom this door has to some extent been opened to endeavour to acquaint others with the fact that there is an inner side to things, and that life becomes truer and fuller in proportion as we penetrate it and make our estimates of all things according to what becomes visible from this interior point of view.

In the widest sense, everything is a symbol of that which constitutes its inner being. All Nature is a gallery of arcana revealing great truths to those who can decipher them. But there is a more precise sense in which our current life is based upon symbols in regard to the most important subjects that can occupy our thoughts: the symbols by which we strive to represent the nature and being of God, and the manner in which the life of man is related to the Divine Life. The whole character of a man's life results from what he really believes on this subject — not his formal statement of belief in a particular creed, but what he realizes as the stage which his mind has actually attained in regard to it.

Has a man's mind only reached the point at which he thinks it is impossible to know anything about God, or to make any use of the knowledge if he had it? Then his whole interior world is in the condition of confusion which must necessarily exist where no spirit of order has yet begun to move upon the chaos in which the elements of being are all disordered — and therefore neutralize one another.

Has he advanced a step further and realized that there is a ruling and ordering power, but beyond this is ignorant of its nature? Then the unknown is, for him, the terrifying; and, amid a tumult of fears and distresses that deprive him of all strength to advance, he spends his life in the endeavour to propitiate this power as something naturally adverse to him instead of knowing that it is the very center of his own life and being.

And so on through every degree, from the lowest depths of ignorance to the greatest heights of intelligence, a man's life must always be the exact reflection of that particular stage which he has reached in his perception of the Divine Nature and of his own relation to it. As we approach the full perception of Truth, so the life-principle within us expands; old bonds and limitations which had no existence in reality fall off from us; and we enter into regions of light, liberty, and power of which we had previously no conception. It is impossible, therefore, to overestimate the importance of being able to realize the symbol as a symbol, and being able to penetrate to the inner substance which it represents. Life itself is to be realized only by the conscious experience of its liveliness in ourselves, and it is the endeavour to translate these experiences into terms which shall suggest a corresponding idea to others that gives rise to all symbolism.

The nearer those we address have approached to the actual experience, the more transparent the symbol becomes, and the further they are from such experience the thicker is the veil. Our whole progress consists in the fuller and fuller translation of symbols into clearer and clearer statements of that for which they stand.

But the first step, without which all succeeding steps must remain impossible, is to convince people that symbols are symbols, and not the very Truth itself. And the difficulty consists in this: that if the symbolism is in any degree adequate it must, in some measure, represent the form of Truth, just as the modeling of a drapery suggests the form of the figure beneath. People in general have a certain consciousness that somehow they are in the presence of Truth; and this leads them to resent any removal of those folds of drapery which have hitherto conveyed this idea to their minds.

There is sufficient indication of the inner Truth in the outward form to afford an excuse for the timorous — and for those who have not sufficient mental energy to think for themselves — to cry out that finality has already been attained, and that any further search into the matter must end in the destruction of Truth. But in raising such an outcry they betray their ignorance of the very nature of Truth — which is that it can never be destroyed: the very fact that truth is Truth makes this impossible. And again they exhibit their ignorance of the first principle of Life — namely, the Law of Growth which, throughout the Universe, perpetually pushes forward into more and more vivid forms of expression. Variety has expansion everywhere and finality nowhere.

Such ignorant objections need not, therefore, alarm us; and we should endeavour to show those who make them that what they fear is the only natural order of the Divine Life which is "over all, through all, and in all".

But we must do this gently, and not by forcibly thrusting upon them the object of their terror and so repelling them from all study of the subject. We should endeavour gradually to lead them to see that there is something interior to what they have hitherto held to be ultimate Truth. We should encourage them to realize that the sensation of emptiness and dissatisfaction, which from time to time will persist in making itself felt in their hearts, is really the spirit within pointing to that inner side of things which alone can satisfactorily account for what we observe on the exterior. By getting to know ourselves from within, we gradually perceive the true nature of our inheritance in the Universal Life which is the Life Everlasting.

Chapter 2
The Science of Spirit

What, then, is this central principle which is at the root of all things? It is Life — but not life as we recognize it in particular forms of manifestation. It is something more interior and concentrated than that. It is that "Unity of the Spirit" which is unity simply because it has not yet passed into diversity. Perhaps this is not an easy idea to grasp, but it is the root of all scientific conception of spirit; for without it there is no common principle to which we can refer the innumerable forms of manifestation that spirit assumes.

It is the conception of Life as the sum-total of all its undistributed powers, being as yet none of these in particular, but all of them in potentiality. This is, no doubt, a highly abstract idea, but it is essentially that of the center from which growth takes place by expansion in every direction. This is that last residuum which defies all our powers of analysis. This is truly "the unknowable", not in the sense of the unthinkable but of the unanalyzable. It is the subject of perception — but not of knowledge — if by knowledge we mean that faculty which estimates the relations between things. Here we have passed beyond any questions of relations, and are face to face with the Absolute.

This innermost of all is Absolute Spirit. It is Life as yet not differentiated into any specific mode; it is the Universal Life which pervades all things and is at the heart of all appearances.

To come into the knowledge of this is to come into the secret of power and to enter into the secret place of Living Spirit. Is it illogical first to call this the unknowable, and then to speak of coming into the knowledge of it? Perhaps so, but no less a writer than St Paul has set the example; for does he not speak of the final result of all searching into the heights and depths and lengths and breadths of the inner side of things as being to attain the knowledge of the Love which passeth knowledge? (Eph 3:14-19) If he is thus boldly illogical in phrase, though not in fact, may we not also speak of knowing "the unknowable"? We may: for this knowledge is the root of all other knowledge.

The presence of this undifferentiated Universal Life-power is the final axiomatic fact to which all our analysis must ultimately conduct us. On whatever plane we make our analysis it must always abut on pure essence, pure energy, pure Being — that which knows itself and recognizes itself, but which cannot dissect itself because it is not built up of parts but is ultimately integral. It is pure Unity.

But analysis which does not lead to synthesis is merely destructive: it is the child wantonly pulling the flower to pieces and throwing away the fragments. It is not the botanist, also pulling the flower to pieces, but building up in his mind from those carefully studied fragments a vast synthesis of the constructive power of Nature, embracing the laws of the formation of all flower-forms. The value of analysis is to lead us to the original starting-point of that which we analyze, and so to teach us the laws by which its final form springs from this center.

Knowing the law of its construction, we turn our analysis into a synthesis, and we thus gain a power of building up which must always be beyond the reach of those who regard "the unknowable" as if it were "not-being".

This idea of the unknowable is the root of all materialism; yet no scientific man, however materialistic his proclivities, treats the unanalyzable residuum thus when he meets it in the experiments of his laboratory. On the contrary, he makes this final unanalyzable fact the basis of his synthesis. He finds that in the last resort it is energy of some kind, whether as heat or as motion; but he does not throw up his scientific pursuits because he cannot analyze it further. He adopts the precisely opposite course, and realizes that the conservation of energy, its indestructibility, and the impossibility of adding to or subtracting from the sum-total of energy in the world, is the one solid and unchanging fact on which alone the edifice of physical science can be built up. He bases all his knowledge upon his knowledge of "the unknowable". And rightly so, for if he could analyses this energy into yet further factors, then the same problem of "the unknowable" would meet him still. All our progress consists in continually pushing the unknowable, in the sense of the unanalyzable residuum, a step further back; but that there should be no ultimate unanalyzable residuum anywhere is an inconceivable idea.

In thus realizing the undifferentiated unity of Living Spirit as the central fact of any system, whether the system of the entire Universe or of a single organism, we are therefore following a strictly scientific method. We pursue our analysis until it necessarily leads us to this final fact, and then we accept this fact as the basis of our synthesis. The Science of Spirit is thus not one whit less scientific than the Science of Matter; and, moreover, it starts from the same initial fact, the fact of a Living Energy which defies definition or explanation wherever we find it. However, Spiritual Science differs from the Science of Matter in that it contemplates this energy under an aspect of responsive intelligence which does not fall within the scope of physical science as such.

The Science of Spirit and the Science of Matter are not opposed. They are complementary, and neither is fully comprehensible without some knowledge of the other. Being really but two portions of one whole, they insensibly shade off into each other in a border-land where no arbitrary line can be drawn between them. Science studied in a truly scientific spirit, following out its own deductions unflinchingly to their legitimate conclusions, will always reveal the twofold aspect of things, the inner and outer; and it is only a truncated and maimed science that refuses to recognize both.

The study of the material world is not mere Materialism if it be allowed to progress to its legitimate issue. Materialism is that limited view of the Universe which will not admit the existence of anything but mechanical effects and mechanical causes; and any system which recognizes no higher power than the physical forces of nature must logically result in having no higher ultimate appeal than to physical force, or to fraud as its alternative.

I speak, of course, of the tendency of the system, not of the morality of individuals, which is often very far in advance of the systems they profess. But as we would avoid the propagation of a mode of thought whose effects history shows only too plainly, whether in the Italy of the Borgias, or the France of the First Revolution, or the Commune of the Franco-Prussian War, we should set ourselves to study that inner and spiritual aspect of things which is the basis of a system whose logical results are truth and love instead of perfidy and violence.

Some of us, doubtless, have often wondered why the Heavenly Jerusalem is described in the Book of Revelations as a cube — "the length and the breadth and the height of it are equal" [Rev. 21:16 — Ed.]. This is because the cube is the figure of perfect stability, and thus represents Truth, which can never be overthrown. Turn it on what side you will, it still remains the perfect cube, always standing upright; you cannot upset it. This figure, then, represents the manifestation in concrete solidity of that central life-giving energy which is not itself any one plane but generates all planes: the planes of the above and below and of all four sides. But it is at the same time a city, a place of habitation; and this is because that which is "within" is the Living Spirit which has its dwelling there.

As one plane of the cube implies all the other planes and also "the within", so any plane of manifestation implies the others and always refers back to that "origin within" which generates them all. Now, if we would make any progress in the spiritual side of science — and every department of science has its spiritual side — we must always keep our minds fixed upon this "innermost within" which contains the potential of all outward manifestation, the "fourth dimension" which generates the cube.

Our common forms of speech show how intuitively we do this. We speak of the spirit in which an act is done, of entering into the spirit of a game, of the spirit of the time, and so on. Everywhere our intuition points out the spirit as the true essence of things; and it is only when we commence arguing about them from without, instead of from within, that our true perception of their nature is lost.

The scientific study of spirit consists in following up intelligently and according to definite method the same principle that now only flashes upon us at intervals fitfully and vaguely. When we once realize that this Universal and unlimited power of spirit is at the root of all things and of ourselves also, then we have obtained the key to the whole position; and, however far we may carry our studies in spiritual science, we shall nowhere find anything else but particular developments of this one Universal principle. "The Kingdom of Heaven is within you".

Chapter 3
Intelligent Order

I have laid stress on the fact that the "innermost within" of all things is Living Spirit, and that the Science of Spirit is distinguished from the Science of Matter in that it contemplates Energy under an aspect of responsive intelligence which does not fall within the scope of physical science as such. These are the two great points to lay hold of if we would retain a clear idea of spiritual science and not be misled by arguments drawn from the physical side of Science only — the liveliness of the originating principle which is at the heart of all things, and its intelligent and responsive nature. Its liveliness is patent to our observation, at any rate from the point where we recognize it in the vegetable kingdom; but its intelligence and responsiveness are not, perhaps, at once so obvious. Nevertheless, a little thought will soon lead us to recognize this also.

No one can deny that there is an intelligent order throughout all Nature, for it requires the highest intelligence of our most highly-trained minds to follow the steps of this Universal intelligence which is always in advance of them. The more deeply we investigate the world we live in, the more clear it must become to us that all our science is the translation into words or numerical symbols of that order which already exists. If the clear statement of this existing order is the highest that the human intellect can reach, this surely argues a corresponding intelligence in the power which gives rise to this great sequence of order and interrelation, so as to constitute one harmonious whole.

Now, unless we fall back on the idea of a workman working upon material external to himself — in which case we have to explain the phenomenon of the workman — the only conception we can form of this power is that it is the Living Spirit inherent in the heart of every atom, giving it outward form and definition, and becoming in it those intrinsic polarities which constitute its characteristic nature.

There is no random work here. Every attraction and repulsion acts with its proper force, collecting the atoms into molecules, the molecules into tissues, the tissues into organs, and the organs into individuals. At each stage of the progress we get the sum of the intelligent forces which operate in the constituent parts, plus a higher degree of intelligence which we may regard as the collective intelligence superior to that of the mere sub-total of the parts — something which belongs to the individual as a whole, and not to the parts as such. These are facts which can be amply proved from physical science; and they also supply a great law in spiritual science, which is that in any collective body, the intelligence of the whole is superior to that of the sum of the parts.

Spirit is at the root of all things, and thoughtful observation shows that its operation is guided by unfailing intelligence which adapts means to ends, and harmonizes the entire Universe of manifested being in those wonderful ways which physical science renders clearer every day. This intelligence must be in the Generating Spirit Itself, for there is no other source from which it could proceed. On these grounds, therefore, we may distinctly affirm that Spirit is intelligent, and that whatever it does is done by the intelligent adaptation of means to ends.

But Spirit is also responsive. And here we have to fall back upon the law stated above, that the mere sum of the intelligence of Spirit in lower degrees of manifestation is not equal to the intelligence of the complex whole, as a whole. This is a radical law which we cannot impress upon our minds too deeply. The degree of spiritual intelligence is marked by the wholeness of the organism through which it finds expression. Hence the more highly organized being has a degree of spirit which is superior to, and is consequently capable of exercising control over, all lower or less fully-integrated degrees of spirit. This being so, we can now begin to see why the spirit that is the "innermost within" of all things is responsive as well as intelligent.

Being intelligent, it knows; and spirit being ultimately all there is, that which it knows is itself. Hence it is that power which recognizes itself; and accordingly its lower powers recognize its higher powers, and by the law of attraction they are bound to respond to the higher degrees of themselves. On this general principle, therefore, spirit, under whatever exterior revealed, is necessarily intelligent and responsive.

But intelligence and responsiveness imply personality; and we may therefore now advance a step further and argue that all spirit contains the elements of personality, even though, in any particular instance, it may not yet be expressed as that individual personality which we find in ourselves.

In short, spirit is always personal in its nature, even when it has not yet attained to that degree of synthesis which is sufficient to render it personal in manifestation. In ourselves the synthesis has proceeded far enough to reach that degree, and therefore we recognize ourselves as the manifestation of that personality which is of the essence of spiritual substance on every plane. Or, to put the whole argument in a simpler form, we may say that our own personality must necessarily have had its origin in that which is personal, on the principle that you cannot get more out of a bag than it contains.

In ourselves, therefore, we find that more perfect synthesis of the spirit into manifested personality which is lacking in the lower kingdoms of nature and, accordingly, since spirit is necessarily that which knows itself and must, therefore, recognize its own degrees in its various modes, the spirit in all degrees below that of the human personality is bound to respond to itself in that superior degree which constitutes human individuality. This is the basis of the power of human thought to externalize itself in infinite forms of its own ordering.

But if the subordination of the lower degrees of spirit to the higher is one of the fundamental laws which lie at the bottom of the creative power of thought, there is another equally fundamental law which places a salutary restraint upon the abuse of that power. It is the law that we can command the powers of the Universal for our own purposes only in proportion as we first realize and obey their generic character. We can employ water for any purpose which does not require it to run uphill, and we can utilize electricity for any purpose that does not require it to pass from a lower to a higher potential.

So with that Universal power which we call the Spirit. It has an inherent generic character with which we must comply if we would employ it for our specific purposes, and this character is summed up in the one word "goodness". The Spirit is Life; hence its generic tendency must always be lifeward or to the increase of the liveliness of every individual. Since it is Universal, it can have no particular interests to serve; and therefore its action must always be equally for the benefit of all. This is the generic character of Spirit: just as water, or electricity, or any other of the physical forces of the Universe, will not work contrary to their generic character, so Spirit will not work contrary to its generic character.

The inference is obvious. If we would use Spirit we must follow the law of the Spirit, which is "Goodness". This is the only limitation. If our originating intention is good, we may employ the spiritual power for what purpose we will. And how is "goodness" to be defined? Simply by the child's definition that what is bad is not good, and that what is good is not bad; we all instinctively know the difference between bad and good. If we will conform to this principle of obedience to the generic law of the Spirit, all that remains is for us to study the law of the proportion which exists between the more and less fully integrated modes of Spirit, and then bring our knowledge to bear with determination.

Chapter 4

The Law of Spirit

The Law of Spirit, to which our investigation has now led us, is of the very widest scope. We have followed it up from the conception of the intelligence of spirit subsisting in the individual atoms to the aggregation of this intelligence as the conscious identity of the individual person.

But there is no reason why this law should cease to operate at this point, or at any point short of the whole. The test of the soundness of any principle is that it can operate as effectively on a large scale as on a small one; that though the nature of its field is determined by the nature of the principle itself, the extent of the field is unlimited. If, therefore, we continue to follow up the law we have been considering, it leads us to the conception of a unit of intelligence as far superior to that of the individual man as the unity of his individual intelligence is superior to that of the intelligence of any single atom of the body. Thus we may conceive of a collective individuality representing the spiritual character of any aggregate of men — the inhabitants of a city, of a district, of a country, or of the entire world.

Nor need the process stop here. On the same principle there would be a superior collective individuality for the humanity of the entire solar system; and finally we reach the conception of a Supreme Intelligence bringing together in itself the collective individualities of all the systems in the Universe.

This is by no means a merely fanciful notion. We find it as the law by which our own conscious individuality is constituted, and we find the analogous principle working universally on the physical plane. It is known to physical science as the "law of inverse squares", by which the forces of reciprocal attraction or repulsion, as the case may be, are not merely equivalent to the sum of the forces emitted by the two bodies concerned, but are equivalent to these two forces multiplied together and divided by the square of the distance between their centers. Hence the resultant power continually rises in a rapidly-increasing ratio as the two reciprocally exciting bodies approach one another.

Since this law is so universal throughout physical nature, the doctrine of continuity affords every ground for supposing that its analogue holds good in respect of spiritual nature. We must never lose sight of the old-world saying that "a truth on one plane is a truth on all". If a principle exists at all, it exists universally.

We must not allow ourselves to be misled by appearances. We must remember that the perceptible results of the working of any principle consists of two factors: the principle itself, or the assertive factor; and the subject-matter on which it acts, or the passive factor. While the former is invariable, the latter is variable; and the operation of the same invariable upon different variables must necessarily produce a variety of results.

This at once becomes evident if we state it mathematically. For example, a, b, or c, multiplied by x, give respectively the results ax, bx, cx, which differ materially from one another though the factor x remains the same.

This law of the generation of power by attraction applies on the spiritual as well as on the physical plane, and acts with the same mathematical precision on both. Thus the human individuality consists, not in the mere aggregation of its parts, whether spiritual or corporeal, but in the unity of power resulting from the intimate association of those parts with one another. According to the law of the generation of power, this unity is infinitely superior, both in intelligence and power, to any less fully integrated mode of spirit. Thus a natural principle, common alike to physical and spiritual law, fully accounts for all claims that have ever been made for the creative power of our thought over all things that come within the circle of our own particular life. Each man is the center of his own universe and has the power, by directing his own thought, to control all things therein.

But, as I have said above, there is no reason why this principle should not be recognized as expanding from the individual until it embraces the entire Universe. Each man, as the center of his own world, is himself centered in a higher system in which he is only one of innumerable similar atoms, and this system again in a higher until we reach the Supreme Center of all things. Intelligence and power increase from center to center in a ratio rising with inconceivable rapidity until they culminate in illimitable intelligence and power commensurate with All-Being.

Now we have seen that the relation of man to the lower modes of spirit is that of superiority and command; but what is his relation to these higher modes? In any harmoniously constituted system, the relation of the part to the whole never interferes with the free operation of the part in the performance of its own functions. On the contrary, it is precisely by means of this relation that each part is maintained in a position to discharge all functions for which it is fitted.

The subordination of the individual man to the Supreme Mind, so far from curtailing his liberty, is the very condition which makes liberty possible — or even life itself. The generic movement of the whole necessarily carries the part along with it. So long as the part allows itself thus to be carried onwards, there will be no hindrance to its free working in any direction for which it is fitted by its own individuality.

This truth was set forth in the old Hindu religion as the Car of Jagannath — an ideal car only, which later ages degraded into a terribly material symbol. "Jagannath" means "Lord of the Universe", and this signifies the Universal Mind. This, by the law of Being, must always move forward regardless of any attempts of individuals to restrain it. Those who mount upon its car move onward with it to endlessly advancing evolution, while those who seek to oppose it must be crushed beneath its wheels, for it is no respecter of persons.

If, therefore, we would employ the Universal Law of Spirit to control our own little individual worlds, we must also recognize it in respect to the Supreme Center around which we ourselves revolve. But we must first abandon the old way of supposing that this Center is a capricious Individuality, external to ourselves, which can be propitiated or cajoled into giving the good which He is not good enough to give of His own proper motion. So long as we retain this infantile idea we have not come into the liberty which results from the knowledge of the certainty of Law.

Supreme Mind is Supreme Law, and can be calculated upon with the same accuracy as when manifested in any of the particular laws of the physical world. The result of studying, understanding, and obeying this Supreme Law is that we we thereby acquire the power to use it. Nor need we fear it with the old fear which comes from ignorance, for we can rely with confidence upon the proposition that the whole can have no interest adverse to the part of which it is composed and, conversely, that the part can have no interest adverse to the whole.

Our ignorance of our relation to the whole may make us appear to have separate interests, but a truer knowledge must always show such an idea to be mistaken. The same responsiveness of spirit which manifests itself as obedience to our wishes when we look to those degrees of spirit which are lower than our own individuality must manifest itself as a necessary inflowing of intelligence and power when we look to the infinity of spirit of which our individuality is a singular expression. In so looking upwards we are looking for the higher degree of ourselves.

The increased vitality of the parts means the increased vitality of the whole. Since it is impossible to conceive of spirit otherwise than as a continually expanding principle of Life, the demand for such increased vitality must, by the inherent nature of spirit, be met by a corresponding supply of continually growing intelligence and power. Thus, by a natural law, the demand creates the supply, and this supply may be freely applied to any and every subject-matter that commends itself to us.

There is no limit to the supply of this energy other than what we ourselves put to it by our thought. Neither is there any limit to the purposes we may make it serve other than the one grand Law of Order, which says that good things used for wrong purposes become evil. Consideration of the intelligent and responsive nature of spirit shows that there can be no limitations but these. The one is a limitation inherent in spirit itself, and the other is a limitation which has no root except in our own ignorance.

It is true that to maintain our healthy action within the circle of our own individual world we must continually move forward with the movement of the larger whole of which we form a part. But this does not imply any restriction of our liberty to make the fullest use of our lives in accordance with those universal principles of life upon which they are founded. There is not one law for the part and another for the whole, but the same Law of Being which permeates both alike.

In proportion, therefore, as we realize the true law of our own individuality, we shall find that it is one with the law of progress for the race. The collective individuality of mankind is only the reproduction on a larger scale of the personal individuality; and whatever action truly develops the inherent powers of the individual must necessarily be in line with that forward march of the Universal Mind which is the evolution of humanity as a whole.

Selfishness is a narrow view of our own nature which loses sight of our place in relation to the whole, not perceiving that it is from this very relation that our life is drawn. It is ignorance of our own possibilities and consequent limitation of our own powers. If, therefore, the evidence of harmonious correlation throughout the physical world leads irresistibly to the inference of intelligent spirit as the innermost within of all things, we must recognize ourselves also as individual manifestations of the same Spirit which expresses Itself throughout the Universe as that power of intelligent responsiveness which is Love.

Chapter 5

The Harmony of Spirit

We find ourselves to be a necessary and integral part of the Infinite Harmony of All-Being. We do not recognize this great truth merely as a vague intuition, but rather as the logical and unavoidable result of the Universal Life-Principle which permeates all Nature. We find our intuition was true because we have discovered the law which gave rise to it. Intuition and investigation both unite in telling us of our own individual place in the great scheme of things. Even the most advanced among us have, as yet, little more than the faintest adumbration of what this place is, but it is clearly a place of power. Towards those higher modes of spirit which we speak of as "the Universal", the law of man's inmost nature makes him as a lens, drawing into the focus of his own individuality all that he will of light and power in streams of inexhaustible supply. Man thus becomes the directive center of energy and order towards the lower modes of spirit which, for each one, form the sphere of his own particular world.

Can we conceive of any position containing greater possibilities than these? The circle of this vital influence may expand as the individual grows into the wider contemplation of his unity with Infinite Being, but it would be impossible to formulate any more comprehensive law of relationship. Emerson has rightly said that a little algebra will often do far more towards clearing our ideas than a large amount of poetic simile. Algebraically it is a self-evident proposition that any difference between various powers of x disappears when they are compared with x multiplied by itself to infinity, because there can be no ratio between any determinate power, however high, and the infinite; and thus the relation between the individual and All-Being must always remain immeasurable.

But this in no way interferes with the law of growth, by which the individual rises to higher and higher powers of his own individuality. The virtual unchangeableness of the relation between all determinate powers of x and infinity does not affect the relations of the different powers of x between themselves: but the fact that multiplication of x by itself to infinity is mentally conceivable is the very proof that there is no limit to the extent to which it is possible to raise x in its determinate powers.

I trust unmathematical readers will pardon my using this method of statement for the benefit of others to whom it will carry conviction. A relation once clearly grasped in its mathematical aspect becomes thenceforth one of the unalterable truths of the Universe, no longer a thing to be argued about but an axiom to be assumed as the foundation on which to build up the edifice of further knowledge. But, laying aside mathematical formulae, we may say that because the Infinite is infinite, there can be no limit to the extent to which the vital principle of growth may draw upon it, and therefore there is no limit to the expansion of the individual's powers. Because we are what we are, we may become what we will.

The Kabbalists tell us of "the lost word", the word of power which mankind has lost. To him who discovers this word all things are possible. Is this mirific word really lost? Yes — and No. It is the open secret of the Universe, and the Bible gives us the key to it. It tells us, "The word is nigh thee, even in thy mouth and in thy heart". It is the most familiar of all words, the word which in our heart we realize as the center of our conscious being, and which is in our mouth a hundred times a day. It is the word "I AM". Because I am what I am, I may be what I will to be. My individuality is one of the modes in which the Infinite expresses Itself, and therefore I am myself that very power which I find to be the innermost within all things.

To me, thus realizing the great unity of all Spirit, the infinite is not the indefinite, for I see it to be the infinite of Myself. It is the very same I AM that I am; and this is not by any act of uncertain favour, but by the law of polarity which is the basis of all Nature. The law of polarity is that law according to which everything attains completion by manifesting itself in the opposite direction to that from which it started. It is the simple law by which there can be no inside without an outside, nor one end of a stick without the opposite end,

Life is motion, and all motion is the appearance of energy at another point. Where any work has been done, it appears under another form than that in which it originated; but wherever it reappears, and in whatever new form, the vivifying energy is still the same. This is nothing else than the scientific doctrine of the conservation of energy, and it is upon this well-recognized principle that our perception of ourselves as integral portions of the great Universal Power is based.

We do well to pay heed to the sayings of the great teachers who have taught that all power is in the "I AM". It is better to accept this teaching by faith in their bare authority rather than not accept it at all; but the more excellent way is to know why they taught thus, and to realize for ourselves this first great law which all the master-minds have realized throughout the ages.

It is indeed true that the "lost word" is the one most familiar to us, ever in our hearts and on our lips. We have lost, not the word, but the realization of its power. And as the infinite depths of meaning which the words I AM carry with them open out to us, we begin to realize the stupendous truth that we are ourselves the very power which we seek.

It is the polarization of Spirit from the Universal into the particular, carrying with it all its inherent powers — just as the smallest flame has all the qualities of fire. The I AM in the individual is none other than the I AM in the Universal. It is the same Power working in the smaller sphere of which the individual is the center. This is the great truth which the ancients set forth under the figure of the Macrocosm and the Microcosm, the lesser I AM reproducing the precise image of the greater. This is what the Bible tells us when it speaks of man as the image of God.

Now the immense practical importance of this principle is that it affords the key to the great law that "as a man thinks, so he is". We know by personal experience that we realize our own liveliness in two ways: by our power to act and by our susceptibility to feel. When we consider Spirit in the absolute, we can conceive of it only as these two modes of liveliness carried to infinity. This, therefore, means infinite susceptibility. There can be no questions as to the degree of sensitiveness, for Spirit is sensitiveness. It is thus infinitely plastic to the slightest touch that is brought to bear upon it; and hence every thought we formulate sends its vibrating currents out into the infinite of Spirit, producing there currents of like quality but of far vaster power.

At every moment we are dealing with an infinitely sensitive medium which stirs creative energies that give form to the slightest of our thought-vibrations. This power is inherent in us because of our spiritual nature; we cannot divest ourselves of it. It is our truly tremendous heritage because it is a power which, if not intelligently brought into lines of orderly activity, will spend its uncontrolled forces in devastating energy. If it is not used to build up, it will destroy.

There is nothing exceptional in this: it is merely the reappearance on the plane of the Universal and undifferentiated of the same principle that pervades all the forces of Nature. Which of these forces is not destructive unless drawn off into some definite direction? Accumulated steam, accumulated electricity, accumulated water, will at length burst forth, destroying everything around. But, drawn off through suitable channels, they become sources of constructive power, inexhaustible as Nature itself.

And here let me pause to draw attention to this idea of accumulation. The greater the accumulation of energy, the greater the danger if it be not directed into a proper order, and the greater the power if it be. Fortunately for mankind the physical forces, such as electricity, do not usually subsist in a highly concentrated form. Occasionally, circumstances concur to produce such concentration; but as a rule, the elements of power are more or less equally dispersed.

Similarly, for the mass of mankind, this spiritual power has not yet reached a very high degree of concentration. Every mind, it is true, must be in some measure a center of concentration, for otherwise it would have no conscious individuality. However, the power of the individualized mind rapidly rises as it recognizes its unity with the infinite Life, and its thought-currents, whether well- or ill-directed, then assume a proportionately greater significance.

Hence the ill effects of wrongly directed thought are in some degree mitigated in the great mass of mankind. Although the thinkers themselves are ignorant of what thought-power is, many causes are in operation to give a right direction to their thoughts. To give a right direction to the thoughts of ignorant thinkers is the purpose of much religious teaching, which the uninstructed must accept by faith in bare authority because they are unable to realize its true import.

Notwithstanding the aids thus afforded to mankind, the general stream of unregulated thought cannot but have an adverse tendency. Hence the great object to which the instructed mind directs its power is to free itself from the entanglements of disordered thought, and to help others to do the same. To escape from this entanglement is to attain perfect Liberty, which is perfect Power.

Chapter 6
Application of Spirit

The entanglement from which we need to escape has its origin in the very same principle which gives rise to liberty and power. It is the same principle applied under inverted conditions. And here I would draw particular attention to the law that any sequence followed out in an inverted order must produce an inverted result, for this goes a long way to explain many of the problems of life.

The physical world affords endless examples of the working of "inversion". In a dynamo the sequence commences with mechanical force which is ultimately transformed into the subtler power of electricity; but invert this order, commence by supplying electricity to a motor, and it becomes converted into mechanical force. In one order, the rotation of a wheel produces electricity; in the opposite order, electricity produces the rotation of a wheel. Or to exhibit the same principle in the simplest arithmetical form, if $10 \div 2 = 5$, then $10 \div 5 = 2$.

"Inversion" is a factor of the greatest magnitude and has to be reckoned with. However, I must here content myself only with indicating the general principle that the same power is capable of producing diametrically opposite effects if it be applied under opposite conditions. We are apt to fall into the mistake of supposing that results of opposite character require powers of opposite character to produce them. Our conceptions of things in general become much simplified when we recognize that this is not the case, but rather that the same power will produce opposite results as it starts from opposite poles.

Accordingly the inverted application of the same principle which gives rise to liberty and power constitutes the entanglement from which we need to be delivered before power and liberty can be attained. This principle is expressed in the law that "as a man thinks, so he is". This is the basic law of the human mind. It is Descartes' "Cogito, ergo sum". If we trace consciousness to its seat, we find that it is purely subjective. Our external senses would cease to exist were it not for the subjective consciousness which perceives what they communicate to it.

The idea conveyed to the subjective consciousness may be false but, until some truer idea is more forcibly impressed in its stead, it remains a substantial reality to the mind which gives it objective existence. I have seen a man speak to the stump of a tree which in the moonlight looked like a person standing in a garden, and repeatedly ask its name and what it wanted. So far as the speaker's conception was concerned, the garden contained a living man who refused to answer.

Thus every mind lives in a world to which its own perceptions give objective reality. Its perceptions may be erroneous, but they nevertheless constitute the very reality of life for the mind that gives form to them. No life is possible other than the life we lead in our own minds. Hence the advance of the whole race depends on substituting the ideas of good, of liberty, and of order for their opposites. This can be done only by giving some sufficient reason for accepting the new idea in place of the old. For each one of us, our beliefs constitute our facts, and these beliefs can be changed only by discovering some ground for a different belief.

This is briefly the rationale of the maxim that "as a man thinks, so he is". All the issues of life proceed from the working of this principle. Man's first perception of the law of cause and effect in relation to his own conduct is that the result always partakes of the quality of the cause. Since his argument is drawn from external observation only, he regards external acts as the only causes he can effectively set in operation. When he attains sufficient moral enlightenment to realize that many of his acts have been such as to merit retribution, he fears retribution as their proper result. Then by reason of the law that "thoughts are things", the evils which he fears take form and plunge him into adverse circumstances. These again prompt him into further wrong acts, and from these come a fresh crop of fears which in their turn become externalized into fresh evils. Thus arises a circulus from which there is no escape so long as the man recognizes nothing but his external acts as a causative power in the world of his surroundings.

This is the Law of Works, the Circle of Karma, the Wheel of Fate, from which there is no escape — because the complete fulfillment of the law of our moral nature today is only sufficient for today and leaves no surplus to compensate the failure of yesterday. This is the necessary law of things as they appear from external observation only; and so long as this conception remains, the law of each man's subjective consciousness makes it a reality for him.

What is needed, therefore, is to establish the conception that external acts are NOT the only causative power, but that there is another law of causation, namely that of pure Thought. This is the Law of Faith and of Liberty, for it introduces us to a power which is able to inaugurate a new sequence of causation not related to any past actions.

This change of mental attitude cannot be brought about till we have laid hold of some fact which is sufficient to afford a reason for the change. We require some solid ground for our belief in this higher law.

Ultimately we find this ground in the great Truth of the eternal relation between spirit in the Universal and in the particular. When we realize that substantially there is nothing else but spirit, and that we ourselves are reproducing in individuality the Intelligence and Love which rule the Universe, we have reached the firm standing ground where we find that we can send forth our Thought to produce any effect we will. We have passed beyond the idea of two opposites requiring reconciliation into that of a duality in which there is no opposition other than that of the inner and the outer of the same unity. This is the polarity which is inherent in all Being. When we realize this unity, our Thought is possessed of illimitable creative power; it is free to range where it will; and it is by no means bound down to accept as inevitable the consequences which, if unchecked by renovated thought, would flow from our past actions.

In its own independent creative power the mind has found the way out of the fatal circle in which its previous ignorance of the highest law had imprisoned it. The Unity of the Spirit is found to result in perfect Liberty. The old sequence of Karma has been cut off, and a new and higher order has been introduced. In the old order the line of thought received its quality from the quality of actions, and since they always fell short of perfection, the development of a higher thought-power from this root was impossible. This is the order in which everything is seen from without. But in the true order everything is seen from within.

It is the thought which determines the quality of the action, and not vice versa. Since thought is free, it is at liberty to direct itself to the highest principles, which thus spontaneously reproduce themselves in the outward acts. Thus both thoughts and actions are brought into harmony with the Universal Mind. The individual realizes that he is no longer bound by the consequences of his former deeds, done in the time of his ignorance. He realizes, indeed, that he was never bound by them except so far as he himself gave them this power by false conceptions of the truth.

Thus recognizing himself for what he really is — the expression of the Infinite Spirit in individual personality — Man finds that he is a free "partaker of Divine nature", not losing his identity but becoming more and more fully himself with an ever-expanding perfection, following out a line of evolution whose possibilities are inexhaustible.

But not all men know this. For the most part they look upon God as an individual Being external to themselves. What the more instructed man sees to be unity of mind and identity of nature appear to the less advanced to be an external reconciliation between opposing personalities. Hence the whole range of conceptions which may be described as "the Messianic Idea".

This idea is not, as some suppose, a misconception of the truth of Being. On the contrary, when rightly understood, it will be found to imply the very widest grasp of that truth. It is only from the platform of this supreme knowledge that an idea so comprehensive in its adaptation to every class of mind could have evolved. It is the translation of the relations arising from the deepest laws of Being into terms which can be realized even by the most unlearned — a translation arranged with such consummate skill that, as the mind grows in spirituality, every stage of advance is met by a corresponding unfolding of the Divine meaning. Even the crudest apprehension of the implied idea is a sufficient basis for an entire renovation of the man's thoughts concerning himself because it gives him a ground from which to think of himself as no longer bound by the law of retribution for past offences, but as free to follow out the new law of Liberty as a child of God.

The man's conception of the modus operandi of this emancipation may take the form of the grossest anthropomorphism or the most childish notions as to the satisfaction of the Divine justice by vicarious substitution: but the practical result will be the same. He has got what satisfies him as a ground for thinking of himself in a perfectly new light; and since the states of our subjective consciousness constitute the realities of our life, to afford him a convincing ground for thinking himself free is to make him free.

With increasing light he may find that his first explanation of the modus operandi was inadequate. But when he reaches this stage, further investigation will show him that the great truth of his liberty rests upon a firmer foundation than the conventional interpretation of traditional dogmas, and that it has its roots in the great laws of Nature which are never doubtful and which can never be overturned. It is precisely because their whole action has its root in the unchangeable laws of Mind that there exists a perpetual necessity for presenting to men something which they can lay hold of as a sufficient ground for that change of mental attitude by which alone they can be rescued from the fatal circle which is figured under the symbol of the Old Serpent.

The hope and adumbration of such a new principle has formed the substance of all religions in all ages, however misapprehended by the ignorant worshippers. Whatever our individual opinions may be as to the historical facts of Christianity, we shall find that the great figure of liberated and perfected humanity which forms its center fulfills this desire of all nations in that it sets forth their great ideal of Divine Power intervening to rescue man by becoming one with Him.

This is the conception presented to us, whether we apprehend it in the most literally material sense, or as the ideal presentation of the deepest philosophic study of mental laws, or in whatever variety of ways we may combine these two extremes. The ultimate idea impressed upon the mind must always be the same: it is that there is a Divine warrant for knowing ourselves to be the children of God and "partakers of the Divine nature". When we thus realize that there is solid ground for believing ourselves free, by force of this very belief, we become free.

The proper outcome of the study of the laws of spirit which constitute the inner side of things is not the gratification of a mere idle curiosity, nor the acquisition of abnormal powers, but the attainment of our spiritual liberty, without which no further progress is possible. When we have reached this goal, the old things have passed away and all things have become new. The mystical seven days of the old creation have been fulfilled, and the first day of the new week dawns upon us with its resurrection to a new life, expressing on the highest plane that great doctrine of the "octave which the science of ancient temples traced through Nature, and which the science of the present day endorses, though ignorant of its supreme significance.

When we have thus been made free by recognizing our oneness with Infinite Being, we have reached the termination of the old series of sequences and have gained the starting-point of the new. The old limitations are found never to have had any existence save in our own misapprehension of the truth, and one by one they fall off as we advance into clearer light. We find that the Life-Spirit we seek is in ourselves. Having this for our center, our relation to all else becomes part of a wondrous living Order in which every part works in sympathy with the whole, the whole in sympathy with every part, in a harmony wide as infinitude, and in which there are no limitations save those imposed by the Law of Love.

I have endeavoured in this short series of articles to sketch briefly the principal points of relation between Spirit in ourselves and in our surroundings. This subject has employed the intelligence of mankind from grey antiquity to the present day, and no one thinker can ever hope to grasp it in all its amplitude. But there are certain broad principles which we must all grasp, however we may specialize our studies in detail, and these I have sought to indicate — with what degree of success the reader must form his own opinion. Let him, however, lay firm hold of the one fundamental truth, and the evolution of further truth from it is only a question of time: that there is only One Spirit, however many the modes of its manifestations, and that "the Unity of the Spirit is the Bond of Peace".

CPSIA information can be obtained at www.ICGtesting.com
Printed in the USA
LVOW03s1906140814

399140LV00007B/288/P

9 781612 034270